ETHICAL ISSUES IN HUMAN GENETICS

Genetic Counseling and the Use
of Genetic Knowledge

CONTRIBUTORS

Henry David Aiken
Daniel Callahan
Alex M. Capron
James F. Crow
David Eaton
John Fletcher
F. Clarke Fraser
Charles Fried
Harold P. Green
James M. Gustafson
Judith Hall
Sir Harold Himsworth
Lee B. Jacoby
Michael M. Kaback
Leon R. Kass

Lord Kilbrandon
David A. Kindig
John W. Littlefield
Herbert A. Lubs
Aubrey Milunsky
Robert S. Morison
Arno Motulsky
Robert Murray
James V. Neel
Paul Ramsey
Victor W. Sidel
Robert L. Sinsheimer
Tracy M. Sonneborn
James R. Sorenson
Robert S. Zeiger

Fogarty International Proceedings No. 13

ETHICAL ISSUES IN HUMAN GENETICS

Genetic Counseling and the Use of Genetic Knowledge

Proceedings of a Symposium Sponsored by the John E. Fogarty International Center for Advanced Study in the Health Sciences and the Institute of Society, Ethics and the Life Sciences October 10-14, 1971

Edited by
Bruce Hilton and Daniel Callahan
Institute of Society, Ethics and the Life Sciences
Hastings-on-Hudson, New York

Maureen Harris and Peter Condliffe
Fogarty International Center
National Institutes of Health
Bethesda, Maryland

Burton Berkley
Office of the General Counsel
National Institutes of Health
Bethesda, Maryland

PLENUM PRESS • NEW YORK-LONDON • 1973

First Printing—February 1973
Second Printing—October 1973
Third Printing—September 1975

Library of Congress Catalog Card Number 72-93443
ISBN 0-306-30715-4

Plenum Press, New York
A Division of Plenum Publishing Corporation
227 West 17th Street, New York, N. Y. 10011

United Kingdom edition published by Plenum Press, London
A Division of Plenum Publishing Company, Ltd.
Davis House (4th Floor), 8 Scrubs Lane, Harlesden, NW 10 6SE, England

CONTENTS

ACKNOWLEDGMENTS

This book could not have been prepared without the sustained efforts of Lou Hurley, Toula Bockting, Virginia Vogel, and Sharmon Sollitto.

PREFACE

In May 1970, the Fogarty International Center held a conference on "Early Diagnosis of Human Genetic Defects", under the chairmanship of Dr. Robert Morison.* This conference dealt primarily with the technical aspects of amniocentesis, analysis of genetic defects by cytogenetic and biochemical techniques, the culture of amniotic fluid cells, the risks of amniocentesis, and the technical and ethical problems that arise during screening for defects in homozygotes and heterozygotes. The last session of this meeting was devoted to ethical issues that have arisen from the development of amniocentesis in combination with genetic analysis which enables a growing list of defects to be diagnosed as early as 16 weeks in pregnancy.

At the close of this meeting in 1970, the chairman, in agreement with other members of the conference, pointed out to the Fogarty International staff that with one exception, a lawyer, all the invited speakers had been medical research workers well known as leaders in their various disciplines of genetics, pediatrics, obstetrics, cytology, research administration, and biochemistry. While several ethicists and lawyers were invited to participate, the composition of the conference clearly reflected a not-unusual situation in which scientists who are the first to know of developments in the laboratory and clinic, discuss the societal aspects of their work among themselves and only later enter into a dialogue with their colleagues in the law, the social sciences, the humanities, and letters. Considering the potential social impact of modern medical research, the Fogarty International Center which is charged with bridging not only this interdisciplinary gap between scholars but with explaining to the public the significance of advanced study in the health sciences, decided to follow up this first conference with a second at which ethicists, lawyers, philosophers, theologians, and other scholars would be invited to participate more fully.

Several members of the Institute of Society, Ethics and the Life Sciences had attended the conference, including the Chairman,

---

*Early Diagnosis of Human Genetic Defects: Scientific and Ethical Considerations, Maureen Harris, editor. Washington, D.C., U.S. Government Printing Office, 1972.

Dr. Robert Morison. Following the conference, the Fogarty Center approached the Director of the Institute and invited him to collaborate in preparing the program for a fuller discussion of the ethical issues. It was agreed that the philosophical, legal, and sociological aspects deserved discussion by acknowledged scholars. The conference, whose proceedings are recorded in this book, was the result of this collaboration between a government agency and a private institute devoted to the illumination of the social implications of advanced medical research.

Until 200 years ago there was no thought that man would ever be able to deliberately modify his own evolution. "Species" as such were seen as immutable. The existence of sports or monstrosities in this fixed pattern began to convince a growing number of skeptics (the Transformationists) that organisms were subject to change, culminating in 1859 in Darwin's famous tract The Origin of Species. With Darwin's work and the population biologists who applied Mendel's principles to it, it became possible to view man's evolutionary potential not as a fixed entity, but one that is constantly undergoing modification through changing patterns of fertility and mortality. Since that time, geneticists have pieced together the mechanism of hereditary transmission and devised sufficiently discriminating tools (karyotyping, amniocentesis, etc.) to allow man to view and, for the first time, to modify his heredity.

At first this intervention will be modest--at the level of single individuals. But any intervention in the birth of what would have been the result of random forces introduces the hand of man in the fundamental process of evolution itself.

To some of us who participated in this present meeting the debate seemed to be over this basic issue. Ought medicine, through applied human genetics, to take part in what Jacques Monod in Chance and Necessity calls "this teleonomic project" by altering either the probability of change or by intervening in the selection process through negative means such as abortion, or, in the future, by directly altering the chemical structure of DNA.

As Monod points out, we now understand biology sufficiently to construct a coherent theory about it. This enables us to predict the probable lines of technological development in biology and medicine even though much experimental detail must be filled in. We are indeed in a situation analogous to that of the physicists following the discovery of nuclear fission by Hahn and Meitner, after which it was certain that an atomic bomb could be constructed if sufficient effort was made. Nirenberg has pointed out the inevitability of technological developments such as cloning, construction of synthetic genes, and other phenomena. Much of this future development is discussed in these proceedings by Sinsheimer.

The conference program committee (Drs. Daniel Callahan, Leon A. Kass, Arno Motulsky, Robert F. Murray, Jr., Robert S. Morison, Blair Sadler, and Peter Condliffe) while cognizant of these future developments, felt that examination of immediate ethical issues presented to the genetic counselor in his practice of medicine was a useful tool for getting at the existing and future predicament. Precedents set now will probably form the basis for future legislation and for legal disposition of future cases arising from the more esoteric forms of genetic intervention. Examination of the legal and ethical consequences of amniocentesis could be helpful, for example, in dealing with the introduction of extra-corporeal fertilization and uterine implantation into gynecological practice along the lines proposed by Edwards and Steptoe in England.

A program was laid out which first summarized the scientific knowledge as it exists today forming the basis of genetic counseling. The significance and meaning of genetic disease was then discussed from the perspectives of the individual patient and that of population groups. The discussion then moved to the philosophical perspectives on the meaning of genetic disease. The ethical aspect was taken up and this led directly into the problem of the right to life and to a consideration of standards for this right. These discussions set the background for direct consideration of the existing legal situation, of privacy in genetic counseling, and the question of who decides to apply the available techniques. After an excursion into potential problems in the future, the final session considered public policy with respect to control of applications of genetic knowledge.

In organizing these discussions the program committee felt they should be addressed to a wide audience of concerned professionals in medicine, the law, and particularly in political-administrative community as well as the interested public. We hope that this volume will serve this purpose of aiding discussion of these difficult areas.

> Peter G. Condliffe
> Daniel Callahan

ETHICAL ISSUES ARISING FROM THE POSSIBLE
USES OF GENETIC KNOWLEDGE

Tracy M. Sonneborn

I realize that I am probably a fool to rush into the ethical domain where angels--the philosphers, ethicists, theologians and lawyers--do not fear to tread. But these ethical problems concern us all, and not the least among us, the geneticists. I submit that after we listen carefully to what the professional theologians, ethicists and philosophers have to say, as many of us have, then we, too, may speak up and tell about our own attempts to see our way through the difficult problems that beset us. This dialogue has now been going on with increasing frequency during the last eight years, and some of my fellow scientists have written and spoken very thoughtfully on the subject. They are not in complete agreement, but neither are the theologians, ethicists, and philosophers. I assume that the purpose of this conference is to encourage further communication between physicians and geneticists, on the one hand, and philosophers, theologians, ethicists and lawyers on the other hand. Perhaps it is significant that a geneticist has been given the opening spot at the conference, but that lawyers and a historian will have the last words.

The present and potential uses of genetic knowledge and technology are, in a general way, widely known. They have been frequently presented to the public by the popular press and other mass communication media. So, I think it is not necessary for me to do more than recall them briefly. Most of the major ethical issues arise directly or indirectly from the genetic knowledge and correlated technologies that are concerned with human procreation. Genetic knowledge permits a degree of counseling to prospective parents in regard to the probabilities for the occurrence of certain traits among their future children. Perhaps the most spectacular technological advances along these lines have been those that are useful in predicting characteristics of a developing baby a considerable time before it is due to be born. Certain abnormal genes and chromosomal conditions can be detected by this technology with virtually 100 percent accuracy. The number of conditions that can be predicted prenatally and the accuracy with which these

1

predictions can be made is increasing every year. Many ethical
issues arise in connection with the interrelations among the
genetic counselor, the physician, the pregnant woman and her
spouse. These will doubtless be brought out in some of the later
papers and discussions. But the major ethical issue is whether
abortion is justified when the child is found to have defective or
abnormal genes or chromosomes. In a beautiful and eminently humane
paper known to many of us, Dr. Lejeune--who has been a pioneer and
remains a leader in the field of human chromosomal abnormalities--
has presented many reasons for doubting the justification of such
induced abortions. Later I shall come back to this problem.

A second and very different set of ethical issues arises from
the possibility of using for genetic purposes forms of procreation
other than the normal one of sexual intercourse between husband and
wife. Among these forms of precreation, only one is at present
feasible; artificial insemination of the woman with sperm from a
donor other than her husband. The other forms of procreation have
been carried out with higher animals; although not yet possible in
man, research toward this objective is in progress. One of them is
fertilization outside of the body, using eggs from any female and
sperm from any male; the fertilized egg, after proceeding to a very
early developmental stage, is then implanted into the uterus of any
properly prepared female. As Arno Motulsky vividly phrased it,
this raises among other ethical problems the problem of "wombs for
rent." The other form of procreation is to remove the nucleus from
any female's egg and replace it by a nucleus obtained from a body
cell of the same or any other individual. This, theoretically,
should result in the development of an individual whose heredity is
identical with that of the individual who provided the donor
nucleus. As you are well aware, this is called cloning and can be
used to produce as many genetically identical individuals as
desired--not merely twins or triplets, but multiplets. Cloning has
been subjected to searching ethical analysis by Kass, Ramsey, and
others.

Finally, a third set of ethical issues is raised by genetic
surgery, which lies still further in the future. Genetic surgery
refers to anticipated possibilities of changing the genetic constitution of the reproductive cells in a person, or by changing it
in the initial or very early stage of development of a new
individual. Doubtless Dr. Sinsheimer will have much to say about
this.

All of the possibilities mentioned, along with simple differential amounts of normal procreation by people with different
genetic endowments, are components of a vision held in some
quarters that foresees man consciously and purposefully guiding his
own future evolution or, as some like to characterize it, trying to
play God. Clearly the ethical issues that arise from these possibilities are among the most important that could be envisaged.
They all deal with problems of life and death, with the character
or quality of life, with the active interference of human beings in

deciding who shall live and who shall die, and with what kinds of people shall live or die. These decisions could affect not only those now living and their children but our successors many generations hence.

These, then, are the major questions, problems, and ethical issues that have been and will continue to be discussed. Yet there is, I believe, a deeper and more encompassing question. The way we answer this question largely determines how we will answer all the others. It is a touchy and highly sensitive question, which is bound to annoy, anger, or infuriate many of us. Perhaps that is why it is so seldom put explicitly and clearly at the center of discussion where it really belongs, although answers to it are tacitly implied by our actions and the principles of action to which we adhere. It is, therefore, with fear and trembling that I put the question before you: Who or what decides what is right or good? By what authority? What do we really mean when we ask about anything--"Is it ethical?" In spite of not being a professional ethicist, I cannot avoid coming always to that central question. Do we assume that there are eternal verities--universal, self-evident, absolute truths about right and good human conduct? Do we assume that they have been transmitted to us from a supernatural divine authority via his mortal servants? Do we assume that knowledge of them is an inherent characteristic of man, knowledge that he can obtain by turning to his conscience? Or does ethics take a different form and have a different authority? If so, what? Or is ethics a chaotic no-man's land without authority of any kind?

The answers given by human beings to these central questions are by no means uniform. Some of us, though profoundly awed by the universe as we apprehend it, do not believe in a supernatural God and we reject divine authority for an ethical code. Nor can we accept the idea of an eternal, universal, absolute ethics imprinted in the conscience of man. We find in comparative religion, in anthropology, and in history the record of diverse ethical codes. We see them as man-made and variable from time to time, from culture to culture. We see them as codes of conduct authorized by common consent, or imposed to regulate particular social orders. Although, as Waddington and others have argued, man is an ethical animal and even an authority acceptor (as well as challenger), the particulars of his conceptions of right and good are varied and changeable. Even within one over-all culture, different groups profess different ethical codes--for example, physicians, corporation executives, lawyers, congressmen, and presidents. It seems to me, therefore, that the authority for ethical decisions, for decisions as to what is right and good, come from man himself, from his own choices, individually and in groups. The function then of conferences such as this is to debate what is right and what is good for man as part of the process of crystallizing individual and group choices which will become the authority for ethical decisions.

Viewing the general situation in this way, I should like now to apply this view to the ethical problems of life and death, of human procreation, that arise from present and potential uses of genetic knowledge. The first problem is abortion. Two opposed solutions to the problem are indicated by news reports. Superior Court Judge Jack G. Marks of Tucson, Arizona, is reported to have appointed a guardian of a nine-week old fetus on the ground that "the fetus has the rights of equal protection of this court." The suit was reported to have been filed by the Planned Parenthood Center of Tucson and by ten physicians in a challenge of the state's abortion laws. According to the papers, the suit claims that the mother of the fetus will probably not die if she gives birth to the child, but that she will be permanently injured. I have seen no mention of whether abnormality of the child is involved; presumably it is not. The issue that appears to be drawn is simply conformity to existing law, based on the sanctity of life versus modification of the law to conform to changing public opinion about the range of applicability of the adversary principle.

The adversary principle has been recognized as valid even by the Judaeo-Christian tradition. Abortion is right if the choice is death of the fetus or death of the mother. Killing has also been justified--albeit regrettably--in self-defense against a life-threatening adversary, both at the level of the individual and, in the case of war, at the level of a nation. The ethical question at issue now is whether the adversary principle should be extended, in the case of a fetus, to situations in which the fetus is deemed to be an adversary against not necessarily the life, but merely the well-being of the parents or society. In the past, man's ethical judgments have changed on the basis of discussion and experience as new situations have arisen--as, for example, in the case of contraception when new methods were developed and new social conditions came into being. At first, argument centered about the right to prevent the initiation of a new life by interposing mechanical blocks between sperm and egg. After long and bitter battles against the law and previous ethical judgments, the issue was in effect decided by widespread practice. More recently the pill, working on a different principle, has been widely accepted. The intrauterine device, which may operate by what amounts to very early abortion, is also accepted by many. Extension to somewhat later abortion is now at issue, as well as the question of how late.

The great numbers and heterogeneity of mankind, as well as the existence of many adventurous, non-conformist or simply desperate people, make it highly likely that new possibilities will be tried by some people regardless of how they stand in the light of current civil, moral, or sacred law. Some of these trials will fail to win general acceptance; others will succeed. Acceptance may at first be limited to special cases and later become more general and comprehensive. Submission to the test of public opinion and practice is sometimes a slow method of change. But a slow pace, permitting time for testing and weighing, affords some protection against precipitous unwise choices. Individuals and society thus have ways of sanctioning uses of new knowledge and technology and, in fact, they do so even if these uses initially conflict with current legal, moral, and religious codes. If the new ethics are eventually judged to operate contrary to the good of man, readjustments can be made. We went through that reversal, for example, in the adoption and then repeal of Prohibition. The touchstone of man's choices, of his ethical choices, is simply his judgment of whether it is right and good for man. Man is the measure of all things.

This I believe to be the way that all of the ethical issues mentioned earlier--abortion, methods of procreation, guiding human evolution--will be decided. I doubt whether man's present choices will be guided by long-range considerations of human evolution, at least not by enough people to have an appreciable effect. Actually, however, that doesn't greatly matter. What does matter are the choices made in each generation with regard only to the procreation of the next generation. People greatly desire not to have defective or abnormal children. Because this hits home hard, I believe man will eventually decide that it is right and good to use for this purpose means offered by genetic knowledge and procreative technology, including the techniques of genetic surgery if and when they become available. I believe that man will, in short, adopt as ethical Bentley Glass' dictum that every child has the right to be free of genetic defect and abnormality insofar as this can be achieved. If people come to desire to have above-average or outstanding children, however defined, with anything like the strength of their desire to avoid having defective and abnormal children, they will find it as easy, or as difficult, to resolve the ethical problem in the one case as in the other, for the problems have much in common. The conscious guiding of human evolution would then be in progress simply by active concern for one's children, without looking further ahead; the guidance could continually adjust to changing conditions and new knowledge.

My thesis, then, is that man develops his ethics by the method of public discussion, by individual decisions and actions, by public acceptance of what appears to be right and good for man, and by rejection of what appears to be wrong or bad. We agree that it is right and good to reduce misery and improve the quality of life for all those who live, by using environmental and social means. We now debate whether it is right and good to use genetic means. Our conceptions of what is ethical, right, and good change in the light of new knowledge and new conditions. What we lack is neither flexibility of mind nor adventurous spirits, but knowledge and experience. If the future can be judged by the present and the past, we shall get that knowledge and experience and eventually authorize the ethics that permits doing what is believed to be right and good for man.

If I have glossed over the pitfalls and difficulties in the process of arriving at particular ethical judgments about specific details of the uses of genetic knowledge and technology, it is not because I am unaware of them. But this, I am happy to say, is not my assignment. These tough problems will occupy us during the next four days--and beyond. As we approach that task, we have no basis for being cocky. We are still full of ignorance in spite of the spectacular increase of knowledge. It would be both unwise and inhumane to proceed without the utmost humility and compassion.

SURVEY OF COUNSELING PRACTICES

F. Clarke Fraser

My task will be to tell what genetic counselors do, pointing out along the way some of the ethical issues that arise, but not saying much about them myself. And since I know our own department best, I shall describe what this genetic counselor does, rather than any other.

We do our counseling in the Department of Medical Genetics in a pediatric hospital, and we get referrals for counseling largely from patients on the wards or in the outpatient departments of the hospital. We also get referrals from physicians outside the hospital, occasionally from adoption agencies, and sometimes from interested individuals directly. The problem usually deals with the question, "Will it happen again?"--"it" being some condition, some disease or defect, about which the parents are worried. Less often it deals with other problems, such as the hazards of cousin marriage or racial characteristics.

To give an idea of the kinds of cases that we see, I analyzed the last 349 cases that were referred specifically for counseling. Table I presents these by mode of inheritance. The message to be gotten from this is that there are a large number of diseases that the counselor deals with, and that this requires a wide body of knowledge and available literature. I went through the list and identified the numbers of cases where amniocentesis might be relevant--that is, where the case can be diagnosed in utero, bio-chemically or by chromosome examination. I put the X-linked ones in here, too, because amniocentesis may come into this picture. It turns out that about one in every six of our cases involves a condition where amniocentesis might be relevant. That is rather higher than I thought it would be. I don't know how other counselors make out in that regard.

The first step in the counseling process is to establish an accurate diagnosis, of course, and I won't go into the problems involved here. Having accepted a valid diagnosis, the next step is to establish the probability of recurrence of the disease, and that involves a number of procedures. The counselor draws on the family history, the diagnosis, the literature, Mendel's laws, the karyotype, and various special tests in order to establish "P" (the

TABLE I.   Categories of Diagnosis for 349 Families Referred Specifically for Counseling

AUTOSOMAL DOMINANT		X-LINKED	
tuberose sclerosis	7	Duchenne muscular dystrophy	10
Huntington's chorea	6	hemophilia	3
osteogenesis imperfecta	6	agammaglobulinemia	2
retinoblastoma	4	other (1 each)	4
aniridia	3		19
Apert's syndrome	3	MULTIFACTORIAL or UNCLEAR	
ectodermal dystrophy (hidrotic)	3	neural tube defects	20
Ehlers-Danlos syndrome	3	mental retardation, non-specific	15
polycystic kidneys	3	multiple congenital anomalies	15
Turner phenotype (Noonan's)	3	convulsive disorders	13
holoprosencephaly	2	congenital heart defect	6
Holt-Oram syndrome	2	limb malformations and mental	
Leber's optic atrophy	2	retardation	5
neurofibromatosis	2	microcephaly	5
mandibulo facial dysostosis	2	de Lange syndrome	3
nerve deafness	2	Goldenhaar's syndrome	3
other (1 each)	18	repeated abortion	3
	71	cerebral palsy	2
AUTOSOMAL RECESSIVE		hemangioma	2
albinism	9	hydrocephalus	2
pancreatic cystic fibrosis	6	leukemia, acute lymphoblastic	2
congenital deafness	5	omphalocoele	2
Friedrich's ataxia	4	Robin's syndrome	2
Werdnig-Hoffman's disease	4	Rubinstein-Taybir	2
Tay-Sachs disease	3	other (1 each)	27
thalassemia	3		129
cataracts	3	CHROMOSOMAL	
PKU	2	trisomy 21	27
ataxia telangiectasia	2	other (1 each)	5
chondrodystrophia calcificans	2		32
deafness, nerve	2	MISCELLANEOUS	
Larsen's syndrome	2	consanguinity	17
retinitis pigmentosa	2	racial ancestry	2
Riley-Day syndrome	2	exposure to mutagens or	
other (1 each)	23	teratogens	2
	74	other (1 each)	3
			24

probability of recurrence). And I am not going to say anything else about that here, since it doesn't involve ethical issues, except occasionally the unethical means the counselor may have to use to get the relevant data from the family history. That is, there are cases where one needs the consent of the person to release information. But the person may not be available to give the consent, and one needs that information to help make the diagnosis or establish the probability. Sometimes one has to take rather circuitous routes to get the information. Amniocentesis, of course, can sometimes establish P as zero or one, and I am leaving that part of the situation to subsequent papers.

The next stage in the procedure is to help the family reach a decision, if they want help in this regard. This, of course, involves all kinds of other considerations besides the probability of recurrence and the severity of the disease--religious, economic, cultural, family, legal, and many others. This is where a number of ethical and moral issues arise. Since these issues are likely to involve the ethics and morals of the counselee or the family being counseled rather than of the counselor, I find that I tend to take a fairly pragmatic view of the situation. I am really not very good at seeing the broad ethical issues and consequences in an individual situation. I tend to try and work towards the best solution for the immediate family as I see it, and rarely, if ever, does this conflict with my own ethics or morals, such as they are. My real problem is in trying to see what the best solution is in terms of the immediate situation.

A few examples will illustrate the kinds of problems that turn up. Until quite recently, for instance, the question of contraception was a problem for many of the parents whom I saw for counseling--parents who decided they did not want further children but were Roman Catholics, living in a country where it was illegal even to give advice about contraception, much less use it. And there were, and I think still are, many children born defective because of the parents' unwillingness to go against the teachings of the church in this regard. Other parents I saw would choose to contravene the church's, or rather the priest's instructions in this regard. More than one mother has said to me, "Is the priest going to take care of my sick children?" But those who did it, I am sure, have suffered discomfort to their consciences. Sometimes a referral to a more sympathetic priest than the one that they had been talking to was the answer.

Now, of course, the problem is much less prevalent. Contraception, as Dr. Sonneborn mentioned in his paper, is much more widely accepted. But the same questions still arise with regard to sterilization and abortion. For instance, Mrs. Carpenter, when she was married, knew she had a fifty-fifty chance of being a carrier of hemophilia; she had an affected uncle and two affected brothers, and the family had received counseling and knew what the genetic situation was. Her first child proved that she was indeed a carrier, so she knew she had a fifty-fifty chance that any subsequent son would have the disease. This was before the days of amniocentesis. She decided that she did not want to take the risk of having another affected child, but being a good Roman Catholic, she adopted the rhythm method in order to achieve her desires. That resulted in hemophiliac son number two. Condoms resulted in the third child, a girl, who was unaffected but may face the same problem when she grows up.

At that point she decided that she had had enough, and applied for a tubal ligation. While her application was being processed, she became pregnant again, this time through a diaphragm, and had to change her application from tubal ligation to termination of pregnancy. The first hospital committee to which she applied said no, that a 25 percent chance of hemophilia was not sufficient grounds for termination of the pregnancy. She reapplied to a second hospital and finally got permission. By that time she was five months pregnant and the baby was moving, and she just couldn't go through with it, quite understandably. The result was that she now has three hemophiliac sons. She loves this little boy, and she is a good mother, but she is quite sure that she would have preferred that he had not been born.

Nowadays things might be quite different in Montreal (at least the West End), both in terms of the difficulty of obtaining consent for a termination and because of the advantages of amniocentesis. But nevertheless, there are still large areas of the world where a woman who wants to have no more children because of a high risk of severe disease may be unable to obtain the means of prevention.

Mrs. Little had a mentally retarded child, nonspecific, then a normal son, and then a third child with chondrodystrophia calcificans, a severe form of dwarfism. The child died in early infancy from this disease, which has a one-in-four risk of recurrence. She asked for advice and was referred to a family planning clinic. Nevertheless a couple of years later she produced twins, one of which died, and one of which has a fairly severe cerebral palsy.

Two years later she became pregnant again and at this point applied for a termination of pregnancy. The chief of the obstetrics department at the hospital she went to said that the genetic grounds weren't enough, and she would have to have a letter from a psychiatrist saying that birth of a subsequent child would be damaging to her health. When she got into the psychiatrist's office, she began to bleed all over his nice new carpet, and in fact was having a threatened abortion, whereupon she was whipped into the obstetrical wing of the nearby hospital (the one that had referred her to the psychiatrist) where they did everything in their power to save the pregnancy--and did so! At seven months she was admitted again with toxemia of pregnancy and at that time the diagnosis of twins was made. She spent most of the next two months in the hospital under careful surveillance to save the babies, and eventually produced two healthy, bouncing baby boys.

The obstetrician, when she came in with the bleeding, said to me that it was extraordinary that although she had wanted a termination, once she started to bleed and thought she was going to lose the baby, she became very concerned and didn't want to lose it. But when I saw Mrs. Little on the wards after the twins were born, she was really very bitter against the hospital staff. Everybody had been concerned about saving the baby, and nobody had thought about her, she said, and I know that she is not looking forward to the prospect of caring for two handicapped children and her healthy son, plus the twin boys. I think that either the obstetrician or I were projecting our own attitudes in this situation, and of course I think it was the obstetrician.

The third case involves Mrs. Davis, who had a fifty-fifty chance of being a carrier for Duchenne-type muscular dystrophy. She had lost a brother with it, and a nephew was in a terminal stage when she became pregnant at age 42 after a 14-year fallow period. She wanted an abortion for many reasons, including the possibility that her son would have muscular dystrophy. Again, this was before amniocentesis, and even before one could measure the creatine phosphokinase and try to establish whether she was a carrier.

She was referred for a termination of pregnancy, but rather than go through all the legal folderol that one has to go through to get a termination, she chose to go to an illegal source for help, and shortly thereafter appeared at the local obstetrical hospital bleeding profusely. The hemorrhage was stopped, thanks to all the bounties of medical practice these days, and she was discharged, only to reappear two nights later with another hemorrhage, because she had gone back to the same abortionist. This time it was life-threatening, but she survived and the pregnancy did not.

Three years later her unmarried teenage daughter became pregnant, and she applied for an abortion for the daughter. At that time we could do enzyme studies and demonstrate that she was indeed a carrier, and the obstetrician, on this ground as well as on sociological grounds, terminated that pregnancy. The obstetrician wanted to sterilize this young lady at the same time, but was prevailed upon not to do so. Following this, incidentally, the girl went on drugs and became severely emotionally disturbed. Apparently an appreciable part of the basis for this disturbance was--although I cannot prove this--the knowledge that she was a carrier of this defective gene. I mention this in passing as an almost untouched and possibly quite serious problem--the problem of the psychological effects of knowing or discovering that you carry a defective lethal gene.

What other problems worry the genetic counselor? There is considerable argument, for instance, as to how directive counseling should be. I disagree with those who say that counseling includes only giving an estimate of P, the recurrence risk, and that is where it stops. I also avoid telling anyone explicitly that they should or should not have further children, or get married, or whatever it is. If they push me about what I think they should do--sometimes they say, "Well, what would you do if you were in my situation?"--I say that I cannot really put myself in their situation because I am not them. If I try to, as best I can, then I tell them I think I would not have a baby, or have one, as the case may be. But it is very difficult to be objective about this, and one must beware of projecting one's own personality into the situation. If you are the kind of person that likes to be a good guy, then you sometimes find yourself being over-optimistic about the advice you are giving, and if you are a hostile kind of person, you may be over-pessimistic.

I try to follow the principle of acting for the good of the immediate family, so I do not bring the question of eugenics into the situation. Sometimes the parents do, however, and if so, I say to them that we really don't know enough about the things that control the frequencies of genes in populations to be able to say anything sensible about the eugenic aspects of their particular action, and that their decision should be based on the future for their own children, rather than on considerations of posterity in general. I also don't hold with the view that suffering is ennobling and that therefore you shouldn't worry about the possible effects of having a baby with a deleterious condition of some sort.

Another problem that counselors worry about is the question of high-risk relatives and how far one should go in counseling the

family. When you see a particular set of parents, it may become
clear from the family history that there are other persons in the
family who are high-risk. For instance, in a sex-linked recessive
type of disease, all the mother's sisters may have a high risk of
being carriers and would presumably benefit from counseling.

One gets into problems of invasion of privacy. Let's look at
another example. I have been following a family with Huntington's
chorea for many years, having been approached first by a young lady
who at the time didn't know what her mother and five sisters had.
And this is one of the instances where I had to adopt illegal
methods of finding out what they had, because all the hospitals
said they couldn't release the information without the consent of
the patient, and the patient was usually dead or incapacitated. It
turned out to be Huntington's chorea, and there was first the problem of whether to tell her or not. After considerable thought, I
did tell her. She is still free of the disease at the age of 35,
but four of her cousins have developed it since I first saw her.
One of them, for instance, recently began to develop the personality changes that are characteristic of the condition. She threw
bottles at her husband and beat up the children--just terrible
behavior. And it was not recognized for what it was.   It is
extraordinary how people refuse to see what they don't want to see.
In spite of her mother having been affected, nobody in the family
recognized what was going on with this lady. I was able to write
to her physician suggesting the significance of the family history,
and it turned out that this has improved the situation considerably. The family and the community, indeed, find her behavior much
easier to cope with and to understand now that they know she is
suffering from a disease and not just being bitchy.

But was this an unjustified invasion of privacy?   And what
about a situation where the counselee doesn't want to contact the
other members of the family because he doesn't want the family to
know that he has had a child with the disease? I think I will
leave these questions to Dr. Shaw.

Finally, I would like to say a few words on the question of
the support of counseling services. Until recently at least, most
counselors did it as a sort of hobby, or at least a very part-time
activity.   They took time out of their teaching or research to see
the occasional patient with a problem, free of charge to the
patient.   Insofar as the state was supporting their research and
teaching, the state paid for this.

Nowadays, of course, counseling may involve expensive diagnostic tests, and the counselor is often an M.D. who is working as
part of a team. The patient does, in fact, get charged a clinic
fee or consultant's fee, at least in some areas. So counseling is
really becoming more and more of a medical service, and is being
treated as such from a financial point of view. As we move more
toward state-supported medicine, with hospital insurance and health
insurance state-supported, this trend will continue. In Canada,
medical care is almost entirely state-supported, and one province

has already recognized medical genetics as a medical specialty. The counselor can charge a consultant's fee for his services--which the patient doesn't pay, except insofar as he contributes through taxes.

With the help of Miss Susan Wright, I recently asked a number of counselors, selected from the National Foundation Directory of Genetic Services, their views on who should do counseling and whether there should be any attempt to assure that only competent counselors did the counseling. As one would expect, the results were extremely heterogeneous and have no statistical validity. I thought I would just mention them here. Of the 26 M.D.'s and 13 Ph.D.'s who answered the questionnaire--which was really not a questionnaire but just a letter with a couple of questions in it-- about half of the M.D.'s had had some specific training in genetic counseling, such as a stay in a medical genetics unit. Most of the Ph.D.'s had not. I expect that this proportion will improve as time goes on. Almost all of them, 31 out of 38, favored some kind of quality control, although there were wide differences as to the nature or extent of it. All the M.D.'s thought that an M.D. was advisable for a genetic counselor, and half of the Ph.D.'s thought it was, too. As to the kind of quality control, the recommended qualifications ranged all the way from "You shouldn't do genetic counseling unless you have an M.D. and Ph.D. and specialty train- ing," to the other extreme, where all you needed was a Ph.D. in genetics. Two of the 12 who expressed an opinion suggested a Board examination. Six thought an internship in a medical genetics unit was the appropriate qualification.

Other suggestions included drawing up a set of guidelines for what a genetic counseling unit ought to have, approval by the American Society of Human Genetics, and perhaps a registry with some kind of accreditation procedure, or a Society of Genetic Counselors, with memberships open to those who were properly quali- fied (in whose eyes?). My personal bent is for the minimum amount of formalization. But I would point out that with the increasing trend toward state-supported medical care, some kind of accredita- tion is likely to become necessary, especially if a fee is charged for the service. If the geneticists don't set it up, someone else probably will.

DISCUSSION

Principal Discussant: Margery W. Shaw

It has been estimated that 25 percent of the patients admitted to a large metropolitan hospital suffer from a genetically-caused or genetically-influenced disease. I suspect that this figure was arrived at by a geneticist rather than a clinician, because it is such a nice Mendelian fraction.

Now let us assume that the house physician who first sees one of these patients on admission recognizes the genetic component of the disease with which he is confronted. He may or may not wish to consult with an expert in medical genetics. But suppose he does, and the genetic counselor now finds himself at the patient's bedside. What can he do? There is, at present, only a limited number of things he can do. Many restrictions, both factual and legal, hamper his ability to do what is best for the patient and best for society.

De Facto Restrictions

De facto restrictions fall into three general categories: diagnosis, risk, and treatment.

The first of these areas, diagnosis, is under active assault, and the ignorance in this area (the absence of facts) is rapidly diminishing. Twenty years ago the genetic counselor could do little more than get an extensive family history, draw a pedigree, determine whether the disease transmission fitted a Mendelian pattern, and quote a risk figure for future children if it did. If the patient had a known genetic disease and was the only affected member of the family, the counselor was forced to "guess" among several possible alternatives: recessive inheritance, new mutation, low penetrance, phenocopy, or illegitimacy. But great strides have been made in genetic diagnosis in the past two decades. We need not be reminded how many "new" genetic and chromosomal diseases have been discovered, how many can now be diagnosed prenatally, how heterozygotes can be detected, and how abnormal gene products can be identified.

Yet there are many genetically-related diseases which do not follow Mendel's laws, or if they do, we are still ignorant about them--a de facto restriction. I am thinking of the diseases responsive to a large environmental component as well as heritability factors, such as birth defects and coronary artery disease, and diseases which are probably polygenically determined, such as diabetes and schizophrenia. In addition, the somatic mutation diseases--cancer, autoimmune conditions, and aging--fall into this large category where our ignorance is abysmal. In these conditions, diagnosis is not so great a problem but calculation of genetic risks can be relatively meaningless. We fall back on empiric risk figures derived from population studies where, no doubt, dozens of genetically distinct diseases are lumped into a single diagnostic pigeonhole. Thus, risk figures are easy to derive for Mendelian diseases, while diagnosis often requires modern sophisticated techniques, whereas in the more common non-Mendelian diseases the diagnosis presents fewer problems but the prognostication for other members of the family and for future offspring is cloudy.

The treatment of genetic disease has lagged far behind diagnosis and determination of risk. A rational therapy can be

devised only when the molecular basis of the disease is understood.
Attempts have been made to eliminate offending molecules from the
diet (galactosemia), replace missing gene products (hemophilia),
suppress abnormal metabolites (hyperuricemia), and eliminate
excessive accumulations (mucopolysaccharidoses). Of course, conventional forms of therapy such as surgical ablation (multiple
polyposis) and organ replacement (polycystic kidneys) are also
used. But for the most part, the limitation of facts restricts our
approaches to gene therapy.

De Jure Restrictions

The outlook for greater knowledge of genetic disease is very
optimistic. But the same cannot be said for legal innovations.
Recently the State of Florida brought a criminal action under an
1866 statute against a young woman who had secured an abortion. If
found guilty, she could be sentenced from two to twenty years in
prison for allowing an illegal operation to be performed upon her
person. In many states the genetic counselor does not have the
option of recommending abortion when a diagnosis following amniocentesis reveals that the fetus is suffering from an incurable,
perhaps fatal, genetic disease. But abortion laws are only a small
segment of the de jure problem.

The "right of privacy" of the individual and privileged
communication in the doctor-patient relationship impose two other
areas of de jure restriction. An individual who is found to harbor
a deleterious gene is not required by law to make this fact known
to his spouse or potential spouse, nor is the doctor free to communicate such a fact to relatives, to public health authorities, or
to society. Yet the opportunity to transmit his defect is, in some
respects, greater than if he suffers a venereal disease which is a
"reportable" disease and under statutory regulation for obtaining a
marriage certificate.

Prevention of medical disease has always been regarded by
society and the medical profession as desirable. Thus, vaccination, quarantine of persons with communicable disease, and
federal control of foods and drugs have all come under judicial
notice. Genetic disease is certainly a "communicable" disease even
though it is transmitted vertically rather than horizontally. But
genetic isolation by compulsory sterilization of individuals with
lethal genes is not as acceptable to our society as physical isolation of the patient with tuberculosis or leprosy. One could
argue that more individual freedoms are encroached upon by quarantine than by sterilization--freedom of movement has always been a
cherished constitutional right.

Opponents of legal restrictions on deleterious genes argue
that it would be difficult to decide which genes are damaging
enough to fall into the category of necessary controls. This
decision of "black" and "white" and "gray" areas is not a new

problem in the law. Cases have always been decided after a determination of facts, and there are no simple rules which are controlling. Although precedent lends great weight, many of our most
far-reaching legal decisions have later been overruled. Even the
highest tribunal in the land has, on numerous occasions, overruled its own previous decisions or found a way to distinguish a
certain set of circumstances from the prevailing law on a subject.
Laws written by both federal and state legislatures are normally
conservative in that only the most flagrant of wrongs to society
are included in the statutory regulations. Thus, even if we can't
decide whether certain genes are deleterious enough to come under
legislative control, we can at least make a start with examples on
which all (or nearly all) would agree. One such example is
Tay-Sachs disease. Here is a clear-cut autosomal recessive disease
which dooms the child to blindness, suffering and death in early
childhood. Is there any rational reason why a fetus should be
deprived of his right not to be born when the only alternative is a
cruel and unusual punishment and a certain death sentence within
months?

Another argument against legal obliteration of deleterious
genes is that perhaps these genes have a beneficial effect in the
heterozygous state. There are at least two counter-arguments to
this theory: first, if the complete extinction of such genes were
accomplished (an unlikely event), they would eventually be replaced
by new mutations. Thus, any possible advantage to the heterozygote
is not lost to the species forever. Second, in the cases where
prenatal tests can distinguish the heterozygote from the homozygote, only the latter need be eliminated, thus preserving the
gene in question for possible evolutionary value to mankind.

Another area of potential judicial attack is the situation in
which an individual knows that he has a gene which will bring
certain harm to his offspring and he chooses, willfully and with
malice, to reproduce. If he has an affected child, it could be
said that he had the requisite legal intent, i.e., a reasonably
prudent man would have anticipated the possibility of such an
outcome. One legal interpretation of such an act is that he has
committed a tort on another human being, and his child has a right
to sue him for the wrong he has perpetrated. Another way of
examining the issue is to consider such an act a crime against
society, subject to punishment. Although Soviet laws are quite
different from American legal codes, it is interesting to note that
recently the Georgian Republic has revised the criminal penalty for
spreading venereal disease. A Georgian found guilty of infecting
another with VD is liable for two years in prison, and those
infecting two or more persons or a minor are subject to a sentence
of five years. And in this example, scienter, or legal knowledge
of the crime, is not a prerequisite for prosecution. Is not the
act of transmitting an undesirable gene to be regarded just as
criminal, and the actor just as culpable?

Before the genetic counselor can be freed of the legal chains which restrain him from counseling in the best interests of his patient and his patient's offspring, society must deal with the basic question of intervention vs. nonintervention in the right to live and the right to die. We will wrestle with this question for the next three days.

Judge Oren Roberts once said, "Justice is the dictate of right, according to the common consent of mankind generally, or that portion of mankind who may be associated in one government, or who may be governed by the same principles and morals." Laws are merely a set of rules, codifying the principles of justice. Our present laws will not be changed, nor new laws written until the "common consent" is achieved. It is our duty, as genetic counselors, to educate our patients concerning the impact of genetic disease on themselves and on society. They, by "common consent," will subject themselves to private controls and help to effect the needed innovations in our laws.

General Discussion

LEJEUNE: If I understood you correctly, Dr. Shaw, you feel that those children which are recognized by amniotic puncture to have Tay-Sachs disease and who will become ill within one year, will die in a difficult condition—then why not discard them earlier?

I think this argument is very weak and the discussion is not necessary because we can entirely prevent Tay-Sachs disease. That was covered by Professor Harris in the last Congress of Human Genetics in Paris. As you know, Tay-Sachs disease is extremely frequent among Ashkenazi Jews and is extremely rare among other populations. Professor Harris proposed just to tell all the Ashkenazi people not to marry an Ashkenazi spouse, and then most cases of Tay-Sachs disease will be eliminated.

It is not racial discrimination because Sephardic Jews do not have the gene, and then if they want to marry within the Jewish community, they can do it without any difficulty. I think this type of approach to fighting a disease should be emphasized much more than puncture-punishing a few disease-disabled children.

SHAW: My assumption was that the fetus was already in the uterus and that the decision of spouses had already been made. Also, if we find a cure or a treatment for Tay-Sachs disease, then this would be one of the decisions that would have to be overruled.

SONNEBORN: I would like to ask whether you aren't making more trouble for the future. If this intermarriage should go on to a large extent, the cure then couldn't be used. If the Jews married non-Jews, then they would be spreading the gene around still further, and it seems to me eventually you would run into the same problem.

LEJEUNE: The impression is that this gene has to be maintained by some heterozygous advantage because it is so deleterious in its homozygous state that it should have disappeared. It is possible that it is a good gene if you have only one and a bad gene if you have two of them.

Remember, it is doing something on the insulating system of the nervous system. It destroys less of the insulating molecule, the sheath around the nerves. Maybe it's a better regulation than the normal stage.

Then the proposal of Professor Harris is very wise, because if this gene is good, it should be spread in the population, but it should be prevented in the homozygous stage. In the long range, let's say, in a hundred thousand years, it will become difficult to prevent homozygosity, because of the high frequency, as you properly stated it. But I don't worry about that very much because at that time—around a hundred thousand years from now—I believe geneticists will have made some progress and perhaps will have taken care of that new difficulty.

FRASER: May I ask what you would do about the carriers who refused to marry outside their race, who in fact may choose to marry someone who is a carrier.

LEJEUNE: I would tell them that they are free to do so, and I would not judge what they do as prejudicial for the next child. They are counting their own quality, that is, the quality of one man and one woman, and they choose that those qualities are more important than the possible defective gene effect which can result in the child. I believe they are right, and I will never quarrel with them about that.

I am not at all condemning them about it. I would just tell them what the risk is, and tell them if they want less risk to their progeny, they had better avoid homogamy for this particular gene.

VESELL: I think Harry Harris' statement was a very witty one that impressed all of us in Paris when we heard him make it. There is no question that as a theoretical approach, this is one way we can eliminate autosomal recessive disorders. However, it is not a practical solution. It is something we know from history that people will not do. They will not marry on the basis of what geneticists tell them their genes may or may not produce.

FRIED: I assume Tay-Sachs disease is something which leads pretty inevitably to an early death, to blindness, and to a short period of extreme misery. Quite apart from the advice Professor

Lejeune would give as to whom you should marry, what would he suggest where there is already a pregnancy? I would like to have that very clear.

LEJEUNE: I think the question is whether I would like to suppress a child or not. My simple answer is definitely not, because we have to recognize one thing which is very frequently overlooked: medicine is essentially and by nature working against natural selection. That is, our duty is the reason why medicine was invented. It was really to fight in the contrary sense of natural selection.

When there is one afflicted person, our duty as medical persons is to treat him as best we can. Maybe we cannot be of any great advantage to him, but we should not condemn him. When medicine is used to reinforce natural selection, it is not any longer medicine; it is eugenics. It doesn't matter if the word is palatable or not; that is what it is.

STEINBERG: I think Professor Lejeune made a fundamental error when he said that medicine works against natural selection. The physician, as does the architect, the maker of clothes, the maker of eye-glasses, works to modify the environment. Natural selection proceeds in a new environment. It is not a question of working for or against natural selection. Everything we do as humans modifies the environment. We have a new nature, and selection acts naturally in this new environment. Therefore, I think your argument collapses.

LEJEUNE: I was just thinking you were giving water to my mill.

CROW: It is my opinion that you, Dr. Lejeune, are using sophisticated genetical and evolutionary arguments to discuss a point which you are really upholding because of a moralistic principle with which I differ.

HOTCHKISS: It seems we are dealing with the difficulty of the conflict between responsibility to individuals and responsibility to society, and I am glad to see it come up so soon. I would like to make one primitive point we could be thinking about right from the beginning--that the gene pool of mankind is public property.

It is natural that, coming from a long history of savage isolation, we should be much concerned with individual freedom and individual inheritance, and that this should encourage biochemists to emphasize the study of individual genes. However, there is another very useful level at which we can deal with the gene, and that is the gene pool. The gene pool exists, it functions, and if you assume mobility of exchange, it can be measured and dealt with as a concrete body, or as sets of them, to which every individual's genes contribute.

I feel that this gene pool will eventually have to be considered as public property held in common, and those of us
interested in social and legal questions, I propose, should begin
thinking how to deal with and protect it as public property. This
could obviate such problems as Dr. Fraser has met--the inability of
the counselor to get information from a hospital (as public
health information, it could easily be obtained), or the problem
of getting it to the family; likewise, informing the spouse, or
some of the other de jure problems Dr. Shaw mentioned.

So I hope that you who are better able to deal with these
levels of the problem might keep this primitive point in mind as we
go ahead.

VALENTI: I am very naive. I thought two people would get
married because they were in love, and I haven't heard this
mentioned.

We have monitored eight pregnancies in the past year, only in
one of which did we diagnose Tay-Sachs disease, and now we have
seven normal children that according to your theory would not even
have been conceived by the two people meeting and not conceding
their love for one another. Totally, I think the number is
thirty-two pregnancies with Tay-Sachs heterozygotic parents, five
of which have been interrupted altogether.

Now, what do you think of the twenty-seven children that
either have been born normal or who are going to be born presumably
normal, if no mistake has been made? Aren't you depriving them of
the right to be born normal, but also depriving them of the right
of even being conceived? I think the limitation of freedom is much
more severe than if you acted the other way around.

LEJEUNE: I would say that with children that are born, I am
very happy: I am very glad that they are born.

Now, let's deal with children which have been eliminated in
utero. They would have been eliminated anyway, because we cannot
cure the disease. Then what you have achieved is just to speed the
process of their death. That is the other thing.

When you speak about the limitation of freedom by the proposal
of Dr. Harris, I think you are entirely wrong. There is no
limitation of freedom in telling people well ahead that if they
want to have the best chance, they could possibly look toward
marriage with a non-related person. Now this gene is frequent
among Ashkenazi and does not exist among Sephardic Jews. Thus,
they could intermarry inside their religion without any pressure
whatsoever and continue to avoid the production of homozygotes.

I agree with what was said by Dr. Sonneborn, that in the long
range, we will come again to random encounter of two heterozygotes,
because the gene is freed. But I strongly maintain that I cannot
believe that our present ignorance would be on the same low
level--I would say on the floor level as we are--with this disease
a hundred thousand years from now.

GUSTAFSON: I would like the chairman to request one of the lawyers present to respond to Dr. Shaw's proposals with reference to alterations in the law.

FRIED: Could you repeat the specific proposals?

SHAW: I really didn't make proposals. They were generalizations. I was trying to point out some restrictions that we are faced with by our present laws: the restrictions concerning sterilization, concerning abortion and the right of being able to go to other members of the family to counsel, and all of the general areas in which we have conflicting problems.

One of the examples is a case where amniocentesis has been performed, and we are faced with a state law which prevents counseling for abortion because it is illegal in that state.

GUSTAFSON: It seems to me, Dr. Shaw, you were saying there are analogies between venereal disease and genetic disease (suggesting genetic disease as a transmissable disease or communicable disease), and thus similar controls might be legally feasible. I would like to see whether, in the judgment of other lawyers present, those analogies carry weight.

WARKANY: Do you have genetic diseases that are transmitted with such certainty as syphilis and gonorrhea?

SHAW: Would some of the medical people help me out? How certain is transmission of syphilis if you are a carrier of syphilis? It is not 100 percent. But there are genetic diseases that do carry 100 percent risk, the chromosomal translocation between a homozygous 13 centric fusion.

WARKANY: Genetically determined disorders which carry a 100 percent risk for the offspring are rare. But when syphilis was as widespread and devastating as it was in past centuries, it was not rare that in an affected family the first pregnancies ended in abortion, then stillborn children were born, followed by syphilitic living children. Furthermore, syphilis was transmitted by one affected mate to the other.

SINGER: I'm a lawyer, and I practice in Washington, D. C. I am bold enough to accept Dr. Gustafson's challenge. Personally, I don't think that discussion of abortion as a serious constraint on medical practice because of abortion laws is any longer very fruitful. I think that the society has moved to the point where abortion, although perhaps not yet accepted in Florida, certainly will become routinely available without legal inhibition.

The question, and the more serious question, it seems to me, is Dr. Shaw's suggestion that there be some sort of institutionalized compulsion for the reporting of genetic information to some kind of public or quasi-public institution, which would then be in a position to make that information available to those to whom it is relevant, such as people intending to marry. It would also compel ultimately--and indeed that "ultimately" would be quite short in my judgment--the performance of certain kinds of tests on the whole population in order to translate the information into a usable form.

Looking at these proposals from the parochial vantage point of a lawyer, one tends to see them primarily as freedom-limiting or freedom-affecting types of proposals. My general attitude on such problems is that some major inefficiencies in government should be preserved if the freedom of individuals is to be preserved. I would to such inefficiencies add certain ignorances or lack of information on the part of governments.

For a variety of nonmedical reasons I would, I think, for the time being strongly oppose any centralization of information. I don't think it can be done successfully on a local basis. The collection of this data, if it were required to be disclosed, probably can be done successfully with various electronic techniques. And I would just rather not have the government quite so well informed, even though one pays a price on a social basis in particular instances.

LUBS: I wanted to ask Professor Lejeune if he provides information about the alternative of amniocentesis and selective abortion to a family with Tay-Sachs if they come asking for counsel. Also, does the lawyer help a counselor who did not provide this information in a country such as France? Could they successfully defend themselves in court if sued by the parents who subsequently had another child with Tay-Sachs?

LEJEUNE: What I do is this: I tell everything I know to the parents, and I tell them that amniocentesis could detect whether the child is affected or not. But I tell them also that I don't do it myself. So there is no ambiguity. They have the factual data, scientific data, and they know what I think about it. But, indeed, I would never conceal any scientific data.

THE CONCERNS OF DOCTORS AND PATIENTS

Judith Hall

I have been asked to discuss the concerns of doctors and patients which lead them to seek genetic counseling. I have interpreted this to mean that I am to deal with the new kinds of concerns which are becoming evident because of new technical developments.

As Dr. Fraser has pointed out, the traditional role of the genetic counselor has been to help an individual who comes because some family member has been defective, and he wants to know if it will happen again. Once an accurate diagnosis has been established--and this is really the crux of being able to give good genetic counseling--the role of the genetic counselor has been that of a neutral educator. Traditionally, he has dealt with four major areas: delineation of the odds and probability for future affected individuals, in terms meaningful for the patient; description of the natural history and complications of the conditions; discussion of possible treatments, whether symptomatic or directed at altering the disease course; and finally, prevention of future affected individuals by pointing out high-risk situations. The good counselor takes as much time as necessary and gives whatever emotional support seems indicated.

The success of this approach has been difficult to evaluate (Carter, 1971; Leonard, 1971). In the studies which have been done, success has been judged by whether patients take high risks, and whether there is ultimately a reduction in the number of genetically predisposed individuals; in other words, whether they abstain from having their own biologic children.

Some attempts have been made to evaluate whether families understand the odds and natural history of the condition about which they received counseling (Leonard, 1971; Sibinga, 1971). These studies suggest that families have very poor basic knowledge of probability and biology, and that traditional counseling may have failed because it assumed the general public has more basic knowledge than it really does.

With the advent of new techniques for earlier and easier detection of homozygotes and carrier states, with the development of methods of treatment which actually alter the course of in-

herited disease, and with the outright prevention of some conditions by amniocentesis and abortion, new concerns and questions
arise. These problems are even more difficult to delineate and
evaluate than the traditional odds and natural history.

They stress our technical skills, our demographic data, and
our psychological insight. These problems also challenge the other
side of the genetic counselor, which is that of investigator, to
more fully explore the new techniques, their potential, and their
effect upon the individual, the family, and society.

The public is well read, and genetic information, not always
scientifically correct, abounds in the lay press. The public
learns about potential applications of genetic engineering from
Time magazine (April 19, 1971), the risks and advantages of cousin
marriages from Playboy (September, 1971), and how to be sure their
baby will be normal from Family Circle (Warshofsky, 1971).

The general public, and particularly the youth, are deeply
concerned about the fate of the world as a whole. In this respect
I might differ with Dr. Sonneborn in that I think the youth,
idealistically at least, are concerned about future generations
other than their own progeny.

The threats of pollution and over-population are evident, but
the continuing process of natural selection and evolution within
that kind of environment is more subtle and unrecognized. Most of
the new questions which are raised have no answers as yet, but
geneticists and genetic counselors should and must be able to speak
to them from the knowledge we do have. We must develop, as well,
methods for assessing the contributions which we do make.

Essentially there are three kinds of voices raising the
questions: the individual as he faces the threat of a genetic
disorder, the physician as he cares for the individual within our
changing society, and the society as it gropes toward the future
and must deal with the multiplicity of various individuals' problems. The genetic counselor has responsibility to all three of
these. Inevitably, because he must deal with each of them, he must
don different caps for dealing with them.

The new genetic counselor must answer the traditional
questions of odds and natural history. He must continue to be an
educator, relaying the information which is available. But he also
has tools for changing the odds and the natural history of many
conditions, the ultimate effect of which he does not as yet understand and can not really predict.

Let me start with what I see, from my perspective, as the
major concerns of the individual seeking genetic counseling today.
In passing, I would mention that I am probably one of the least
qualified persons here to speak about genetic counseling. Although
I have worked in two large referral centers, I lack in years of
experience. But perhaps that allows me more empathy with the mili-
tant youth, the struggling young scientist, the everyday housewife,
and the expectant mother.

In the past, the individual came to the genetic counselor asking, "A genetic defect has occurred in my family. Will it occur again?" Now he asks, "How can I be sure my baby will be normal?"

Concerned, educated parents are planning for children more carefully and, therefore, each child is more important and more valuable, and the parents have greater expectations of him. Because having each child can be an active choice, parents want to be sure that their child starts off as healthy and normal as possible. The individual who has experimented with drugs, who has been exposed to environmental toxins, or has taken mutagenic therapeutic agents, wants to know how those will affect his offspring. If an inherited condition already exists, the individual wants to know if he can be sure his child will not have it. Parents are willing to go through arduous testing and uncomfortable procedures, perhaps even repeated abortions, to assure a chance for a normal, healthy child.

As you know, technical developments allow us to go beyond predicting odds in probably as many as 70 conditions and actually identify affected individuals and abort them. But we are unable to assure a normal child. It is important that our limitations be stressed, that the individual parents know we can only identify specific conditions at risk, that the parents understand that there is perhaps a 3 percent to 6 percent risk with every pregnancy for some major defect.

As we attempt to assess our counseling practices, we will need to clearly define the patient's initial questions, his initial state of knowledge, and his initial attitudes towards the condition in question. A simple questionnaire may suffice.

Many new types of screening programs are being established to help ensure the normal children for which parents are asking, such as the postnatal amino acid screening of the newborn, the intra-uterine amniocentesis of mothers over 45, the preconception Tay-Sachs screening for carriers to identify potential high-risk parents.

Traditionally, the genetic counselor has been limited to families which already had affected individuals, but the new programs are actively trying to prevent disease in families where it has not occurred before. Such programs are complicated by the general population's lack of knowledge concerning the nature of specific defects. Many individuals will be frightened to learn they are carriers; others will have no concept of the severity of a specific condition. The effectiveness of these programs, in terms of prevention, awaits years of experience and analysis. They can only be as effective as our techniques are reliable. And it is extremely important that our analysis of these screening programs include the detrimental effect such programs have in terms of worry and guilt for previously unknown carriers.

How will we judge their effectiveness? By the old standard of reduction in the number of genetically predisposed individuals? Or by a new standard of number of normal individuals produced? Or by still another standard of which program brings about the least suffering for families or for society?

A second area of concern for the individual is his feelings about the condition he carries or which has occurred in his offspring. The genetic counselor has always had to help the individual deal with feelings of guilt about carrying "bad genes." However, the new techniques, procedures, and screening programs have identified a whole group of silent carriers and made them vulnerable to a host of new psychiatric problems. The guilt and humiliation of having one's inadequacies exposed, even if they are only pieces of DNA we call genes, may be an increasing problem.

How shall we evaluate this problem? Tests and procedures, even when fully explained, arouse fear in patients. Concern that an amniocentesis will harm the baby is perhaps not unfounded as yet. How can we assess the effect of this fear versus the results in normal children?

Abortion, no matter how routinely it is done presently, can never be taken for granted psychologically. In our psychologic evaluation we must make a clear distinction between abortions done as contraceptive measures and those done for genetic indications. The first are done because children are unwanted, the second because normal children are wanted.

Perhaps abortions done for genetic indication raise an even greater possibility of psychologic problems. Mothers love their children, even unborn children, even unwanted, malformed, defective children. They want the best for their children. They want them to suffer as little as possible. The best way, with the least amount of suffering, may well be to never live at all. But that is not a straightforward emotional conclusion to the pregnant mother, particularly if she already has an affected child or knows one well. That child is an individual she may love deeply.

And how does the pregnant mother rationalize the abortion of a similar child she would surely love, much less a normal child, in her attempt to get a genetically approved baby? How does she feel about the loss of a normal carrier when heterozygotes and homozygotes cannot be distinguished? How does she feel about the loss of a possibly normal male in a sex-linked condition, or a perfectly normal twin?

As our techniques improve, some of these problems will be solved by better detection of carriers and perhaps by preconception selection, but the need for better emotional adjustments to abortion will persist, and just as much so, our need to evaluate it, so that we can be better counselors.

In passing, I might point out that most genetic counselors are men, and most individuals seeking abortions are women.

It is indeed trite to say that times are changing and that women's roles in society are changing, but it is a fact, the analysis of which may help the genetic counselor to deal more effectively with the modern women's psychological problems. Men's and women's emotional responses are still, at this time in history, different, despite Women's Lib.

And men have different kinds of concerns because they are not the bearers of the children. Their concerns are perhaps more pragmatic, more futuristic, less emotional, and immediate. Men may well ask if they have the right to ask for abortions. They may ask what is their responsibility toward children produced by artifical insemination. They may ask if the donors of sperm for artifical insemination have been screened for the genetic defect which they are trying to avoid. These are not only emotional but legal questions with which the genetic counselor may have to deal.

And, after the ordeal of amniocentesis and subsequent birth, psychological problems may well persist, even though an apparently normal infant is born. This child is highly valued, but when he cries all night, when he has a temper tantrum, when he wrecks his father's antique watch, when he turns out to be a little less than perfect or, worse yet, actually has some defect which was unpredictable, the parents will naturally be angry, frustrated, and feel shortchanged.

It seems an equally natural response on the part of the parents to blame the genetic counselor for this imperfect child, to relinquish responsibility for his inadequacies, to wish to rid themselves of him now in a sort of postnatal abortion.

The genetic counselor may lack the experience to handle these types of complicated psychiatric problems, but he must be alert to their existence and attempt to evaluate their long-term effects and obviously have reliable referral facilities available. I think we will find an essential part of our assessment of the new genetic practices will be to ask the psychologists and psychiatrists to set up programs which evaluate the emotional impact of the new genetic counseling. Screening for attitudes, defense mechanisms, and family dynamics may be part of our initial evaluation of families, and hopefully we could then learn how families and individuals change with counseling.

A third area of concern for the individual is to what extent the genetic counselor will invade his privacy. This has been mentioned already this morning. In the past, genetic counselors have dealt only with those individuals who came to them. Now our screening programs are turning up unexpected affected individuals, suggesting relatives who need screening, and family histories suggesting high-risk individuals.

What is the responsibility of the genetic counselor to these people? Will he cause more problems, or fewer, by becoming involved? Can an individual still expect confidentiality about his defect when he seeks out consultation? Does privileged communication still exist? Or is it inevitable that his family will be screened?

Because of the initial success of some screening programs, and because of the emotional appeal of preventing birth defects, we can anticipate more and more screening programs to become enacted as

laws unless we speak directly against their being legislated, for
it will be argued that if a screening program is left to voluntary
involvement, many possibly affected individuals will be missed.

I might point out that because of the rapidly changing
standard of behavior in our society, any screening program must
take into account the increasing number of premarital and extra-
marital conceptions which would make screening at marriage
unreliable.

The screening programs are of two types, those to identify
affected, untreated living individuals, and those to identify
either carriers or unborn affected individuals in high-risk
pregnancies. The aim of the first type is to provide therapy. The
aim of the second is to avoid an affected child.

One might ask: If screening is required by law, can or should
abortion and therapy be required by law? Perhaps by educating the
public, the patients and physicians, screening to prevent affected
individuals will be fully utilized voluntarily by the appropriate
population at risk, while screening programs to treat unidentified
affected individuals could be required of all individuals at an
appropriate age. This may not solve the problem of individuals
feeling that their privacy has been invaded, but education should
help.

In the meantime, it is our job to attempt to deal with and
attempt to evaluate what the sequellae of invasion of privacy are
for the individual. And I think the psychologists and psychiatrists will help us in this evaluation.

I would like to turn now to the concerns of physicians which
cause them to refer patients for genetic counseling. In general
they are seeking expert advice in a specialized area. The
practicing physician is having to turn from treating a few types of
infectious disease in large numbers of patients to treating large
numbers of diseases, each in a very few individuals. At the same
time, medicine is becoming less acute and more preventive. The
modern practitioner cannot possibly know all of the ever-expanding
range of genetic conditions, much less how to treat them. He may
feel unqualified to handle some aspect of the traditional counseling of odds and natural history, but more likely he wants to
establish the diagnosis and assure the patient of the latest
developments in therapy and prevention.

Over the last 20 years, the number of genetic counselors has
grown from a handful to many hundreds of centers and thousands of
trained individuals. How does the physician know who is qualified?
Dr. Fraser has asked this question also.

Many criteria have been suggested, such as specialized training, being a physician, having access to specialized diagnostic and
therapeutic procedures, knowing the complicated mathematics of
certain types of probability predictions, having psychiatric
training, knowing institutions for referral and adoption, and being
equipped to give family planning and contraceptive advice.

In fact, we have no specific standards required of genetic counselors, and as yet we have made no attempt to compare the relative effectiveness of various individuals, various centers, or techniques of counseling. If we could, would we judge qualifications by the ability to diagnose, or to treat, or to prevent, or to help the family adjust to its problems?

Which is the most important to the referring physician who has the continuing care of the individual? It would be relatively easy to ask the physicians directly what it is they want from us and whether they feel they have gotten it.

Physicians need to be educated about the new developments in genetics. Postgraduate courses in genetic diseases and counseling fulfill some of the educational needs of physicians, but we rarely ask them what they have understood from such a course. A test at the end of such a course? Never, because it would tell us that we have failed as educators, and it might jeopardize our relationship with the practitioner. And consequently, we don't really know how good a job as educators we have done.

But more specifically, the education of the practicing physician should occur with every case he refers. He needs to have a clear definition, if not diagnosis, of the patient's condition. He needs to have all the details of the counseling which occurred with his patient. He needs to understand the rationale for the counseling, because ultimately he will be the educator of that patient. He needs to be supplied with the details of management and the interpretation of laboratory data for the continuing care of the patient.

Many times we fail to supply that information, but only extremely rarely do we attempt to assess whether it has been understood and utilized. Whether it has helped the physician in his management of the patient, again, a telephone call, a simple questionnaire, might tell us.

An area of concern to both the genetic counselor and the physician is the need for a better understanding of the natural history of specific disease entities. The variations of expression and the possible complications of many conditions are poorly recorded in the literature. Further, a comparison of psychological effects of various disease processes upon the involved families, or a comparison of family dynamics in different types of inheritance patterns has never been adequately described. The physician can provide an extremely useful service if he is made aware of the need for this type of information and cordially invited to cooperate in such endeavors. In this respect we have failed to utilize referring physicians and to make them recognize their contributions to our progress.

Finally, an area of concern for the physician, to which I alluded earlier, is the patient-physician relationship and how this may change with the new developments in genetic disease. Traditionally the physician has been the advocate of the individual, the

patient. He has sought the best care and treatment for that
patient, regardless of cost, effect on society, or ultimate value
of the individual to society. The effectiveness of medical care
has been measured by the quality of care delivered to the
individual. But now we are beginning to think in terms of public
health, of evaluating how health care is delivered to the masses.
We often lose the individual relationship, and we ask: How does
this kind of care that I give the individual affect society and
other family members?

The physician-patient relationship, which takes enormous time
and energy to maintain, is being lost in the busy practice. So,
not only does the individual patient suffer by the loss of his
advocate, but the physician is caught in the bind of too little
time, responsibilities to the family's finances, and a concern for
society's resources.

The physician's role is complicated further by medical-legal
restrictions. It is only a matter of time until an older mother
sues her obstetrician for failing to inform her of her increased
risk of having a mongoloid child and offering her amniocentesis and
abortion, or a high-risk relative of an affected individual sues a
physician for not informing him of his risk.

So we must ask: What is the physician's responsibility to the
family of an affected individual? How much can he be expected to
become involved? Is that not prying? Is this invasion of privacy
or the physician's responsibility?

In our changing times these are difficult questions, but
certainly the genetic counselor must become involved in setting
standards to guide the practitioner. We must be willing to be the
first to take the responsibility of invasion of privacy as well as
to evaluate its effect.

Finally, I would like to mention a group of concerns which
belong not only to the individual patient and the physician, but
also deal with the interrelationship of the individual and the
physician within society as a whole.

Probably we would all agree that one of the major problems
facing the world is the population explosion. If society's aim is
to reduce the number of births, certainly we will have an increased
concern about the quality of the fewer children born. The aim of
screening programs is just that, but are there other ways of
improving quality? How, and in whom, will we utilize genetic
engineering?

Will we make second-class or less privileged citizens by our
concern for quality? Will we deny mentally retarded or handicapped
individuals the right to procreate? Will treated PKU girls be
allowed to carry pregnancies to term, even though almost every
child will be retarded?

We are all aware of the population geneticists' calculations
that with a given family size and the abortion of homozygous
defective conditions, we will eventually increase the gene

frequencies for those defective conditions. This means that those screening programs which are aimed at increasing the quality of our children may, by their very nature, eventually lead to an increasing number of abortions. Procreation will inevitably become more and more a laboratory science in order to obtain normal babies.

Are we willing to pay this price? Some people have advocated the abortion of carriers for deleterious conditions. Not only would such a project be overwhelming because of the numbers involved, but we do not know what role the heterozygote plays in preserving flexibility in the process of natural selection. We would not be sure whether we might be changing the gene pool in a detrimental way.

What will happen as we decrease the population growth rate and families become smaller? The usual forces of natural selection cannot work. But selection has probably changed with the advent of urban living and modern medicine. Selection is probably already taking place for those individuals who can tolerate crowding, pollutants, ghetto living, and noises. In the past it has been thought that man's selective advantage has been his ability to alter his environment, but we may be coming to an age when the environment will be so constant that we may not need this ability or the flexibility of the heterozygote.

We do not know what the future holds. And even more importantly, we do not begin to know which part of our inheritance or our genetic make-up will serve us best in the future.

What is the role of the genetic counselor in these matters? Can he be the advocate of the individual? Can he be the advocate of the physician? Can he be the advocate of society? Can he be these all at the same time?

Surely we have too little knowledge to make definitive statements. However, we will be called upon to provide information, the information that is available at this time, for the formulation of regulations and laws. Within ten years, laws concerning population control and required screening programs will probably be forthcoming. Abortion laws regarding genetic conditions are already available in most states. If workable, theoretically acceptable programs are to be enacted, we must be in the forefront of the planning.

In closing, it is obvious that I raise many more questions than answers. The concerns of the individuals and the physicians are many. The answers to their questions and problems are unknown. We are only beginning to define the problems raised by recent advances in genetics. It will be many years before we can assess the new role of the genetic counselor. But there is no question that the primary roles of the genetic counselor have been and will continue to be those of the educator and investigator.

It seems surprising, however, that as investigators the genetic counselors have failed in the past to evaluate how they might themselves be better educators. We have failed to utilize the wealth of modern educational techniques and equipment. We have failed to assess our limitations and our strengths and our ability to deal with patients' psychological problems.

The need to further educate patients and physicians is obvious, but the need to educate legislators and the public is just as critical. We must develop methods for evaluating how successful we are in our attempts to educate.

REFERENCES

Carter, C. O. (1971). *Lancet 1*, 281.
Leonard, C. and B. Childs (1971). *Unpublished data.*
Playboy Advisor (1971). *Playboy (Sept.).*
Sibinga, M. and C. J. Freedman (1971). *Pediatrics 48*, 216.
Time Editors (1971). *Time*, (April 19), p. 33.
Warshofsky, F., (1971). *Family Circle*, (April), p. 82.

DISCUSSION

Principal Discussant: Barbara R. Migeon

My comments have to do with the aspects of Dr. Hall's paper dealing with the attempts of the genetic counselor to educate his patient regarding the nature of the genetic disease and the probability of its recurrence--to illustrate several of the points she made.

It seems that physicians and geneticists, although indoctrinated in the scientific method, have considered genetic counseling out of the realm of science--more of an art or service. As a consequence, very few attempts have been made to evaluate the process. As Dr. Hall noted, when evaluation is attempted one has had difficulty in deciding which criteria to use and the evaluation is usually based on whether or not the parents take high risks. Until recently, there has been no attempt to determine whether the decision made by individuals regarding family planning had anything to do with their exposure to genetic counseling, or whether these were really determined by factors independent of the facts. Are decisions made consistent with the facts, or are they influenced by preconceptions and fantasies? How well do patients comprehend the barrage of education we are presently providing?

Fortunately, two excellent recent studies have addressed themselves to these questions. The first was undertaken by Drs. Sibinga and Friedman at St. Christopher's Hospital for Children in Philadelphia and published in the August issue of *Pediatrics* (48, 216, 1971). It deals with the complexities of parental understanding of phenylketonuria. Drs. Sibinga and Friedman point out that communication of medical information from physician to parents is often complicated by the parents' insufficient ability to understand the information or by their tendency to distort it.

The subjects of their study were 40 mothers and 39 fathers representing 42 families of children with classical phenylketonuria who attended the Hospital clinic. The physicians responsible for the medical management of these children had repeatedly informed the parents of the basic facts, genetic and metabolic, about their child's disease and treatment. In addition to frequent discussions, the parents were given pamphlets containing the pertinent material concerning the disease. However, when parents were asked to write in essay form their understanding of the nature of the disease, potential consequences and treatment, only 19 percent were able to give adequate answers.

The second study was carried out at the Johns Hopkins Hospital by Dr. Claire Leonard and Dr. Barton Childs, who have permitted me to present some of their unpublished data. Again, this study involves families of patients with relatively well-defined genetic diseases. Drs. Leonard and Childs attempted to determine whether extensive genetic counseling had been effective in informing parents of the nature of their child's disease and in influencing their family planning attitudes as well as their actual reproductive behavior.

The subjects of the Leonard-Childs study were 78 families, including: all families of patients attending the Hopkins Cystic Fibrosis Clinic; all families of patients being followed for phenylketonuria; and 15 families of infants with Down's syndrome, patients of the Genetic Counseling Clinic of Sinai Hospital. Families of children with connective tissue disorders were used as a non-genetic control population. The diseases studied vary in recurrence risk and in regard to the burden imposed by the child's illness as well as the treatability of the disease. Again, the type of genetic counseling has been, by most current standards, more than adequate, since it involved repeated person-to-person communication of pertinent counseling material reinforced by innumerable educational pamphlets provided by the various foundations involved. Moreover, in the case of PKU, parent group sessions had been held to help in providing the emotional reinforcement and support deemed necessary. The data were obtained through personal interviews carried out by Dr. Leonard, as well as from a short questionnaire on probability which was completed at leisure and returned in person or by mail subsequently. The interview involved questions relating to the nature of the disease, reasons for limiting family size, prior and present means of contraception, the risk of recurrence, as well as questions designed to assess the parents' general biological and genetic knowledge.

The results indicated that the parents had little knowledge of the disease in question and of probability in general, and were lacking in general biogenetic information. There was a striking reduction in the number of additional children born to these families, but the reasons for family limitation were often not related to the risk of recurrence, which was poorly conceptualized, but instead to the burden of the disease.

The implications of the results of these studies seem clear. We should direct more effort toward the need. Our efforts should perhaps be directed, not toward the establishment of more genetic counseling facilities, but to providing facilities to promote comprehension of the important facts of human biology--basic knowledge which will prepare individuals to comprehend the kinds of information we are prepared and preparing to give them.

What is needed is more objective studies of the counseling procedure relevant to the proper timing of counseling and effective means to communicate the information we wish to impart to patients which take into account their pre-existing knowledge and misconceptions. It seems clear that one of the serious stumbling blocks to effective counseling is the lack of sophistication among our patients regarding genetics and human physiology, despite their current exposure to these subjects in newspapers and magazines. Our growing body of genetic knowledge, to be effectively communicated, needs to be attached to a pre-existing foundation.

It seems imperative to me that we recognize the need and initiate action to provide the basic facts of human biology to as many people as possible, preferably introduced and developed as part of elementary school curricula, so that the next generation will understand what chromosomes are and what genes do, which will help them acquire a rational basis for important decisions which they may have to make.

General Discussion

CARTER: There is some misapprehension on Mrs. Hall's part in suggesting that we judged the success of our efforts by the proportion of high-risk parents who decided to have no children. That was not our criterion. Our criterion was the proportion of parents who had been able to take sensible and responsible decisions on the basis of the information we had given them, decisions about which they were still happy when we saw them five to ten years after we had initially counseled them.

We did not criticize their decisions. We have no criticism of high-risk parents who have planned more children. That is their right. We were pleased, however, that in no case did parents who had a high risk of a child who would have a prolonged handicap plan a further child. Quite a number had taken a risk on something like Tay-Sachs disease where the child, if affected, would die young, and we did not criticize them.

A second quite different point is: How does the general practitioner know who is the appropriate counselor?

The National Health Service in England has dealt with this in the following way. The Central Advisory Council to the Ministry of

Health has sent to every doctor in the United Kingdom a small pamphlet setting out very simply the principles of genetics, what genetic counseling can do, and which are appropriate families, in a broad way, to refer to a clinic. Listed at the back are the individual clinics now established.

There is at least one clinic in each of the hospital administrative regions, so every general practitioner knows who is the appropriate genetic counselor to whom he can refer parents with a genetic problem.

SONNEBORN: Do you have any way of knowing what proportion of the physicians who receive that information have acted on it, and who would not have acted on it if they hadn't gotten it? That is, how many of them throw it in the wastebasket or look at it and forget it?

CARTER: I can't fully answer that question. The general practitioners get these little pamphlets on various topics from the Ministry about twice a year. Probably in many cases the pamphlets go into the bottom drawer of the practitioner's desk. I doubt they are thrown away. When the practitioner has a patient with a specific problem, he fishes the pamphlet out of the bottom drawer and looks up the appropriate clinic.

This isn't done just once. This pamphlet was sent around in 1967, and early in 1972 there will be a new edition, bringing it up to date, including a paragraph on prenatal diagnosis. This will reinforce the message.

SONNEBORN: Do you think part of the success might be due to the simplicity of the information in the pamphlet to begin with-- that it is not too ambitious?

CARTER: Yes. We are dealing with a generation of family doctors who, most of them, have had no training or even education in medical genetics. The new generation of doctors, of course, mostly has had standard courses of lectures. But the older generation hasn't, so we have to keep it simple.

SONNEBORN: Has there been any increase in the number of people referred to genetic counseling centers, which might be an indirect way of knowing to what extent the Ministry documents have had an impact on the local physician?

CARTER: Yes. The increase has come about gradually. It didn't come immediately after the issue of the pamphlet. We are now seeing three or four times as many patients as we were before the issue of the pamphlet, and this is the experience of other clinics.

But at the same time, as pediatricians get better informed, we also tend to get better selected cases.

BERKLEY: I am the legal advisor to NIH, and I would like to make a comment to Dr. Migeon that as a lawyer, without a terribly acceptable definition of a chromosome, although I have a vague idea of what it is--I think I can understand the general problems involved with genetic defects and their recurrence.

I wonder if possibly the fault might not lie in the fact that your counseling, or the counseling in the studies you are talking about, was too technical. If I came in and were given a lot of detailed technical, scientific information which I considered to be irrelevant to determining what I wanted to do in the future, I am not sure that it would sink in with me either. The most important things you want to get across are the dangers involved, and the percentages--the risk factor of recurrence--and what can be done, whereas the basic technical, scientific understanding is something which is not all that significant. And as a non-scientist, I think that to say people should know more about science is something unrealistic. The counseling should be less technically scientific and more down to the layman's level.

MIGEON: The information given was not any more than anyone might expect that a parent would want to know about his child's disease. However, one needs to have a kind of gut understanding of biological facts before this kind of information can be truly comprehended. To know you have an extra chromosome without knowing what a chromosome is, seems inadequate.

BERKLEY: It is more important to know what it is that an extra chromosome does to a person. You can call it an extra widget, but if I know that if I have an extra widget, my children are going to be deformed in a certain manner, that is more important than knowing what the widget is.

NEEL: We have been doing genetic counseling for some 30 years at Michigan, and it is very easy to document from the records its increasing complexity. Twenty-five years ago, about all we could deal with were these probabilities. But now with carrier detection and prenatal diagnosis, this is becoming a highly sophisticated activity indeed, and perhaps as sophisticated as any branch of medical science.

I hesitate to get into cost accounting, but the entities we are trying to deal with are entities which have a tremendous impact economically on society and on the family.

Now, it is inevitable that the problem of regulation of genetic counseling is going to arise. We just can't turn our backs on it any longer. In this country we have a girls' school which is offering a master's degree in genetic counseling. I am not quite sure what happens to these young ladies, but this is a fact.

Dr. Carter's statement implies to me that there must be some kind of an accreditation procedure in England and Scotland at the

present time. I can't believe that whoever is compiling this list
is not doing some kind of accreditation.

I wonder if you would speak to that point.

CARTER: In Britain we do not have accreditation. However,
the list of clinics in the Ministry's pamphlet is compiled by
reference to the senior administrative medical officer of the
regions. If a clinic is set up in, say, Manchester, this is done
by the Manchester Regional Hospital Board. There are fifteen of
these boards in England and Wales, five in Scotland and one in
Ulster. Obviously, the board will not select a man who is
incompetent. They will get the best man they can, and this will
usually be the head of the university medical school's department
of genetics. Those in charge of the regional clinics are all medically qualified and all have training in medical genetics.

MORISON: As a teacher of biology, I would like to ask if
there could be a little expansion of the last suggestion, that some
of these basic biological facts should get tucked back into high
school. For example, was there any breakdown of the population
studied in relation to the kinds of courses they may have had,
either in biology or in probability, in college or in high school,
or in the elementary years, and whether this made any difference?

I am particularly concerned about the probability aspects. It
has seemed to me--and I guess I have said it now in print about
three times--that we would be better off if we taught probability
in high school than if we taught Euclid. After all, we don't live
in a Euclidian world any more, but we do live in one in which
questions involving probability play an increasing role. Nobody
ever seems to take me up on this suggestion.

I am not sure that it is easy to get into anybody's mind what
statistics derived from 100,000 cases have to do with a particular
case. The real question I am asking is: What kind of breakdown do
you have on the educational experience of your population, and does
it have any correlation whatsoever with the way they behave?

MIGEON: Let me repeat that the study is not my own, so I
don't have all the raw data at hand. There was an attempt to
evaluate the influence of education, but not specifically in relation to whether the people took courses in genetics or biology.
There was a greater correlation between level of education and the
ability to answer questions in the Baltimore study than in the
Philadelphia study, where a greater tendency to distort information
was observed among parents with higher I.Q.'s.

VESELL: Do you think that some of this failure to penetrate
is denial or rejection of the illness?

It may be part of the defense mechanism of an individual who
has one or several children with phenylketonuria to deny knowledge

of it, thereby rejecting any guilt that might be associated with the transmission of a defective gene. In order to correct the situation that you say exists, do you have counselors give courses until parents get 80 percent or above in their answers to these questions?

MIGEON: Reinforcement, such as the group therapy session with the PKU parent group, contributes to understanding of the disease. Of course, there must be emotional components. There are also preconceived ideas due to religious beliefs.

Regarding probability, one of the parents who frequented the race track wasn't able to define 30-to-1 odds, so that an aptitude for gambling is not necessarily an indication that one can understand what risk figures mean.

MURRAY: I wonder if we aren't perhaps placing too much of the burden on the patient. Physicians are often notoriously poor at giving directions, even when instructing patients about taking aspirin or antacids. This might suggest that M.D.'s ought not do the direct counseling, because of the difficulty many of us have in communicating.

The language that is used in counseling is critical. How you say the thing is very important, and it might very well be that the people who should do the talking to the patient are people who can talk to him in his own language. Physicians have great difficulty in speaking in four- and five-letter words and in brief sentences. If we place more emphasis on the communications aspect of counseling, we might do a better job of getting information across.

FLETCHER: I applaud any and all efforts to study the effectiveness of genetic counseling. It is intriguing to me that in the first two studies that are cited, it is basic knowledge or biologic information that is the subject of evaluation, not the patient's knowledge of the alternatives available to him or her.

I hypothesize that it is at least as important, if not more important, to study for the effectiveness of the counseling procedure than the ability to repeat information.

I am very glad you brought these studies to my attention, and I think there is a lot more to be gleaned from this discussion.

HAMILTON: To further that last point about studying not the patient or the knowledge he gains, but the process of educating him, what about getting two parents and exposing them first to one doctor who gives them factual information, and then seeing what kinds of decisions they might make. Then expose the same parents to a psychologist who might ask them to begin to express their feelings and, in an attitude of some acceptance, see if their decisions about the pregnancy would change. Then expose them to group sessions where two or three other couples, who had made recent decisions with regard to having or not having children with similar diseases, would discuss their experience.

Finally, I doubt an evaluation five or ten years after a decision is made about a pregnancy has much value. Most people learn to live reasonably well with whatever decisions they make. Therefore, I would look more toward an evaluation of the teaching procedure right at the time.

SINGER: First, I would like to comment briefly on what Canon Hamilton said.

I would be appalled at the notion of running a single set of parents through a variety of counseling procedures as some kind of experimental technique to see which information technique is the most satisfactory. I think there has to be a simpler and better way than to play on the miseries of those parents, or exploit them.

Seriously, I would like to ask questions which are perhaps somewhat broader than the techniques of counseling.

Dr. Hall said in her statement--and it is an extremely prevalent notion--that because of our concerns with population limitation, we have focused more attention on the quality of the population that will be born. I simply don't understand the causal nexus between those two statements. Both statements may be true, that we are focusing more on quality and that we are more concerned about quantity, but the causal nexus escapes me. This may be a function of my own ignorance, but people state it as delivered truth.

MACINTYRE: The assumption appears to be that if the time comes when, because of societal pressures, each couple is expected to produce no more than a limited number of children, two for example, there will be an increase in parental concern for the normalcy of each child, over that usually exhibited, because of the feeling that there will be no chance to compensate for a defective child by producing a normal one subsequently.

Whether or not this attitude is logical, I believe that it exists. We have heard it from several patients. Furthermore, we have sensed a feeling of need on the part of parents who have produced a defective child, to compensate for it with subsequent pregnancies, provided some reassurance can be given that the risk of an additional defective child is not great.

SINGER: Are there any data on how frequently the defective child is the last child?

MIGEON: In the Baltimore study the burden of the disease had a devastating effect in limiting family size. Thirty-one out of 39 children with cystic fibrosis were the last children. Half of the families with mongolism, where the abnormality was of the ordinary 21 trisomic variety carrying a relatively small risk, decided they weren't willing to take the risk. The control population, families of children with connective tissue diseases carrying essentially no genetic risk, decided not to take that risk either because of the burden of the disease.

MCLAREN: I thought there was also evidence for reproductive compensation, in the sense that for some conditions parents who had a defective child then went on to have another child that they wouldn't have had otherwise. This factor would have to be taken into account in considering the rate of spread of genes.

NEEL: There is pretty good evidence of reproductive compensation in the case of a child who dies early. For instance, this comes out of our studies of consanguinity effects in Japan. There is a tendency to fill in for a child who dies early. To the extent that children with genetic defects die early, then there might be reproductive compensation. But, I know of no evidence that the presence of a child who lingers on also results in reproductive compensation.

HALL: I wanted to reinforce Dr. Migeon's comments, especially from a lot of experiences in a children's hospital.

You have to divide the genetic counseling into two groups, those who come to you specifically for counseling, and those who have it more or less forced upon them because they acquired a certain disease, and because of the disease they come to you for counseling.

In the former group, around 50 percent are influenced by the counseling one way or another, and 50 percent are not. But among those who come to you because the disease is diagnosed in the hospital or immediately afterwards, the influence of counseling is very poor. The reason for this is that most of these families have a great deal of difficulty accepting the diagnosis that you have made of a bad disease. They tend to reject it; they certainly do not think that it is genetic, and you cannot convince them of this until some time has passed.

One of our faults, perhaps, is that we tend to want to throw the genetic counseling in very shortly after the diagnosis has been made, because we feel it is our duty to give them the whole picture. After six months or a year, after a certain amount of acceptance of a disease, such as cystic fibrosis, they are more likely to want to come back to us for reconsideration of the genetic aspects in future children.

My experience with this personally has been that they do not usually listen to us very effectively the first time. Even when they come to us, they do not; and one must re-discuss this with them at a later time, maybe a month later. I usually always ask them when I sit down, "Tell me, what did I tell you last time?" This was perhaps a month previously, and most of them will give me a completely garbled version of what I know, because I have taped what I have actually told them. So you probably give them more credit for understanding what you are trying to say than is due, because most of the time they don't take it in, and certainly they don't take it in on the first occasion.

MELLMAN: The theory of probability is something the medical profession has tended to reject, and the evidence for this is reflected by medical students' not electing more of their curricula of courses in statistics.

The medical profession does not like the idea of probability; they like the idea of absolutism. They like absolutism because this is more appealing to their patients.

There are now two types of genetic counseling, one probabilistic and the other tending to be absolute. Decisions are often made on relative risks, and this has always been very difficult for physicians and patients to understand and to apply in decision-making. The evidence is very clear that if a couple has a mongoloid child and are told the risk is one-in-a-thousand for recurrence, they are still often not going to take the risk, because they are faced with the impact of a mongoloid child in their home.

And now we are introducing an absolute system where, by prenatal diagnosis, we can say, "Your next child will or will not be a mongol." This approach is more attractive to the medical profession, and they have seized upon this with great excitement. We are faced now with a general clamor for absolutism in counseling, and it is obviously not available for most of the problems we have in genetics.

We must, therefore, face up to the educational need. Perhaps probability must be taught before the stage of medical education, before there are certain psychological sets. Are we really doing the job of saying we have to get education at the level where minds are still receptive to these ideas? And for this subject, this might be at the high school or college level, not in medical school.

SONNEBORN: I have had some experience with trying to get conceptions of probability across to college students who are brilliant in every other respect, and 25 percent I can't touch. I think it is too late for them.

CHEZ: We are talking of two things. The first is the fact that anxiety certainly impedes communication between that person who is anxious and the person who is making that person anxious. For instance, data has been published showing that when you present a diagnosis of cancer to a patient, nothing else is heard for several minutes and you might as well stop talking at that point.

Somehow the concept persists that the granting of a medical license also presents the person with a license to teach. This concept that physicians are educators persists in spite of the fact

that all of us who have spent our four years in medical school know
how inadequate the presentation of the curriculum is. Furthermore,
we could acquire the same data if we were to return to the medical
school and partake of the present curriculum. The point is, if you
take the time to use some of the modern educational devices our
children are receiving in the grammar schools and high schools, you
will find physicians are not the best people to educate their
patients, and you will find there are ways to create active learn-
ers rather than passive recipients of the information.

Perhaps one of the most humbling experiences, for those of you
in the room who have not tried it, is to take a portable TV play-
back unit into your office next time you give genetic counseling to
a patient. Then watch yourself in a more leisurely moment,
preferably with some scotch in your hand, so you can see how you
failed repeatedly to pick up verbal and non-verbal communication
and how you have failed in this particular aspect of total patient
care.

NEEL: Someone should respond to Mr. Singer and his comments
about playing on people's misery.

Suggestions were made about improvement in genetic counseling.
As I understand it, the physician discharges his responsibility
when he delivers the best care which he has available at the time.
In the courts this is usually interpreted as acceptable care as
judged by community standards.

What was proposed was to deliver the best care, and then to
attempt to improve on it by further sessions. And it is difficult
for me to see this as playing on people's misery.

MCLAREN: Could I support Dr. Neel very strongly in this and,
in particular, make the point that people who are under emotional
stress usually find reassurance in discussion, including group
discussion.

PRENATAL GENETIC DIAGNOSIS:
STATUS AND PROBLEMS

John W. Littlefield, Aubrey Milunsky,

and Lee B. Jacoby

More clearly than traditional genetic counseling in the past, prenatal genetic diagnosis has focused attention on ethical issues concerning abortion, because this technique makes it possible to state with certainty if a fetus will be affected with one of many genetic disorders, rather than simply advise as to a statistical risk. In this more defined situation, it is difficult for the individual doctor, as well as for society in general, to avoid assuming a more clear-cut advisory role. To set the stage for a discussion of these and related ethical problems, I will present some facts as to the current usage of amniocentesis and a few remarks as to the direction it will probably take in the future.

In a word, this new diagnostic technique involves sampling the amniotic fluid, and especially the fetal cells therein, at about 16 weeks gestation in order to preview the sex, chromosomes, and certain of the enzymes of the fetus. So far the frequency of complications to mother or fetus from amniocentesis appears to be very low, and only a very few diagnostic mistakes are known to have occurred--mistakes which could probably now be avoided.

Last summer we asked a number of the genetics clinics in the U.S.A. to summarize their experience with prenatal diagnosis. Table I shows that up to that time, 677 pregnancies were studied in 14 centers, and of course there have been more elsewhere as well. Three-quarters of the cases (509 cases) have involved the question of a chromosome disorder; in Table II this group is separated into three main indications, familial translocations, pregnancy in an older woman, and previous child with trisomy 21, plus a miscellaneous group. Thus, as would have been predicted, the most common indication has been older maternal age (234 cases); we have estimated (Milunsky et al., 1970) that the woman pregnant at age 40 or older runs a 1 in 40 chance that her offspring will have a serious chromosome disorder such as trisomies 13, 18 or 21, XXY or XXX. So far, the risk of amniocentesis at 16 weeks appears so low that we

Table I.   Partial Listing of U.S. Experience with Prenatal Diagnosis

DISORDERS	TOTAL CASES	MAJOR CENTERS	
Chromosomal	509	Bloom, A. D.	Ann Arbor
		Epstein, C.	San Francisco
Sex-Linked	49	Hirschhorn, K.	New York
		Hug, G.	Cincinnati
Metabolic	119	Mcintyre, N.	Cleveland
		Milunsky, A.	Boston
		Nadler, H. L.	Chicago
		New, M.	New York
		O'Brien, J. S.	San Diego
		Rattazzi, M.	Buffalo
		Robinson, A.	Denver
		Rosenberg, L. E.	New Haven
		Scott, R.	Seattle
		Volk, B. W.	Brooklyn
Total	677		

feel all women pregnant at 40 or older should be offered this test, and perhaps those over age 35 as well.   Indeed since serious chromosome disorders occur overall at a frequency of 1 in 200 live infants, it may become wise to offer amniocentesis to all pregnant women when and if data is obtained establishing more definitely the low frequency of immediate and/or long-term complications of amniocentesis.   In Table II, for 1 of the 6 affected fetuses in this group, the parents did not wish the pregnancy terminated. This may represent a change of mind, as many centers feel that amniocentesis should not be done unless parents are prepared to

Table II.   Prenatal Diagnosis for Chromosomal Disorders

Indication	Cases	Affected Fetuses	Aborted	Diagnosis of Disorder Confirmed
Translocation Carrier	50	9	9	9
Maternal Age 35 years	234	6	5	5
Previous Trisomy 21	182	3	2	1
Miscellaneous	43	1	1	-
Total	509	19	7	15

take appropriate action. Other geneticists feel differently on this point, however.

Three fetuses with trisomy 21 were discovered in the 182 pregnancies in women who had previously had an offspring with the same disorder. Probably the main reason for amniocentesis in this group had been to allay anxiety in the mother, but this relatively high frequency is an added indication if confirmed in a larger series of cases. Again, one family decided against termination. In this and the miscellaneous group, one abortus was unfortunately not examined in order to confirm the diagnosis, but otherwise all diagnoses were correct, including that of the normal infants delivered to date. This was true also for the translocation carrier group of 50 amniocenteses and 9 affected fetuses. These latter families are, of course, particularly appropriate for amniocentesis, and we feel strongly that geneticists should search out potential translocation carriers to advise them. Of course, it should be widely appreciated that prenatal diagnosis is possible only if both chromosomes participating in the translocation can be identified. The new chromosome stains may help in this regard.

Another caution concerning the prenatal diagnosis of chromosome disorders is the frequent occurrence of tetraploidy in amniotic fluid cell cultures (Milunsky et al., 1971), as shown in Table III, which includes our recent experience. Skin fibroblast cultures usually contain about 3 percent tetraploid cells. The surprisingly high frequency in Table III perhaps indicates that some cells derive from the amnion, since tetraploidy is common in this organ.

Forty-nine amniocenteses were done for X-linked disorders, with abortion of 20 male fetuses out of 27, and confirmation of male sex in the 19 abortions examined. One hundred and nineteen amniocenteses were done for 21 different inherited metabolic disorders, especially Tay-Sachs Disease (52 cases), Pompe's disease (24 cases), the mucopolysaccharidoses (11 cases), and maple syrup urine disease (6 cases). Thirty-three affected fetuses were diagnosed, 27 aborted, with one error recognized (a misdiagnosis of Tay-Sachs).

The list of inherited metabolic disorders diagnosed or potentially diagnosable in utero continues to grow, as shown in Table IV. Recent additions include fucosidosis, mannosidosis, more of

Table III. Tetraploidy in Cultured Amniotic Fluid Cells

Cases	Percent Tetraploid Cells
22	less than 10
19	10 - 25
12	25 - 50
3	50 - 75
0	75 -100

Table IV.   Inherited Metabolic Disorders Diagnosable Prenatally

Acatalasemia	Hyperlysinemia
Argininosuccinic aciduria	Hypervalinemia
Chediak-Higashi syndrome	I-cell disease
Citrullinemia	Ketotic hyperglycinemia
Congenital erythropoietic	Krabbe's disease
porphyria	Lesch-Nyhan syndrome
Cystinosis	Lysosomal acid phosphatase deficiency
Fabry's disease	Mannosidosis
Fucosidosis	Maple syrup urine disease
Galactosemia	Metachromatic leukodystrophy
Gaucher's disease	Methylamalonic aciduria
Glucose-6-PO4 dehydrogenase	Mucopolysaccharidoses (Types 1-6)
deficiency	Niemann-Pick disease
Glycogen storage diseases	Ornithine-α-keto acid transaminase
(Types 2,3&4)	deficiency
Gm1 gangliosidoses (Types 1)	Orotic aciduria
Gm2 gangliosidoses (Types 1&3)	Pyruvate decarboxylase deficiency
Homocystinuria	Refsum's disease
	Xeroderma pigmentosum

the glycogen storage diseases, various gangliosidoses, and several new amino acid disorders. All but two of these disorders (Morquio's and Chediak-Higashi syndromes) are evidenced by the deficiency of a specific enzyme or another specific biochemical feature. We have emphasized elsewhere the importance for these tests of choosing as controls cultured amniotic fluid cells of comparable gestational age, total age in culture, and position in the lag-log-stationary growth cycle (Littlefield, 1971). Cystic fibrosis is still conspicuously absent from Table IV, but will probably be added in a year or so.

Prenatal diagnosis has been reviewed repeatedly in recent months (Nadler and Gerbie, 1970; Emery, 1970; Milunsky et al., 1970; Nadler, 1971; Milunsky and Littlefield, 1972) and we want to concentrate here upon only a few developments.

First, for the inherited metabolic disorders, there is a great need for miniaturized enzyme or kinetic assays to shorten the time required for prenatal diagnosis. At the invitation of Dr. R. S. Wilroy, we were recently given the opportunity to diagnose the genotype of a fetus in a family at risk for recurrence of argininosuccinic aciduria. This time the amniotic fluid cells grew slowly, and it was only after seven weeks in culture, as the cells were becoming senescent, that we had enough for Dr. V. Shih to carry out her argininosuccinase microassay, which established that the fetus was unaffected. It seemed likely that an earlier diagnosis might have been obtained if the cells were exposed to C^{14}-citrulline, which would be converted to C^{14}-argininosuccinic acid and, in cells containing argininosuccinase, to C^{14}-arginine for incorporation into protein. Therefore skin fibroblasts from a normal control, a patient with citrullinemia (Tedesco and Mellman, 1967) and a patient with argininosuccinic aciduria were exposed to C^{14}-citrulline in arginine-deficient medium for 24 hours, and then the C^{14} in protein determined on each culture. H^3-leucine was included too, so that the results could be expressed as the ratio of the incorporation of C^{14}-citrulline to H^3-leucine, if variation in growth rate occurred between the cultures. The results are shown in Figure 1. The incorporation of H^3-leucine was linear over the 24-hour period and similar in all the cultures, although other experiments showed that the growth of the cells from the patients with citrullinemia and argininosuccinic aciduria subsequently slowed in arginine-deficient medium. C^{14}-citrulline incorporation paralleled that of H^3-leucine in the control culture, but did not occur at all in the cells from the patient with citrullinemia and only gradually in the cells from the patient with argininosuccinic aciduria. In other experiments, similar "leakiness", as expected clinically and theoretically, occurred in cells from patients in three other kindreds with argininosuccinic aciduria. Several heterozygotes gave nonoverlapping intermediate values. After a 4-hour incubation period for maximal discrimination, we examined amniotic fluid cells cultured from three pregnancies terminated for various reasons and from the fetus in question. The average of two assays on the latter cells was 59% of the average of the control values, indicating the fetus to be a heterozygote (Jacoby et al., 1972). This was confirmed subsequently by argininosuccinase assay

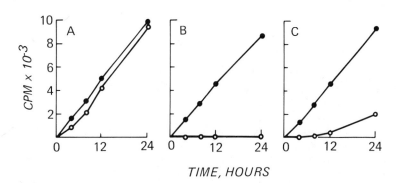

TIME, HOURS

FIGURE 1. Incorporation of H^3-leucine (●) and C^{14}-citrulline (o) into trichloroacetic acid-precipitable material in cells from a normal control (A), a patient with citrullinemia (B), and a patient with argininosuccinic aciduria (C). One hundred thousand cells in Eagle's medium were inoculated into 30 mm plastic petri dishes containing 22 mm cover slips. 48 hours later when the cells were growing exponentially, they were refed with arginine-deficient medium containing the radioisotopes. After 4 or more hours of incubation at 37 degrees, the cover slips were washed in saline and several times with cold acid, dried and counted. All assays were performed in duplicate, and iced controls subtracted. From Jacoby et al. (1972).

of cord blood. Of course, considerably more experience with this technique is needed, but it requires only a total of 10^5 cells in contrast to 10^7 needed for the enzyme microassay, and it should be possible about two weeks earlier. The same assay could be used for the prenatal diagnosis of citrullinemia. Similar miniature assays would be most helpful for other inborn errors.

Probably in the long run the best method to screen for many metabolic diseases at once will not be multiple individual enzyme or kinetic microanalyses as this one, but rather a simultaneous analysis of the concentrations of many metabolites. Automated technology to determine this sort of profile of body fluid or cell constituents is now becoming available. Probably these analyses would best be done not on amniotic fluid itself but on cultured amniotic fluid cells which are removed from the correcting influence of the mother.

Next, we want to discuss the status of prenatal diagnosis for three common hematological disorders, sickle cell anemia, hemophilia, and glucose-6-phosphate dehydrogenase deficiency. Only the latter can now be diagnosed directly in cultured amniotic fluid cells, and generally this deficiency is not serious enough to warrant amniocentesis. In regard to hemophilia, human skin fibroblasts contain a clotting factor similar if not identical to Factor VIII, fibroblasts cultured from hemophiliacs contain an equal amount of the same factor, and so do cultured amniotic fluid cells (Zacharski et al., 1969; Green et al., 1971). Therefore it seems unlikely that it will be possible to distinguish in utero between an affected and a normal male fetus. However, the locus for Factor VIII is closely linked on the X-chromosome to that for glucose-6-phosphate dehydrogenase. It has recently been emphasized by several geneticists that the prenatal diagnosis of hemophilia is now possible with a high degree of accuracy for women who are heterozygous at the dehydrogenase locus and who have had one son with hemophilia or are known to be carriers of hemophilia from other linkage relationships.

It seems quite likely that the prenatal diagnosis of sickle cell anemia will become practical within the next year or so. Hollenberg, Kaback and Kazazian (1971) have now confirmed earlier reports of the presence of measurable amounts of adult hemoglobin in the peripheral blood of 9- to 18-week human fetuses and have focused on this hemoglobin by examining its rate of synthesis and by blocking the synthesis of fetal hemoglobin. The technique is so sensitive that, by using only 10 microliters of fetal blood, a fetus with sickle cell trait can be distinguished from one with sickle cell anemia. To obtain this amount of blood from a 16-week fetus may well be possible from the placenta, which can be localized at this time in pregnancy through ultrasound (Miller, 1971). Since about 1 in 500 Black infants in the U.S.A. has sickle cell anemia, the ability to diagnose this disorder in utero would markedly stimulate the initiation of sickle trait screening programs, as well as put a strain on our current facilities for prenatal diagnosis.

Looking further into the future, one wonders if it will ever be possible to diagnose in utero serious autosomal dominant conditions such as neurofibromatosis, tuberous sclerosis, retinoblastoma, and Huntington's chorea. As with hemophilia, the discovery of close linkage to markers manifest in amniotic fluid cells would be of great help (Renwich, 1969). More precise would be detection of the effect of the gene itself, but what would one look for in an amniotic cell? Perhaps these cells could be coupled somehow to differentiated "indicator" cells, or alternatively to cells which already manifest cytopathology characteristics of the disorder. Thus, it is possible that amniotic fluid cells from a fetus affected with a dominant disorder such as retinoblastoma might cause neoplastic growth of normal retinal cells in culture, or conversely fail to suppress the neoplastic growth of retinoblastoma cells. This effect might occur if the two cells were in contact or might require cell fusion. Possibly the best indicator in some instances would actually be a whole mouse embryo. In this case the human amniotic fluid cell could be fused with a fertilized mouse egg (Graham, 1969) or injected into a mouse blastocyst (Gardner, 1968). Then the egg or blastocyst would be reimplanted, and after a few weeks further development, the embryonic or newborn mouse examined for some sort of characteristic histopathology.

Current and future problems concerning prenatal diagnosis are listed in Table V. In regard to ethical issues, it is important to separate abortion for severe genetic diseases, with which we are most concerned and which is widely accepted medically and legally in the U.S.A., from abortion "on demand" for social reasons. In regard to societal issues, it seems to us inevitable for practical reasons that society will gradually take a more active role in encouraging abortion for these severe untreatable conditions, just as it must do so for population control, but of course others disagree with this point of view. Until a consensus evolves on these issues--and each society will evolve a different one-- the safest and wisest role for the physician seems simply to supply the family with complete information and let them make the decision for or against amniocentesis and possibly abortion. This information should include the nature of the disease and the risks not only genetic but also those of amniocentesis, abortion in the second trimester, the possible occurrence of twins, and various other congenital disorders which cannot be detected.

Little is known about optimal methods for genetic counseling beyond the impression that it is often ineffective and poorly comprehended; especially will this be so when dealing with emotionally-charged topics such as amniocentesis and abortion. The legal problems listed in Table V are familiar, and as for population genetic effects, Motulsky has shown that prenatal diagnosis will cause neither a marked increase in the pool of deleterious genes

Table V.   Problems Concerning Prenatal Diagnosis

Overall Considerations

Ethical issues about abortion
Roles of society and the physician

Medical and Legal Problems

Counseling methods, psychological effects, etc.
Informed consent, responsibilities, privacy, etc.
Population genetic effects

Needed Technical Developments

Definition and lessening of risks
Earlier test results
Increased number of disorders detectable
Research on prenatal and postnatal treatment

Public Health Aspects

Selection, coordination and support of facilities
Cost/benefit ratios
Registries and quality control
Professional and public education

---

nor a marked decrease in the number of affected children unless it is coupled with a program for carrier detection (see also Crow, this volume). In this larger context, prenatal diagnosis becomes one of several alternatives available to a couple found to be "at risk" for producing offspring with a genetic disorder. However, if ultimately screening for all chromosome and metabolic disorders could be done from amniotic fluid cells, the routine monitoring of pregnancies in this way would have advantages over carrier screening programs in detecting fresh mutations and chromosome errors and in circumventing the problem of illegitimacy.

In regard to the definition and lessening of immediate and long-term risks of amniocentesis, it is heartening that the U.S. Public Health Service has recently established registries for amniocentesis in a number of genetics clinics. The risk of Rh sensitization by amniocentesis has recently been appreciated (Queenan et al., 1971). Evaluation of the need to routinely localize the placenta by ultrasound, improved techniques for abortion in the second trimester, and further understanding of amniotic fluid physiology are all desirable. Improvements in the treatments of severe genetic disorders in utero and postnatally are badly needed, to provide in at least a few situations an alternative to abortion. In this regard enzyme therapy or tissue transplantation seems to us likely to be more useful than gene therapy (Fox and Littlefield, 1971).

Finally, in the United States many of the major facilities for amniocentesis are being coordinated presently through privately-supported networks, but eventually public support seems both appropriate and essential. Cost accounting will unfortunately be necessary. Professional and especially public education will be required. In the long run, this should be part of education in human genetics in general, which in turn should form just part of a much larger program of education in all aspects of human biology, offered at all levels of schooling.

ACKNOWLEDGEMENTS

This paper is copyrighted by Excerpta Medica, 1972, and is reprinted with permission from the Proceedings of the 4th International Congress on Human Rights. Studies mentioned in this article were supported by U.S.P.H.S. grants AM 13655 and HD 05515 and U.S.P.H.S. research fellowship GM 32919. We are grateful to the individuals listed in Table I for the information which they supplied.

REFERENCES

Emery, A.E.H. (1970). In *Modern Trends in Human Genetics,* Vol. I, A.E.H. Emery, editor. London, Appleton-Century-Crofts.
Fox, M. S. and Littlefield, J.W. (1971). *Science, 173,* 195.
Gardner, R. L. (1968). *Nature, 220,* 596.
Graham, C.F. (1969). In *Heterospecific Genome Interaction,* Wistar Inst. Symp. Monograph No. 9, V. Defendi, editor. Philadelphia, Wistar Institute Press.
Green, D., C. Ryan, N. Malandruccolo, and H. L. Nadler (1971). *Blood, 37,* 47.
Hollenberg, M.D., M.M. Kaback, and H.H. Kazazian, Jr. (1971). Synthesis of adult hemoglobin by reticulocytes from the human fetus at midtrimester. *Science,* in press.
Jacoby, L.B., J.W. Littlefield, A. Milunsky, V.E. Shih, and R. S. Wilroy, Jr. (1972). *Am. J. Human Genet.,* in press.
Littlefield, J.W. (1971). *Birth Defects: Orig. Art. Ser.,* 7 (5), 15.
Miller, D.J. (1971). *Birth Defects: Orig. Art. Ser.* 7 (5), 33.
Milunsky, A., L. Atkins, and J.W. Littlefield (1971). *J. Pediat., 79,* 303.
Milunsky, A., and J.W. Littlefield (1972). *Ann. Rev. Med.,* in press.
Milunsky, A., J.W. Littlefield, J.N. Kanfer, E.H. Kolodny, V.E. Shih, and L. Atkins (1970). *New Eng. J. Med., 283,* 1370, 1441, and 1498.
Nadler, H.L. (1971). *Birth Defects: Orig. Art. Ser.* 7 (5), 5.
Nadler, H.L, and A.B. Gerbie (1970). *New Eng. J. Med., 282,* 596.
Queenan, J.T., S. Shah, S. Kubarych, and B. Holland (1971). *Lancet, i,* 815.
Renwick, J.H. (1969). *Lancet, ii,* 386.
Tedesco, T.A. and W.J. Mellman (1967). *Proc. Nat. Acad. Sci., 57,* 829.
Zacharski, L.R., E.J.W. Bowie, J.L. Titus and C.A. Owen, Jr. (1969). *Mayo Clinic Proceedings, 44,* 784.

DISCUSSION

HIMSWORTH: I have been serving on a committee in the United Kingdom considering the time in pregnancy when viability could be presumed and, therefore, the question of when abortion could be done was considered. In the United Kingdom, viability of a fetus is now officially 28 term weeks. Many obstetricians, backed by the World Health Organization, want to reduce the number of weeks to 20. Thus, there is a distinct possibility that the more complicated investigations on fetal cells may not be completed until you are past the time at which a legal abortion can be performed. How much time is required to make a diagnosis based on karyotype and to do biochemical investigations? Are we in a time margin which will give us great difficulties?

LITTLEFIELD: The data suggest that the 14- to 16-week gestation period is the earliest that amniocentesis can be done safely because of the increased amount of amniotic fluid at that time. One is certainly faced with a problem in terms of the time required for biochemical analyses. A chromosomal diagnosis is usually available in two weeks, but with the assays currently available and the number of cells required, biochemical diagnosis may take six to eight weeks. This is why we urge miniaturization of assays. One might encounter the problem you mention, i.e., the legality of abortions at 20 weeks versus later gestation. So far as I know, laws vary across the United States on this, with pressures to raise or lower the legal time limit for abortion. I hope very much that we can shorten the period of diagnosis to solve this problem.

HIMSWORTH: So with present techniques, if legal viability is 20 weeks, some of the diagnoses will not be made in time.

VALENTI: I agree with Dr. Littlefield that women over the age of 35 should be given the opportunity and advantage of an early diagnostic amniocentesis. Some 30 such women have been subjected to the procedure in my laboratory. My observations are not included in the data that Dr. Littlefield has collected from different centers around this country.

Amniocentesis should be performed even if the parents are not prepared at the time to have the pregnancy interrupted--in case of a positive prenatal diagnosis. Not only can they change their minds once the diagnosis becomes known, but if the fetus is found to be normal, the minimal risk involved with the technique is amply justified by the peace of mind gained by the mother-to-be for as long as five remaining months of gestation. A mother of a Tay-Sachs child whom we studied, in fact, changed her mind after the results of the amniocentesis.

Of 90 successful amniocenteses performed in my laboratory, three times a female karyotype was not confirmed at birth. Fortunately, in each instance, a normal baby was delivered. Probably the cells that we studied were of maternal origin. I have seen tetraploid cells in my cultures of amniotic fluid only very rarely.

The permissiveness of the abortion laws in many states may take away from some of our control over the indications to early amniocentesis. The procedure, at least in theory, should not be applied for the sole purpose of satisfying the parents' curiosity as to the sex of the unborn child.

Extenuating circumstances though may exist which may change our attitude in this respect. I would like to offer to you two significant examples. A young pregnant woman asked me to determine prenatally her baby's sex. She was firmly convinced that the birth of a girl would seriously compromise her marriage. To my refusal, she reacted by threatening to have her pregnancy interrupted anyway. I relented, and fortunately diagnosed a male fetus who was delivered some four months later. Another mother-to-be, having given birth to two boys affected by progressive muscular dystrophy, asked to have the sex of her unborn baby determined. Review of the slides from muscular biopsies done on the two boys revealed polymyositis, which is not hereditary. She did not believe it, and insisted on having her pregnancy interrupted if amniocentesis was not performed. Happily the prenatal diagnosis was of a female fetus, and pregnancy went to term. In these two instances, I have become the attorney for the defendant, namely, the fetus _in utero_. This is somewhat a paradoxical situation which, I am sure, will present itself again in the future.

STETTEN: What steps are being taken to provide extended follow-up of children who have undergone amniocentesis _in utero_ and are not aborted, to ascertain long-term effects of the procedure on physical and mental well-being? Also, what control group is visualized to compare these data with, since these are confessedly a high-risk population?

LUBS: The proposition to study them on a long-term basis was dropped, so that information won't be forthcoming.

MELLMAN: A study sponsored by the National Institute of Child Health and Human Development provides for an evaluation of a baby born after amniocentesis--at birth and at one year. This is the extent of it. The control population is the most vexatious problem because of the difficulty of getting proper controls of the same high-risk group. Attempts are being made to match pregnancies by monitoring the next patient in the same center, who is similar in terms of maternal age, gestational age, etc., and to follow those control patients in a similar fashion.

BEARN: I would like to emphasize the possible long-term consequences of amniocentesis. Suppose, for instance, amnio-centesis lowered the IQ of the child by five points. This would be very, very hard to pick up. Are there any kinds of long-term studies directed toward this aim?

MELLMAN: This question has been side-stepped for the moment because it was considered important to first establish some type of program of recording and collecting short-term experiences on amniocentesis. I think that an eventual goal of this program includes this long-term risk question, but it is certainly not in the current program.

HALL: I wanted to ask what attempts have been made in this network of amniocentesis centers to evaluate this aspect of the mothers' attitudes, the psychological attitudes, the defense mechanisms they are using. Is this being regularly done? Are the mothers being evaluated? Are the families being evaluated in this regard?

LITTLEFIELD: I'm afraid not. These things take money, and they haven't been done.

SINGER: Dr. Littlefield suggested that amniocentesis should be routinely offered to pregnant women over age 40 and perhaps even to women of age 35. This suggests that the procedure has been sufficiently well established in the minds of the medical profession so that it is now good, routine medical practice. If this is true, is the failure to offer such a procedure malpractice, or at what point does that kind of consideration enter into the physician's mind?

FRIED: A New Jersey case made the point that you cannot sue a doctor for not giving advice regarding an abortion, but that was a case where an abortion would have been illegal. If the abortion had been legal, I think there is a basis for a suit saying that the doctor did not provide complete information.

MELLMAN: There is another aspect and that is, when amniocentesis is offered, it is offered in the context that, say, mongolism is something that should be prevented. The question is, then--Does a mongol have a right to be born, and is he likely to take action against a doctor or his parents for either being aborted or being allowed to be born?

HARRIS: American courts have denied all recent claims by children against parents, physicians, or hospitals for "wrongful life," that is, for being born with physical or social handicaps. For example, Gleitman v. Cosgrove and Stewart v. Long Island College Hospital involved suits by defective children born to mothers who had contracted measles early in pregnancy. The children claimed the physicians failed to reveal the risks of measles and thus prevented the abortion of the defective children.

Zepeda <u>v</u>. <u>Zepeda</u> and <u>Williams</u> <u>v</u>. <u>the State of N.Y.</u> involved children with claims for having been born illegitimately. In all these cases the courts ruled that they could not weigh the value of life with physical or social impairments against the nonexistence of life, and disallowed the claims of the children.

SINGER: If failure to offer amniocentesis constitutes malpractice, then how would you ever obtain controls, i.e., following similar high-risk pregnancies where the procedure is not offered?

SCHULMAN: A fairly suitable control group might be the normal siblings born before amniocentesis was offered. This is not a perfect control group, but it might be well to ascertain the neurological and developmental status of these people so they could be compared.

NEEL: Actually this would be a poor control group because it misses the age factor which is so important in mongolism.

MELLMAN: I think Mr. Singer has touched on a very important problem which we are already seeing. In our search for controls, we have gone to other doctors to find women of the same maternal age and gestational age. We have found difficulty with this approach because the doctor isn't enthusiastic about the procedure and doesn't tell his patients about it.

BERKLEY: In order to get a control group and to protect the doctor from possible malpractice prosecution by the parents or by the child, informed consent of the members of the control group would have to be obtained where it would be explained to the prospective parents that the wife could have had amniocentesis.

VESELL: Do physicians performing amniocentesis obtain informed consent, an operative permit, or neither?

LITTLEFIELD: There is a lot of difference. Dr. Macintyre and Dr. Epstein have forms for informed consent. We advise the obstetricians who do our punctures to have a form signed.

MACINTYRE: I felt that a special "Informed Consent and Release" form was important in the case of prenatal evaluations because of the special conditions which exist in such cases, particularly the fact that you cannot do a physical diagnosis on your patient, and there is a highly emotional aura surrounding the entire evaluation. Our form was checked carefully by our hospital attorneys. It serves two purposes in that it assures that I explain carefully the various possible hazards and limitations of amniocentesis and the laboratory evaluations, and it serves as legal protection for the obstetrician and for me and my laboratory.

One thing that we make very clear is that defective babies are born for many reasons and that it is impossible for us to guarantee that the baby will be normal.

VESELL: I see an ethical dilemma because you expect that women who have amniocentesis will then be willing to go through an abortion. I don't think this is a free choice. An informed consent should provide freedom of choice and also the right to withdraw from a study or procedure whenever the patient wishes.

LITTLEFIELD: We think a woman should not run the slight but unknown risk of amniocentesis unless she plans probably to act on the information. All centers don't feel that way about it, however.

LUDMERER: In considering these ethical and legal questions, should we distinguish among diseases of varying severity? For example, can a physician be sued for failing to inform the patient that she is going to have a Tay-Sachs child, but not be sued if he fails to inform her that her baby will have a less severe genetic disease, such as sickle cell?

FRIED: One can make ethical distinctions in terms of diseases, and we do, I think, make them. Where adults have been afflicted with a disease involving diminished mental or physical capacity, one would say that to terminate life would be murder. But we have moved quite rapidly to the position where judging a person dead, who has an irreversible loss of brain function, is not murder. There is the germ of a distinction. If we are willing to do that with adults, surely we ought at least to be willing to consider distinctions about the potential capabilities of fetuses. It would be the strangest of anomolies if we would be prepared to terminate the life of an adult because we say, "This is no longer a human being," and yet, with exactly the same prognosis, take an enormously hidebound rule to a fetus. So there is room for distinctions to be made.

LEJEUNE: I would take exception to what you say about mental damage and not continuing to make a body survive. This is very different from interrupting a life. If the former were not sustained by a special apparatus, he would have died. But this is enormously different from saying, "This one could have lived if we didn't do anything, but we will suppress him." I will not accept a similarity between the two cases.

FRIED: Just to clarify a point, the definition of death in terms of a flat encephalogram has been peddled, I believe, in connection with transplant technologies, so that it is not quite the passive relationship which was suggested, because one of the consequences of finding this flat encephalogram and concluding this is no longer a person is that you take out his heart. And that is by no means a passive letting nature take its course.

BERKLEY: I would just like to make a point in this running battle. Turning off the machine that is preserving what could be called life is just as much of an active, voluntary act as performing an abortion. I think you are deluding yourself to feel that these situations are morally different.

THE SIGNIFICANCE OF GENETIC DISEASE

Arno Motulsky

NATURE AND TYPES OF GENETIC DISEASE

Genetic disease can be divided into four broad categories. The easiest category to comprehend for the nongeneticist is gross chromosomal aberrations, such as addition or lack of a chromosome, which may cause disease. The classic example is Down's syndrome, caused by an additional chromosome number 21. This trisomy leads to abnormal development during fetal life and is associated with a rather characteristic appearance, severe mental retardation, and a variety of other somatic stigmata. Everyone would agree that a patient with Down's syndrome is very abnormal or sick. However, other chromosomal aberrations may or may not lead to "disease." For instance, is a patient with the "XYY syndrome" sick? As a group, such patients have a somewhat increased tendency to criminal behavior, but many are quite normal. Although affected with a clear-cut chromosomal aberration, most patients with the XYY pattern cannot be called "diseased." What about the XXY pattern, Klinefelter's syndrome? Here we have infertile men often carrying some somatic stigmata. Statistically, such patients may be a little more dull than the rest of the population, but many individuals with Klinefelter's syndrome are not "sick." The decision to label a given patient as "sick," therefore, is somewhat arbitrary.

The second category of genetic diseases is monogenic abnormalities. These may be transmitted as autosomal dominant, autosomal recessive, X-linked recessive, or X-linked dominant traits. Victor McKusick of Johns Hopkins University in Baltimore publishes a catalogue of these traits. The most recent edition lists about 1800 different monogenic traits (McKusick, 1971). Not all of these traits, however, can be called diseases. A significant percentage of entries in the catalogue are morphologic or biochemical variants where an affected person is different but would not be considered sick.

With recent emphasis on medical genetics, many more genetic diseases are being discovered and many inborn errors of metabolism have become defined as enzyme deficiencies. There is thus rapid accretion in the number of "bona fide" genetic disease states.

Today, many biochemical variants not associated with disease are being found.

A third well-defined genetic disease category is immunologic materno-fetal incompatibility. Here, genetically conditioned incompatibility exists between mother and fetus, which may lead to serious damage of the fetus. Rh disease of the newborn is the best example. There are other rarer types of such incompatibilities. Physicians often do not think about such conditions as genetic disease.

Lastly, there are polygenic or multi-factorial diseases. Most of the common ailments of middle age, such as diabetes, hypertension and atherosclerosis, appear to have this type of causation. An unknown number of largely undefined genetic factors interact with largely unknown and undefined metabolic factors. We are ignorant about the etiology of most of these diseases. The common birth defects fall in this category also. Here again, genetic factors of unknown nature interact with unknown environmental factors. Are we sure that the birth defects really are polygenic? There is evidence from family and twin studies which fits this mechanism but the clear, crisp evidence that we have about chromosomal abnormalities, single gene abnormalities and immunologic incompatibility does not exist. A variety of common mental diseases, including much of mental retardation and schizophrenia, probably also fall in the category of polygenic disease. An important task of the future is to determine the specific genes which make certain individuals susceptible to these conditions. There are some indications of the data to be expected. Individuals with blood group O are more likely to develop peptic ulcer. Also, nonsecretors, individuals lacking the gene determining secretion of blood group substances, are more susceptible to peptic ulcers than secretors. Thus, a few monogenic traits which cause susceptibility to peptic ulcer are being determined. The breakthrough in understanding polygenic inheritance will come from analysis of the single genes which are involved in multigenic inheritance. Hopefully in many instances the number of such genes may not be as large as supposed by classical geneticists. In diseases, unlike in normal quantitative traits such as height, a relatively small number of genes may be involved.

FREQUENCY OF GENETIC DISEASES

The answer to the question--"What is the frequency and extent of genetic disease in the population?"--is hard to give. We can find out with some precision if we consider only monogenic and chromosomal diseases, but if polygenic disease and malformation are included among genetic disease, we are on less certain grounds. Admitting that all biologic variation has a genetic basis and that the causes of many diseases are related to such variation, most diseases are "genetic." The statement that 25 percent of all

diseases are genetic should be flexible since it depends on where
we set our boundaries and how we define genetic disease. The
figure can be set both higher and lower.

Estimates have been taken of hospital admissions in pediatric
hospitals. About 6 to 9 percent of all patients seem to have a
clear-cut, well-defined genetic disease (Childs, Bearn, and Miller,
1972). Bearn has done a study on adult patients in the internal
medicine ward of Cornell University Hospital and found 1-1/2 to 2
percent of patients with clear-cut genetic disease. Again, the
data are based on hospital-centered studies and are not true epidemiologic estimates. Studies of diseases coming to the attention of
medical geneticists also are not trustworthy. Rare, exotic, esoteric, and poorly understood cases tend to be referred to medical
geneticists more readily than patients who have a genetic disease
well understood by the general medical profession, such as hemophilia or cystic fibrosis. Professional medical geneticists,
therefore, will see an unrepresentative sample of genetic disease
in their personal practices. A well-controlled study based on
clear definition is needed.

DEFINITION OF "DISEASE"

The precise definition of "disease", regardless of etiology,
is difficult. Consider blood pressure. It is generally recognized
that blood pressure levels in a population follow a normal distribution curve. The cut-off at which we label a given patient hyper-
tensive is fairly arbitrary. It is based on that blood pressure
level at which patients are likely to develop complications in the
future. However, no clear consensus exists about this level.

Similar principles apply to a variety of other diseases. For
instance, data on I.Q. levels and mental retardation are of
interest. Using an arbitrary cut-off point of the normal I.Q.
level, a certain number of individuals will be assigned to the
mental retardate category. Since 60 to 80 percent of the variance
in I.Q. can be assigned to genetic factors, many of these people
are "mentally retarded" because they lack some of the genes that
make for "brightness." The proportion of severely mentally retarded
exceeds the expected number under the polygenic model. These
patients are affected with conditions such as trisomy 21, phenylketonuria, other inborn errors of metabolism, and infectious or
traumatic nervous system damage. Clearly, there is a qualitative
difference in the nature of mental retardation of such patients as
compared with those who make up the lower end of the I.Q. distribution curve. Height is another example. Stature is normally
distributed and a certain number of individuals will be short. At
what point do we label someone a dwarf? The exact level chosen is
arbitrary. Sometimes we can clearly distinguish between health and
disease because we can find qualitative differences. In many
instances, as indicated, such distinctions are difficult. Our con-

cept of what constitutes disease under such circumstances is based on somewhat arbitrary definitions.

The confusion about "disease" and "nondisease" is particularly acute in psychiatric disorders. Depression is a good example. Some depressions may represent the lower end of the normal distribution curve of feeling tone and may affect anyone because of an overwhelming grief-producing event in the environment. In other cases there may be a genetically-determined biochemical abnormality which leads to depression even in the absence of strong environmental determinants. At present, the differentiation of the qualitatively abnormal organic types of depression from so-called "reactive" depression often is difficult. However such distinctions will remove from the real "disease" category a considerable number of people who only differ quantitatively but not qualitatively from the rest of the population. Until recently, many psychiatrists have rejected ideas that some patients might owe their symptoms to qualitative differences in their brain chemistry.

The genetics of hypercholesterolemia is another illustration of these principles. The cholesterol level in a western population follows a unimodal distribution curve somewhat skewed to higher levels. By arbitrary definition, we label the upper 5 to 10 percent of the curve as hypercholesterolemics. As shown by correlation studies, hypercholesterolemia may be caused by a polygenic mechanism in some individuals who happen to have inherited a set of genes (involved in the many steps of cholesterol biosynthesis) which places them at the upper levels of distribution. Dietary factors also may play a role. In some individuals the presence of a single gene leads to hypercholesterolemia without detailed family studies.

GENETIC TRAITS VERSUS GENETIC DISEASE

Some inherited characteristics do not necessarily lead to disease. For instance, various groups are starting to test Black communities for the sickle cell trait without clear definition of the objectives of such programs. The impression is left that the sickle cell trait is a mild form of sickle cell disease. This means that 10 percent of the Black population are educated to believe that they are "sick" in some way. Yet, the sickle cell trait is a perfectly innocuous trait, except under very unusual circumstances. Someone who has the sickle cell trait is not sick; he or she is well. It is possible that such programs may be doing more harm than good by implying ill health when it does not exist. Screening programs for the sickle trait designed for genetic counseling are very worthwhile but require a great deal of education. In marriages of two sickle cell trait carriers, 25 percent of the offspring will develop sickle cell anemia. The implications of this fact need to be given to those who have the sickle cell trait. Benign genetic traits are not uncommon and all of us carry several recessive genes. We need to teach that being a heterozygote carrier for a disease does not imply illness in such a person.

BURDEN OF GENETIC DISEASE

The total impact of genetic disease on patients and their families becomes an important consideration in genetic counseling. The birth of a child with trisomy 13 and severe malformations leading to death in early infancy is a tremendous shock for the parents. This burden, however, is small compared to that incurred when a child with trisomy 21 is born. Such patients live for a long time and give their families prolonged distress. In trisomy 21 the distress largely affects the family rather than the patient. In other instances, if a patient is severely crippled but is normal mentally, both the patient and his family are affected by the nature of the disease.

What factors enter into determining the total impact on the family and to the patient? Severity, chronicity, age of onset, mortality, morbidity, presence or absence of chronic pain, mental retardation, and cosmetic disfiguration may alter the burden in different ways.

What is the effect on other children in the family? What are the medical costs? Does the condition involve seeing a doctor or hospital frequently? Can the condition be cured? Pyloric stenosis has strong genetic determinants but can be treated relatively simply by an operation at birth. Cleft lip and epilepsy have genetic components but can be treated. These diseases therefore are less of a problem than illness associated with mental retardation and/or crippling damage.

FAMILY DETECTION IN GENETIC DISEASE

In a number of genetic diseases, we know that a relative of a patient has a high risk of being affected. By testing family members at risk, new cases can be found. It is useful to categorize three disease groups: treatable diseases, avoidable diseases and untreatable diseases.

Many would agree that in a treatable disease with a high risk for other family members to be affected, one should go "all out" to find those who are affected and treat them before they are seriously ill. An example is Wilson's disease. This condition is associated with copper infiltration of the brain and liver, and sibs have a 25 percent chance of being affected. The disease is fatal if untreated. Treatment consists in removal of copper by drugs. Another example is hereditary polyposis which predisposes to cancer of the colon in all cases. There is a 50 percent chance of its occurrence in a first degree relative. Affected patients require prophylactic removal of the colon.

In avoidable disease, our duties also are clear. Porphyria is
an autosomal dominant disease. With exposure to barbiturates, the
chance is high that latent disease might be precipitated. It is
therefore important to warn relatives against taking such drugs.
In patients with a pharmacogenetic abnormality such as G6PD
deficiency or pseudocholinesterase abnormality, it is important to
check relatives, find those who are affected, and warn them about
harmful drugs. In translocation mongolism, the chance of carriers
having an affected child is relatively high. It is easy to detect
such carriers by chromosomal examination which needs to be done not
only in the immediate family, but also in more distant relatives.
Therapeutic abortion of affected babies can be offered.

What are our responsibilities if relatives are located far
away in Canada, in Europe, or all over the United States? It is
difficult logistically to approach all family members, and yet no
one else will be doing this task. Centralized registries may be one
solution to this problem. Can we be sued, if located in Seattle,
for not studying a cousin in Alabama who might be a carrier?   Or
could the distant relative sue us for meddling by bringing up matters he may not want to know about? These are difficult questions.

I feel uncomfortable about detection of patients in diseases
where no treatment is available. Take Huntington's chorea. We can
do neurologic examinations in the family members of affected
patients and may detect individuals who are in the early stages of
the disease.   Are we doing them a favor by implying that in a few
years they will be as sick as the proband? The patient may have a
dominantly inherited myocardopathy. Are we helping family members
when we detect early stages of the disease by cardiologic tests
with the implication that such patients may die of heart disease in
a few years? Polycystic kidneys--a common autosomal dominant leading to kidney failure in middle age--is another example. We can
detect the disease relatively easily by X-ray examinations many
years before symptoms develop.   As long as we cannot provide
treatment such as kidney transplantation, do we really help these
patients by early diagnosis?

In some cases there may be so much dread of a given disease in
all relatives that testing may be worthwhile to rule out the
disease in those not affected so that full assurance of good health
can be given. Unfortunately, tests often are not clear-cut, thus
making it difficult to be sure about the absence of disease.

Many patients may not want to transmit such diseases to their
children. If a person wants to face his responsibility to the next
generation squarely, it is better to know. On the other hand,
finding an untreatable, dreaded illness in someone who is quite
well does not promote happiness. However, if we do not study these
diseases in their early manifestations, clues as to treatment or
prevention may be missed. For those of us who are not only genetic
counselors but also clinical investigators, these are difficult
problems.

SOME PROBLEMS OF COUNSELING IN GENETIC DISEASE

Ideally, genetic counselors should be physicans. An appropriate diagnosis is a sine qua non of good counseling and requires,
under optimal circumstances, physicians who know about genetic
diseases. Teams where nonphysician geneticists work with doctors
are a second best choice.

In communicating with patients, we always try to see both
husband and wife. When we discuss risks, we emphasize both positive
and negative aspects. If the risk of recurrence is 25 percent, we
can tell the parents that there is a 75 percent chance that the
child will be well. We explain these risks in different ways to
make parents understand what probabilities mean and use examples
borrowed from games of chance such as dice throwing.

It is important that the genetic counselor not have any
preconceived idea about the course patients should take, and all
alternatives should be mentioned. These include sterilization,
artificial insemination, various birth control measures and
adoption.

Patients and doctors like objective tests. It often is quite
clear that a patient is affected with a monogenic disease with a
recurrence risk of 25 or 50 percent. After such information is
transmitted, we are sometimes asked, "How do you know? Our doctor
said that you would do chromosome tests to find out." Unfortunately, in practically all Mendelian traits a chromosomal test will
be normal. In our mechanically-oriented civilization, patients and
most doctors prefer objective test results to genetic possibilities. The great success of amniocentesis lies in the transformation of likelihood into certainty by a test.

Families often ask, "How frequent is the disease?" Misery
likes company. Telling patients that one has seen several other
families with the disease gives some comfort that they are not
alone in their misfortune. Usually the recurrence risk is less
than expected. Often, family members have heard old wives' tales
and think the risk is 100 percent.

It is important for counselors to sharply distinguish between
the genetic risk of transmitting a given gene and the risk of a
patient developing a disease. For instance, in the autosomal
dominantly transmitted Waardenberg's syndrome, the trait (pigmen-
tary anomalies, such as white forelock) is passed on to 50 percent
of the offspring. However, the accompanying deafness is the most
serious component of the syndrome. Fortunately, only a relatively
small proportion (10 to 20 percent) of those who carry the gene are
deaf. When quoting recurrence risks, we need to be quite explicit.

Differentiation between absolute and relative risks is
required. A recurrence risk in a family may be a hundred times that
of controls. This sounds frightening. If, in fact, the disease
frequency is one in 10,000 people, the real risk in that family is
only one in 100 (1/10,000 x 100). The risk of recurrence is only

one percent--a very small absolute risk.   Families need to be   told
these absolute risks.

SUMMARY

   The nature and types of genetic disease have been illustrated.
The difficulties of defining genetic disease are stressed since
most diseases have some genetic components. Graded variation in
quantitative traits makes it often difficult to decide whether
health or disease is present in a given individual. Even clearly
"abnormal" chromosomal states such as XYY may not be associated
with disease.   The extent of genetic disease in a population is
difficult to estimate because of these problems.   Heterozygote
states such as the sickling trait may be common in some populations
and must be distinguished from the much rarer sickle cell disease.
   Some commonly raised general problems in genetic counseling
have been discussed.   The impact of genetic disease on a patient
and his family varies depending on the severity, age of onset,
treatability and mortality of the disease. Search for latent or
early genetic disease is mandatory in relatives of affected
patients if the condition is treatable or avoidable. In incurable
genetic illness, early detection may be questionable from the
patient's point of view.

REFERENCES

Childs, B., A. Bearn, and S. Miller (1972). In Mutagenic Effects of
    Environmental Contaminants. New York, Academic Press.
McKusick, V. (1971). Mendelian Inheritance in Man, 3rd edition.
    Baltimore, Johns Hopkins Press.

DISCUSSION

   CARTER: I might mention two situations in the United Kingdom.
First, to what extent should one volunteer information on genetic
risks when he makes a diagnosis of a genetic disorder? This is
difficult, but we do it always for the young adult male with
hemophilia.   Hemophilia is now treated in regional centers where
the patient is given a booklet explaining the genetics of the
condition.   At the same time, he is given a card which he carries
around with him, so that if he is found unconscious in the street,
one will know he is a hemophiliac. The risks to his children and
grandchildren are also explained to him.
   A second point is about registers. Dr. Alan Emery, Professor
of Human Genetics in Edinburgh, has investigated the proportion of
patients who are counseled, and he found that in a particular
series there were three people at high risk in the family for every
one he saw at the genetic clinic. So I think there is need for a

registry, not necessarily to trace and counsel these other people at risk, but to tell their doctors. Then the decision as to what should be done rests, as it should, with the family doctor. He may decide to keep quiet about it or may decide that he should refer the person involved for counseling.

Having a registry system also has the advantage that one can contact people at the age when they need genetic counseling. One will know automatically that there are 30 individuals in the country who are 18 or 19 years old with 50 percent risk of Huntington's chorea.

GUSTAFSON: I have three observations about Dr. Motulsky's presentation that I think point to some central matters for our discussion. One pertains to the problem of determining what constitutes health. There seems to be an arbitrary point on a statistical norm which indicates health or lack of health. What about a further step, namely, a person's right to life? If one can call the fetus a person for the moment, is its life dependent upon a decision which is fairly arbitrary with reference to health or disease? That is, we have gone a step beyond health by saying that the value of a person's life, or his right to life, is determined by a relatively arbitrary judgment pertaining to a statistical norm. Other ethical considerations must necessarily be brought to bear in such an important decision.

My second observation refers to the status that desire and feeling have in relation to ethics. From Dr. Motulsky's presentation, one could infer that anything a person did not desire to do, he had no obligation to do; or that anything a person did not feel was for his interest or the immediate interests of those around him, he had no obligation to do. I suspect physicians feel obligated to say some things here that they don't have any immediate desire to say to a patient. They don't conduct their own affairs simply on the basis of doing what makes them feel good or offers them certain kinds of immediate awards. So I raise the questions: What is the status of desire, and are there any things we are obliged to do that we don't have an immediate desire to do?

My third observation pertains to the problem of stress. Is it quantifiable? We seem to assume a quantifiable quality, so to speak, in trying to determine what is undue or bearable stress. We should be clearer as to what kind of stress is bearable. Also, what is the cost to other persons by avoiding the particular kind of stress that we think we have a right to avoid? For abortion, perhaps it is necessary to recognize some cost to a fetal life in terms of relieving stress, or potential stress, to a family. So the questions are: What stress is bearable, and what is the cost to others in deciding what stress you have a right to avoid?

HIMSWORTH: What is sick and what is not sick? This is a particularly important question because, for example, when one sees a chromosome abnormality, there is an awful tendency to think that must mean the person is going to be abnormal. But it is quite clear in genetics that the experience of the individual doctor is limited. To get the real perspective of what a particular chromosome abnormality means requires a lot of pooled experience, not only numbers, but also follow-up. The making of purely professional, objective assessments of national consequence of having an abnormality is becoming a corporate professional responsibility. Assessments of that nature are what the public could properly expect us to produce.

I would like to ensure that the physician, who may have to advise that an abortion ought to be done, has access to the best opinion available and doesn't just assume that an abnormality in the fetal cells is an indication for terminating life. I feel quite strongly that corporate assessments of the best possible professional opinion should be made available because a physician can't be a specialist in everything. Some professional organization should be responsible for producing these assessments.

SINGER: It has been suggested here that physicians are wise enough to decide when and what to tell the patient or the patient's relatives. Clearly, with the development of amniocentesis and quicker procedures for gaining information, in the case, say, of the over-35 pregnant woman, one will find not only presence or absence of Down's, but also a great deal of other information. Dr. Carter seems willing to disclose certain information to the patient's family doctor but not to the patient directly. By what right should information, under any circumstances, be withheld from the patient? I am not sure that I can see any circumstances under which the physician should not disclose truthfully and fully to the patient his condition.

MACINTYRE: One example is nondisjunctional, nonfamilial Down's syndrome. There is ample evidence that the nondisjunctional event is either always or almost always associated with ovogenesis rather than spermatogenesis. Nevertheless, I see no good reasons for making this point to a man and wife who have produced a mongoloid child. I think it is important that they face the problem as a couple, and if I were to place the "blame" on the mother, there would be a real risk of initiating an insidious kind of condemnation, either verbalized or non-verbalized. I don't believe that any benefit can be derived from disclosing that the problem probably stemmed from the mother, and I do believe that such information can do a lot of harm.

FRIED: That example is really very striking because what do you suppose would happen to those patients' confidence in you and in the very sound advice that you gave them, that they must meet this as a couple, if they should later happen to read in the newspaper that, in fact, it is the woman's fault. Wouldn't they feel deceived, and wouldn't they further feel that the deception was somewhat material? Would not their reading of this in fact be a true reading, and the reason you withheld this information was because it was relevant? I think there is an enormous risk of undermining your own credibility by withholding information which people, after all, are very likely to get.

MACINTYRE: Your point is well taken. I should have made the additional point that if parents ask me the specific question, I give them a truthful answer, but that includes the fact that we don't have any proof that nondisjunction doesn't happen in spermatogenesis in such cases, even though the data imply that it is far more frequent in ovogenesis. However, there are situations in which to tell a couple all that we know about the probable bases for a problem can be damaging to them, and if such full disclosure is of no conceivable benefit, I feel we should protect them from such damage. I have never had a couple return to me saying that they had read an article in a magazine implying that mongolism usually is related to a problem in the mother and asking me why I didn't point this out. However, if this should happen, I would tell them that the information probably is correct for the majority of cases, but that in any specific case, we have no proof that the accident couldn't have occurred in the father. I have had no indication that my method of handling this situation has ever led my patients to lose confidence in me, and I don't believe that it ever has because of the care with which I make my statements. However, even if there is a slight chance that my failure to disclose all of the scientific information about nondisjunction would occasionally jeopardize confidence in me, I still would continue to handle counseling in the same fashion in order to prevent the "accusation syndrome" from developing in most cases.

FRIED: What I was suggesting is that their confidence in your very sound advice that they should view this as a couple would be put in jeopardy. That is the point.

MACINTYRE: I don't place a great deal of stress on the concept of viewing the problem as a couple. I merely stay clear of making points which would make it impossible for them to do so.

BEARN: Isn't it true that probably every physician has been confronted with this same problem? How much should he tell the patient? It is a very difficult matter. Most physicians approach the problem with great humility, and probably the most they can hope for is that by the end of their lives they haven't done much harm.

LEJEUNE: Physicians' telling what they know is much more important in the case of the older mother. We need not tell who is responsible for the actual segregation in the child--the father or the mother. But we have to tell them that the risk is greater, the

older the mother. That information is very useful to them. A very
important case is translocation. When we find a child trisomic by
translocation, we look at the parents. Sometimes it is de novo:
the parents are normal, and the translocation is an accident.   But
in roughly half of the cases, one of the parents has a
translocation. We have to tell the couple that there is a risk,
but never tell a spouse that the other is a carrier. We explain to
the carrier that he or she has a translocation and what the risks
are. And then we tell them we can do two things: we can say
nothing to the spouse; or the carrier can tell the spouse, and they
can come back together and we will explain exactly what is the
matter. In no case has the carrier said, "Don't say anything." In
every case they say, "I will tell my spouse immediately, and we
will come together so you can explain to both of us." And this
proved that the truth is not damaging if given at the consideration
of one member of the couple. If it were released by us directly to
the normal person, probably it would be damaging. But because it
is the carrier who said to the other, "I am the carrier, now we
have to understand the matter"--it seems the harm done is the
smallest possible.

     VESELL: I have heard of a diagnosis of severe chromosomal
abnormality made on the basis of karyotype analysis on only a
single culture of amniotic fluid. The pregnancy was interrupted by
abortion, and an entirely normal fetus was found. What should the
parents be told?

     CONDLIFFE: Is this any different from appendectomies in which
perhaps one appendix in every five removed is not diseased?   The
surgeon has intervened usually for a good reason, and no damage is
done, but there were risks. I think in many cases nothing at all
is said to the patient.

     LILEY: The problem of what to tell is not restricted to
genetic disorders. The obstetrician or gynecologist faces this in
questions of infertility: Which is the person at fault? Sometimes
it is brutally obvious to the people, but when it is not, Dr.
Lejeune's advice on how to inform the couple is very good. It is
often not the truth that is harmful but the way it is presented.
     One thing that has been mentioned several times is
communicating with the patient's physician. Of course, it
overlooks that doctors today don't have patients; rather patients
have doctors, and the patient is the safest recipient of this
information anyway. This is true of particularly rare blood
phenotypes, people who are grave transfusion risks. Some
acceptable technique--and it may vary with patients--has to be
found to convey information to individual patients. It is a
problem in blood banking when, say, a positive WR is discovered in
a voluntary donor, but it is a problem you can't dodge simply
because the news is unpleasant.

SINGER: If the indication for doing amniocentesis is age of the mother, presumably you don't look for that one indication. Presumably you do a much broader analysis.

I assume the techniques will become, if not perfect, much better and more perfect than they are. And if you find not Down's but something else, what do you do? I don't think the law says anything yet.

BEARN: This is occurring in routine biochemical screening of blood samples from hospital patients. Sometimes it is cheaper to perform 15 tests rather than the three or four which are specifically indicated. What do you do when you suddenly find somebody with moderately elevated uric acid? You have to decide how far to investigate a purely biochemical abnormality. It could cost a great deal of money chasing symptomless biochemical trivia which are of no concern to the patient and which you can do nothing about.

LEJEUNE: For practical purposes, you cannot screen amniotic fluid for all detectable diseases, because that would mean perhaps 10 or 100 liters of amniotic fluid. Only rarely can you do more than a chromosome analysis and one biochemical assay.

LITTLEFIELD: If we did discover another unexpected homozygous affected situation, obviously we have to tell the parents about it. The problem is more than the handling of information on carrier states. For example, nobody agrees as to what you should tell the carrier of the sickle cell trait. Even if carriers are not liable to various problems, or even though we don't have prenatal diagnosis yet for sickle cell anemia, there is still the basic problem: Are you or are you not obliged to tell people if you find out they have a trait that raises problems about their reproduction? This is in part a legal question.

MIGEON: It seems that we don't have sufficient information about how a parent reacts to learning that he or his spouse carries mutant genes or abnormal chromosomes. Is there a difference in the acceptance of this information when one parent carries the defect rather than both? We need to study precisely how such information is accepted before we concern ourselves with the legal implications of withholding information.

POPULATION PERSPECTIVE

James F. Crow

The principal social issue in human population genetics, I think, is this: How much responsibility should this generation accept for the germ plasm that it will transmit to the future and over which it has temporary custody? To what extent should society infringe on the individual freedom of this generation in order to have a better supply of genes for future generations?

It is clear enough that the current practice is to accept no significant responsibility and to infringe hardly at all. This is not surprising. We have traditionally given little consideration to the future in other kinds of decisions. I am personally annoyed with my great-grandparents who didn't stop to consider whether I might want to see buffalo and passenger pigeons when they laid waste to this country. Serious, widespread concern for the future is a rather new thing even in areas like conservation and population numbers.

There are many reasons not to rush headlong into a eugenics program: society's uncertainty about desirable ends; doubts about our ability to foresee all the consequences; fear of social or political ramifications of a program that could make a significant biological impact; and the belief that new knowledge will render our current attempts obsolete. Yet I am somewhat surprised that most biologists, including geneticists, are hardly willing even to discuss the subject.

I don't know whether future generations will regard us as people who selfishly pursued our own immediate objectives without trying to foresee even the most obvious consequences, or as wise men who judiciously refrained from ill-considered attempts to act beyond their knowledge and wisdom. I tend to belong to the school that wants to place the present individual first and long-range social consequences second in social decisions, but I don't want to ignore eugenic considerations.

I wish to deal here not with population trends in general but with the narrower question of the influence of genetic counseling and particularly of amniocentesis. It is easy to give a first approximation. Since the fraction of the population which receives any genetic counseling is minute, so is the statistical impact thereof. This raises another ethical issue that has been stated most emphatically by Richard Lewontin: Is it ethical to devote so much attention to very rare diseases? However, genetic knowledge and genetic counseling are certain to increase, and I should like to discuss several consequences that seem to be predictable.

RELAXED SELECTION

The first of these is relaxed selection. The effect of a cure or a treatment or a general rise in the living standard is typically to change a condition that has formerly reduced survival and reproduction into one where these are much less reduced. On the average, this means less natural selection against the causative genes. Can this be quantified? In simple cases, yes. In most cases, no. For a single dominant gene one can use the following argument, and I am considering the simplest case.

Suppose this dominant gene is so harmful that it causes the death or the infertility of its carrier. If we now discover a cure for the disease, the person who has inherited the gene and otherwise would not have reproduced, now reproduces at the normal rate. This would double the incidence of the trait in the next generation because, in addition to the inherited cases, there would be the new mutations that normally occur. In each successive generation the new mutations would be added to the incidence in the previous generation. However, I have taken the most extreme example. If the disease is less severe or the cure is less complete, the change is proportionately less. The increase in the next generation is proportional to the improvement in fitness brought about by the treatment.

The issue for society is partly resolved by the consideration of the individual. The person who has been cured of a genetic disease knows, if his counselor has told him, that his children have a 50 percent chance of inheriting the disease. He is likely to make the decision to reproduce or not in accordance with his own experience. If he finds the treated disease is easy to live with and his own life has been rewarding, he will have little hesitancy in exposing his children to a high risk of the same condition. Contrarywise, if his own life has been miserable, he will probably choose not to reproduce.

An example is pyloric stenosis, a formerly fatal obstruction of the digestive tract of newborn infants that is now corrected by surgery. The operation has now been performed for some 40 or 50 years, and the children of persons who were operated on frequently have the condition. So these cases are added on to the others that come from parents who were normal as infants.

In this instance, the interest of society and the welfare of the individual run very closely parallel, and a decision made by the individual in the interest of his own children is what society as a whole would like to have done. A conflict of interest could arise if society assumes responsibility for the costs. If the treatment is very expensive and utilizes very scarce resources, but is not unpleasant for the recipient, the individual with the disease may wish to reproduce while society prefers that he not. Society may somehow have to place restrictions on reproduction or make the appropriate plans to allocate more resources to this disease in future generations.

For a disease such as pyloric stenosis, it would seem to me the appropriate social attitude is simply to budget the proper number of surgeons next generation and the correspondingly higher costs of medical care that come from the predictable increase.

In the case of a recessive condition, the situation is quite strikingly different. The proportion that is added on to the next generation is the amount of improvement multiplied by the square of the gene frequency. This leads to an increase in the next generation of approximately twice the gene frequency times the amount of improvement that has been effected by the treatment. For a trait with a one percent gene frequency, that is, 1 in 10,000 people have the disease, this means approximately a two percent increase next generation. So if the frequency of the disease otherwise would have been 1 in 10,000, it will now be 1.02 in 10,000. I regard this as not very important compared with the immediate benefits to the individuals involved if this is successful treatment.

So to contrast dominant deleterious diseases and rare recessive conditions, in the former case there would be substantial percentage increase in the next generation, but it is likely to be self-correcting in the sense that the individual has a large interest in his own children. In the case of the recessive disease, the increase is very slight, and the individual will probably have little personal interest because it is likely not to be his immediate descendants that are affected by the gene.

I am making one assumption that should be stated at the outset. I am paying less attention to very long-range trends than is sometimes done. My own concern is with the next few generations, perhaps the next 15 or 20, but not the next 100 or 1,000, which seem too remote to try to foresee.

What can I say in a more general way than by picking isolated examples? One thing is that an environmental improvement, medical or otherwise, must be permanent. If, after several generations of treatment, it is necessary to go back to the earlier environment with no treatment, there will be an accumulated gene frequency enhancement all expressed at once. So the institution of a program of treatment should imply some thought to its continuance (or a eugenic alternative).

What if selection is completely relaxed, or medical care becomes perfect, or economic progress improves the living standard until every genotype has an equal chance of surviving and zero population growth comes into effect? What are the predictable consequences of this? We can judge something of the less extreme changes by asking what the most extreme effects would be. No selection at all would mean that gene frequencies would no longer change in a systematic way. They would change by whatever amount chance alone would dictate, but this is capricious and nondirectional. The gene frequencies would stay right where they are as far as any selective processes are concerned. However, the one thing that would not be changed is mutation, and in the absence of selection, the chief influence in changing gene frequencies in future generations would be mutation. So, to the extent that medicine and population regulation equalize the output of all genotypes, to that extent mutation becomes the cause of increased incidence of disease in the future.

One can ask about subtle forms of selection, such as selection of heterozygotes for rare harmful diseases. It is always possible that they are favorable. It is also possible that they once were, but no longer are, i.e., factors causing the high frequency of a particular gene are no longer existent or no longer desirable. I am not greatly worried about the loss of beneficial effects of heterozygotes for rare diseases should these genes become extinct because of genetic counseling. This seems to me like a distinctly second order beneficial effect as compared to the first order detrimental effect of the homozygous gene.

CARRIER DETECTION

If we can detect a dominant trait in utero, then we can reduce the frequency of that particular trait instantly, that is in one generation, to whatever the incidence is due to new mutations. And in fact, if the embryonic detecting system also detects new mutants, it would be possible to prevent the trait entirely. We are nowhere near this situation for any trait that I know of, but at least insofar as the techniques become effective, the eugenic effect as far as I can see is all to the good.

If the trait is caused by a recessive gene on the X chromosome, the reduction in the trait frequency due to carrier detection would also be within a single generation. If heterozygous mothers were detected and affected male embryos aborted, the population incidence would drop to the value of the female mutation rate.

The more challenging questions have to do with what happens when one detects carriers of recessive traits. I am going to consider that in the present generation there are only two kinds of reproducing individuals, those that are heterozygous (Aa) for the deleterious gene and those that are homozygous (AA) for the normal gene. The "a" gene is the harmful recessive gene that is being detected in carriers and possibly in embryos. The frequency of the Aa type is 2p, and the frequency of the AA type is 1-2p. The gene frequency among reproducing adults is "p".

In Table I five different situations are considered.

Table 1. Changes in the frequency of a rare recessive gene with various results of genetic counseling. The gene frequency is counted in the adult stage.

Initial gene frequency

Aa: 2p
AA: 1−2p

Marriage frequencies

Aa x Aa: $4p^2$
Aa x AA: $4p(1-2p)$
AA x AA: $(1-2p)^2$

	Adult gene frequency		Numerical example p = 0.01	
	After 1 generation	After n generations	After 1 generation	After 10 generations
1. Complete cure, or avoidance of marriage between heterozygotes	$2p^2 + p(1-2p)$ = p	p	0.0100	0.0100
2. Abortion or pre-adult death of affected homozygotes	$\dfrac{p^2 + p(1-2p)}{3p^2 + 4p(1-2p) + (1-2p)^2}$ = $\dfrac{p}{1+p}$	$\dfrac{p}{1+np}$	0.0099	0.0091
3. No children from Aa x Aa marriages	$\dfrac{p(1-2p)}{4p(1-2p) + (1-2p)^2}$ = $\dfrac{p}{1+2p}$	$\dfrac{p}{1+2np}$	0.0098	0.0083
4. Artificial insemination in Aa x Aa marriages	$p^2 + p(1-2p)$ = $p(1-p)$	$\sim p(1-np)$	0.0099	0.0090
5. Abortion with complete compensation	$\dfrac{4}{3}p^2 + p(1-2p)$ = $p\left(1 - \dfrac{2p}{3}\right)$	$\sim p\left(1 - \dfrac{2np}{3}\right)$	0.0099	0.0093

The first situation is no selection, where either the trait is completely cured so that reproduction is normal or marriages between heterozygotes are avoided. The frequency of the gene in the next generation under these circumstances won't change. The frequency of affected individuals, however, will be zero because they have been cured or not born. If the population goes back to the situation where they are no longer being treated and marries at random, then the incidence of the trait will be the square of the gene frequency.

The second circumstance is complete selection, in which homozygous recessive genotypes do not reproduce. This can be either because they were aborted or because they die at some later date or are sterile. If this happens the adult gene frequency will drop to $p/(1+p)$ next generation, e.g., if $p=0.01$, in the next generation the gene frequency would be reduced to 0.0099.

The third circumstance is that heterozygotes married to each other decide to have no children at all. (I ignore the possibility that all heterozygotes, whoever they are married to, decide to have no children, since we all carry recessive genes). No reproduction in marriages between carriers will change the gene frequency from p to $p/(1 + 2p)$.

A fourth possibility, whenever husband and wife are both carriers, is artificial insemination with sperm from a donor who is free of the recessive gene, which leads to gene frequency of $p(1-p)$.

The fifth possibility is abortion with compensation. In this case the affected embryos are aborted, but each aborted fetus is replaced by another conception until the total number of children born is the same as if there had been no abnormal fetuses. The frequency next generation is $p(1-2p/3)$. However, complete compensation is rather unlikely to happen.

Table I also gives numerical examples for $p=0.01$. If the disease is completely repaired, then the gene frequency in the next generation is still 0.01. Under the circumstance of complete selection, p becomes 0.0099. Under the third circumstance, that the parents decide to have no children at all, this becomes 0.0098. With artificial insemination, the fourth possibility, the value is 0.0099. In fact, artificial insemination is almost indistinguishable from complete selection or non-compensated abortion. With compensation, the gene frequency is still 0.0099.

Table II considers the effect of mutation on the process, or the effect of whatever else it is that is keeping this gene at a high frequency (e.g., heterozygote advantage). We don't know, for a trait like phenylketonuria or Tay-Sachs or any of the rest of these, whether the gene is getting more frequent or less frequent. The main point I am trying to emphasize is that the change in gene frequency due to any of these five circumstances is less than two percent. If the population were to return to random mating and no selection, the trait frequency would change less than four percent.

Table 2. Same as Table 1 except for the additional assumption of mutation at rate m, or equivalent selection favoring heterozygotes.

	Gene frequency		Numerical examples			
			$m = 10^{-4}$ or het. adv. = 0.01		$m = 10^{-5}$ or het. adv. = 0.003	
	After 1 gen	After n gens	After 1 gen	After 10 gens	After 1 gen	After 10 gens
1.	$p + m$	$p + nm$	0.0101	0.0110	0.0100	0.0101
2.	$\dfrac{p}{1+p} + m$	$\sim \dfrac{p}{1+np} + nm$	0.0100	0.0100	0.0099	0.0092
3.	$\dfrac{p}{1+2p} + m$	$\sim \dfrac{p}{1+2np} + nm$	0.0099	0.0093	0.0098	0.0084
4.	$p(1-p) + m$	$\sim p(1-np) + nm$	0.0100	0.0100	0.0099	0.0091
5.	$p\left(1 - \dfrac{2p}{3}\right) + m$	$\sim p\left(1 - \dfrac{2np}{3}\right) + nm$	0.01003	0.0103	0.0099	0.0094

Thus, immediate humanitarian considerations in this issue far outweigh any eugenic considerations for the foreseeable future.

If we ask about the very long future, I would still argue for humanitarian considerations in the current generation on the grounds that we are learning more, and what we decide to do that is wrong this generation can be reversed next generation if a wiser course of action at that time becomes apparent. It is hard for me to imagine any circumstances under which the humanitarian considerations now do not outweigh the small frequency changes illustrated in Tables I and II.

I want to put in a plea for showing greater respect for empirical information than we often do. Two carriers of phenylketonuria, for example, have a risk of one-fourth that a given child will have PKU. This comes out of Mendelian theory and, of course, it is a very solid expectation. But so far as any particular child is concerned, it is simply a probability. I see no important distinction between a probability that is based on Mendelian theory and one that is based on empiricism or experience, providing the two have the same level of exactness. I realize that probability based on experience is likely to be heterogeneous and that, when I say the over-all risk is 30 percent, I mean it is a mixture of probable causes with heterogeneous risks averaging 30 percent. Nevertheless, as far as this child is concerned, on the basis of information we have at this particular time, that is the best prognostication we can make.

For example, from empirical data, when both parents and one child are mentally retarded, the risk of a second affected child is about 70 percent in the next pregnancy. So if you recommend non-reproduction to parents that have a one-fourth risk, I assume on the basis of empirical data you would recommend this to people who have a 70 percent risk. Yet I don't think this is always practiced. Whatever the arguments are for counseling with PKU, they must be three times as great for unexplained mental retardation, as illustrated in the above example, although only empirical data exist.

MUTATION

One very predictable consequence of medical success is that mutation is likely to become a more important component of disease. Thus an important question is the emphasis that should be given to protection from environmental mutagens. How much should we lower the living standard this generation to protect future generations from mutagens? This, too, can be discussed as an ethical issue of the benefits for one generation balanced against the risk to another generation.

I am inclined to believe that the optimum human mutation rate is zero, not the current spontaneous rate, and I would suggest that the perfect anti-mutagen is almost as important to discover as the perfect contraceptive.

The reason for saying this is that we don't really know what an optimum mutation rate is from the standpoint of very long-range evolution. It is just possible that, if we are asking about our biological fate 10,000 or 100,000 generations in the future, a somewhat higher or somewhat lower mutation rate would change the odds of being able to adapt biologically. My concern again is with the part of the future for which we have some reason for legitimate concern, or the part of the future that we have some predictive power over, and that seems to me to be the course of the next few dozen generations.

We have such an enormous store of genetic variability in the population now, most of which is pre-tested by having stayed around several generations, that we have a body of genes that will enable us to do anything that our society or any reasonable society is ever likely to want to do. We could transform the population if we so choose in quite striking directions. I don't think we need any new mutations but if we decide that we do, mutagenesis is the one technique we have at our disposal and could use instantly. I end with the admonition that the mutation rate is one more human population problem.

DISCUSSION

STETTEN: You indicated that the optimal mutation rate is zero. Are we so sure that the situation today is the best that nature can produce that we would like to cut off the change from this point forward?

CROW: The only reasonable answer to that is no. Yet, I think that our rate of change in the future by natural selection will be so slow that other things (e.g., environmental changes and cultural heritages) will be much more important. I am concerned primarily with the next few hundred years.

KABACK: We have considered the genetic impact of screening and prevention of one recessive disorder, Tay-Sachs disease. If one were to screen every married Ashkenazi Jew of child-bearing age in the United States, abort each pregnancy in which a homozygous recessive fetus is identified, and enable each couple in the population (including doubly heterozygous couples) to have two unaffected children, it would take 8,750 years to double the carrier rate in the American Ashkenazi Jewish population as the result of the slight increase in heterozygous children which would result. This data would strongly support the "humanitarian approach" you have outlined.

THE MEANING AND SIGNIFICANCE OF GENETIC DISEASE: PHILOSOPHICAL PERSPECTIVES

Daniel Callahan

I want to raise here the question of why we are concerned with genetic disease and how we might appropriately look upon it. I will leave to others a treatment of the various ethical problems which the detection and treatment of genetic disease pose. Instead, I will focus my attention on the kind of human, social and cultural perspectives brought to bear on genetic disease, and the way in which they tend to establish the framework within which ethical issues are discerned and handled. This is important not only because these perspectives are interesting in themselves, but also because I am convinced that ethical systems, codes, and insights spring ultimately from assessments of the meaning and significance of human existence. All of us, I believe, have certain images of life, certain fundamental stances toward reality, certain sets of assumptions about the nature of things. Taken together, they help to determine the way questions are framed, priorities of interest established, emotional commitments made, fears, hopes and anxieties aroused. The first question I want to pose concerning genetic disease is this: What image of human existence is pertinent as a framework for determining our response to the reality of genetic disease?

When I was about seven I was approached one day on a playground by a very odd-looking boy of perhaps twelve or thirteen, stumbling, misshapen and with a rather silly, though friendly, smile on his face. My reaction was a mixture of horror, fear, and curiosity. I wanted to stare at him and study him, but at the same time I wanted to run home as fast as I could. I resolved the dilemma at first by moving carefully backwards as he kept coming toward me, trying to keep him at a safe distance. But he kept coming and, eventually, I did run home, certain that if I did not he would "get me." He represented an alien, utterly inexplicable phenomenon.

No one, of course, had told me about Down's syndrome, and no one did for many years after. My parents said vaguely that he was "sick" and that "he wouldn't hurt me," but little more. That he

83

was the child of a close neighbor, usually hidden, was something I had to deduce for myself. All the adults in the neighborhood, it seems, knew about him, but all tacitly engaged in a highly successful conspiracy to say nothing about the matter--indeed, to evade all pointed questions asked by innocent children. Eventually, the mongoloid I had encountered simply disappeared, no doubt into some institution.

I mention this incident because it seems to me to sum up one pervasive, almost instinctual human reaction to genetic disease. The defective human being has historically seemed a mysterious, awesome, terrifying creature--almost a separate, subhuman species--to be shunned altogether, explained away by means of elaborate religious mythologies, or given a special meaning, either as an omen of good or of evil. Of course, we now know more about genetic disease. We have some notion of why these hitherto strange creatures issue forth from the womb as defectives, and we think we have some ways of coping with what we are now able to classify as an abnormality.

But it would be a mistake to think that the old sense of mystery, awe, and terror does not live on. Surely the pervasive parental fear of bearing a defective child is not just because of the troubles of raising such a child, though that is a most serious matter. The fear seems much deeper than that, as if a defective child would represent a supreme undoing of the parents' image of themselves and reality. I am reminded of the conviction of many philosophers of antiquity that there is an irrational, irreducible surd element in the universe, which constantly breaks through our visions and structures of ordered rationality. Genetic disease, long before it was labeled as that, was a case in point. One might in the instance of a hunting accident be able to discern a causal logic; the accident, however unacceptable, at least made sense. Genetic disease made no sense whatever; a defective child just arrived, out of some primeval darkness. A terror before the darkness still endures.

Yet, unlike our ancestors, we are no longer willing to be cowed. We are beginning to fight back, and the steps being taken follow a familiar script. We try to understand the mystery, by turning it into a problem rather than a mystery; then, with our cool-headed, rational explanation in hand we set ourselves to doing something about it--we label it a "disease" and then we try to "conquer" it. The change in our image of reality is evident here. Our ancestors had no choice but to be terrorized, and thus in compensation to find some symbolic means by which the philosophical absurdity of the defective existence could be understood and lived with. For our part, we act--fast, hard, and with all the technical means at our disposal.

The results are becoming evident. We are beginning to understand genetic disease, to know how to diagnose its presence, and, in some cases, how to cure it. Increasingly, it is becoming possible for those who do not want to bear defective children not to bear them. Since no one wants to bear such a child, just as they do not want to contract cancer or coronary disease, we are all that much the better off.

Yet at the level of broad philosophical perspective, I believe we should anticipate some problems. The conquest of genetic disease proceeds from the optimistic assumption that physical reality can be understood and that its aberrations can be minimized or eliminated. Nature can be brought to heel. That has been the assumption of the medical sciences generally, and its successes have served as the best possible arguments against those who still believe there is a surd element in reality. Unfortunately, though, the fact of the matter is that we have just begun the conquest of genetic disease; it may be decades or centuries before the last defective child is born into the world. If a heuristic optimism is a necessity in order that the struggle against the disease is to go forward, this ought not to blind us to the fact that there is far more of what we do not know than of what we do, and far more genetic diseases that we have not conquered than we have.

In the meantime, during a great transition period which has no discernible end point, what ought to be the philosophical signi-ficance we attribute to genetic disease and genetically defective human beings? What ought our image of the world be and what place ought genetic disease to have within it? Let me point to some items on the present cultural horizon which seem to me to bespeak some dilemmas which need to be considered.

First, we still speak much of freedom of parental choice in the use of genetic information. And it is still common for genetic counselors to reassure parents that a defective fetus or child is "not their fault." Yet it is possible to detect tendencies which could eventually rob people of their choice and "blame" them for the defective children they bring into the world. If there is something of a paradox here at first sight, it soon disappears. For the corollary to giving people freedom of choice is to make them responsible for the choices they make. It is then only a very short step to begin distinguishing between responsible and irre-sponsible choices; social pressure begins to put in an appear-ance. Thus, while in principle the parents of a fetus with a detected case of Down's syndrome are still left free to decide whether to carry it to term, it is not difficult to discern an undercurrent in counseling literature and discussion that would classify such a decision as irresponsible. This is amplified in a subtle way. Abortion is said to be "medically indicated" in such cases, as if what is essentially an ethical decision has now become nothing but medical.

I am not concerned here with whether the decision in this or similar circumstances is irresponsible, or whether an abortion ought to be performed. I only want to point out that if and when we begin holding parents responsible for the children they bring into the world, and blaming them for what we take to be irre-sponsible choices, we may then have a result worse than that which

flowed from the superstition of our ancestors. We will then share
with our ancestors the view that a defective child is a curse but
then, unlike them, provide no comfort whatever other than the
ascetic reward of praise or blame for socially acceptable behavior
in the face of the curse. In a word, it is simply not clear to me
that in this circumstance an image of the world which, based on
fierce rationality, would hold every person responsible for every
jot and title of his or her behavior is altogether preferable to
one which, while it could give them no choice, did not judge them
either. And, of course, if we begin blaming those who make what we
term "irresponsible" choices, then the freedom of choice now
extolled in genetic counseling would become a mockery.

Second, while it has no doubt always been the case that
parents of defective children have had to count the financial
costs, the introduction of modern cost-accounting and cost-benefit
analysis into the genetic equation adds a distinctively different
element. We can now, quite literally, put a price on everyone's
head, working out the long-term financial costs to individuals and
societies of caring for a defective child.

But let us observe a curiosity. It was counted a great
advance of the modern mind when a bookkeeping God, with his
minutely maintained ledger of good and bad deeds, was noisily
rejected. Yet here we are, beginning to keep our own books, and
using them increasingly as a determinant in deciding whether or not
defectives should be allowed the privilege of birth, and their
parents the privilege of parenthood. Moreover, we seem to have
forgotten the reason why the bookkeeping God was rejected--because
it seemed eminently unjust, insensitive, and outrageous that a
scorecard be kept on human lives. Indeed, we are even worse than
that old God; for at least in his ledger everything was supposedly
recorded. But our cost-benefit analysis totes up one item only--
what the financial liability of the defective will be, what he will
cost us in terms of taxes, institutional facilities, the time of
medical personnel, and so on. Needless to say, this kind of
reckoning is prone to be weak in comparing the costs of the
defective against the cost of other patently foolish public and
private expenditures which are accepted with barely a word of
protest. What is society spending on cosmetics this year? Nor
does this kind of reckoning have much to say about ways of recon-
structing the social and political order to make possible a more
humane treatment of those considered a social liability--the poor,
the aged, the unfit. No, for the kind of cost-benefit analysis
which seems to be emerging in genetic calculations goes only in the
cost direction; it is seemingly assumed that the benefits to a
society which decided simply to bear the costs of humane care are
either nonexistent or simply too intangible to be worth much
bother.

Third, behind the human horror at genetic defectiveness lurks,
one must suppose, an image of the perfect human being. The very

language of "defect," "abnormality," "disease," and "risk" presupposes such an image, a kind of prototype of perfection. In the
past there seemed little which could be done to realize the
prototype; it was contemplated as a platonic form, well out of
reach. Eventually, a kind of wisdom developed. Since it appeared
clear that, even if there is a perfect human being to be conceived
or imagined, the price of pursuing and imposing it is very high in
terms of the ways it can change our response to actually existing
human beings. Human diversity began to be appreciated and justified. In fact, behind modern society's at least verbal commitment to civil rights, to justice for all, lies a rejection of
images of individual perfection and uniformity. A similar pattern
has been manifest in even the purely scientific sphere, with a
rejection in biology and zoology of monotypical modes of analysis
and classification (which stressed a fixed, static concept of type)
in favor of a populationist approach (which makes room for a richer
appreciation of individual variation).

Yet because of the advances in the detection and cure of
genetic disease--the ghost of the perfect human being, once
sensibly laid to rest, is putting in his appearance again. And I
believe we are beginning to see evidence of what this means: a
heightened anxiety on the part of prospective parents about bearing
a defective child, increased social pressure against those who
would bear a child deviating from the norm of perfection, and, at
what I hope is not the leading edge but a fringe only, hints that
the sensible society of the future will of course deny parents the
right to bring into the world any child who could not measure up,
who would be a burden upon society.

There have surely been abuses and a good deal of plain
silliness in recent rejections of purported ethical absolutes and
ethical objectivity, of fixed codes, of rigid notions of the
"human" and the "non-human," of the worthy and the unworthy, of
static notions of perfection and imperfection. But on the whole,
this rejection has helped to soften life, to provide a defense
against the totalitarian reformer, to widen our appreciation of the
value of human differences, variations and dissimilarities, to lead
us to construct visions of political and social orders which can
encompass and profit from variety. An image of man based on a
pluralistic rather than a monistic conception of reality has been
hard-won. It would be a supreme irony if, in the name of even
greater progress, there was reintroduced the old monistic, monotypical kind of thinking, this time, as before, in the name of
value, good order, and a mythical notion of perfection.

Fourth, every image of the world and reality carries with it a
correlative view of the nature of human community. It is not for
nothing that political reformers and revolutionaries (think only of
Karl Marx) have felt that the condition for a change in ethical and
political thinking is, first of all, a change in metaphysical
thinking. An egalitarian social structure can, only with diffi-

culty and patch-work logic, be built upon a metaphysic of fixed
hierarchical realities. Participatory democracy has nothing going
for it in a society which secretly believes that some people are
inherently lower than others and thus not fit to govern themselves.

It would be a mistake to say that past human societies adapted
happily and well to the reality of genetic disease and defect. Yet
there did develop the humane response that society as a whole
should share the burden of caring for the defective, that the
parents or family should not be left with sole responsibility for
the care and survival of the defective. Moreover, in laws against
infanticide, child neglect and abuse, there was reflected a belief
that society has an obligation toward children, an obligation which
holds good regardless of their physical or mental condition. We
can see in these historical developments a concept of community and
society which tried to respond to human diversity, even that diversity represented by the grossly abnormal. So, too, it was perceived that any effective recognition of diversity--which means a
recognition of actual inequalities of individual assets and
liabilities in society--required a joint sharing of responsibility
by all for all, so that those least equipped by nature or nurture
to function would not be inevitable losers.

This cultural development represented a great milestone in
human history, even if our society and most others have hardly
succeeded in living up to the obligations which it entailed. We
created public instituions for defectives, only too often to treat
them like animals once we gave them the benefit of admission to
those institutions. Nonetheless, the introduction of the very
notion of common and public responsibility represented a triumph of
great magnitude. A triumph, I am sorry to say, which would all be
for nothing if we accept the idea that defectives and their parents
have no right to burden the rest of us with their troubles, or that
it is naive to find a social solution for a problem which can be
done away with by a scientific solution.

I would not want to be misunderstood here. Nothing I have
said should be construed as an objection to the further development
and refinement of genetic knowledge and the art of genetic counseling. On the contrary, the suffering brought on by genetic disease
warrants nothing less than a full-scale social, scientific and
economic effort to eliminate, cure or alleviate these afflictions. My concern, rather, is with the spirit in which such an
effort is undertaken, with the kind of philosophical perspective
which should lie behind it, and with the social context in which it
is carried out.

Genetic disease will not be done away with overnight, if ever.
At the simplest level, there is at least a requirement that
people's hopes not be raised too high too precipitately; that will
just set the stage for even more suffering. More important though
is the question of how we are to continue living in the company of
genetic disease, even as vigorous steps are taken to minimize its
impact. As Professor Crow has emphasized, the reality of genetic

disease is that it is a recurrent disease brought about by the continued reintroduction of defective genes by mutation. The overarching dilemma I have tried to sketch comes to this: How can we manage both to live humanely with genetic disease and yet to conquer it at the same time? Both goals seem imperative and yet the logic of each is different. We cure disease by ceasing to romanticize it, by gathering our powers to attack it, by making it an enemy to be conquered. We learn to live with a disease, however, in a very different way; by trying to accept and cherish those who manifest the disease, by shaping social structures and institutions which will soften the individual suffering brought on by the disease, by refusing to make the bearer of the disease our economic, social, or political enemy.

Our communal task, I believe, is to find a way of combining both logics. That will not be easy, if only because most people find it easier to cope with one idea than with two at the same time. It will mean, for instance, simultaneously working to improve the societal treatment and respect accorded those born with defects, and working to extend our genetic knowledge and applying it to genetic counseling. It will mean taking the idea of free choice seriously, allowing parents to make their own choice without penalizing them socially for the choices they make, or condemning them for those choices which will increase the financial costs to society. Part of the very meaning of human community, I would contend, entails a willingness of society to bear the social costs of individual freedom.

It will mean some care in the way we use language. As physical organisms we stand "at risk" of genetic disease, as do our children and our descendants; as cultural beings, however, we stand "at risk" also in another sense, of seeing our values, our better instincts, and our humanity diseased and crippled. If odds are to be calculated, then let both sets of risks be included in our general equation. Moreover, if the "risk" of genetic disease is to be calculated, and better calculated, let it be remembered that no set of mathematical statistics can, by themselves, "indicate" what we ought to do in response to the realities they delineate. That requires the introduction of ethical premises, and those premises, in turn, require some coherent notion of what the human good is. When we speak of the good of "the patient," let it not be the case, in the first place, that we use the term "patient" only for those we think desirable to treat (using some clinical term for the rest--fetus, conceptus, neonate); or, in the second place, that the decision if and how to treat a patient not be made a matter of how we, as individuals or community, happen to feel about the intrinsic worth of that patient. Beyond that, particular care is needed when we speak of someone or some group's "good." It is not all that easy to know what is good for the individual, for the family and for society, though one might gather otherwise in light of the many confident statements made on the subject. As a descriptive term indicating deviation from a statistical mean, the word "abnormal" can be very helpful; as a philosophical term, indicating some mandatory level of social and genetic fitness--a prototype of human perfection--it can be very hazardous.

To conquer a disease is to reflect a view of the world. It is also to create a partially new world and a new view of human possibilities. How we go about dealing with genetic disease--the kinds of counseling techniques developed, the professional consensuses which emerge, the attitudes developed toward carriers of defects and toward the children many of them will bear, the kinds of choices which emerge and the positions taken on the nature of those choices--will both reflect one world and bring another into being. That is a heavy burden to bear and we had better be aware of it.

DISCUSSION

Principal Discussant: David Brock

A central dilemma in the current use of genetic knowledge has been stated succinctly by Dr. Callahan. How, he asks, can we manage both to live humanely with genetic disease and yet to conquer it? Given that counseling--at present the principal outlet for the prevention of genetic disease--is in the widest possible sense a beneficial occupation, how can we extend and develop it without impairing our own humanity? Can we avoid the dehumanization which comes when mystery gives way to mastery? Can we apply genetic counseling at the population level without endangering an essential feature of democratic and liberal societies, that painfully constructed coexistence of different views of the nature of man? Questions of power are involved here, the concentration of power through knowledge in the hands of a few and the impact this may have on a pluralistic society. Power and coercion, efficiency and dehumanization, these are the themes which I shall try to develop in this commentary.

When a new area of knowledge is developed intensively, it is often accompanied by a growing rigidity in attitudes. In medical genetics we are beginning to see this in the tendency to classify diseases according to severity. It is not an overt classification, but almost instinctive, demanded by a need for immediate advice and action. At both ends of the spectrum of genetic disease, general agreement on prognosis and action exists; few would wish a child to be born who will have Tay-Sachs disease or generalized gangliosidosis, while most counselors would reassure parents whose children may have methaemoglobinaemia or alkaptonuria. But most genetic diseases lie somewhere between these extremes, in the realm where it should remain possible to argue the case either way and where the outcome of the argument depends as much on the physician's ethical preconceptions as on his medical experience. As the number of well-described disorders increases and as they become complicated by heterogeneity, they will inevitably pass out of the direct experience of any one counselor. He will need to acquire his knowledge from the medical literature and his colleagues, and it would be foolish not to expect him to be influenced by the unstated value judgments implicit in any comprehensive description of a disease.

So many counseling situations are profoundly difficult to resolve even at the most practical level. How, for example, should a counselor respond to a late onset dominant of variable expressivity like myotonic dystrophy? Should he emphasize the potential gravity of the later stages of the disease in the interests of the unborn and society at large, and scare the parent away from reproduction? Or should his first responsibility be the traditional one, the patient before him (who may well be dead before any children reach the age of clinical symptoms), so that he tempers his counsel with massive reassurance. Dilemmas like these cry out for codification, for the efficient transmission of one man's experience to another, and for accepted and standardized procedural steps. And yet any standardization, while relieving burdens on an individual counselor, will serve to diminish the flexibility which so often lies at the bottom of the truly humane response.

I am not convinced that the growing science of antenatal diagnosis substantially alters this difficulty; in some ways it compounds it. Various lists have now been published of the medical indications for amniocentesis, and most of these include as one of the categories, a family history of a gene-transmitted abnormality. What is presumably meant is an abnormality which in the informed view of the parents would constitute an intolerable burden for the child and family. But if the genetic disorder falls in the middle of the spectrum of severity, in the realm where reasonable alternative views of burden may be held (I would think that Fabry's disease might be considered as a real example here), then antenatal detection is merely delaying the decision in the hope that it can be avoided. But when it cannot be avoided--the fetus is demonstrated to be affected--then the act of amniocentesis (coupled to the technology of the biochemical detection of inborn errors of metabolism) has already made the decision, and possibly made it in a direction which would not have been made in the genetic counseling office. Of course one can argue that amniocentesis should never be performed without a clear idea of what is going to be done with the various possible outcomes of the tests (including ambiguity). But this is to ignore the powerful attraction of procrastination in the face of a supremely difficult problem, a procrastination which may well cause the problem to disappear, but which may also force decisions to be taken in a situation of great stress. In the latter case--a mother who had hoped that antenatal diagnosis would be able to reassure her and had been disappointed--there will be a strong tendency to invoke precedent and to reach for the guidance of what had been done before--in fact, a situation of enhanced rigidity.

Much of what I have been saying about rigidity turns on the question of whether genetic counseling is a system of information-giving or a system of advice-giving. There are many who claim that counseling involves only two elements--accurate diagnosis and as precise as possible a statement of risks--and that this can and should be kept entirely factual. This seems to me like saying that history is facts and that no one should write it who has any kind of bias. An admirable statement were it not for the exclusion of the human element. I think we have to recognize that there are two features about the medical profession today which make pure information-giving difficult, perhaps impossible, and I would argue, undesirable. The first is the almost God-like status which most patients attribute to their doctors, a status founded in the first place on specialized knowledge about life-and-death issues, but which has been compounded by other features of the contemporary scene (in particular the decline of other traditional high-status figures--the priest, the village teacher) so that what is now demanded is not facts but wisdom. The other is the exclusiveness of the medical profession, which through its emphasis on the clinical presentation has always maintained that its practitioners have a fund of experience which cannot be gained by others who have not been through the same process. Across this gulf it is very difficult to transmit information about prognosis (indeed, it is difficult to transmit information from any professional group to a lay group); inevitably, patients will come away from the counseling office feeling that they don't have all the knowledge they want, and that their doctor is in a better position than they are to make a decision.

Taking this point further, one could argue that if efficiency in combating genetic disease is our goal, much genetic counseling could be done by machine. The only precise form of diagnosis for an inborn error of metabolism is a biochemical one. One can envisage an automatic heterozygote detector to which prospective marriage partners gave a sample of blood and receive back counseling information on a punched card. And yet I, for one, recoil from this prospect, for I believe that one of the most important things which the counselor brings to the genetic clinic is his value framework. His role is certainly to confirm diagnoses (though increasingly this will be done in the biochemistry laboratory) and to calculate risks (which is hardly intellectually taxing when the diagnosis is made). But these are so often with reference to ultimates--crippling disorders, wasting diseases, idiot children--a whole spectrum of situations which raise questions about the framework of life. If his counsel is to be meaningful, his patient's worries must interact with his value system and his comments must proceed from a mature life-view. I don't think it matters too much whether his belief structure coincides with that of his patient; what is important is that the value-judgment element in statements of prognosis be apparent. This is of course asking a great deal of genetic counselors and may well impair efficiency, but it seems to me the only way of preventing counseling from becoming a machine-like operation.

Already in the medical literature there are a number of publications asking questions about the effectiveness of genetic counseling. This is quite proper; anyone systematically involved in a course of action which concerns people as intimately as counseling does is obliged from time to time to try to assess his impact. But we should be clear that these questions are asked very largely from the standpoint of society; how many cases of serious genetic disease have been averted, how many children with grave diseases have been born who might not have been born, and what is the cost to society of ignored statements of risk? Because the gap between the medical literature and the lay literature is a small one nowadays, particularly with respect to conclusions reached (indeed, some scientists have found it profitable to combine their results and conclusions and announce this as achievement through the news media before putting the details before their peers), there is a very real danger that the public will see only one aspect of counseling, then question the apparently low efficiencies achieved and exert pressures for greater effectiveness. To keep the humane side of counseling before the public eye, indeed to present the humane side, we need to start grappling with the much more difficult question of at what cost to the patient's psychological well-being has any reduction in genetic disease been achieved.

This leads into the central and most difficult concept which pervades current applications of genetic knowledge--the concept of benefit. At a simplistic level, we can distinguish three levels of beneficiaries: the child, the parents, and society. But then the tangle begins, and I must confess that I have very great difficulty in comprehending philosophical analyses of statements such as "the benefit to the unborn in not being born," or, for that matter, in following the legal arguments in a suit by a child against its parents for ignoring genetic risks. Perhaps I can sidestep the issue and fall back on the practical by remarking that is seems to be that most people are agreed that prospective children have a basic right to reasonable mental and physical health, and that they are disagreed only as to the mechanisms for achieving this. I am not sure that we need to be sophisticated and skillful in sorting out the strands of greater good and lesser good, if counselors feel instinctively that it is right to advise the denial of life to a prospective child with a substantial risk of a deleterious genotype, provided that parental well-being can be accommodated to the decision.

This is the level at which concepts of benefit and practical genetic counseling interact most closely--the level of the parents. They are the ones who ultimately make the decision, however much or however little they may have been influenced by the words or suggestions of the counselor. They are also beneficiaries-- recipients of a curious kind of benefit that is essentially negative and rests on the assumption that suffering is evil and that happiness is a highly-prized end of human existence. Society is prepared to buy this happiness for parents at the cost of feticide; it further spares their anguish by calling it termination of pregnancy, knowing that for many of us a fetus is a being while pregnancy is only a state. Now I am not arguing against abortion; I am convinced that it has done far more good than harm. But I believe that because the fetus cannot argue its own case, and because we cannot properly argue the case for the fetus, we must continue to scrutinize most carefully the motives of the next level of beneficiaries--the parents. Dr. Callahan has already mentioned one important factor in this regard--the undoing of parental self-image which a defective child might induce--and one wonders if at times abortion may not be a substitute for an overdue coming to terms with reality. There are all sorts of cross-currents which disturb clear thinking about parental benefit: the importance of lineage or breeding in our cultural tradition, so that defects are taken as marks of genetic poverty; and the confusion of risk and challenge, so that we respond instinctively to 'loaded' situations by trying to overcome them. And then there is the arrogance of science. With one breath we are saying that we are the new masters and that nature has yielded its secrets to the scientific onslaught, with another breath that there is little we can do about genetic risk except pin it with greater precision on individual people or couples. One is a call for pride, the other a call for humility. Counseling must be conducted with an awareness of our powerlessness in the face of nature's inequalities which is quite alien to other branches of science. Our ancestors, in their ignorance of the causes of disease, were able at times to accept suffering with a humility which verged on the noble. We are increasingly disinclined to accept any suffering at all. This can create severe tensions in the counseling office; the tension of rising expectations generated by the scientific onslaught meeting the brutal facts of the inequality of nature.

Part of the reason for this tension is produced by our insistence on introducing the population perspective when thinking about the benefit of genetic counseling. We talk of conquering disease--abolishing Tay-Sachs or eliminating Down's syndrome--even when the motivation is a personal rather than a eugenic one. The imagery is unfortunate, for surely the special feature of genetic disease qua disease is that we can no more conquer it by current technology than we can conquer the Viet Cong by dropping bombs on Hanoi. I think the analogy is an apt one for both ideas raise expectations in the mind of the public which can never be fully realized. When disappointed, their response may be for escalation; in the case of genetic disease, a demand for coercion and legislation. What worries me particularly is that we are moving into an age of apocalyptic vision about mankind's future--population explosion, rapidly depleting food and fuel resources, increasing pollution--and there is a growing tendency to think 'big' in biological problems and to see genetic disease as just another aspect of the pollution problem. As such, it is soluble by the kinds of methods used in other forms of pollution, i.e., legislation of the prescriptive type. I see no justification for approaching the problem in this way; if I understand Dr. Crow correctly, he is saying that there are really few situations where the results are so beneficial that they would remotely justify the coercive means required.

Instead, there is a very real danger that the type of imagery which pervades the population perspective--embodied in words and phrases like abolish, eliminate, eradicate, conquer, deteriorating gene pool, lethal load--will induce the wrong kinds of action and will do so because policy lines seem clearer and less fraught with ethical dilemmas. The population approach to Tay-Sachs disease is to screen all Ashkenazi Jews for carrier status and through counseling and monitoring of at-risk pregnancies, to seek to reduce the frequency of this appalling disorder. As such, it is a heroic undertaking and worthy of our fullest support. But should the population prove indifferent, should the results fall short of the high expectations which advance publicity has already generated, then we must be prepared to resist any suggestions for coercive reinforcement. Though the methodology of the approach is scaled to the population level, the aims remain the alleviation of individual suffering. In the last resort, we must continue to fall back to the basic concept of genetic counseling as an expression of man's humanity to man.

General Discussion

LUDMERER: The feeling I have had in the recent discussions of genetic counseling is that many regard it as somewhat sinister. This disturbs me because historically the development of genetic counseling has been just the opposite.

If I may illustrate, the first genetic counseling in this country was performed by institutions of what sometimes is called the old eugenics movement.

The eugenicists, many of them, were the reformers of their day. They came from what is sometimes called the humane movement of the late 19th century, representing a whole new group of professions: trained prison wardens, trained prison physicians, superintendents of homes for paupers, delinquents, and alcoholics. These reformers gave the first impulse to the eugenics movement in this country as well as to genetic counseling. In the course of their work, they came to feel that all social inadequacy is caused by poor heredity, and accordingly they began to claim that social problems could be solved only by eugenic reform. Many were fascist types who advocated state control and compulsory sterilization. Eventually, in this country and elsewhere, their views fell into disrepute.

In the 1930's there emerged a group of people who created the institutions which conduct genetic counseling today. These individuals explicitly repudiated the compulsory approach of the earlier eugenicists and urged voluntary compliance instead. They stressed that eugenics could exist only in a democracy.

I do not mean to minimize the importance of the many ethical questions which concern genetic counseling, and I do not mean to minimize the danger that such counseling might be abused. But the whole development of genetic counseling has been toward greater humanitarianism, greater compassion, and greater democracy.

MACINTYRE: I would like to stress one point here that Dr. Kaback touched briefly upon in support of the positive aspects of prenatal diagnosis.

Those of us who are involved in such diagnoses do not deserve to be classified as hand-maidens to the abortionists because, in fact, just the reverse is true. The cases which come to us with a high genetic risk involved and in which pregnancy has already been initiated, would all end in therapeutic abortion if prenatal evaluations were not available. These interruptions of pregnancy would be accomplished because of the known risk and the anxiety which it generates. Furthermore, they would be accomplished even with the knowledge that the fetus might be normal. Therefore, each prenatal diagnosis which predicts normal development for the fetus is literally saving the life of the child.

Furthermore, even in cases of a 50 percent risk such as would theoretically be present with a reciprocal translocation carrier parent, the actual number of tested fetuses that prove to be genetically unbalanced is significantly less than expected. It is felt that this apparent discrepancy probably results from the fact that embryos which are badly unbalanced genetically are aborted spontaneously very early in gestation. Therefore, results of the prenatal diagnoses are weighed heavily in favor of saving babies.

KABACK: I would like to respond to several comments made by Dr. Brock. First, I concur with his feeling that genetic screening could conceivably lead us away from humanitarian considerations into things smacking of eugenics. The possibilities of legislated and socially-justified programs of enforced screening would be quite dangerous as well, in my opinion.

I do not agree that an autosomal recessive disease cannot be prevented--for at least the most part. Certainly, this is one of the goals of the screening program for Tay-Sachs disease. It is probably true that genetic disease cannot be 100 percent prevented, but a significant reduction in the incidence of such diseases can result from mass screening.

I do wish to take some exception with the phrase, "advance publicity," that was used. In fact, if genetic screening and the prevention of genetic diseases is to become feasible, mechanisms for effective education of the public must be developed. Genetic screening and prevention on a volunteer, informed-consent basis, at least, cannot be achieved if people do not understand exactly what it is that we are doing. The information must be delivered effectively.

Perhaps the very best ammunition against what Dr. Brock has cautioned us, i.e., legislated genetics, will be the high compliance which can result on an informed-consent basis after an effective educational program. In the Tay-Sachs Program in Maryland, nearly 25 percent of a projected population of 30,000 individuals of child-bearing age in the at-risk population of greater Baltimore have responded for screening in the first few months. Obviously, I do not believe 100 percent compliance can be achieved for such screening. But if high response rates can be achieved by informed consent, we may have the very ammunition to go to legislatures and insist that one need not legislate such genetics--but rather that effective education is more desirable, whether it be for Tay-Sachs, cystic fibrosis, sickle cell anemia, or what have you.

"Advance publicity" regarding the Tay-Sachs Program was not that at all. In fact, not the slightest information was available in the public media for a period of one and one-half years during formulation phases of our program. It was not until just prior to the screening programs in the community that the mass media were utilized. Obviously, many other means of education were used in addition to the media, that is: physicians, religious leaders, organizational leaders, etc.

We must develop the mechanisms for effective education of the public. This should enable individuals to make their own decisions as to whether or not their genes should be evaluated. I believe it is most important to emphasize that we do not know whether or not this is the case at this time. In addition, we do not know if mass genetic screening is in the best interest of the public. What we must do is to evaluate these questions, to ascertain whether or not the public is benefited by such programs, and if not, we must have the wisdom to back off appropriately.

BROCK: I will take your point about education. I foresee the other side of this. As you are aware, your attempts to put this over to the whole population did generate a certain amount of what can only be described as unfortunate publicity. I think at this stage of the game one can put that aside and hope the press will get educated to the aims of these programs and not sensationalize them in any way.

We must make it clear to those in a legislative position that we do not expect to eradicate genetic disease completely and that we cannot remove it, at least in the near future, because of the mutation rate. We can cut down the incidence of certain diseases, but there will always be a residual level, and this does not mean that the program has been unsuccessful.

CAPRON: I would like to ask Dr. Brock for a clarification of the choices which he believes are open to the genetic counselor. I took his computer diagnosis and punch card to be somewhat facetious, but I wasn't sure if he had in mind another formulation, one of information-giving rather than "I will leave it in the doctor's hands." Or does he believe that, given the doctor-patient interaction, the latter is the only one which we can expect will ever occur, and that if we expect the choices to be made by the patients, we are merely fooling ourselves?

BROCK: Take the example of myotonic dystrophy. A man in his early thirties just contracting the disease comes in for counseling. In the interest of efficiency, surely the genetic counselor should describe in very real terms what is going to happen to him, what the prognosis is. If he doesn't do it, this man who is minimally affected at the time simply cannot see the need to curtail his reproduction. He can't see that there is any point in doing this, unless it is spelled out to him in very clear terms what the eventual outcome of this disease is going to be. And yet this would seem to me to be totally inhumane.

MOTULSKY: You have an alternative to what you can tell this man.   You can tell him, "Your case is rather mild. Many people with the disease have a mild case. However, the disease can be very bad." Then proceed to tell him about severely affected cases.
You don't have to take the props out from under a man. I try to give patients some hope. Giving the patient the truth and all the unadorned facts is erring against the ethos of medicine by which we try to help the patient. Sometimes, withholding of all information is in the best interest of the patient. If I think it is better that a man not be told that he has cancer, I will not tell him. As a physician, I have to make this decision myself. It is hard. I can share and discuss with my colleagues, but ulti- mately it is my decision. To give the whole truth to every patient is not humane.

BEARN: I would like very much to endorse what Dr. Motulsky says. I think this is exactly right.

NEEL: Dr. Callahan has spoken about what we might call the syndrome of the rejection of the abnormal child, which is certainly a problem in the culture today. I have been very much impressed by Edmund Leech's 1967 Leith Lectures. He is a social anthropologist who looked at what was going on in the world from that perspective under the title "A Runaway World." One of his points relates to the collapse of the kinship system, which was so important to man for a long time. With the mobility of society, which takes us out of communities where we have built up those kinds of friendships that sustain us, increasingly the small nuclear family is turned inward on itself in times of trouble.

And I think this growing demand, then, that the geneticist offer a way out, may reflect part of the general social dilemma of our time, of an inwardly turned family now assuming in the present society burdens which individual families haven't really had to assume. What I am doing is getting in a plug against compartmentalizing our thinking.

CROW: I don't regard these as different approaches. I am very much wedded to a cost-benefit approach to problems, and in this instance it seems to me the cost-benefit ratio is clear. Present humanitarian considerations outweigh the future increase in the disease. I have the same feeling about the radiation issue. One balances the benefits of increased radiation against the calculated cost. I think the difficulties in making the calculation should not negate the principle by which we do it.

I wanted to ask Dr. Callahan about a point where I think I disagree with him. It seems to me perfectly reasonable to say that Tay-Sachs disease is abnormal, without asking about what constitutes the ideal or the normal man. I am as much for genetic variability and phenotypic variability as the next person--and yet there are things that are clearly abnormal, and we wouldn't have much difficulty in agreeing on them.

CALLAHAN: When one starts using "abnormal" to attribute value or worth to different sorts of lives--at that point, one is on very dangerous ground. Statistically and humanly, Tay-Sachs is obviously an abnormality. But this is not to say the child with Tay-Sachs is an unworthy human being. That is the distinction I am most concerned to make.

MCLAREN: Could I, as a non-medical, ask my medical colleagues whether doctors are, in fact, bound by a professional code of conduct--for example, the Hippocratic Oath, which says that the welfare of the individual patient is paramount and outweighs any responsibility to society? Or is this left to the individual doctor to resolve?

I was curious about this, for instance, in connection with Dr. Clarke Fraser's reference to the obstetrician who was planning to sterilize the unmarried girl who was a carrier of muscular dystrophy.

BEARN: Physicians, quite clearly in my view, have their primary responsibility to the patient. A patient comes to a physician because he needs help. Any time a patient were to gain the impression that he was being treated as a statistical unit of society, and that society's good, not his good, was the goal of the physician, he would quite properly lose confidence in his physician and in medicine as a profession. (Notification of patients with certain infectious diseases has as its object the prevention of disease in the individual patients.)

There is no law, of course, which forbids the physician, as an informed scientist, to discuss the possible long-term genetic consequences of any decision the patient may make. This is a different matter.

LEJEUNE: One thing struck me very much in Professor Callahan's presentation. He said the words were very important, and this thing was explained plainly. To give an example, for most of the people a child with an extra chromosome is just a Mongol, a trisomic 21. If we speak of him as Christopher or Michael, his name, that makes a great difference.

The second thing which struck me was that you asked how we can fight against genetic disease and still behave humanely. I think the way we can do that was found long ago: as medical men we have to hate the diseases but love the disabled. If we don't use that yardstick, we are not doing medicine.

HIMSWORTH: I would think, myself, that the consensus of opinion amongst medical people was that their primary duty was always to the individual. I think the reason for that is that the duty to society has always been felt to be a shared duty.

HOTCHKISS: We should not be speaking as though benefiting the individual and society were always in conflict. In attempting to abolish a disease, it may be quite true that even guaranteeing that no affected children are to be born makes very small inroads on the "p"--the proportion of the people in a future generation who are at risk. But if you have learned to screen and make these inroads in individual families, you can expect to apply them to that next generation. And so what you can abolish is the suffering which, largely speaking, is to abolish the disease, both socially and individually.

MOTULSKY: I would like to clarify one point in my discussion. The point was that in general, the yardstick of disease is made by the patient or physician or by society. Rarely do we have an absolute yardstick, especially for quantitative and polygenic multifactorial diseases. I think it should be added that if we take a disease like sickle cell or phenylketonuria or any single gene disease, there is a clear qualitative distinction between the abnormal and the normal. We can, in fact, make these distinctions. We can see that there is an additional chromosome, and in some cases like Down's syndrome it makes a tremendous impact, while in some instances--some mentioned XXY or XYY--it makes less impact. So there are definitions. But in terms of monogenic diseases, there are clear qualitative diseases. We can tell. In the large residue of disease we don't have this knowledge, and there the flexible standard arises.

GENETIC COUNSELING AND THE USES OF GENETIC KNOWLEDGE — AN ETHICAL OVERVIEW

James M. Gustafson

To prepare a paper which has an "overview" as its assigned topic is not without difficulties. The task could easily be executed in high level generalizations couched in philosophical and theological language; it is more demanding to relate the overview to genetic counseling. To say something fresh and novel is also difficult, since the major ethical issues in genetic counseling, while couched in precise alternatives offered by scientific work, are probably as old as the earliest human reflections on what is morally good and bad, what is morally right and wrong. Previous papers I have written have dealt more extensively with some ethical issues (Gustafson, 1970, 1971).

My intention in this paper is to state sharply a few ethical issues I find in the literature on the uses of genetic knowledge-- literature written by scientists and non-scientists alike. I take my cue from Dr. Robert S. Morison (1972): ". . .It appears that (the method of science) has at least two contributions to make to the progress of ethics. The first may be a rather equivocal one-- the very power of science requires us to think more adequately about ethical matters if we are to survive. The second point (is) the ability of science to reduce abstract questions of right and wrong to a series of rather clearly defined situations in which decisions must be reached in relatively concrete terms. There are those who will deplore even this, since the over-all result is to reinforce the utilitarian view of ethics and to cast doubt upon the existence of absolute truths of any kind--scientific, moral, or aesthetic. Just as in a dice game known as bedoux, there is no hand which beats all other hands, so in a relativistic world there is no good that supersedes all other good."

Morison's first point is well taken--the power of science requires more adequate ethical thinking. His second point is less persuasive; I suspect abstract questions of right and wrong have always been engendered by very concrete situations and in concrete terms, though biological research does refine and extend the arena of choice. I believe he is correct in suggesting that a utilitarian view of ethics is reinforced by scientists, though whether this is on scientific or other grounds we shall have to examine. Whether the relativity of truths leads us to a situation in which one cannot discriminate between values, and whether no good (or goods) supersede any other goods is still under debate.

Both from conversations with genetic counselors and from the literature, I would judge that the major persisting matter of moral choice is whether preference should be given to the individual, or to a community, in the decision. The "community" in the decision might be the family involved, the society of which the family is a part, or the whole of the human race. The use of the word "preference" is deliberate, for the tension between individual and community exists in various specifications of "preference"; it exists whether one speaks of the "rights" of individuals and communities, the "claims," the "consequences for," the "benefit of," or any other term.

Within the tension between the individual and communities, there are various ways in which it is stated. It might be the rights of an individual to life against potential "costs" to his family or the state; it might be the "rights" of the human race to survive against the rights of the fetal carrier of a genetic disease to live, etc. To state the tension as one between individual and a community, however, is too simple. In many decisions one is engaged in the question of which of alternate communities is to be given preference, and on what grounds.

I shall attempt to sharpen the issues by means of a series of propositions designed to make us confront the need to give reasons for our choices, no matter which of the propositions we are most prone to accept.

A. The first set of propositions is designed to distinguish between a way of thinking that has as its base line the inherent and inalienable rights of individuals, and one that has as its base line the consequences of various courses of action.

A.1. In genetic counseling and in therapy using genetic knowledge, there are inherent and inalienable rights of individuals which limit the morally acceptable course of action. Such procedures are deemed to be morally wrong regardless of their possible beneficial consequences for others. Two examples come to mind.

a. The unconditional right of fetal life to come to full term, to birth (the unconditional right thus excluding consideration of genetic defects).

b. The unconditional rights of parents to conceive and bring the fruits of conception into the world.

In a strong and consistent representation of this point of view, there would be no concessions to the possible beneficial or painful consequences that would mitigate the prior claims of these

rights.   Subsequently,   we   shall   look at some reasons why such a
position is held.

A.2.   There are no inalienable or inherent individual   rights.
In   genetic   counseling and therapy, all parties are concerned with
(a) the minimization of undesirable consequences, or (b) with   the
maximization of   desirable consequences. (The distinction between
the aim of minimizing the bad and maximizing the good is a   crucial
one;   it marks the division between negative and positive eugenics,
between planning and control to avoid bad consequences,   and planning and control to intervene in the development of man for presumably   the good of   individuals or the race.) Four examples of the
minimization of undesirable consequences which are used to   justify
interventions follow.

a.   Consequences for the   child   if   it   is born: its
physical suffering as in Tay-Sachs disease; its inability to live a
"fully   human   life" as in mongolism. (Note the differences in the
judgments that would support each of these two instances.)
b.   Consequences for parents: the personal anguish   and
suffering they will have to endure if a seriously defective child
is born; the economic costs for medical and other services.
c.   Consequences for civil society: the   social   and
economic costs involved in caring for defectives; the allocation of
scarce   resources   to   maintain   the   lives of relatively useless,
unproductive persons.
d.   Consequences for the human race and its future,   the
biological   community of man: the potential costs for the survival
of the race if the minimization of inherited defects is   not   taken
into account.

My assessment of the   literature and of conversations with
genetic counselors leads me to state that most writers and practitioners do not radicalize either of the two base lines.   That   is,
they do not work with simple logical consistency from either basic
principle taken by itself. It is also my assessment, however, that
most persons choose or accept one base line or   the   other,   making
qualifications or exceptions in the   light of the other. Some
examination of the reasons persons choose each base line might help
to see wherein lie the differences in practical and concrete
judgments.
Why do some persons opt for the language of individual rights
as the primary language to be used? One reason appeals to the
consequences for persons and societies when that   language   is   not
basic. The question becomes this: If one permits the camel's nose
of the primacy of consequences to come under the tent of societies
which protect inherent individual rights, does the whole frame   and
fabric of protection of the individual collapse? Has one established a principle that the value of a person is to be judged by
his genotype, or his potential costs or usefulness to society? If

one has established this principle, does it lead to the judgment
that the right to life is conferred upon persons by parents, by the
medical profession, or by the state? And if the right to life is a
conferred, and not an inherent right, how does one avoid the
consequences of a race-hygiene by all-powerful groups who decide on
pseudo-scientific grounds (or scientific ones) which human beings,
or classes of human beings, shall live? In short, does the erosion
of individual rights to life, regardless of defects, lead to their
disappearance--and to all powerful professions or states which
dictate who shall live?

It is clear that the wedge argument, the camel's nose argument, is not persuasive to those whose base line is consequences.
They can turn the pattern of argument back onto the defenders of
individual rights, and inquire about the consequences for societies
if there were no limitations of individual rights for the sake of
communal welfare. Granted that limitations are accepted, for
example, with reference to social justice (no person has a right to
arbitrarily exclude others from his payrolls because of their
race), what is now being asked for is an extension of limitations,
preferably by consent, into a realm of life in which there was no
need for it previously. Or, at least, with new knowledge we are
aware of needs which we could not meet in earlier ignorance.

They might wish to counter the wedge argument by a sociological argument, namely, that the frame and fabric of the tent is
malleable but firm, and that the concern for consequences will not
make it collapse. The culturally held values, impregnated in the
consciences of individuals, in the civil and criminal laws of
society, and in social institutions are to be considered as
seriously as the logical extensions of isolated moral principles.
These values will lead to resistance to excesses in the society,
just as they set limits to the activities of practitioners of
genetic counseling--who, for example, adhere to the principle of
informed consent (based on individual rights) in their dealing with
patients.

They might further argue that "new occasions teach new
duties," that under the circumstances of new knowledge of genetics
--both individual and population--the range of choices for persons
is expanded, and thus persons' range of values is practically
altered. Humans are no longer fated by chance, either individually
or collectively, to the degree they formerly were. They can know
potential consequences of certain births for themselves and for
others, and thus can and will alter their allegiances to individual
rights that appear to be tied to the fatedness of certain effects.
And, in the light of pending crises for the human race (there is
always room for argument about whether we are in a crisis, or how
soon it will come), the overriding value of survival demands
limitation of what were judged to be individual rights under other
circumstances. There is and there must be an alteration in the

shape of the tent, perhaps requiring alteration in its frame and its fabric.

But not all adherents to the base line of individual rights would rationally justify their position only by appeals to potential consequences, if the consequences line became the base. There are profound beliefs, stated by some as intuitions, and by others in theological and philosophical terms, which support their positions. On the intuitive level, Edward Shils can ask--"Is human life really sacred?"--and respond to his own question--"I answer that it is, self-evidently...Its sacredness is the most primordial of experiences, and the fact that many human beings act contrarily, or do not apprehend it, does not impugn the sacredness of life" (Shils, 1968). This affirmation and appeal to the self-evidence of the sacredness of human life does not entail individual rights to life in a strict sense (nor does Shils make that claim), but it suggests a pattern of justification. Do individuals have an inherent right to life regardless of their genotypes? Answer: "They do, self-evidently." The appeal to self-evidence may not be persuasive, so it might be bolstered by claims that once individuals come to independent existence, they strongly desire to preserve their lives and to fulfill their lives in meaningful ways, regardless of their defects. But perhaps at a crucial point in any choice of values or in any ethical point of view, there is an appeal, like that to self-evidence, which cannot be argued persuasively for all rational men. And certainly one would have to acknowledge that the "belief" that all men are created with certain inalienable rights has had a profound effect on the shaping of American culture, even if this belief is not persuasively justified in the eyes of those for whom rights to life depend upon predictable qualitative consequences for the individual and for others.

But appeal to "self-evidence," a primal intuition, is not the only one that is made. The western religious traditions, while rooted in the social notions of a "people," a community, whether the people of Israel, the Christian community, or the whole human community, have lent great support to individual rights to life. That history, often oversimplified by its defenders and critics alike, is too complex to trace here. And the arguments within it--for example, whether the unconditional right to physical life is an absolute value, or an "almost absolute value," or a value relative to other things God values for man, e.g., a quality of "fullness of life"--would be of no great interest to many who read this paper. It is also clear that through history the Christian community has had a rather shocking record of the practice of suppression of the rights to life, as well as other rights. I only note that appeals can be made to the western religious teachings for some support.

Another strand of ethical thought, namely the natural law tradition, in some forms and interpretations gives priority to

unconditional rights to life of individual human beings. Its
history is complex also, and its interpretations vary; indeed it
can be argued that even in some of its Thomistic forms, where there
is a clash between the community and the individual, the community
in the end prevails.

Without amplification of these appeals to more general levels
of justification for adherence to individual rights, I wish only to
make the point that beyond the practical, moral judgments of
whether a genetically defective fetus should live are other
"levels" of justification, of appeal, which support the practical
judgments. The arguments about ethical issues in the uses of
genetic knowledge often reflect consciously defended or tacitly
held beliefs about wherein lies the moral right and good.

We can now return to ask why some persons opt for the base
line of judging desirable and undesirable consequences in their
reflections about the uses of genetic knowledge. Why do some work
from my proposition A.II. above? Why does the language of "good"
and "bad" effects supersede the language of "right" and "wrong"
actions?

Without being historically, philosophically, and theologically
thorough, I wish to indicate what I think are the most frequent
answers to these questions. I suspect one answer is a conviction
that persons have fundamental orientations, or purposes, and that
the point of morality is to fulfill those purposes. Why might the
option of abortion of a genetically defective fetus be considered
to be morally permissible? Because persons, minimally stated, are
oriented toward the least possible suffering (an end that they
have) for others and for themselves. This purpose, or this end,
provides the justification for the act of abortion. (In another
sphere of experience, the issue came up dramatically in Swedish
society recently when a young man killed a truck driver at the
driver's request, in order that the driver would not have to suffer
the anguish of his fate, namely, being trapped in a fire that would
inevitably burn him to death.) "The least possible suffering" as
an end, as a purpose, is minimal; the ends or purposes of men have
been stated much more positively when philosophers have asked what
men seek as an end in itself and not as a means to any other end:
for Aristotle it was eudaemonia, happiness; for the utilitarians it
was pleasure; for some theologians it was blessedness, a vision of
God.

Perhaps it is too strong, too metaphysical to say that there
is a conviction that persons have fundamental orientations or
purposes. If it is, another frame of reference can lead to the
same conclusion about least possible suffering. That might be that
persons are "coping" with life, seeking to interact with difficulties and opportunities in such a way that they can survive with the
least amount of anguish and pain. They are not seeking to fulfill
purposes so much as they are trying to find solutions that they can
"live with" to ambiguities and to threats to their personal and
social equilibrium or adjustment. The point of morality would then

be to facilitate this process of adjustment, to make life bearable
in the face of suffering, and to make it rewarding in the face of
opportunities. Empirical support can be given for this view of
what life is all about. For example, if given a real choice between
the anguish and expenses involved in bringing a child with Tay-
Sachs disease into the world or aborting it in the fetal stage,
many persons will choose the latter.

Those who make judgments about acts through assessments of
their consequences are aware of the slippery criteria for assessing
the beneficial as against the bad effects of an action. As critics
of the ethics of consequences have long pointed out, one is in a
game of trying to quantify elusive qualities such as suffering,
happiness, or pleasure. Even given the greater accuracy of predict-
ability of some consequences through scientific study of genetics,
there is no certain resolution of the question of whether having a
mongoloid child, for example, is to be judged a moral evil--to the
child, to the parents, or to the society. That to have a "normal"
child is "better" than to have a mongoloid no one will dispute.
But the judgments about economic and social costs, about parental
anguish, about deficiency in capacity to be fully human, are not
readily translated into clear-cut moral terms.

Thus the critic will say that the criteria are too relative,
the reliance upon feelings or intuition too irrational, the compar-
isons between various desirable consequences and various undesirable consequences, not to mention the weighing of the desirable
against the undesirable, are too impressionistic to make sound
moral judgments possible.

This is old territory. But it is territory on which a fundamental conflict in genetic counseling and therapy still exists.
Subsequently, I shall indicate some possible ways of overcoming it.
Before doing that, however, I wish to state the conflict that
perhaps is even knottier--not between rights and consequences, but
between consequences for an individual and consequences for a
group.

B. The conflict between the individual and the group cuts
across the distinctions between rights and consequences. Conflicts
exist in rights as well as in values; we have not spelled out all
the alternatives here. The question I wish to raise here is whether
numbers count and how much they count. If the rights of an individual conflict with the rights of five other persons to life,
which has precedence? Or, to put the question in terms of consequences, if the beneficial consequences for one individual are
costly in terms of the subsequent consequences to many persons,
which has precedence?   This is an old moral issue, preceding the
utilitarian principle of "the greatest good for the greatest
number" by hundreds of years. For example, there is a discussion
in the Talmud of the question of whether one Jew is obligated to
die as a ransom in order to save the lives of other Jews. "It was
taught: If a company of men travelling on a journey were held up

by Gentiles, who said to them, 'Give us one of you and we will kill him, and if not, we will kill all of you,' let them all be killed and let them not betray to them one soul of Israel" (Jacobs, 1957). The passage continues to develop an exception and differing interpretations of the teaching. Jacobs' essay is important for showing a distinction in Jewish ethics between what was normally expected (that one is not under obligation to give up his life for a friend) and teachings that "saints" ought to follow.

Put in propositional form and confined to the language of consequences (omitting rights), the opposing points of view can be stated as follows.

B.1. The cost or benefits for other persons involved does not make any difference in judging the morality of a proposed procedure resulting from genetic knowledge. The primary concern is for the benefit of the individual patient.

> Example: In a case of a genetically defective fetus,
> (here significant qualifications might be made with
> reference to what constitutes a defect and how serious it
> is), the aim of medical procedures is to save that life,
> and to exercise all possible therapeutic procedures
> toward that end, regardless of various forms of "cost"
> (a) to others neglected by the attention given to that
> individual, (b) to family, insurance companies, and the
> state in caring for the child, and (c) to possible future
> generations if the patient should survive and be a
> carrier of the defect.

B.2. The moral permissibility of a proposed procedure resulting from genetic knowledge is to be calculated in terms of the greatest good to the greatest number. In population genetics this involves an assessment of benefits and costs for future as well as present generations.

> Example: If, on the basis of amniocentesis, a fetus is
> known to have a genetic defect which, if carried into
> future generations would seriously (the judgment of
> degree of seriousness is a matter for discussion) affect
> the well-being (another matter of judgment) of future
> individuals, and of the human race, the greatest good for
> the greatest number dictates that abortion is desirable,
> if not obligatory.

At this point we can recall Morison's statement that the overall result of the effects of the method of science on ethics "is to reinforce the utilitarian view of ethics." As I noted earlier, it is not altogether clear whether that reinforcement is entailed by science, or whether certain ethical preferences on the part of scientists, to be sure, supported by certain uses of scientific data, are not more determinative of the reinforcement. Perhaps in genetics, when one is thinking in broad and long-range terms, the crucial value is the survival of the human race. Believing that the human race ought to survive, for whatever reasons, that value gets translated into utilitarian terms of the greatest good for the greatest number, or minimally stated, the least possible threat to the smallest number.

Whether the threats to survival are at a critical stage is an issue open for discussion. How the issue is decided, to be sure, is a matter of assessing data, extrapolating from the known present to the unknown future, accounting for elements of chance which would qualify predictions, etc. I have a growing conviction, however, that the same evidences, and perhaps even the same predictions, can evoke different attitudes in scientists and non-scientists alike. One can find an attitude near that of apocalypticism about the genetic future of the race, and one can find an attitude near that of complacency, with various others between. Some other factors, perhaps moral beliefs, perhaps basic views of how much humans are egocentric and short-sighted or capable of disinterested concern for others and for the future, perhaps quasi-metaphysical or quasi-theological beliefs about whether one can or cannot have confidence in the development of life toward human survival (whether chance and randomness are to be trusted more than human manipulation), are finally decisive in determing an evaluation of how critical the state of affairs now is.

The criterion of physical survival for the race, however, cannot be readily applied to arenas of smaller numbers or shorter time, in which the utilitarian view is also often applied. Whether, for example, the abortion of a mongoloid fetus serves the greatest "good" for the greatest number depends on the analysis of what constitutes "good," or benefits, how one assesses their qualities, and indeed their quantities, and on who gets included in the "number" and over what span of time. This is not the time or place to rehearse the generations of critical analysis of the notion of good: its ambiguities, and the necessary distinctions; whether it should ever be used as a noun, or only as an adjective, and even as an adjective how to compare the "good" of physical life with the "costs" of maintaining it, etc. There may be cases in which the criterion appears to be more immediately applicable (Tay-Sachs disease might be one) than it is to others. I wish only to suggest that scientific knowledge does not necessarily convert into utilitarian ethics without remainder, and that there are many non-scientific judgments made in (a) the adoption of utilitarian ethics as a sufficient basis for practical moral judgments in genetic counseling, and (b) in the application of its criteria to particular cases if it is adopted.

Yet, there are few, if any, who would say that numbers never count in making moral judgments. There are probably few persons who do not find voluntary self-sacrifice for the sake of saving the lives of others to be, in principle, commendable--an act (in a sense) beyond the requirements of the law. Whether particular acts of self-sacrifice are commended, such as self-immolations with the intention to increase resistance to the war in Vietnam, is more complex. But many who would say that it is commendable to give one's life voluntarily that others might live, would balk at others deciding that a life ought to be taken for the sake of others. If my death could save ten lives, or if my not having children could prevent genetic defects in future generations, do others have the right (they may have the power) to kill me, or to perform surgery so that I cannot perpetrate defects in the future? "Informed consent" is the principle still practiced to preserve the value of voluntarism.

The point to this discussion is to indicate that the thorny old chestnut of who should decide, and on what warrants, cannot be forgotten even in discussions of how much numbers count. I suspect that whether others feel free to assume that power as a moral right is relative to the circumstances of cases; where human survival is clearly at stake, it is clearer than where it is a matter of relieving bearable suffering and anguish. Thus the assessment of circumstances--their seriousness with reference to things valued--will be a crucial factor even for those who minimize the significance of numbers in moral discourse.

These issues we live with every day, and further rehearsal of them has perhaps long ago reached a point of diminishing returns.

C. I wish now to suggest some procedures that might help us practically to overcome some differences of agreement.

C.1. While it does not resolve all the differences between well-intentioned, rational men, I believe there is merit in Bernard Gert's argument that we are more likely to come to agreement on evils to be avoided than we are on goods to be achieved (Gert, 1970). Gert's five rules--"Don't kill, Don't cause pain, Don't disable, Don't deprive of freedom or opportunity, Don't deprive of pleasure"--are not applicable in a simple way to the uses of genetic knowledge, as he would be the first to admit. And some would wish not to have rules at all in judging what is right to do. But the basic thrust behind his formulation might be worthy of exploration in genetic ethics. Can we proceed to seek agreement on what consequences are to be avoided? I am not certain how far we would get; perhaps no further than if we tried to compose the goal of the genetically best human race. In efforts to delineate posi- tive goods, or goals, the plurality of values has to be recognized, and there is no natural harmony between these values. The same problem would occur if we sought to specify precisely the evils we would seek to avoid causing. We would necessarily get into a quantification problem of which evils are the greatest and for whom.

I make the suggestion, however, in the aspiration that if we could come to some agreement on minimal objectives, a modest but significant achievement would be made. While the resolution of particular cases would not be automatic or devoid of judgments relative to circumstances, we might achieve a common orientation. Where matters of public policy are concerned, certainly it is at least prudent to have some agreement on evils to be avoided.

C.2. I have noted that I do not find actual writings which take either the line of individual rights, or the line of common good, without some qualification of one by the other. Two ways of working seem implicit in this practice; a brief outline of these procedures might be clarifying. Both stand between the extremes of "pure" intuitionism on the one hand, and exceptionless moral rules on the other hand.

a. One procedure is to discover or establish certain rules, either pertaining to protection of individual rights, or to protection of consequences for individuals, or to development of the common good. To such rules one would recognize exceptions. Indeed, to follow another formulation by Gert, public advocacy for the exception would be an obligation. The genetic counselor would be obliged to state why, under certain conditions, he violated the agreed-upon rules.

Certainly this is the case already in medical practice. Through thought and the accumulation of professional custom, certain rules are formulated which cover most known cases of medical practice. Alteration in practice requires advocacy in the light of new knowledge, individual instances, and personal judgment about what one ought to do.

The advantage of the procedure of rules with publicly advocated exceptions is that it guards against individual idiosyncracies and fallibilities. It provides a framework within which genetic counselors can function with confidence in most cases and gives them a basis for support for their judgments. The requirement of advocacy also protects against the possible errors of intuitive judgments.

b. The second procedure is to formulate certain values to be achieved (either evils to be avoided or positive benefits to be sought), certain rights to be protected, etc., and recognize both their plurality and their conflicts. Let us call them, for shorthand purposes, principles. One would recognize them not as rules with possible exceptions (though that would be the effect in ordinary cases) but as points of orientation toward responsible moral decisions in particular cases. Robert A. Dahl makes the point in a pithy way in the context of his recent discussion of democratic government: "Principles provide an orientation, not a path; a compass, not a map" (Dahl, 1970). Whether one might argue more for a map function than merely a compass function is an important issue, but for my general point it need not be discussed.

My main point is that, particularly in the early stages of the development of a science and its application, we might use moral values and principles as orientations to decisions. That this would rely upon previous experience in similar cases is evident. That it would permit more latitude for individual decisions in individual cases than the procedure of rule with exceptions is also evident. For some, this latitude would be too extensive, too permissive, too subject to intuitive justifications, too idiosyncratic, and its errors too costly to tolerate. The requirement of advocacy or justification can very well be made here as well; indeed, a conference such as this is an arena of advocacy.

It may be that in the final analysis these two procedures are compatible, the first operating in normal circumstances and the second in exploratory or novel circumstances. It would be my judgment that in an area such as the uses of genetic knowledge, where so many different moral points of view are brought to bear, some agreement on procedures might facilitate efforts to overcome moral disagreements. Where participants have differing but overlapping moral commitments, it would be foolish to proceed by trying to convert to unanimity of fundamental commitments. However, it is wise to recognize that such commitments exist and to analyze how they affect particular judgments. A more modest aspiration is in order: namely, an effort to come to such stages and areas of agreement as we can and to find procedures that are mildly effective and acceptable in order to proceed with our common interdisciplinary work.

REFERENCES

Dahl, Robert A. (1970). *After the Revolution?* New Haven, Yale University Press. *Citation from page 104.*
Gert, Bernard (1970). *The Moral Rules.* New York, Harper and Row. *Citation from page 69.*
Gustafson, J. M. (1970). *Basic Ethical Issues in the Biomedical Field,* in *Soundings: An Interdisciplinary Journal,* vol. LXX, no. 2, pp. 151-180.
Gustafson, J. M. (1972). *Genetic Engineering and the Normative View of the Human,* in the *Boston University Conference on The Dignity of Man,* held December 1969 (in press).
Gustafson, J. M. (1971). *What is Normatively Human, American Ecclesiastical Review,* CLXV, 192-207.
Jacobs, Louis (1957). *Greater Love Hath No Man...,The Jewish Point of View of Self-Sacrifice, Judaism 6,* 41-47. *Citation from page 45. Quotation from the Jerusalem Talmud, Terumot 8, 12 and Tos. Ter. 7, 23.*
Morison, R. (1972). *Introduction,* in *Early Diagnosis of Human Genetic Defects,* Maureen Harris, editor. *Washington, D.C., U.S. Government Printing Office.*

Shils, Edward (1968). The Sanctity of Life, in Life or Death: Ethics and
Options, Daniel H. Labby, editor. Seattle; University of Washington
Press. Citation from pp. 18-19.

DISCUSSION

Principal Discussant: Jerome Lejeune

I am not at all an ethicist. As you possibly know, not even a gene ethicist. I only try to be a geneticist.

Dr. Gustafson has said that there are guidelines, that there are rules with exceptions, and that we should try to do our best in those ways.   He mentioned disposal of trisomic 21 fetuses (i.e., abortion). I would like to ask whether he would have said the same thing about disposal of trisomic 21 children (i.e., infanticide). I think it is a very important point, because we have to know whether, with scientific progress, there is a dividing line between abortion and infanticide. I would like to know whether the same arguments would apply to infanticide as he supposes apply to abortion. My personal feeling is that this is the crux of the matter.

I would come to very simple points now. When we discuss problems concerning adults and children, the National Institutes of Health is quite generally preferred. But when dealing with tiny fellows, especially the not-yet-born, the National Institute of Death finds some supporters. The reason for this divergence seems to lie in the question: Are they human or not? If already human, help and heal is the goal. If not yet human, discard and destroy is the solution. Hence, my question about abortion versus infanticide problems. My personal feeling is that we should elaborate our decision on scientific grounds only -- using all the scientific information we can gather.

Let us take the example of trisomy 21, observed by amniocentesis.   Looking at the chromosomes and detecting the extra 21, we say very safely "The child who will develop here will be a trisomic 21." But this phrase does not convey all the information. We have not seen only the extra 21; we have also seen all the 46 other chromosomes and concluded that they were human, because if they had been mouse or monkey chromosomes, we would have noticed. Hence, genetically speaking we have got two answers: first, here is a human being developing; second, he is affected by trisomy 21. All the discussion springs from the fact that some people note only the extra chromosome, and others look at the whole set.

I have never believed myself the ensoulment theories (whether theological or materialistic), pretending that the developing thing in utero will become a man some day, but is not yet human before a given step has been reached. Indeed, this "given step" varies broadly from specialist to specialist. But that is not the question. What seems obvious to me, from all we know about genetics, is simply this: if a fertilized egg is not by itself a full human being, it could never become a man, because something would have to be added to it; and we know that does not happen.

General Discussion

GUSTAFSON: I wish to address the problem of the distinction between abortion and infanticide because I recognize that it is one of the slippery slopes one gets onto if no single principle decides all cases. There is no question that one can avoid that issue if one states that from the moment of conception one is dealing with the human being and that there are no conditions under which a human life can be taken. Then one can be very consistent and say, "No abortion; obviously no infanticide," and everything is very clear-cut.

I would argue that certainly we are dealing with capacities for full humanity from the moment of conception, and therefore one has always to argue what conditions are sufficient to warrant taking human life.

The ethical tradition in the West has always argued that under certain conditions, it is morally justifiable to take a human life. What are those conditions? The argument has to be translated into more ethical terms: What rights would override the right of that individual to life, or what benefits for others would override the right of that individual to life?

With regard to abortion and infanticide, I would argue that once an infant is born, it has a different status than it has in utero—although it is human in both cases—and that it has a different kind of claim to life. Thus, I would not argue for infanticide.

My main point is that there would be a presumption in favor of saving human life, but then one asks under what conditions is it morally permissible to take it?

HIMSWORTH: I thought that Professor Lejeune brought things at one stage down to a critical question when he said, "What is the difference between a fetus with mongolism and a newborn baby with mongolism? And if you can kill one, why can't you kill the other?"

In this connection, I would like to ask Professor Gustafson one thing. You were talking about the inalienable right to live. And you used this particular phrase—"once it has come to an independent existence."

I want to be certain that I wouldn't be unfair in assuming that you intentionally used the words, "once it has come to an independent existence," and that you were drawing a distinction.

GUSTAFSON: Yes, I was very careful in saying what I said there, but that begs a lot of questions. And that is your point: What is that moment of independent existence?

HIMSWORTH: It is the crux of the question.

GUSTAFSON: It is the crux of the question. That is a slippery slope, too. None of us ever comes to independent existence in a broad sense. We are always dependent upon others for our existence. There is no moment in which any individual has a totally independent existence, if that means he is able to exist merely by reference to his own resources and not rely upon resources of others for his own existence. So we have to recognize that we make a judgment about a point like that.

Now, it may be logically absurd to use the same word "independent" in the same way in different contexts. I would take it that a conceptus has an independent existence relative to sperm and egg. There is an entity there which can be differentiated from the conditions out of which it emerged.

Then it comes down to the judgment that at the moment of birth there is a greater degree of independence than _in_ _utero_. At that juncture, I take it, other sorts of arguments now pertain, because the kind of dependence and the degree of dependence has altered to some extent. So I use that very deliberately.

HOTCHKISS: At this slippery interface between the potential human being and the actual human, there is another aspect of independent existence which has been in my mind.

Perhaps even closer to the crux of the matter is that the supposedly independent existence of the Down's syndrome infant requires eventually a great deal more attention, care, and support from the family and society than that of the normal one. So we should not make the mistake of projecting each potential human being into an idealized, fully-rounded and fully participating human being, but should carefully consider just which human values we are bound to conserve.

In fact, through medical insight and experience, it is possible, for this and numerous other serious disorders, to make fairly predictable projections for an affected individual. And it is just these which bring us to the problem.

I think we should also remember that not only is the fertilized human ovum a potential human being, but within the perhaps not-distant future we may look upon the white cells or any nucleated cells, cells discarded during menstruation or at surgery, even the hapless haploid sperm cell, as potential human cells, valuable material, and if one were so minded, capable by the arts that may be developed, of growing into a human being. So these are things, too, that have potential often wasted.

We must also think of such abnormal potential as that of the tumor cell which will undoubtedly be capable of growing and gaining, and leading a very happy life from a tumorous point of view, although it is something that we have already made the decision should often be sacrificed as a damaged part. Why? To support better the potential of the almost intact being who remains, and it is clear that we are careless in not supporting adequately that potential in all too many cases.

CROW: This is purely a pragmatic issue, but in the court decision in Wisconsin a few months back, the decision was made that the criterion should be quickening rather than capability of independent existence. I am told that this was chosen on the grounds that the criterion should not change from year-to-year with the improvement of medical skills.

EATON: This may muddy the water up more, but I think what is coming down is not a discussion about when human life begins, but a differentiation between human life and human personality. In many ways the world in general, and the Western world in particular, has used the word "human life" sort of synonomously with human personality. And I am not too sure that that is a correct analysis. I am wondering what a geneticist does when he is confronted with arguments that there is a difference between human life and human personality.

A person who is born can be so oppressed and subjected and taken through various forms of behavioral mechanisms and adjustments that many philosophers and psychologists would argue that you have a human living organism, in terms of his organic and protoplasmic structure, but that you don't have a human being in terms of personality.

LEJEUNE: Whether we consider, as geneticists, that there is a distinction between life and personality depends really on how much we believe in biological determinants. If we believe in biological determinants, then the whole thing is settled after the genome is established, if not disturbed, that is. You cannot make the distinction that psychiatrists would propose, as you said, because in these terms, a newborn has no personality. This would be a scientific mystery as far as our science is now.

It is dangerous to say that a newborn, if properly maltreated, will never become a human being, because it would mean that any maltreated child is not a human being and then can be discarded by any means. This kind of view is not only entirely illogical, if you make a difference between the personality and the fact of her life; it is contrary to all the biological science now available.

MELLMAN: In the United States there has been a tendency to treat mongolism as a curse, a reflection of some evil that was inflicted on a family for a reason. As a result, there has been an impulse to rid ourselves of mongolism, both as individuals and society. Perhaps we are now getting away from this, because we have scientific evidence to refute this, and a very significant change may be developing in the personality of our society and its view of mongolism. Therefore, I am asking whether we are acting in response to an old tradition, a wrong premise.

SCHULMAN: I would like to tell a story which highlights to me the great difficulties in making a distinction as to viability and inviability in justifying abortion. And I might say that I speak from the point of view of someone who does not find abortion ethically unacceptable.

About a year ago in New York City, a legal abortion by saline installation was carried out. A fetus was passed—a dead fetus—along with a live infant. There had been a double amniotic sac. The saline had been injected into only one sac. The fetus who was born alive lived, with intensive pediatric care, for several days, and no one thought of killing it.

I wonder really what is the distinction between the one that got the salt and the one that didn't. I don't know.

VASTYAN: I wanted to address my question to Professor Gustafson. We use the word "viability." Aren't we in a very real way talking about potentiality?

In medical practice I think potentiality becomes a norm. Pneumonia, the old man's friend, is rarely treated for the 80-year-old man with metastases throughout his body. Nor is it very conceivable that a child, newborn, with Tay-Sachs disease, diagnosed with a cardiac problem or an intestinal obstruction is going to be rushed to surgery.

How much of a part does potentiality play as an ethical norm? Has this been elucidated at all?

GUSTAFSON: Potentiality has been used as a sort of ethical norm. If one thinks not merely about what one is dealing with at a given moment of development, but also about what that can become, there is a sense then in which a judgment of what a person can become is involved.

If this line of discussion is followed, one has to say that there are different stages at which different potentialities have different possibilities of realization. The fertilized egg has a different potential than an unfertilized egg. One then makes his judgments about what to do with a fertilized egg in the light of what it might become.

There are real differences at this juncture between termination of life near the point of death and termination of life at its beginning. The kinds of potentialities, the range of potentialities, and the time span for development of potentialities, is different.

I have been in discussions, for example, in which people have said that if a flat EEG becomes a basis for the determination of the right to no longer sustain life, would it not be possible to say that before there is measurable brain activity in the fetus, on the same principle, you could abort a fetus.

That is one of the places in which I say potentiality makes a difference. With reference to the fetus, there is a capacity there. (I prefer to use the language of "capacity" rather than "potentiality.") There is a capacity there for development over a long range of time and the fulfillment of certain human possibilities that is not present at the other end, and therefore that makes a difference.

FRIED: It is true that scientists, at least recently, have had a kind of preference for utilitarian ethics. I think it is demonstrably false that there is any necessary connection or logical connection between the two positions.

But I would like to draw attention to a paradox in utilitarian ethics which provides some support to the ideas Professor Lejeune was alluding to.

The usual formulation one gets of the utilitarian ethic is the greatest good to the greatest number. The first question one is brought to ask is: Assuming even that we can find some way of adding your good to my good and to everyone else's good and finding some common currency for all of our goods, does that therefore mean that 8 million units of good are better than 7 million? In fact, the whole thing tends to infinity, and if we therefore have a population tending in size to infinity, existing at the most marginal level of consciousness (and therefore enjoyment), would that be better because the sum of good would be greater? That is an obvious absurdity.

Therefore, the attempt was made to say, "It doesn't really mean the greatest good to the greatest number," and the most honest of the utilitarians, John Stuart Mill, quickly made the point, "No, no, it is the sum divided by the number of individuals; it is the average. We want the highest average. We want to maximize the average."

That, too, leads to some odd paradoxes because in that case it means that a very small population with a very high level of well-being is preferable to a larger one. But that is perhaps not even a paradox, and we would perhaps be willing to accept that--indeed, are moving toward acceptance of it. But it would also mean that the surprise, unannounced killing of people also is a useful thing to do because, having killed them, they no longer figure as denominators to the equation, and if the result is to keep the numerator constant, we are indeed maximizing the quantity. Again, that is a result one doesn't quite want to accept.

There are those who are prepared to swallow that and who would say that the reason, therefore, that we don't kill is because in fact as you reduce the denominator you are also reducing the numerator because of the insecurity effects on those who are left alive, and so on. But there is a certain element of the ad hoc to those arguments.

The point that emerges from these paradoxes in utilitarianism--which is really only on the surface a coherent theory and only on the surface appears to be a nice way of turning ethics into numbers--is that there is no real sense, no real ethical sense, in talking about maximizing happiness unless you take as given the fact of individuals.

Otherwise, what you are doing is making your ethical value out of an abstraction. That is what the Bentham formula is--making a value out of an abstraction. Simply, you say that there should be the greatest sum total of happiness, and it is apparently irrelevant how happy the individuals are. The individuals disappear. What is of value is the size of that number. And that obviously is not ethics any more. It is some kind of an abstraction, completely devoid of the concern for individuals which is what ethics is about.

Ethics assumes that individuals exist, and then proceeds to think about that, rather than ethics being a way of maximizing some quantity without regard for individuals--because that becomes really a nonsensical procedure. There really are problems about who are individuals and when do they come into existence--because this is the substance of ethics.

MORISON: Professor Gustafson may remember more clearly than I do what I said 14 months ago, but I don't think I said there is any logical connection between science and utilitarian ethics. I was taking a more practical and pragmatic point of view. In the first place it is true, for reasons that are probably too long and complicated to go into, that science tends to support the point of view of Peter Abelard towards the status of universals. This point of view, in turn, makes it difficult to talk in terms of a deductive sort of ethics based upon immutable principles.

The second point is a much more practical one; science makes it apparently much easier than it used to be to trace the consequences of acts over a longer chain, so one can compare a larger set of results of a larger number of options with one another. As science has made it easier to predict the consequences of a given act, it has simultaneously strengthened the position of those who hold that the best way of making an ethical judgment is through careful assessment of the probable results of the various choices, rather than by an appeal to some a priori principle.

SINSHEIMER: I just wanted to make a brief comment to Dr. Lejeune. In the real world, in many instances, the distinctions that we draw are ultimately arbitrary. Of course, there is a continuum from the unfertilized egg to the conceptus, and so on. And the distinction therefore between infanticide and abortion is largely in the mind of the beholder. That gets down to the matter of the social personality, the set of our culture that Dr. Mellman mentioned. But in utilitarian terms, that is a very useful distinction.

One other comment to Dr. Fried--the calculation of utilitarian value is much more complicated than you made it out. There are all kinds of non-linear interactions and, as we have come to learn increasingly, everything we do in the end comes back to act on everything we do, and that has to be taken into account.

SCREENING: A PRACTITIONER'S VIEW

Robert Murray

Although I am to discuss screening from the perspective of the practitioner, I must also include some discussion of genetic counseling, for the two ought to be tied together. If they are not, then the patient is done an obvious disservice.

In looking at the ethical aspects of the screening and counseling process, I have adopted in the simplified fashion an approach used by the Population Task Force of the Institute of Society, Ethics and the Life Sciences. This involves an evaluation of the degree to which certain aspects of screening and counseling affect ethical values that to me seem important to the patient, the family, and the community. Such values are survival, justice, freedom, well-being, truth-telling, and the general welfare. There are many problems inherent in trying to define precisely these terms, and I will make no attempt to do so. I think the broad general meanings that are usually applied will allow most people to understand what I am going to say. This kind of approach is intended only to provide flexible guidelines and directions, in the sense mentioned by Dr. Gustafson (this volume), to the practitioner involved in screening and counseling when he is faced with some of the ethical conflicts that arise in specific cases, since each case is a unique situation.

The cornerstone of medical practice has been the doctor-patient relationship, and modern medical practice continues to emphasize the physician's responsibility to each individual patient. He must not only treat the patient's ills but, further, must do no harm. I quote the Hippocratic Oath: "I will follow that system of regimen which, according to my ability and judgment, I consider for the benefit of my patients, and abstain from whatever is deleterious and mischievous." There are occasions when, in the act of abstaining from whatever is deleterious and mischievous, the physician may withhold information or even treatment which he judges would do a given patient more harm than good. But always at the center of the clinician's concern is the individual--that particular patient with whom he is immediately concerned--for he must answer to that individual for his actions. His interests have in the past extended beyond the individual usually only when communicable or infectious diseases or toxic environmental agents have been involved which might have constituted immediate danger to individual members of the larger community.

Large-scale screening for genetic disorders is another instance in which the focus of the physician has extended beyond the individual to the group. Here the group may be the family, the community, or even all of mankind. The difference is that the conditions about which the physician is concerned are not communicable or dangerous in the immediate sense, but rather in a futuristic sense. Only a minority, and in many cases a small minority, of the total population is usually threatened with involvement. The threat to the group is more nebulous when compared to the threat of death from communicable disease. But just as the emphasis when working with the community on communicable disorders is on prevention, the emphasis in screening for genetic disorders is not primarily on treatment of disease but prevention of disease, and even the prevention of the birth of potentially diseased individuals.

In the past, the clinician has thought of the prevention of disease in a positive sense. Disease has been prevented by treating the living patient or his environment in a specific manner rather than by eliminating him. Smallpox, for example, has been prevented by immunizing the subject in such a way that contact with the infectious agent does not result in clinical disease. The mental retardation that will almost always occur in phenylketonuria or galactosemia is prevented by removing phenylalanine, in the first instance, and galactose, in the second instance, from the environment of infants who have the specific mutations that produce these metabolic errors.

It is the treatment and possibly the prevention of disease in this latter sense that has excited intense interest in and promoted the development of the massive programs of screening for diseases that are presumably the result of mutant genes or other aberrations in the genetic material. The dream of the physician is, after all, the prevention of the manifestation of disease rather than its cure after it has been found. What could be better than to check all newborn infants at birth for as many biochemical and chromosomal defects as possible? One would not only identify those neonates who are diseased, but would be able to assure the parents of those who are not affected that they need not worry--at least about those conditions which have been tested for.

It is essential in those cases where genetic disease or a mutant gene product has been identified, that there be therapy or a positive course of action for the condition. And herein lies a part of the dilemma of the clinician. In most of the cases where genetic disease or potential for disease is detected, there is no effective therapy or direct course of action available for the patient. If the patient's prognosis is very poor and death ensues rapidly as a result of the disease, the absence of effective therapy may not be seen as oppressive. But if the condition is chronic, debilitating, slowly progressive, like, for example, muscular dystrophy of the Duchenne type or sickle cell disease, and there is no effective therapy available, knowing about the condition prior to its clinical manifestation may merely provoke increased patient or parental anxiety without offering any positive reassurance. There will be little benefit to the patient and, for a time at least, some possible degree of harm to the parents and patient, depending upon their emotional stability.

It could be argued that diagnosis of the genetic defect before the fact of overt disease infringes upon the ethical values of security and well-being and perhaps even the freedom of parents and of the patient. For, although prior knowledge of the defect supports the ethical value of truth-telling, it does so at the expense of two or perhaps even three other very important ethical values. To the physician, as with other scientists and scholars, knowledge is in and of itself of value. But this is a purist's point of view. Many utilitarians and many of today's modern youth ask of knowledge, "What good is it?" This is a valid question asked by many parents. Some two or three years ago, we briefly saw in our Heredity Clinic a four- or five-year-old Caucasian girl who had odd pigmentation of her skin and hair. She was requested to return to the clinic for further diagnostic study which would have included skin biopsy. But her mother refused to bring her back again. In trying to persuade her to return, we told her that we wished to know for certain what her daughter's skin disorder was. Her reply was, "If you can't cure her or make her skin more normal, what is the good of knowing? It may help you, but not me or her."

For many parents, knowledge of the potential problem disturbs their well-being, without providing any other practical benefits. Knowing ahead of time without there being some way of altering the course of the disorder is, to them, more an academic exercise than a benefit. For in this instance knowing infringes on the pleasure and well-being of parents, at least until such time as the first signs or symptoms of a particular condition appear. After all, in some cases like this, ignorance is bliss.

It is in this instance that one special aspect of genetic counseling assumes importance. For where, on one hand, the physician takes away from the well-being of parents by informing them of their child's condition, he can enhance their well-being by assuring them of their innocence in the causation of the condition--by making it clear that it was a consequence of fate, and by helping them appreciate what they can do to help their child, even when there is no effective treatment for the condition. He can help them look at their child as a human being to be helped, not pitied, and he can help them avoid the self-pity that so often occurs.

The fact that most hereditary disorders now detected by screening have no effective therapy has been responsible for the emphasis on intrauterine diagnosis followed by therapeutic abortion. But "therapeutic" in this instance applies to the mother and father, not to the embryo, which is the disease. Furthermore, it

has emphasized the necessity for the identification of these clinically normal carriers of mutant genes, more specifically those
that are autosomal recessives, so that the conception of individuals with genetic disease might be prevented.

Let us look at some ethical values in the screening and
counseling of diseased or potentially diseased individuals. The
practitioner has always been bound by an ethical obligation to
protect the security of the patient by maintaining his privacy. He
has recently supported the invasion of such privacy by the compulsory screening for PKU now practiced in many states, since only by
early detection can the patient receive effective therapy. The
benefit at issue, that of normal mental development, is well worth
the right of privacy infringed upon.

The benefit of normal mental development and function to the
patient is also considered more important by the practitioner than
the detriment to the population that may occur because the treated
patient is likely to contribute to an increase in the frequency of
mutant genes. The physician knows what will happen to the
untreated patient, but he cannot be certain what the long-term
effects of increased mutant gene frequency will be. The human
benefits of enhanced freedom, increased well-being and survival
outweigh, in the minds of many, if not most, practitioners, those
suspected but uncertain dangers to the human gene pool which are
very long-range ones and for which solutions may or may not be
found.

Screening for hereditary disease is then a mixed blessing.
Where specific therapy exists, the ethical benefits far outweigh
the risks and disvalues that result. Where there is no therapy, it
may be that the emotional burdens imposed by prior knowledge
without definitive therapy being available may not be worth the
emotional trauma that prevents there being at least a brief period
during which parents can enjoy a positive sense of well-being in
their relations to their child. The physician may exert a negative
influence in the course of truth-telling or bringing truth to the
parents, but he can bring positive benefits through effective
counseling.

Now let's consider the dilemma of the carrier. The clinician
is vitally interested in the development of screening programs to
detect the clinically normal, heterozygous carriers of hereditary
biochemical abnormalities, but he must consider the process from
the point of view of both the carrier and the non-carrier.
Subjects who are identified as non-carriers will have their state
of being enhanced, their freedom increased, and their faith in
science and medicine enhanced since they have received genetic good
news. But what of the person who is detected as a carrier? He is
usually unprepared for the disappointing news that he receives
unless he already knows that he has a positive family history.
Even individuals who are knowledgeable about a particular condition
like, for example, sickle cell trait, may be unable to
immediately accept the news that they are carriers.

An example of this occurred on a recent Washington, D.C., television program on sickle cell anemia. One enthusiastic volunteer worker was emphasizing the importance of everyone's knowing whether or not he or she had the sickle cell trait. To dramatize this the volunteer, who didn't know her hemoglobin type, had a sample of blood taken at the beginning of the program and a sickling test performed during the show. She was shocked into speechlessness when she was told that the test was definitely positive.

What options are open to the individual identified as a carrier? Let us assume that the carrier of this trait, say sickle cell trait, wishes to act on the information provided in a positive way, possibly to prevent the birth of a child with sickle cell anemia.

1. Since the freedom of mating of the carrier is compromised, he or she might inquire of all prospective mates, perhaps on the first date, of his or her carrier status. In the United States, roughly one in ten Black men will be eliminated as a mate for a Black female carrier of sickle cell trait. Other persons carrying hemoglobin C or beta thalassemia genes will also be eliminated since offspring doubly heterozygous for these conditions will have serious clinical disease. Of course, this kind of practice might tend to squelch social relationships.

2. The carrier might just take a chance and then check the carrier status of the spouse after marriage. The chances are roughly nine in ten for a noncarrier-carrier marriage in sickle cell trait. If they have not had this good fortune and two carriers have married, then they must either: (a) not have any children of their own, or, (b) be able to detect the potential disease condition antenatally in order to prevent the birth of a child through therapeutic abortion. Option (b) is not yet possible with sickle cell anemia, and I am not as optimistic as some are that we will soon have a reliable method of intrauterine diagnosis.

3. If there should be some effective way to treat the condition--and in the case of sickle cell anemia there is not as yet--they need worry only about the exorbitant cost of medical care in this country.

The practitioner is confident when he is able to detect the carrier state of a hereditary disease for which there is specific medical therapy, or where therapeutic abortion might be employed as a preventive measure. The mass screening program of Kaback and his colleagues to detect carriers of Tay-Sachs disease in the Baltimore-Washington Jewish population is an example. This kind of program has been justified because it costs less than the hospital care of the Tay-Sachs patient until his death, and because it spares the parents the anguish of the miserably ill child, thereby enhancing the general welfare of the community and the freedom and well-being of the parents.

The ethical aspects of making such life-or-death decisions on the basis of primarily financial considerations has already been discussed. Suffice it to say that there is ethical support for screening in cases like this because the well-being and freedom of the parents and the general welfare of the community is enhanced. On the other hand, there is ethical conflict for the practitioner when he detects the carrier state in disorders like sickle cell trait, where there is no medical therapeutic alternative and the freedom and well-being of patient and perhaps the general welfare of the community may be reduced. For after all, an effective program of counseling of sickle cell trait subjects will result in a very slow increase of the frequency of the sickle gene in the population.

In developing mass screening programs for carriers, some specific questions must be answered before effective programs are instituted. Who is to be tested? Should testing be voluntary or compulsory? What should be done with the information obtained from testing? What will be the attitude of the public and their peers toward the individual who is identified as a carrier?

At first glance, it would seem logical that testing should be done only in high-risk populations where the carrier frequency is significantly high. Jewish groups would be tested for the carrier state for ethnically frequent conditions like Tay-Sachs disease. Blacks would be tested for sickle cell trait. And if testing is voluntary this might be an ethically acceptable approach to screening. But if testing for traits like this should be made compulsory, and there is evidence that people are already starting to do this, e.g., in New York state, it might happen that children identified as carriers would be stigmatized as different and as being undesirable parents or as being weaker or less fit. Compulsory screening only in specific ethnic groups might also tend to reinforce racist or separatist doctrines.

A recent advertisement placed in Ebony Magazine for the purpose of raising money for sickle cell research characterized carriers of sickle cell trait as being weak. It is particularly apropos because of Dr. Callahan's comments about fighting disease, and I quote:

"It's a killer. One out of every ten Black Americans carries a blood trait that threatens to cripple or kill. It's called sickle cell disease, because it creates deformed 'sickle-shaped' red blood cells.

"It can weaken those it doesn't kill. Even those with the milder form of sickle cell disease--the 'trait'-- suffer. Usually they must avoid strenuous activities and consult their doctors on a regular basis."

This was not sponsored by the American Medical Association--it was sponsored, surprisingly enough, by American Express, and is tied to the purchase of their American Express Money Orders. The purchase price of every American Express Money Order used will be donated to the drive. So if you send your subscription in on an American Express Money Order, the cost of that money order will be used in supporting the fight against sickle cell disease.

Another comment I would like to make with reference to stigmatization has to do with the discussion of cloning at a recent meeting. It was suggested by one speaker that perhaps it would be more emotionally acceptable if we started off by cloning people like Raquel Welch. I wonder if we would consider cloning her if we found she was a carrier for hemophilia.

The large-scale screening programs must be combined with extensive educational programs in order to avoid misinformation and negative labeling of carriers of hereditary traits that might result. There might also be a tendency to extrapolate from reports of death in four Black recruits possibly associated with the sickle cell trait that have appeared in recent medical literature.

The information from screening must be transmitted to the individual or his parents, depending upon his age, but it is not enough to report that the screening test is positive or negative. The patient must be educated about the meaning of the carrier state from a medical and genetic point of view, and he should also learn about the range of severity of the disease as it occurs in the homozygous state. He must understand the condition well enough to make an intelligent decision based on the information he has been given. If this is to be the patient's decision--and I believe it should be--the physician must be careful not to directly influence, at least not knowingly so, that decision, unless he has a very good reason to do so.

I do not believe that this data should be placed in large, centralized computers, as has been suggested by some, because of the problems of maintaining the confidentiality of such data.

THE RIGHT NOT TO KNOW

Physicians have generally supported the right of the individual to have access to medical information when it was in his own best interests. This would be especially true when the patient's well-being, freedom, and happiness were being enhanced, but he just as vigorously protects the individual's right not to know if these same values would be enhanced.

If I do not happen to know that my wife and I are carriers of a particular autosomal recessive trait, we are free to go ahead and conceive our own natural children. We might be among the lucky ones and have our first two or three children be phenotypically normal. On the other hand, if we learned through a screening program that we are carriers, our freedom to act would be compromised if we were concerned citizens. In this particular instance we would have greater freedom through ignorance, as well as a

better state of mind to pursue our needs as parents. By the same
token those who know of their carrier state also have a right to
know who else are carriers so they might make an intelligent choice
of a mate. One might readily imagine the situation of an
individual who not only doesn't know but doesn't wish to know his
carrier status.

And what about the rights of society? Doesn't the couple have
some obligation not to knowingly produce offspring that will be a
drain on the resources of society? On the other hand, the right of
parents to have, if they are capable, their own natural child, even
an abnormal one, perhaps ought to take precedence over their obligation to society. Through no fault of their own, the freedom,
justice and well-being of carriers would be abridged, presumably to
further the general welfare of society.

The primarily financial cost to society of supporting a less
fit individual is, in my estimation, far outweighed by the ethical
and emotional cost to the couple denied a child. One might just as
well--as some have at times advocated and some states have tried to
legislate--deny the birthright to some couples because they are
extremely poor. Those who claim that society's right to maximize
its quality should take precedence over the rights of the individuals who make it up, must demonstrate clearly what they mean by
this and show exactly how this can be reliably accomplished.

ILLUSTRATIVE CASES

I should like to illustrate the kinds of conflicts that might
arise in the course of screening. These cases did not really occur
as the result of a screening program, but they show the kinds of
problems that one might be confronted with as a consequence of such
a program. All of them involve the detection of the sickle cell
trait.

Case 1

The first case is that of the husband of a childless
young Black couple who came to the heredity clinic at Howard
University because he learned that he and his wife both carried the
sickle cell trait and his wife, who badly wanted her own natural
children, was so disheartened by the news that she actually refused
to come to the clinic. They were under the impression that sickle
cell anemia was a horrible crippling disease, absolutely fatal,
about which nothing could be done. After a thorough discussion of
the range of severity of the disease, the origin and significance
of the sickle cell gene, and what the genetic possibilities were, I
reviewed with this man his perception of the situation. He seemed
much less discouraged and said that he would like to talk to his
wife about "taking a chance and trying for one natural child."
Regardless of the phenotype of this child, he thought that they

would adopt other children. It was clear when he left that this young man still had a great deal of the emotional conflict to work out in his own mind. One could multiply this particular situation many times over when many of the new screening programs get into full swing.

Case 2

A 27-year-old Black female brought her year-old infant to the hospital because of anemia and failure to thrive. During his workup the child was found to have sickle cell anemia. Sickling tests were done on the mother and the putative father, the woman's common-law husband. The mother's test was positive but the father's sickle cell prep was negative. The mother was told that the test was inconsistent with her common-law husband being the father of the child but the woman swore, "on her mother's grave," that he had to be the father. This is a very strong oath in the Black community—I don't know about other communities—and rather than dismiss this case as just another case of non-paternity, hemoglobin electrophoresis was performed. The common-law red cells contained only five percent of the hemoglobin as sickle cell hemoglobin which was probably insufficient to cause his red cells to sickle under reduced oxygen tension. In this instance the physician avoided producing family discord by heeding the mother's insistence and performing more careful studies. This case further illustrates the kind of serious errors that can occur when a screening test has false negative results. The physician must be extremely cautious in cases where non-paternity appears to be involved. Where there is a conflict between human relations, well-being, and total scientific truth, I have tended to sacrifice the truth, as in this next case.

Case 3

A Black couple was being interviewed to determine the psychological effects of sickle cell anemia on their four-year-old child. The mother volunteeered that only she had the sickle cell trait. This was verified by hemoglobin electrophoresis. It was clear from subsequent discussions that this couple did not under-stand the genetics of sickle cell anemia. It seemed that an en-tirely lucid explanation of the genetics would raise the question of non-paternity and perhaps lead to the disruption of what appeared, at least to me and the social worker in our clinic, to be a very compatible family relationship. It was explained to them that an egg from the mother containing a sickle cell gene was fertilized by a sperm in which a fresh mutation producing a sickle cell gene had occurred. It was not pointed out that mutations are extremely rare. They were not interested in further genetic coun-seling since they had already completed their family.

SUMMARY

The physician should consider the needs of the community in developing new programs of genetic screening, but the ethical considerations and the needs of the individual patient or couple must still come first. It is probably unjustified on ethical grounds to mount large-scale screening programs for disease or carrier detection in conditions where the patients and carriers cannot be offered specific medical therapeutic alternatives, including intrauterine diagnosis and abortion.

It is, on the one hand, unjust that everyone cannot yet know his or her mutant gene carrier status and also unfair that those whose mutant carrier status can be determined may be stigmatized. It is probably also unjustified at this time to make screening programs compulsory. Even large-scale educational programs can result in a kind of indirect coercion from peer group pressure that might be exerted.

The current state of genetic knowledge is such that we cannot and should not use any kind of coercive methods, either direct or indirect, to insist that carrier couples should not have children in those cases where intrauterine diagnosis is not yet available.

I would suggest that the counselor ought sometimes to counsel ignorance rather than revealing the total truth in the interest of the well-being and freedom of the patient. Knowledge is not always good. The whole truth is not always the best thing for everyone. Although our knowledge is limited, I believe we know more about the needs for stable human relations than we do about the beneficial or detrimental effects of particular kinds of mutant genes in the long run. The admonition to do no harm might well serve to continue as a rule of thumb in our naive and fumbling attempts to apply in a beneficial sense the rapid advances occurring in our knowledge of human genetics.

Finally, let us not forget that as important as our concerns about the correct appplication of genetic advances continues to be, these must be kept in their proper perspective, for there are pressing problems of high infant mortality in the Black population, as well as malnutrition, overcrowding and social and economic unrest that we now have the power to correct, if we but apply ourselves to the task. If we do not devote at least a significant portion of our energies to these problems, we shall be acting unethically and inhumanely.

THE JOHN F. KENNEDY INSTITUTE TAY-SACHS PROGRAM: PRACTICAL AND ETHICAL ISSUES IN AN ADULT GENETIC SCREENING PROGRAM

Michael M. Kaback and Robert S. Zeiger

INTRODUCTION

The challenge invoked by an informed-consent, adult-oriented, genetic screening program directed at the prevention of a fatal inherited disorder of childhood generates a number of critical questions, some practical and others of an ethical nature. The science or art of screening large populations of healthy individuals for the carrier state for a genetic disorder is without precedent or established guidelines. In such a novel medical-service program, practical expertise is nonexistent.

Tay-Sachs disease is a devastating autosomal recessive neurodegenerative disorder and the most common of the sphingolipidoses. Since the initial descriptions of the disease by Warren Tay and Bernard Sachs in the latter part of the 19th century, several thousand infants have been born destined to die with this disease. This severe gangliosidosis (considered such due to the abnormal storage of the sphingolipid, GM2 ganglioside, in the central nervous system and other tissues), first manifests itself at the age of three to six months in the form of mild motor weakness and hyperacusis (increased startle response to sounds) in an otherwise happy and playful infant. These early symptoms and the parent's initial concerns are usually dispelled at first by the family physician. However, as the degenerative process proceeds, the motor weakness becomes relentlessly more obvious and usually, by eight to twelve months of age, it is medically obvious that the child is failing. The infant, who may have crawled, sat unaided, or even pulled to a standing position, rapidly deteriorates both mentally and physically by about one year of age. The previously playful and happy infant now no longer smiles, no longer reacts playfully, no longer recognizes or sees his parents and, in fact, rapidly loses all contact with his environment. Poor muscle tone

131

soon leads to generalized paralysis; feeding difficulties secondary
to ineffective deglutination progresses to inanition. The child
with Tay-Sachs disease remains in this totally deteriorated mental
and physical state until death occurs, usually due to aspiration
pneumonia by the age of three to five years. Longevity of the
child with this condition usually is dependent entirely upon the
type of care attended the child, that is, the better the child is
cared for, the longer the child survives.

Rare genetic diseases like Tay-Sachs disease (unfortunately,
there are too many) are mass tragedies, far transcending the
affected child. The tragedy extends to the parents, the siblings,
the relatives, and friends of the family. As well as it can be
evaluated, the infant with Tay-Sachs disease does not suffer pain.
In fact, one might speculate that the suffering is primarily that
of the parents and family rather than of the child itself. The
ability of the parents to cope with this human tragedy is complicated by the dearth of hospital facilities willing to care for
these children's acute needs for prolonged periods. Moreover, the
hospital costs for care of these children may reach $20,000-$40,000
per year, the financial burden being assumed by the parents, family
funds, insurance, or by some public agency. In short, the already
massive personal tragedy for the family must in our present social
system be joined by this social and financial tragedy as well.

In a retrospective epidemiological study of Tay-Sachs disease
in 88 families (Slome, 1933), it was found that 82 percent of the
cases of the disease represented initial occurrences within the
kindred. It should be emphasized, therefore, that a preventive
program, initiated after the occurrence of the proband case, would
prevent only eighteen percent of the cases of Tay-Sachs disease.
Obviously, it would be more optimal if a preventive mechanism were
applicable prior to the proband case. Such a program might dramatically reduce the incidence of the disease or even prevent it
completely.

THE PROGRAM

In the Baltimore-Washington area, we have recently initiated a
pilot screening program directed at the prevention of Tay-Sachs
disease. The emphasis of our program is directed at Tay-Sachs
disease, since this disorder is currently the only condition which
meets three necessary prerequisites for prospective prevention:

1. The Disease Occurs Predominantly in a Defined and
   Accessible Population.

The relative incidence of affected children with Tay-Sachs
disease is 100 times greater in Ashkenazi Jews than in any other
populations. These are Jewish individuals whose ancestry is from

Central and Eastern Europe, and more than 90 percent of American Jews are of such heritage. The estimated carrier rate in this group is 1 in 30 individuals (Aronson, 1964). This heterozygote frequency is 10 times higher than that estimated for non-Jews or for Sephardic or Oriental Jews. Based on the estimated heterozygote frequency, the chances of an Ashkenazi Jewish couple being at risk for Tay-Sachs disease (both parents are carriers) would be approximately 1 in 900 couples (1/30 x 1/30). Since the disease is inherited as an autosomal recessive condition, the chances of this carrier-carrier couple bearing a child with Tay-Sachs disease would be 25 percent with each pregnancy. Therefore, the overall risk for any Ashkenazi Jewish couple having a child with this tragic disease is 1 in 3600 children (1/30 x 1/30 x 1/4). The incidence of the disease in all other populations would be 100 times less or about 1 in 360,000 births. It has been calculated that about 50 children with Tay-Sachs disease will be born in the United States each year. Of these, 40 to 45 will be Jewish children with Central and Eastern European ancestors.

2. A Simple, Accurate, and Inexpensive Test is Available for the Detection of the Heterozygous State.

In 1969, Okada and O'Brien demonstrated that the activity of hexosaminidase A (Hex A) was absent in children with Tay-Sachs disease. Moreover, they subsequently showed that a statistically significant reduction in Hex A occurs in the tissues (serum, white blood cells, and fibroblasts) of parents (obligate heterozygotes) of Tay-Sachs children (O'Brien et al., 1970). The method described by O'Brien and his co-workers is readily adaptable to high volume screening. We have successfully developed an automated method for this purpose in our facility (Kaback and Lash, 1971). With the automated serum assay, a practical and inexpensive test is, therefore, available for mass heterozygote screening.

3. The Disease Can be Accurately and Safely Detected in the Affected Fetus Early in Pregnancy.

By assaying cultured amniotic fluid cells and/or supernatant amniotic fluid for hexosaminidase A activity in samples of amniotic fluid obtained by transabdominal amniocentesis in the early second trimester of pregnancy, a highly accurate method is available for the detection of this disease in the fetus. Several groups have already demonstrated that Tay-Sachs disease can be diagnosed in the fetus with a high level of accuracy in at-risk pregnancies (Schneck et al., 1970; O'Brien et al., 1971). Normal or heterozygous fetuses have been shown to possess hexosaminidase A levels in readily measurable quantities, while enzyme activity is absent in amniotic fluid and cells from fetuses with Tay-Sachs disease.

The three prerequisites provide the basis for the screening program. Simply stated, by applying the carrier detection test to child-bearing age individuals in the at-risk population, one should be able to define those rare couples in which both husband and wife are carriers of the Tay-Sachs gene. These are the only couples at risk for Tay-Sachs disease in their children. By then monitoring each pregnancy in these couples only, one should be able to selectively prevent Tay-Sachs disease in their offspring, and also enable these couples to have only unaffected children.

THE ISSUES

The advent and development of intrauterine diagnosis critically provides the at-risk couple with a positive alternative or a mechanism by which the selective birth of only unaffected children can be achieved. Statistically, three out of four of the monitored at-risk pregnancies will result in an unaffected child; for the unfortunate pregnancy that carries a Tay-Sachs fetus, the parents can, if they so choose, terminate that pregnancy.

The moral-ethical questions raised by termination of pregnancy for invariably fatal disorders in the fetus are many. It is not the purpose of this discussion to deal extensively with this fiery issue. We wish to state, however, that the choice of terminating such a doomed pregnancy should, it would seem, be primarily within the auspices of the moral, religious, and ethical consciences of the individuals who would most acutely suffer the tragedy of the disease, that is, the parents. In a very real sense, termination of pregnancy in this way limits the tragedy of Tay-Sachs disease to one, the fetus.

An obvious goal of this program is the definition of couples at risk for Tay-Sachs in their offspring prior to the birth of an affected child. It must be underscored that the abortion of fetuses affected with Tay-Sachs disease is not the emphasis of the screening program. Rather, it is strongly suggested that abortion serves only as a means to the goal of enabling families to have healthy children. In this context, it is important to note that previous epidemiologic studies (Myrianthopoulos, 1966) indicate that in the past, families who have had Tay-Sachs children stop having subsequent offspring, once counseled as to the recurrence risks in further pregnancies. It is, therefore, most critical to emphasize that as the result of a prospective prevention program, more children will be born than would be born without it and the children will be uniformly unaffected with this condition.

Selective abortion is not the ultimate answer to Tay-Sachs disease. Clearly, control of this disorder through abortion should not continue in lieu of continued efforts to develop effective therapy or even cure for this disease. This would clearly be a more satisfactory answer. However, until such a therapy or cure is available for this devastating disease, selective abortion of the affected fetus seems a reasonable and humane alternative.

A genetic screening program for the purpose of genetic counseling of adult individuals should require the availability of a positive alternative if the results of such testing are positive. If the mechanism is available by which individuals found to be at risk for a given condition can have unaffected children, screening of large populations for heterozygosity seems warranted. On the other hand, where this positive alternative is not available, serious questions can be raised. The possible fear, anxiety, and apprehension generated by learning of one's less-than-perfect genetic endowment, coupled with the foreseeable tragedy of subsequent affected offspring, is assuredly very real if no such positive alternative for childbearing exists. On the other hand, where the mechanism for successful childbearing is available, the impact of positive information as to the carrier state for a lethal recessive gene should be less likely to generate these reactions. In fact, the families identified to date as carrier-carrier couples at risk for Tay-Sachs offspring have received this information with apparent gratitude and appreciation and with no overt signs of fear or apprehension at first analysis.

The mass screening program for the detection of heterozygotes for Tay-Sachs disease fulfills the previously defined criteria. The technology is available for the prevention of this disease. Moreover, the mechanism by which at-risk couples can bear their own children, without ever suffering the anguish and tragedy of Tay-Sachs disease, expresses the credo upon which this program was promulgated.

DEVELOPMENTAL ASPECTS

The planning and development of the John F. Kennedy Institute Tay-Sachs Disease Program was, for practical purposes, divided into six phases as illustrated in Figure 1. These divisions were quite empirical as precedents and guidelines were unavailable. The emphasis in the planning stages was to anticipate and attempt to alleviate or reckon with those "theoretical" problems which we envisioned might occur.

The goals of any screening program must be carefully formulated prior to the inception of the program. It is the goals which define the methods by which they may be achieved. It is important to distinguish the difference beween making a service available and "taking it to the community." In addition to the immediate goals of detecting at-risk couples and reducing the incidence of Tay-Sachs disease, it was hoped that the screening program also might function as a prototype for Tay-Sachs screening in other areas and as a means of evaluating the possible social and psychological impact associated with genetic screening of this kind. In addition, and most importantly, it was felt from the out-set that the principles of delivery of a genetic screening program, using Tay-Sachs disease as the prototype, might serve an important precedent for screening programs directed at the prevention of other genetic diseases such as sickle cell anemia, cystic fibrosis, and so forth.

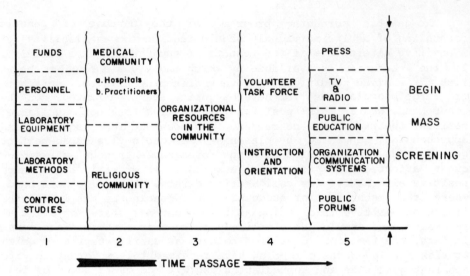

FIG. 1.   Strategy and kinetics of the Baltimore-Washington Tay-Sachs
Screening Program. Phases one through five for this program
required approximately 16 months (further discussion in text).

PHASE ONE: METHODS, FUNDS, AND PERSONNEL

It is obvious but nevertheless critical to first ascertain the
accuracy of the methodology employed in mass screening. The technical procedures adapted for performing enzymatic assays must be
standardized anew in each laboratory to assure accuracy, repro-
ducibility, and reliability of results. The methods selected for
screening must be evaluated in control studies and shown to effectively detect the heterozygous state. A detailed description of
the evaluation of the Hex A assay now used routinely in our
screening program has been presented elsewhere (Kaback and Zeiger,
1971). The test is highly accurate, reproducible, and now
automated. As many as 300 individuals can be screened daily in our
facility.

In order to avoid false-negatives, which any screening program
must consider, an arbitrary "inconclusive range" was established
for a certain range of values resulting from serum screening tests.
About four percent of all individuals tested fall within this
"inconclusive range" after the initial analysis. Ninety-six
percent of those individuals screened can be identified as carriers
or non-carriers on primary serum screening tests. All serum
samples are evaluated blindly and the statistical data are analyzed
completely prior to individual identification. Individuals found
to fall within the arbitrarily-defined inconclusive range (primar-

ily to avoid false-negatives) are contacted and then re-evaluated by the more accurate but laborious white blood cell hexosaminidase A determination. (The leukocyte method is technically prohibitive for primary mass screening purposes at this time). With follow-up leukocyte analyses for the inconclusive group, a clear indication as to the carrier or non-carrier status of each individual is obtained. Of the 8,000 individuals who have now been screened, three remain inconclusive after repeated serum and leukocyte analyses. It is predicted that these individuals may represent genetic heterogenity in the population since similar inconclusive levels in leukocytes and serum have been found in other family members of these individuals.

In a few individuals, particularly some women on birth control medication, serum hexosaminidase A assay may indicate a carrier genotype when leukocyte and family studies define the person to be a non-carrier. The problem of dealing with such false positive carrier tests may be considerable, particularly in terms of possible family implications. Where both "natural" parents are shown to be non-carriers (by both serum and white blood cell testing), an "apparent" carrier-offspring could be explained by a false positive test, spontaneous mutation, incorrect paternal parent, or possible unknown infant exchange in the newborn nursery. Needless to say, this situation must be dealt with most carefully without necessarily going into all of the above possibilities with the family. On two occasions, a proven carrier (by serum and white blood cell testing) was found to have two non-carrier parents.

Since the possibility of a false-positive carrier test exists (with serum testing only), all couples designated carrier/carrier, carrier/inconclusive, or inconclusive/inconclusive by serum assay are re-evaluated by the more accurate white blood cell analysis to assure the diagnosis. In addition, parental testing, if possible, is strongly recommended to further corroborate the carrier status of both members of an at-risk couple. With this combination of rapid serum evaluation backed up by the white blood cell assay and parental studies, the program is able to make a genetic designation in essentially all individuals tested.

Perhaps the single most critical aspect of any screening program is the commitment and responsibilities of the professional personnel. Specifically, a physician or team of physicians must be available to provide appropriate genetic counseling. Since it is the counseling responsibilities which create the greatest weight in this program, the commitment of the counselors must be substantial. Information, in large measure of a potentially threatening nature, must be related to families in a highly individualized fashion. In all couples where any question may remain after the initial testing is completed as to risks for affected offspring, this counseling is done by direct contact rather than by mailed information. Obviously, individualization of such discussions must be the rule, since no two individuals will comprehend and respond to this kind of factual and scientific data in the same manner.

Several situations have recurred with a high potential for provoking anxiety and concern, and which require extensive counseling efforts. These include discussions with women who voluntarily come to be screened, but who are too far along in pregnancy (greater than five months), making the screening test ill-advised for her or her husband; the notification of couples in which both members are found to be heterozygotes or one inconclusive and one heterozygous as to follow-up testing, amniocentesis, etc.; the couple in which the husband is found to be a carrier while his wife is in early pregnancy and has not yet been tested. It would appear that intensive counseling in these situations minimizes anxiety to a large degree. In fact, the anticipated anxiety may be much greater than that observed. It would appear that if individuals have been properly educated, this information is received without undue fear or anxiety.

The generation of funds to support the screening program was not really an issue of major ethical concern. Since the screening program was envisioned as a pilot effort and because of the inherent difficulties in gaining rapid governmental support, the primary assistance for the initiation of this program came from the community involved. More recently, the Maryland State Department of Health and Mental Hygiene has given some additional support to our program.

PHASE TWO: EDUCATION AND PARTICIPATION OF
             MEDICAL AND RELIGIOUS COMMUNITIES

The second stage of planning was directed at gaining the support and assistance of the medical and religious communities. Medical practitioners, in large measure, are unfamiliar or inexperienced with rare genetic disorders like Tay-Sachs disease. Moreover, recent medical advances or breakthroughs might not come to their attention. Additionally, their specific familiarity with medical genetics is often quite meager, since less than 25 percent of American medical schools (as of 10 years ago) offered any formal curriculum in this subject.

The practicing medical community, therefore, was first educated about the disease and oriented to the screening program. If they were to function as an instrumental force in public education, this was an essential prerequisite. Such a step is mandatory since, once informed of the program, the individuals in the community might be expected to contact their family physician for advice. The uninformed or busy physician might respond by claiming, "This is a rare disease. Don't worry about it. It's just another ivory-tower scientist with a high-browed idea about community medicine." On the other hand, the previously informed physician will react to his patient's inquiries in an enlightened and compassionate manner saying, "This is a rare disease and probably nothing to worry about. The chances are very remote (1 in

900) that this is going to be of any significance to you.   But it is important that you be tested since it conceivably could be beneficial."

The religious community must also play a vital role in such a program, since genetic screening and its implications, in large measure, deal with moral-ethical related issues.   Moreover, the religious leaders are considered the "experts" in these areas within the community.   The religious leaders were, therefore, addressed individually and in groups months before the program was publicly announced.   It was obvious that the support and enthusiasm of religious leaders was essential for the program to attain any social impact in our area.   The overwhelming majority of the rabbinate in the Baltimore-Washington area reacted very positively and have given the program both their moral and active support. Through personal contacts and sermons, the rabbis have advanced the program and helped in the education of the public.   Since the screening for at-risk couples cannot be limited with respect to time, there must, in addition, be a mechanism for the continuation of this service.   It was anticipated that after the initial thrust of screening had reached the existing married couples of child-bearing age in the community, it would be necessary only to screen newly married couples to maintain an on-going check on this disease.   Since nearly all Jewish couples are married by a rabbi, it seemed extremely practical for the rabbinate to function as the needed link for counseling each newly married Jewish couple as to the advisability of being screened for the Tay-Sachs gene.   Other possible mechanisms for the continuation of the screening, which we feel are less suitable, will be discussed subsequently.

PHASES THREE AND FOUR: MANPOWER--THE ORGANIZATIONAL RESOURCES

The organizational resources in the community provide the real manpower for the program.   It is unrealistic to believe that scientists alone can ever deliver this type of genetic service without the full assistance of the community.   To optimize the program's impact, it is essential that the community participate in the development, the organization, and the delivery of the service.   A diagramatized formulation of the organizational workings and participation in our program is depicted in Figure 2.   This has been an integral feature of the Tay-Sachs Program and is probably responsible for much of its initial success.   Through workshops and addresses to multiple community organizations and organizational representatives about the Tay-Sachs Program and its needs in the months prior to its public inception, it was possible to generate from each of some 100 organizations in the Baltimore-Washington community a 10 to 20 member Tay-Sachs task force group from each organization.   Accordingly, there are now approximately 1,000 lay individuals (primarily housewives) who have been specifically educated in the Tay-Sachs Program.   This task force group is

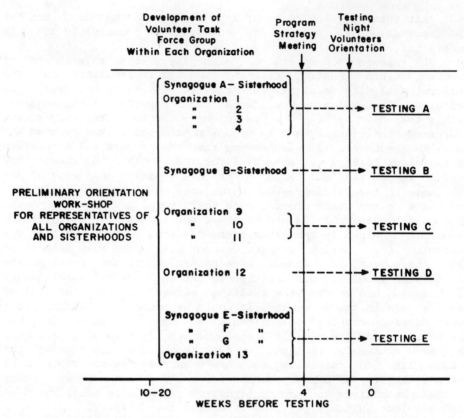

FIG. 2.   Schematic reproduction of mechanisms of participation of
         multiple community organizations in the Tay-Sachs Program (further
         discussion in text).

extremely knowledgeable about Tay-Sachs disease and the screening
program, not in terms of molecular biology, but in practical terms.
They have become familiar with the facts as to the characteristics
of the disease, carrier rates, predilection, the meaning of an
at-risk couple, as well as the "philosophy" of the program. These
small, well-informed, task-force groups become the program's
emissaries to their own organizations and to their community.
    The Tay-Sachs Program, in essence, functions through a
multi-organizational process to deliver this genetic service to
individual groups and community members.   Several organizations
participate closely for a two- to three-month period until their
respective groups have been tested (Figure 2).   In this way,
organizational interest is garnered personally by the organization's own members. Moreover, the Tay-Sachs Program does not usurp
the other interests of each organization and requires their participation for only a limited time.   Through sisterhoods and non-
synagogue affiliated organizations, a large percentage of the

at-risk population can be reached. In addition, through other social contacts, acquaintances, and through public educational means (press, TV, etc.), individuals not affiliated with such organizations can also become informed and tested.

PHASE FIVE: PUBLIC EDUCATION

Public education began only after the first four phases were completed and solidified. A very real ethical question, practical and not theoretical in nature, pertains to the manner in which a large community should be educated about simple genetics, about a specific rare genetic disease that may affect them, and about how to educate the community sufficiently in order to motivate them to voluntarily submit to a blood test for this purpose. How does one most effectively carry out such an educational program? How does one educate the public so that sufficient concern is generated in the community (to achieve relatively high compliance) without creating significant fear?

The line between an educational process which generates concern versus that which frightens individuals may be quite tenuous. Each individual's response to this type of information will necessarily be different. Some will understand its intent while others may become unduly anxious. Again, this dilemma necessitates considerable versatility and individuality-of-approach in the physician's interaction with community members. Every opportunity must be sought, after the educational material is employed and before testing is performed, to permit the individual a means for clarification, should issues remain unclear. This is, therefore, one of the areas in which the physician-counselor plays the most vital role. As a physician, he must be alert to inappropriate anxiety and fear in any individual. Our thoughts are, therefore, very much in accord with the comments of Doctors Murray and Motulsky (this volume) as to the need for a physician's participation in such a service.

A multi-faceted saturation approach to genetic education has been adopted by the Program (Figure 3). Physicians have been provided with informational brochures to be distributed to their patients; rabbis have voluntarily corresponded with their congregation both by letter and by sermon; the organization task forces have manned telephone squads, held community forums, and distributed flyers and letters, and the mass media has contributed its expertise and energy for the purpose of educating the public as to the genetic concepts related to Tay-Sachs disease and how it can be prevented. Moreover, ample resources have been made available for channeling and answering questions generated by this educational process.

As our understanding of genetic disorders advances in the immediate future and its clinical application becomes a reality, a well-informed medical and lay community will be essential for

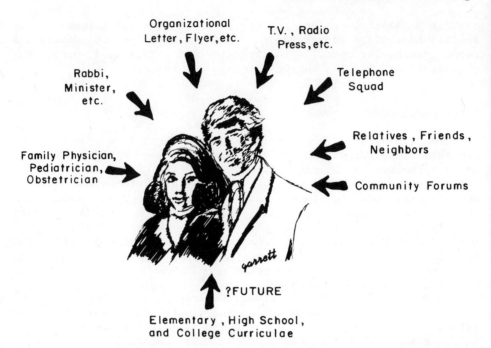

FIG. 3. Multiple mechanisms for genetic education of the public utilized
in the Baltimore-Washington Tay-Sachs Program.

effective implementation of future breakthroughs. This might best
be achieved if simple concepts of human biology and genetics become
part of our elementary and high school curricula. If voluntary
participation is desired in this and in future genetic screening
programs, previous knowledge related to such matters would greatly
minimize the problems.

PHASE SIX: MASS TESTING

Community testing began approximately one and one-half years
after the program was formulated. Since the first testing on May
2, 1971, in which 1800 persons came for testing, the program has
tested approximately 8,000 individuals; the manner in which
community facilities (synagogues, community centers, etc.) have
been employed in each of these testings is shown in Figure 4. The
efficiency of this system is quite excellent and can be measured
perhaps by the mere 10 to 20 minutes required for a couple to be
screened at a testing attended by 500 to 1,000 individuals. The
manpower for these testings again is derived from the volunteer
groups in addition to the 10 to 20 volunteer physicians who perform
the venipunctures. Sixty to 100 lay volunteer workers are the
critical individuals who provide the high level of efficiency in
the delivery of this service.

An anticipated problem that materialized with the initiation of testing was its attraction for pregnant families. Approximately one-third of the 1800 persons attending the first testing were in this category. In pregnant women, the serum Hex A is inaccurate (a high frequency of false-positives). However, the white blood cell assay remains valid. To circumvent these difficulties, only husbands of women less than four months pregnant were tested at the mass screening sessions. Those pregnant women whose husbands were found to be carriers or inconclusives (as determined within the first few days after the testings) were contacted by phone and the woman then evaluated by white blood cell assay. In this manner, if both mates were found to be carriers, there would still be sufficient time to perform amniocentesis, cultivate the amniotic fluid cells, and ascertain the status of the fetus in that pregnancy. Couples in which the woman was more than four months pregnant were not screened because there was not sufficient time to perform all the necessary procedures. Rather than raise the spectrum of a possible genetic defect in their offspring, such couples were counseled as to the remoteness of these possibilities and that it was preferable not to test either the husband or wife until the pregnancy was completed. Each couple was personally counseled at the testing site. From the responses of these couples, it appeared that the counseling was effective in allaying obvious anxiety.

A very real ethical-moral issue generated by screening programs pertains to the methods of attracting the public. Some have

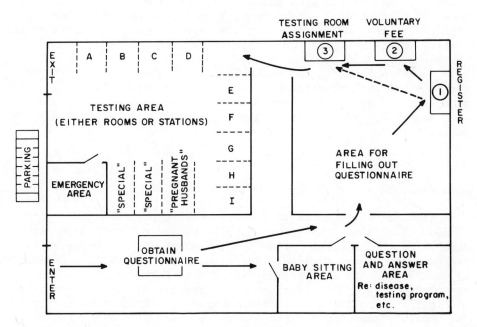

FIG.4.   Typical lay-out of a community facility for the genetic screening
         program (further discussion in text).

espoused the virtues of specific screening legislation, thereby making testing compulsory for certain or all individuals. The dangers (political, social, ethical, and psychological) inherent in legislated genetics, in our opinion, far outweigh its benefits in compliance. Adult-oriented screening programs can function effectively (as the initial experience with our program suggests) on a voluntary basis after appropriate education, commitment, and effort are generated. The motto, "Educate, not legislate," comes to mind in this context.

As alluded to earlier, perhaps the single most difficult and delicate task in a genetic screening program is the manner of delivering the results. This must be approached with great care, understanding, and personal attention so that anxiety is minimized and, at the same time, some degree of optimism is fostered. Much needs to be learned about the psychological and social impact of genetic screening. Evaluation of this impact is thereby a very real responsibility of all screening programs. It is very much an objective of the Tay-Sachs screening program that these concepts be critically evaluated. We are now beginning to explore these areas. It is hoped that certain of the principles which evolve from the Tay-Sachs program will be applicable to screening programs for other genetic diseases as well.

To date, the John F. Kennedy Institute Tay-Sachs Program has detected ten couples at risk for bearing children with Tay-Sachs disease. None have a previous history of the disease in their immediate families. Such couples may now have only unaffected children if they so desire without ever having to suffer the anguish of learning that a seemingly healthy infant is doomed with Tay-Sachs disease.

Recent scientific and technological achievements portend much for the future prospects of this "new medicine." Genetics, medicine, and the social sciences must now begin to explore together the means by which these achievements can best be applied to the service of man.

ACKNOWLEDGMENTS

Studies described in this paper were supported by the John F. Kennedy Institute Tay-Sachs Fund, The Aaron and Lillian Strauss Foundation, and a grant from the Maryland State Department of Health and Mental Hygiene. The authors acknowledge the dedicated support of the National Capital Tay-Sachs Foundation as well as many additional organizations and individuals in the Baltimore-Washington communities. To Donna German as Program Coordinator, Marguerite Sonneborn, Linda Reynolds, and Doctor L. Pallan, we express our thanks for their expert technical assistance.

REFERENCES

Aronson, S. M. (1964). In Tay-Sachs Disease. B. W. Volk (ed). New York, Grune and Stratton.

Kaback, M. M. and E. Lash (1971) (in preparation).

Kaback, M. M. and R. S. Zeiger (1971). In Sphingolipids, Sphingolipidoses, and Allied Disorders. B. W. Volk and S. M. Aronson (eds.). New York, Plenum Publishing Co. (in press).

Myrianthopoulos, N. C., and S. M. Aronson. (1966). Amer. J. Hum. Gen. 18: 313.

O'Brien, J. S., S. Okada, A. Chen, and D. L. Fillerup. (1970). New Eng. J. Med. 283: 15.

O'Brien, J. S., S. Okada, D. L. Fillerup, M. L. Veath, B. Adornato, P. H. Brenner, J. G. Leroy (1971). Science 172: 61.

Okada, S., and J. S. O'Brien, (1969). Science 165: 698.

Schneck, L., J. Friedland, C. Valenti, M. Adachi, D. Amsterdam, and B. W. Volk. (1970). Lancet I: 582.

Slome, D. (1933). J. Genetics 27: 363.

SCREENING: AN ETHICIST'S VIEW

Paul Ramsey

INTRODUCTION

Possibly there is an irrepressible conflict between the first and the second Articles of the Nuremberg Medical Code. The first and best known Article expresses the requirement of an informed consent--to which we may add a well-founded implied consent(Alexander, 1966a, 1966b; Ramsey, 1970). The second Article states the requirement that an experiment on human subjects "should be such as to yield fruitful results for the good of society, unprocurable by any other methods or means of study, and not random and unnecessary in nature."

There is a possible collision between these two requirements. One of the Articles places an independent limit upon the use of the other. A major task in the ethical practice of medicine is to harmonize these requirements and to stay within the boundaries of permissable practice fixed by both together.

Beecher (1959, 1970) repeatedly emphasized what is needed for human experimentation to be ethically permissible: if a screening program is moral, it is moral in its inception; it does not become moral because it happens to produce good results. Screening should be judged not by the standard of the second Article alone, but by the first Article as well (with appropriate addition of well-founded implied consent).

Beecher does not deny that the researcher has a moral responsibility to see that his research is likely to be for the good of society. He simply believes that, regardless of the total net good that may come from it, an experiment or other medical procedure is immoral in its inception unless, chiefly, it is based on some reasonable facsimile of a valid consent on the part of every individual admitted to it. If not, medical goods would be sought regardless of the number who are made menial to the greatest net good. The "bonum communum" would not include and flow back upon all concerned. Still, the medical benefits might be greatly increased for fewer than all concerned, for less than the "greatest number". This would happen if ever we are morally permitted to employ "statistical morality" and cost/effectiveness studies as the chief standards of appraisal, or if ever we are morally permitted to overlook a single individual in determining whose the benefits shall be.

We need to examine certain typical varieties of screening situations and procedures with a view to sorting out the relevant moral features of each. I choose to discuss four cases: (1) screening in the case of contagious diseases, (2) certain public health measures, such as fluoridation or mass vaccination, (3) screening connected with genetic counseling, and (4) screening the unborn and the newly born. In addition to good results, the test will be whether we can identify patients through screening with their validly implied consents and in the medical interest of each individual. The minimum test will be that the screening do no harm. A screen cannot be morally justified by a social-costs analysis alone or by establishing a statistical connection among the individuals in a group proposed for screening: the latter casts the net too widely and can only lead to doctoring of patients without their agreement (actual or implied); consent for the screen itself cannot be adequately construed merely from a statistical incidence of the disease. A low incidence of damage from the procedure cannot measure up to the minimum standard that medical practice do no harm in the case of individuals incompetent to give expressed consent to screening for non-contagious diseases.

Unless these principles of medical ethics are abrogated, my conclusions are, to state them in advance of analysis or argument, that screening for contagious diseases (and vaccination against them) and screening as an extension of genetic counseling, having in view informed decisions about parenthood, are clearly justified, if not obligatory; that proxy consent to screen for non-contagious illnesses in individuals, born or unborn, who are unable to consent is warranted if the objective is treatment and if no harm is done by the procedure to another life who needs neither help nor the screen; that intrauterine screening by amniocentesis is ethically most problematic if, indeed, it is not to be morally censured; and, finally, that publicly authorized health-connected measures are a "borderline" case in the practice of medicine, if such measures do a comparatively small amount of harm along with the greater good they do.

SCREENING FOR CONTAGIOUS DISEASES

Seeking patients among a population who are all at some significant risk of contagious disease is to be likened to Good Samaritan medicine in cases of highway accidents. It is also to be likened to adult proxy-consent medically in behalf of a child or otherwise incompetent patient, submitting him at some risk to investigational therapy. Either an actual illness or a risk of infection justify implying the consent of patients who cannot expressly give consent. Unconscious patients, incompetent patients and unknown patients in widespread contagious diseases may all be assumed to consent to medical treatment. An injured man who is unconscious, we rightly assume, "consents" to be treated. So also, we rightly assume, a child suffering from some malady would want it investigated so that it might be treated. Nor is it a false presumption that we may properly construe the consent of asymptomatic persons in the case of contagious diseases. Each member of the population suffers the incidence of danger that all suffer. Everyone's consent to be relieved of that risk to himself may be implied, and mass screening may be used if feasible.

The foregoing justification of mass screening argues from the implied consent of the unknown patient. It is not solely or primarily a protection-of-society-from-contagious-diseases argument. The latter, taken alone, would be the utilitarian view, and such justification cannot be claimed for screening and public health measures where some concerned may be harmed if the survival of a given human society is not at stake but only the greater elective good of the community. A "protection of society" argument, justifying the acceptance of doing possible harm to some when survival from a plague is the overriding need, would also fulfill the conditions for constructively assuming consent of every member of a population who are subject to an actual risk of infection. The latter seems crucial in any justification of screening as a practice of medicine.

HEALTH-RELATED PUBLIC POLICIES: BORDERLINE CASES

It is more difficult to justify the fluoridation of drinking water for the prevention of tooth decay without apparent patient consent and plainly against the expressed dissent of some. People do not ordinarily catch tooth decay from one another, nor are they in desperate straits, and fluoridation is not the only recourse. Still, fluoridation can truly be said to be in behalf of everyone on whom it is imposed. The common good, it can be argued, flows back without exception upon everyone in the population.

Nevertheless, if the "borderline" case of fluoridation is to be justified under the foregoing moral reasoning, one minimal condition must be verified: there should be no discernible additional risk brought by the procedure upon any of the patients. If there are no risks, then people's "consents" to be treated can validly be construed where there is weighty public interest. The same minimum moral justification--all concerned are helped, none is harmed medically--is sufficient to warrant the imposition of sewer systems by political authority as a public health measure.

At this point, our moral argument leads us into some complex socio-medical problems. I have called fluoridation a "borderline case" of possibly justifiable medical practice. Perhaps instead we should say that fluoridation is not an action falling within the practice of medicine; it is rather a public policy that is health-connected, such as school lunch programs, chlorination, spraying land against insects, noise abatement, pollution control, etc. If we think of such measures as health-connected public policies and not as medical practices, then those who perform them are public functionaries and not physicians, and the ethics of a physician should be distinguished from those of an agent of public authority. Unless the minimum condition of no additional risk is met in the "borderline" cases of health-connected actions of public authority, it is hard to see how there remains any relic of the patient-physician relationship, in which persons with health needs seek care and make decisions balancing the risks to themselves. Instead, certain experts would have calculated for them the statistical incidence of, say, periodontal trouble in the population and, without actual or implied patient consent, weighed this against the risks of fluoridation. In medicine, this would be an opening toward what in the political order is correctly called totalitarianism, i.e., doing the "greatest good altogether" without the actual or soundly implied individual consent of "all concerned."

The foregoing cases have sorted out the important questions to be asked about screening those who are incapable of giving consent. If they are not even remotely the possible beneficiaries of the screening in question, then to presume their consent is a false presumption. If they may be harmed, then to presume their consent is a violent presumption, which would advance physical health at the expense of the moral "health" of our society and of medical practice. It would be to advance the total aggregate physical health of our society by using (at possible cost) those who were linked by only a mathematical incidence to the many (who are being helped). The fundamental question at issue is whether screening other than for contagious diseases begins with all the "patients" of this procedure and not only with the undiscovered patients. In the borderline case, the question is whether screening on the way to the greater medical good altogether begins with the "patients" of the procedure in the (least) sense that no one concerned will be harmed without his will.

GENETIC COUNSELING WITH PRE-PARENTHOOD SCREENING

Screening with a view to the prevention of conception seems clearly justified, if not indeed positively mandated. In this case, patients are given knowledge they need to know for respon-sible parenthood," i.e., to embrace responsibility for not trans-mitting knowable defects to their children. If the available information is good enough and the need serious, I can see no overriding objection to mass screening that may aid people to make responsible marriages and better decisions about having or not having children. Such screening connected with genetic counseling need not, for any moral reason I can see, be limited to special populations.

While I approve in principle of screening with the prevention of conception in view, it nevertheless should be said that since there are other values in life besides the biological perfection of the individual, some severe qualification may have to be introduced. In the face of mounting possibilities for mass screening, we need to keep in mind that coercion is still an evil. Also, in the face of mounting genetic information, there may indeed be a "right not to know," if all of life's spontaneities are not to be toned down to the impersonal level of the laboratory or all of us learn to smell disease everywhere. For genetics in the future, as for multiphasic health testing, at some point we may have to judge the human costs and benefits of medicine as a whole in comparison with other human needs. Concerning, in particular, future applications of genetic knowledge, we may need to appraise the human costs to follow from a widely held elevation in our expectations of human "normality," with its concomitant lessening of our care for "abnormals" or acceptance of them.

SCREENING THE UNBORN OR THE NEWLY BORN

Ponder Scriver's (1972) ironic remark: "Many of us wonder whether the individual has any real place in the political and constitutional fabric of modern society. Yet advances in human genetics have achieved at least one goal, and that is to generate concern for our 'mutants.'" We need to know that, by the use of novel procedures of screening, each individual is accorded a real place in the fabric of medical care. Does everyone count equally as one? Or is the aim to increase the total "quality of life," the net greatest health regardless of numbers, or for fewer than "all concerned"? If the latter is the case, then screening is of a piece with the vanishing of the individual into the mass at other places in the fabric of modern society.

This is an especially poignant problem in regard to screening the unborn or the newly born, because these patients do not suffer from a contagious disease, often their treatment is not in view and a validly implied consent is therefore absent, and sometimes normals may be harmed by the screen or by its follow-up. If harmed by the screen or by treatment mistakenly begun, this may be correctable in the case of the newly born. Such is not now possible in the case of intrauterine screening of the unborn; and treatment is often not the aim.

Then, it seems, physicians can resort to statistical morality, cost-effectiveness analyses, and to an ethics of the "greatest net benefit." This ethics is open to decisive objection, for two reasons: (1) the benefits may not be comparable, and because of the incomparability of relative goods, "the greatest good altogether" is an empty term. (2) even if the benefits were comparable on a single scale, the benefitees are irreducibly different, noninterchangeable human lives. Because the patients subjected to screening cannot morally form a real aggregate, again the "greatest net benefit" is an empty term.

I shall try to show the force of these objections by commenting upon some moral quandaries that arise in screening the unborn and the newly born: first, the problem of false-positives in screening new-borns and mistaken identification in amniocentesis, followed by abortion, second, the difficulty of "quantifying the qualities," or comparing the impairments, and the tendency of physicians to obscure this difficulty by using "incidence of risk" figures when the depth of what is at risk is of equal or far greater importance. The first point will show that an ethics of the "greatest good altogether," standing alone, cannot avoid interchanging non-interchangeable lives. The second point will show that an ethics of the "greatest good altogether" can suffice if and only if it can be demonstrated that benefits (or impairments) are comparable and can be weighed in the same scale. Thus I shall speak first of the wrongfulness of aggregating "benefitees" together and treating some unjustly; then of our failure to know how to quantify and compare impairments (the ones to be treated and the ones that may be induced). "Incidence of risks" statements hide both problems from view.

1. Physicians engaged in screening sometimes seem more troubled by false-negatives than by false-positives in the outcome of their tests. Janeway (1971) feels that "the screening test must be over-sensitive, so that it identifies all cases. There should be a number of false-positive, but no false-negative tests." On its face, that seems to be a prescription expressive only of concern for the greatest aggregate of cases found of the disease, regardless of those who were in no sense benefitted but rather were used, inconvenienced and possibly hurt by the procedure itself. The true-positive and false-negative count for more than one, the false-positive counts for less, in this screening-design and the values it enshrines.

There is point in saying, as does Rosenberg (1972), that "some false positive tests are permissible because a presumptive diagnosis should always be confirmed by appropriate, definite laboratory examination"--where this is a possible part of the procedure and is not harmful. But in PKU screening, the fate of some false-positives (to which Rosenberg refers when he points out that "a child with a transient neonatal elevation of plasma phenylalanine may be harmed as much by low phenylalanine diet as a child with true PKU will be harmed by unrestricted phenylalanine intake") argues against the comparative greater acceptability of false-positives over false-negatives. Unless each false-positive can be protected from harmful, inappropriate "treatment," an ethical assessment must disagree with the judgment that "false-negatives are much more serious because affected patients may not be diagnosed until symptoms appear--the exact antithesis of the screening concept."

That last statement discloses the moral features of some screening concepts. The idea seems to be that patients are wronged if they are not found and helped or if there is any failure to relieve their natural estate, and that the greatest medical relief must be delivered, even at cost to false-positives. Of course, it cannot be denied that the net benefits may be greater even when inconvenience and harm to false-positives is subtracted. Still, I suggest that older moralists had a truer view, when they distinguished between sins of omission and sins of commission--which screening seems to reverse, whenever failure to find the patient is felt to be more grievous than finding the wrong one. This point is most important and it may by itself morally forbid many sorts of screening. This can be seen when we note that "a test accurate 99.99 percent of the time for a disease occurring once in 20,000 persons should find one "false-positive for each one affected" (Knox, 1970). That means that the incidence of "commission" from using the screen would be the same as the incidence of "omission" from not screening.

It can, of course, be argued that relieving the need of the true-positive is much "greater" than the inconvenience, disvalue or harm brought upon the false-positive. If this is said, the rejoinder must be that if the quality of the benefits (and the harm) can be weighed in the same balance, whose they shall be cannot. The "benefitees" are irreducibly different. Even if the suffering can be compared, the sufferers cannot and they cannot be interchanged or aggregated. Only a statistical morality of the greatest net relief of suffering regardless of who gains, who loses, can suppose otherwise. Medical ethics to date has been based on the premise that we are not to choose martyrs for the sake of medical advancement or for the good of others without their understanding or validly implied consent (and even then, not if there is likelihood of serious harm).

The problem of false-positives is, of course, more serious in the case of screening the unborn, where abortion is the "remedy" and not simply mistaken treatment that can be withdrawn after the original test is disconfirmed. For example, sex chromatin tests are used to determine the sex of a fetus whose mother is a carrier of hemophilia or of Duchenne muscular dystrophy. Here there is no confusion of actually existent and unconnected patients; there is only one patient under investigation. Even if all errors in diagnosing sex were eliminated, a normal male fetus may be destroyed instead of the affected male that was the object of the search. In this case, one fetus is given the treatment said to be justified if a different one had been there. The fetus is interchanged with another one who is non-existent. The fetus in this case might have had some cause for celebration if there had been misdiagnosis because of "maternal cell contamination" in the fluid, and he had been taken for a girl.

Kaback and Leonard (1972) have said that, if all pregnancies are monitored, "the rare normal pregnancy that would be lost" would

be "an undefendable catastrophy." Even in screening "high risk"
populations, I see no moral reasoning or morally relevant factual
features that would support any other verdict. In mass or in
selective screening, the moral gap is equally wide and the connection equally insubstantial between one "benefitee" and another.
The connection between normals in the case of more limited populations is simply stronger in the mind of the observing statistician.
What is required to justify the "undefendable catastrophy" is an
undefendable system of ethics which derives its warrants from
aggregated increments of betterment, whether experienced in one or
another life. This flawed statistical morality is illustrated by
determining the sex of the fetus in order to screen for X-linked
traits. To screen by means of sex determination and to catch a
normal male fetus in a statistical net is in no instance to deliver
medical care in his case. Such mistaken identification is rather
like operating on the wrong patient--which no one would excuse by
saying that the condition to be remedied was graver than the
operation.

2. Next, let us ask whether natural defects and induced
damages can be compared on a single scale or summed up any more
than the patients screened ought to be. This seems to be so only
because incidence of risk fails to take into account what may be at
risk: if one skims the surface of incomparable traumas or benefits,
then, of course, they can be compared.

One argument for not doing amniocentesis until one can distinguish the affected and the heterozygous is that there would be a
75 percent chance of abortion being recommended in each pregnancy
and "the trauma of five successive abortions might even be greater
than having a child with one of these disorders" (Kaback and
Leonard, 1972). That comparison seems plausible, but is it really
rational? Is it not obvious that non-medical decision swayed in
unknown ways by idiosyncratic feeling is needed decisively to fill
out the "reasons," to choose among grave and incomparable traumas?

Fraser reported a case of a woman with a risk of 1 in 20 of
having a second child with cleft lip; she found such a risk "so
formidable" that she determined to have no more children, and had
an illegal abortion when she accidentally became pregnant. It
seems to me unrealistic for Fraser, as reported, to comment: "It
seems we failed to convey a realistic view of the risks in this
case" (Stock, 1969). What are realistic and what are formidable
odds? What is or is not judged to be a formidable impairment can
vary widely; and, as this instance shows, it may be no answer to
say that the probability of its occurring was slight.

There are physicians convinced that the risk of damage to the
woman or to the fetus from amniocentesis is about one to two percent. These physicians then require that the risk that the fetus
will be genetically defective must be higher than one or two
percent for amniocentesis to be indicated. Further decrease in the
incidence of risk from amniocentesis compared with the incidence of

genetic defects waiting to be discovered antenatally may, indeed, be taken by a maximum-benefits ethics to be the way to determine the population to be screened. "If the risk of amniocentesis is indeed as low as appears, and the overall frequency of a serious chromosome disorder is about 1:200 live births, the possibility arises that all pregnant women should be offered this diagnostic test" (Milunsky et al., 1970).

Incidence seems to be an odd point to light upon in balancing the two risks, since surely the depth of the genetic deformity and the depth of damage that might be caused by amniocentesis are at least equally important in a risks/costs/benefits analysis. Physicians should not avoid facing the "quantity of the quality" problem by concentrating on the quantifiable and comparable incidence, while neglecting the gravity of the afflictions to be treated or induced.

Why intrude the principle of equality in the balancing test, insisting that the incidence of induced damage from the procedure not exceed the incidence of probable genetic defect? Is that not a reflection of an "old ethics" applicable to a single patient at risk? Why don't physicians shift to a "new ethics" that attempts to calculate the balance of net worth altogether? Why not stress balancing the enormity of the impairments instead of the incidence of risks? There is evidence that the woman or the parents consider more than the incidence of risk; they decide according to some sort of "weighing" the depth of the risk; they feel they are "quantifying the disqualities." Carter and his colleagues found that parental decisions were a function of whether the child would be at risk of a serious and a long-term handicap. Muscular dystrophy always deterred, but parents' decisions varied when an affected child would die early (not a long-term impairment!), when the condition was relatively mild, when treatment was available, and when prognosis of treatment was improving (cystic fibrosis)(Carter et al., 1971). Why may not the physicians' decision to expose normals to the risks of amniocentesis be measured according to the serious and long-term defect the procedure is designed to detect? After all, a small risk of grave injury is a great risk. The conclusion seems ineluctable that screening by amniocentesis should sometimes be undertaken at great risk, that is, if anyone can-- which they cannot--quantify and compare these disparate disqualities and if anyone should--which they should not--forget the fact that the lives in question are not interchangeable.

On the other hand, one can argue that amniocentesis ought never to be done because of the depth of possible induced damage (however small the incidence of risk). Nadler (1972) completely excludes, as defects possibly produced by amniocentesis, only anomalies which are established in the fetus before 12 weeks, i.e., prior to the time at which amniocentesis is performed. "There is no way with present studies, our own included, of establishing, ten or fifteen years from now, if these children lose 5 or 10 I. Q. points." "The risks of 'induced' congenital malformations are difficult to determine and the subtle damage in terms of loss of intelligence is almost impossible to evaluate." If such grave damage from the procedure has not been excluded, intrauterine screening can hardly be justified by comparing only the probabilities.

SHADES OF DOUBT ABOUT STATISTICAL MORALITY AMONG
PROPONENTS OF INTRAUTERINE SCREENING

The requirements of non-statistical moral reasoning are observably at work in the conscientious judgments of physicians performing amniocentesis followed by abortion as the remedy. Physicians have stumbled upon questions of value when they thought they were discussing purely scientific or medical issues. Intrauterine screening, perhaps uniquely, has brought physicians, and others as well, to a point at which moral choice must begin where medical judgment ceases.

We have already noticed this in the intrusion of the principle of equality in balancing a small incidence of induced damage against a small incidence of natural genetic defect. Physicians are disinclined to let the gravity of the impairment of an affected abnormal, if he is not detected, raise the ante of the risks they are willing to bring by screening procedures upon normal unborns. This they should be willing to do, in the logic of the matter, if the standard were, without qualification, greatest net medical benefit.

Generally, the conscience of a physician is formed to believe that no useless risk should be taken; since amniocentesis brings some risk upon the woman and the unborn child, these risks should not be taken unless some action follows. This pattern of physician judgment would dictate, for example, that if only intrauterine therapy for the unborn were possible (not abortion), this should be agreed to by the woman or the parents before the procedure is done. Neither the procedure nor the risk should be useless.

Blending with this is the view that there should be no procedure and no risk unless genetic abortion is agreed to as the right action or as the only available action (in the absence of corrective therapy). There are also physicians who, in justifying amniocentesis, concentrate on the objective of enabling a woman to have a normal child or the eugenic goal of getting rid of abnormals, enhancing the "quality of life," etc.

Along this entire spectrum (except, perhaps, the last rare position), physicians are under the necessity of calling upon patient-decision to determine benefit as never before in the history of medicine. More is sought than the patient's concurrence in a medical decision. This must be the case because of the incomparable impairments and non-exchangeable patients involved.

The impossibility of composing an ordinary medical decision out of incomparable impairments or by aggregating incomparable

benefitees impels some physicians to require in advance a decision
to abort if an affected fetus is found. In fact, if abortion did
not exist, it would have to be invented--not only to prevent the
birth of abnormals when identified, but also to cover the unavoidable contradictions in conscience when unknown risks and risks of
unknown damage are visited upon normals. Therefore, physicians
swiftly resort to a comparison of those most incomparable "impairments": death and a life so defective that it is deemed by others
to be a life not worth having. Since this is in no way a medical
decision--whether or not it is a judgment any man can make--
physicians at this point need someone else to make the judgment and
to strengthen them in the performance of amniocentesis at risk.
So, in the interim between the old medical ethics and the coming
medical ethics, the woman or the parents must be empowered to make
the decision that cannot be made on accessible rational or medical
grounds, to choose the doctoring to be done. For example, Nadler
(1972) stated quite frankly that physicians have preferred patients
who are going to abort because "this has been for our own peace of
mind in terms of justifying the unknown risks of the procedure and
to some extent its reliability."

It seems also generally agreed among most physicians engaged
in amniocentesis that medicine should enable a woman to have a
normal child, however extraordinary the means to that end. Here
medicine may succeed in doing what religion never could: make
procreation the chief end of womankind! The power of this presup-
posed, nearly absolute value is, to say the least, remarkable among
physicians. It calls for some explanation: in the environment of
values needed to support the present practice of amniocentesis, the
explanation may be that, as in the case of the decision to abort
abnormals, physicians are aware that they need to rely on someone
else to provide the means to make amniocentesis good medicine.

Fuchs (1972) claimed that amniocentesis was contraindicated
unless the risks of a particular genetic disorder are greater than
the risks of the procedure to normals (which he estimated to be two
percent). He thus adopted a cautious approach to doing the procedure, based on stressing the incidence rather than the seriousness
of risk. However, Fuchs stated that amniocentesis should not be
undertaken, at risk to a normal fetus, unless the woman and her
physician had made a "firm decision" to "interrupt the pregnancy"
if a positive diagnosis of a particular disease were made. Is this
not a direct comparison of induced injury with natural defect
despite the fact that two different, uninterchangeable lives are
the sufferers in question?

Under these circumstances, it is understandable that physicians need desperately to believe that a woman's "right" to have a
normal child is overriding of all else, and that amniocentesis is
in fact a life-saving procedure. "The onus is on us to help this
(high risk) couple in every possible way to have a normal child.
The families that we are dealing with are families that are
incredibly desirous of having a normal child" (Kaback and Leonard,

1972). In the culture of screening there has been an extraordinary elevation to an absolute of a woman's right to have a normal child by any means. Not only is the woman incredibly desirous of having a normal child, the doctor needs this as well, to palliate his conscience for the risk and the outcome for other "benefitees" of the procedure. Getting the woman a normal child is needed to absolve the rare and unavoidable failure of the procedure or the inability of statistical morality to extend medical care to all concerned. Thus, it is ineffective to say that "most of the women screened should not have been pregnant in the first place. All women who would have genetically high risk pregnancies should be offered sterilization or an effective method of contraception" (Evans, 1971).

Macintyre (1972) has said that "the amniocentesis technique itself generates a significant amount of anxiety, and the individuals who are generating it are obligated to do something about its treatment." Rather, the technique generates its own absolution: by generating the anxiety which then requires the answer the procedure provides, amniocentesis is both self-justifying and self-propelled.

Of course, doctors reserve a place for independent medical judgment concerning whether the procedure is "indicated." Women are not admitted merely at their request, for example to determine the sex of a child to abort the wrong gendered ones. Yet patient desires have already been given the decisive role because it is a moral decision, not a medical judgment. Because of the physician's uncertainty about whether he has the knowledge on which to make a medical decision, and because amniocentesis seems to have been loosed from the moorings of assured medical-ethical principles, the woman's or the parents' decision takes primary responsibility. Probabilities or "statistical morality" cannot provide the doctor with warrants which approach the kind of medical judgments he is accustomed to make. Therefore, the woman's or the parent's choices must be empowered to take up where reason and medicine left off; their non-rational, non-medical choices are needed to fill the gap between amniocentesis and a determination of the "therapy" to be administered. The patient's decision is needed to reduce to practical certainty anything doubtful about "low risk" or "high risk" predictions (which, any gambler knows, tells us nothing about any particular case) of qualitatively different impairments (which not even gamblers know the odds on). The doctors' decisional murkiness and their moral quandaries in screening by amniocentesis seem to suggest that the practice itself should be questioned.

THE EFFECT OF SCREENING ON OUR CONCEPT OF NORMALITY
AND ON THE TREATMENT OF ABNORMALS

Intrauterine monitoring aims to prevent the birth of abnormal children. As screening becomes a part of standard medical prac-

tice, the concept of "normality" sufficient to make life worth
living is bound to be "upgraded", and the acceptance of "abnormality" and care for abnormals is bound to be degraded in our society.
This problem is all the more urgent in view of the obvious fact
that intrauterine screening can never fully succeed; there will
always be defective children who will slip through the net or who
are injured by the procedure itself. In addition, new mutations
will cause defective offspring to be born to couples who cannot be
identified as "high risk." Moreover, the majority of malformed or
mentally retarded children do not have either a chromosome anomaly
or an inborn error of metabolism (Carter, 1972). If medicine
becomes oriented toward finding a few abnormals and great publicity
is given to this accomplishment, what will this do to the care of
abnormal children? Will a woman encouraged to abort an abnormal
child accept the burden of caring for an abnormal one which was not
aborted?

Intrauterine screening seems destined to degrade society's
willingness to accept and care for abnormal children and, at the
same time, to enlarge the category of unacceptable abnormality,
while narrowing the range of acceptable normality. This seems a
prescription for continued generation of abnormal children by a
reevaluation of what is "abnormal." Who can say that society's
repulsion to disease and feeling that lack of biological perfection
is unacceptable will not extend to carriers? Moreover, where the
non-medical decision to accept a low or high risk of abnormality is
being placed on parents, how can determination of the sex of their
children be long withheld?

Our aversion to abnormality may soon deny them the decision
not to terminate a pregnancy. If our society is no longer tolerant
of a known abnormal fetus how long will we tolerate the same abnormality visibly before our eyes in an incubator? Carter (1972) has
asked, "Are we going to be faced with demands to do away with a
child with 21-trisomy syndrome whose mother was 34 years old during
her pregnancy and therefore was denied the benefits of prenatal
diagnosis" (because the line was drawn at women 35 years old and
above)?

I myself would oppose on moral grounds screening procedures
that mix together normals and abnormals merely on the grounds of
the mathematical incidence of both among the offspring of a special
population of their parents, when the "remedy" is the destruction
of abnormals, and incidentally of mistakenly identified normals.

Intrauterine screening has been promoted because it guarantees
the greatest net "normal" health in the born population, regardless
of the number of abnormal patients that have to be excluded to
attain that end. Inexorably that places a question mark beside
every person who does not meet the standard applied earlier in this
procedure, and this means that abnormals must become outcasts in
our society. It raises the standard of "normality" which every
individual must meet in order to have a life deemed by others to be
worth living and to be deserving of care in the human community.

The erosion of care for abnormals and a more exacting requirement of normality would have to be counted as disadvantages far out-weighing the momentary benefits claimed for this practice in medicine.

It would seem to me to be more honest and forthright, for those who espouse screening procedures aimed at securing greater net normality and the least total suffering from abnormality, to advocate that an individual shall not be certified to be among us--counting equally--until two days after birth, or when he can have his first "check-up" to determine whether he can qualify for the "quality of life" we mean to enhance. A similar recommendation was made by Williams (1957) and it seems a harshly logical sugges-tion which anyone should consider who is now content with half-way measures or with an interims-ethik in the matter of preventing suffering from human abnormalities. The "upgrading" of the concept of acceptable normality and the degrading of care for human abnor-mality must be counted as a consequence of amniocentesis, when this has in view the destruction and not the treatment of the needy patient. It might be better to take up the idea unambiguously by screening everyone to see whether we really mean to be Utilitarians who judge everything by the standard of the greatest net anything (whatever we agree on) regardless of numbers.

REFERENCES

Alexander, Leo (1966a). *Limitations of Experimentation on Human Beings with Special Reference to Psychiatric Patients.* Diseases of the Nervous System, Vol. 27, p. 62.
_____ (1966b). *Limitations in Experimental Research on Human Beings.* Lex et Scientia, Vol. 3, No. 1, p. 16.
Beecher, Henry K. (1959). *Experimentation in Man.* Journal of the American Medical Association, Vol. 165, No. 5, p. 468.
_____ (1970). *Research and the Individual.* Boston, Little, Brown & Co., pp. 77, 232; see also pp. 14, 47-49, 51-52, 70.
Carter, C. O. (1972). In *Early Diagnosis of Human Genetic Defects,* Maureen Harris, editor. Washington, D.C.: U.S. Government Printing Office.
Carter, C. O., et al., (1971). Genetic Clinic: A Follow-up. The Lancet (Feb. 6), p. 281.
Evans, T. N. (1971). Quoted in Albert B. Gerbie et al., Amniocentesis in Genetic Counseling. American Journal of Obstetrics and Gynecology (Mar. 1), p. 765.
Fuchs, Fritz (1972). In *Early Diagnosis of Human Genetic Defects,* Maureen Harris, editor. Washington, D.C.: U.S. Government Printing Office.
Janeway, Charles A. (1971). Screening for Inherited Diseases. Editorial, The New England Journal of Medicine, Vol. 284, p. 787.
Kaback, Michael M. (1972). In *Early Diagnosis of Human Genetic Defects,* Maureen Harris, editor. Washington, D.C.: U.S. Government Printing Office.
Knox, W. Eugene (1970). What's New in PKU. The New England Journal of Medicine, Vol. 283, p. 1404.

Macintyre, M. Neil (1972). In *Early Diagnosis of Human Genetic Defects*,
    Maureen Harris, editor. Washington, D.C.: U.S. Government Printing
    Office.
Milunsky, Aubrey, J. W. Littlefield, et al., (1970). *Prenatal Genetic
    Diagnosis (Third of three parts).* The New England Journal of
    Medicine, Vol. 283, p. 1498.
Nadler, Henry (1972). In *Early Diagnosis of Human Genetic Defects*,
    Maureen Harris, editor. Washington, D. C.: U.S. Government
    Printing Office.
Ramsey, Paul (1970). *The Patient as Person: Explorations of Medical
    Ethics.* New Haven, Yale University Press.
Rosenberg, Leon (1972). In *Early Diagnosis of Human Genetic Defects*,
    Maureen Harris, editor. Washington, D. C.: U.S. Government
    Printing Office.
Scriver, Charles (1972). In *Early Diagnosis of Human Genetic Defects*,
    Maureen Harris, editor. Washington, D. C.: U.S. Government
    Printing Office.
Stock, Robert W. (1969). *Will the Baby Be Normal?* New York Times
    Magazine (Mar. 23), p. 25.
Williams, Glanville (1957). *The Sanctity of Life and the Criminal Law.*
    New York, Alfred A. Knopf, pp. 17-24, 349-350.

DISCUSSION

KABACK: Genetic counseling applied after the birth of a proband individual is distinct from prospective counseling associated with mass public screening. If "genetic counseling" is the purpose for mass heterozygote screening, then there is an ethical issue associated with screening individuals for genetic disorders in which no positive alternatives are available to those found to be at risk for the disorder. Sickle cell anemia may be the best example. Suppose married couples in the Black population were screened to identify doubly heterozygous couples. Some serious questions can be raised about such an effort, since the couples found to be at risk (perhaps as many as 1 in 100 Black couples) would have one of the following alternatives as the result of being served "by modern medicine in all its benevolence":

(1) have no children,
(2) abort each pregnancy should a pregnancy occur,
(3) take their chances (having been informed that there is a
    75 percent chance with each pregnancy that their offspring
    would not be affected),
(4) artificial insemination,
(5) adopt children.

This last alternative deserves further comment. I do not believe that adoption will be an available alternative much longer in our society. Adoption of Black children is perhaps only still available because the services of most abortion clinics have not yet reached all individuals in our society. This, however, is changing dramatically, and I believe that as abortion on demand becomes available throughout our society, there will be fewer children available for adoption to any group. This will leave only four alternatives, all of which are negative alternatives in terms of the human psyche. If the couple is going to wind up taking their chances, perhaps it would have been best not to screen them in the first place.

I very much support our interest and concern for the development of positive alternatives for couples found to be at risk for genetic diseases. For instance, when amniocentesis or some intrauterine method is available for fetal detection of genetic disease, then I support screening of adult individuals to define at-risk couples. This enables those identified as at-risk to selectively have their own children, none of whom would be affected with the disease in question. This positive emphasis is really the crux of what intrauterine diagnosis is all about--not the abortion of affected fetuses, but the life of unaffected children.

A "positive alternative" for sickle cell disease and others will be available. Even with such mechanisms, screening must be given careful consideration.

MELLMAN: Artificial insemination with screened semen is a viable option after screening and detection of marriages of two heterozygotes.

MURRAY: That is something the couple, themselves, would have to decide, but it is an option which would not be readily accepted.

KABACK: A method for in utero detection of sickle cell anemia is currently available, however, it requires small samples of fetal blood obtained between the 12th and 20th week of fetal life, for which we do not as yet have a safe and reliable method. This is a technical problem involving tolerance of the human uterus for manipulation and penetration. If we can develop a mechanism for fetal blood sampling, prenatal detection of sickle cell anemia could be achieved. This would then provide an acceptable basis for mass screening in the adult Black community, since a positive alternative would be available to couples found to be at risk for sickle cell anemia in their offspring.

MOTULSKY: The present emotional climate of screening studies is such that to say, "There is ill health associated with the sickling trait," plays into the hands of people who place ads in EBONY magazine about sickle cell trait weakening you so that you have to see a physician regularly. Such an advertisement is outright irresponsible because the facts are that the vast majority of sickle trait carriers are quite healthy, they are not weakened, and they do not need to see a physician regularly.

Two studies are available. One is an autopsy study in which there was no difference among normals and sickle cell trait carriers coming to autopsy, which suggests no differences in mortality. The second was a prevalence study in California of sickle cell trait at various ages. Again, no differences in sickle cell trait frequency were found.

There may be a minor disadvantage to the sickling trait, but to stress this point now is incorrect. We need carefully controlled, large-scale prospective studies of how the sickling trait affects health in large populations--to find out whether or not there is a slight health hazard.

MURRAY: One has to consider the sickle cell trait in the context of the total health problem of the population. There is evidence that in the Black population there is a higher risk of death at all ages from hypertension, tuberculosis, and other diseases. For these there is therapy available, but for the sickle cell trait there is no therapy. So you are merely adding to the burden of the individual without adding any positive benefit. In addition, you further stigmatize such individuals. Take Tay-Sachs disease, for example. The Jewish minority group has suffered social injustice and now, if somebody starts studying carriers of Tay-Sachs disease and finds reduced survival of carriers, certain groups in this country may use this information to further stigmatize the Jewish population.

We are in a position to undo previous social injustice, but we are also in a position to add to social injustice if we aren't careful. The shortening of life span that might be due to sickle cell trait is not that significant in terms of other health problems.

KASS: Stigmatization and other evils that could result from compulsory screening might equally occur in the absence of compulsion, if widespread genetic screening becomes accepted, for example, as part of routine medical practice. One political factor may be pushing us in this direction. The United States is now moving toward a comprehensive national health insurance program, probably under the auspices of the Federal Government. It is very likely that the insurers will specify the diseases for which they will bear the costs of adult screening and amniocentesis, as well as the conditions for which they will pay for postnatal and institutional care of children born with genetic disease. The insurers might even decide not to pay for the care of children whose diseases were detectable by amniocentesis, or at least for those cases where insurance had paid for amniocentesis but the prospective parents refused to abort the child. These purely economic considerations would greatly influence both patients and genetic counselors. The result might well be universal, routine screening, equivalent to mandatory screening brought about by legislation, and with the same problems.

MURRAY: There is another aspect of compulsion, that of the peer group, which might occur in mass screening such as in Dr. Kaback's program. "If everybody is doing it, why aren't you?" There is also the bandwagon approach. "You are not a concerned citizen if you don't join in and be screened." This is not direct coercion, but it is a kind of coercion which is used in advertising, and one has to be cautious about it.

KABACK: Mutual or community coercion raises the issue of the definition of the goals of a mass screening program. If one believes mass screening is of positive value for individuals, then one must try to generate a mechanism of education which will get to as many people as possible and achieve a high compliance rate. This raises the dilemma of testing because of concern versus testing because of coercion and fear. In the Tay-Sachs program, we have implemented a broad saturation approach to genetic education, and this may have caused some mutual coercion, the degree of which must be evaluated.

LEJEUNE: Dr. Kaback, I don't see how you can say you are not screening for abortion purposes, because you are coming to abortion once you have detected an affected fetus. I would consider that you are screening if you are doing it on young people before marriage, but you cannot say that you are not advocating abortion of Tay-Sachs children.

KABACK: I do not agree. Let me elaborate. Approximately 40 pregnancies have been monitored to date because these families had previous children with Tay-Sachs disease. Of these, eight or nine fetuses have been identified with Tay-Sachs disease and abortion carried out. Of the remaining pregnancies, 21 have now come to term and uniformly resulted in children free of Tay-Sachs disease as predicted. That is what I am talking about when I say the program is not directed at abortion. It is directed at those 21 children who did not have Tay-Sachs disease who otherwise might not have been born. The statistics are clear that in the past, families who had Tay-Sachs children tended not to have subsequent children. Now the data will change since these families can now have children and only children free of Tay-Sachs disease. In fact, as the result of such programs, more children will be born and the children will be uniformly healthier.

LEJEUNE: You will kill them in utero.

KABACK: But that may be very different from the families who would otherwise suffer the greatest tragedy if the fetus were born and then went on to die after three to four years with Tay-Sachs disease. This mechanism is much more likely to restrict the tragedy to one, the Tay-Sachs fetus.

FRIED: Why did you choose to screen only couples that have already married?

KABACK: We now have a positive alternative for a couple in which both husband and wife are carriers. If such a positive alternative exists, I do not see the need for screening prior to marriage. The positive alternative is, of course, the mechanism for having as many children as they wish, none of whom will suffer with Tay-Sachs disease. Accordingly, because of limited funds, personnel, and facilities, our program was directed at testing individuals who conceivably would benefit most from this testing, i.e., married individuals of child-bearing age. In certain instances, however, we have tested single individuals prior to marriage and also engaged couples, but I have some serious concerns about the possible effects of genetic information on interpersonal relationships prior to marriage.

LEJEUNE: A positive alternative, but at the expense of those who will be discarded.

KABACK: If you mean by "discard," to abort a fetus who will suffer a uniformly fatal disease, that is correct.

WARKANY: You mentioned that rabbis cooperated with you. I wonder if there were orthodox rabbis who opposed your program?

KABACK: Dr. Warkany's question deals with the fact that, in the interpretation of some rabbis in the orthodox Jewish group, abortion is not a viable alternative after the 40th day of pregnancy. This tenet is not held by the conservative or reformed rabbis. Judaism is guided by the Talmud, which is a book of laws. The Talmud allows for the interpretation of its laws not only by rabbis, but by each individual Jew as well. Therefore, many orthodox rabbis have interpreted the information in a way in which they have been totally agreeable to screening and also the idea of abortion of a Tay-Sachs fetus as well. In discussions with most orthodox rabbis, I have pointed out that the blood test is a screening test by which people are given information. It is not a test that necessitates abortion. Rather, it provides information to people who may then elect to choose different alternatives. Actually, two orthodox synagogues in Baltimore have grouped together to support a mass screening of their congregations. For Hasidic Jews, the most orthodox, abortion and birth control are not accepted mechanisms. However, here again, the screening test is only a means of providing information concerning having or not having children with Tay-Sachs disease. It is not about abortion.

FRASER: Dr. Ramsey, would you elaborate on individuals not being "interchangeable"?

RAMSEY: The interchangeability of non-interchangeable individuals is a crucial point, and Dr. Gustafson put before you a spectrum of possible opinions in his overview paper. He distinguished an ethic based on individual human rights from an ethic oriented toward consequences or net good. He eliminated the extremes and said he knew no consequence- or good-oriented ethic that was not also a factor in a concern for the individual, and no ethic based on individual rights that does not also make significant reference to net good. Dr. Gustafson said that one way in which a good-oriented, net-benefits ethic shows it has concern for the individual patient is its reference to a valid consent. Some forms of screening must be a good-oriented ethic; they must either do harm to some of the lives involved or they do not obtain the grounds for a valid consent. As long as these principles remain in medical ethics as the way the individual is to be viewed, simply calculating the sum total of good to be done by screening is to go to a consequence-ethic. I tried to analyze the morality of screening to require us to pay attention to all of the patients in a screening situation. To do no harm to anyone concerned is a minimum condition.

MACINTYRE: In the history of medicine, we have many times instigated new procedures which have had obvious benefit to certain individuals without overlooking the fact that there might be some possible long-term problems which might arise. All of the data thus far indicate that prenatal chromosome analysis is a very reliable technique. The unlikely possibility of a long-term effect, such as reducing the mentality of an individual by a few IQ points, cannot be discounted completely. However, when one considers the positive value of prenatal diagnosis, I do not believe that the technique should be denied to those individuals who want it and need it because of the possibility of unlikely, subtle and, for the most part, immeasurable long-term ill-effects. There are known pitfalls and limitations in prenatal diagnosis, and it is important that we recognize them, but they should not be used as a basis for overstating a point.

RAMSEY: My point simply depends upon there being the possibility of misdiagnosis, however small. And I was asking you to consider whether or not a life was wholly excluded on the way toward the greatest good. Considering the low risk of the procedure, one can compare it with the great good being done. But if there remains the slightest reference to the individual, the damage from the procedure has to be compared with the natural defect that, in an individual case, is being interchanged and relieved.

That simply is my point, beginning with the minimum principle of medical ethics that one do no harm and with the somewhat more positive principle that one must have a sound reason for presuming a valid implied consent. That, I argue, cannot be established by the incidence of non-actual connection between individuals; such connection is not to be compared to a real shared risk in the case of screening for contagious diseases.

CROW: I would like to ask Dr. Ramsey what his position on abortion is.

RAMSEY: What I say about screening does not involve my view on abortion. My argument is simply that screening without an im-plied consent, with possible damage or whatever risk to potential lives, must meet the objections not only of a religious ethic but of most philosophers today who know that the utilitarian norm of "greatest good altogether" is no way to go about making ethical decisions.

My argument has force against any view of unborn life except one--namely, that the unborn life counts for nothing--in which case the damage and the need for implied consent would not be there. We would have a situation like the one that I deplore now. That is, a misalliance between freedom to determine when a pregnancy is medically unacceptable and the freedom of individualistic judgment to discard an unwanted pregnancy.

The grounds for determining a medically unacceptable pregnancy are going more and more toward doctoring the wishes of people in determining which child is wanted and which is unwanted, rather than using medical-ethical reasons for judging whether screening and the follow-up procedure are acceptable and judging on medical grounds which is an unacceptable pregnancy and which is a subjectively unwanted one.

THE HUMAN RIGHT TO LIFE: ITS NATURE AND ORIGIN

Sir Harold Himsworth

For the last two thousand years we have had people debating what we meant by "right" and what we meant by "life." It seemed to me, therefore, that before we started off, we might try to see what men meant by the bare bones of these terms.

Suppose you were commissioned to write a universal dictionary and you had to define the word "right" and the word "life" in a way that would be acceptable in Bangkok, Cairo, Rome, and New York--What would be the bare bones of the definition you gave?

I am not concerned with values. I am simply concerned with the mechanics, so to speak, of the meaning. Let us take the question of human right first.

I think that we might agree that when a man talks about having a right to something, what he is trying to convey to us is that he believes that he has reason to expect that the society to which he belongs will agree to what he wishes. Similarly, when he talks of the rights of others, he believes the society of which they are members will allow that certain expectations on their behalf are justifiable. It seems to me, therefore, that this idea of mutual expectation in respect to certain ideas is at the basis of this question of right. There has to be a consensus on the matter in question.

Thus, if I expect to be allowed to walk into a shop and take things without paying for them, the consensus of opinion in our society will speedily disabuse me of my right to do that. On the other hand, if I go into a shop and pay for things, I think I shall have the backing of the consensus in this society if I claim that I have a right to keep that for which I have paid.

It seems, therefore, that the distinguishing element in the idea of a right is that it is an expectation supported by consensus in the society to which the man belongs. Without that proviso, an expectation is no more than a personal, private desire. But with that expectation, the wish graduates to the status of an entitlement that applies to all individuals in that particular society.

But the consensus of what is legitimate and what is not--is not the same in different societies. Thus, in a society in which monogamy is the accepted practice, to have more than one wife at the same time is a crime. In one in which polygamy is accepted, to have a plurality of wives is a right.

So I suggest the following as a purely dictionary definition of what is a right: "A right is an expectation in respect to matters affecting the interests of the individuals within a particular society which the consensus of opinion in that society accepts as justifiable."

That, I suggest, would apply in Bangkok as well as in New York.

Now, what about the question of life?

I would like to get one point out of the way first. I am simply talking of what Professor Aiken called biological life, which you will remember he said was the infrastructure upon which a full life was built. There can be no full life without biological life.

The term "life" can be used in several senses, but I am concerned with only two. It can be used in the concrete sense, meaning the state of being alive, or it can be used in an abstract sense to mean a force, a principal, an entity which, when present in the body, produces the state of being alive. That is the kind of sense we use it in when we say that life has departed--that is the abstract sense, and with that I am not concerned. Therefore, I shall confine my remarks to the concrete, biological sense.

The man in the street by tradition is accustomed to distinguishing quite sharply between the state of being alive and the state of being dead. But we, as biologists, know that this no longer holds. We have been driven inescapably to recognize that parts of the body can be alive while the rest isn't. If I happen to have a fatal coronary at this particular minute and any of you have appropriate needles handy, you can take samples of my tissues and put them into tissue culture and they will grow. Similarly, if there happens to be a suitable recipient at the NIH, you might be able to get one of my kidneys out fast enough to implant it in him when my kidney will live. So we are thus driven inescapably to recognize that from the standpoint of the whole individual, the state of being alive depends not merely on the component parts being alive, but also on the ability of the organism so to integrate the actions of these that the body as a whole can function as one unit.

So it seems to me that any definition, insofar as it applies to whole organisms, must include some idea of the integration of function.

We might say, therefore, that we define the state of being alive as that in which an organism is capable of maintaining the integrated functions of its various living component parts so that it may, itself, operate as a single unit. And per contra, we can define the state of being dead as that in which the organism has lost the ability to function as an integrated whole even though some of its organs and tissues are still alive.

In relation to our particular problem, however, we are concerned not with dying, but with coming alive. Or to put it in another way, our concern is with the process of developing that state of integrated function in the body which we recognize when we say that this individual fetus, as distinct from that organ or that tissue, is alive.

I think it is impossible to talk about function apart from considering the purpose which a function subserves. And if we ask ourselves what is the purpose of fetal development in a multicellular organism, the answer is self-evident. It is to produce another individual of that species which is capable of functioning as a self-sustaining whole independently of any connection with its mother.

On that basis, I think you can draw a distinction between a viable and a pre-viable fetus. A viable fetus on this basis is one which has attained a state of development at which it can maintain the operation of its component parts so that it is capable of functioning, or capable of being made to function, as a self-sustaining whole independently of any connection with its mother. And the pre-viable fetus, by contrast, is one that, although some of its component parts may be alive, has not developed to that stage.

I do not think we can escape from recognizing, physiologically speaking, that there are degrees in the process of becoming alive. There is a phase before organs are differentiated when only tissues exist. There is one when there are individual organs, such as the heart or the lungs, but others are as yet imperfectly developed or incapable of function.

Then there is the phase when, although these organs are there, the fetus has not developed to the extent that it is capable of functioning as an integrated whole independently of its physical connection with the mother.

If you want to go on, there is a later phase in which the fetus (or baby) is capable of functioning independently of a physical connection with the mother but is still dependent on her ministrations for its subsistence.

And finally, you have the stage when the baby (or child) can fend for itself.

Now, I repeat that I am talking of the physiological aspects of life. It would seem that on this basis, there is a scale of "aliveness" and that the units in which this scale is drawn up are those of the capacity for independent existence.

Society has already drawn tacit distinctions in the status of a fetus at different stages of its development by setting limits for the time in pregnancy when abortion can be undertaken. In the United Kingdom, this is 28 weeks; in New York State, 24; and in Maryland, 20.

So on the strict understanding that I am speaking physiologically, and expressing no opinion on values, I would therefore propose the following as a definition of "life" for my dictionary. "Life, insofar as it concerns whole organisms, is that state of being in which the organism is capable of functioning as an integrated whole and is thus able, or capable of being made able, to support an independent, self-sustaining existence."

LIFE AND THE RIGHT TO LIFE

Henry David Aiken

The aim of this paper is, in the first instance, one of clarification. That is, the aim of one whose philosophical vocation is
directed not   so   much   to questions of scientific fact, simply as
such, as to questions concerning the manner in which the conceptual
schemes are employed in science, and to the ways in which results
achieved through their employment affect other activities, particularly those bearing upon our ordinary conduct as human beings. But
the task of clarification subtends that of conduct: we want to go
to our various enterprises with clearer heads so that we may make
less confused and more rational decisions of policy.

Now in our thinking about the right to life and of the myriad
problems which it raises, we frequently fail to distinguish two
senses of the term "life" which, although undoubtedly related, have
quite different meanings. Thus, for example, we often say of someone that he has led a full life, that his life was unfulfilled, or
that he is full of life or lively. What do such locutions connote?
For one thing life is not merely a matter of being alive in some
purely biological or bio-physical sense of the term. Something can
be alive or be capable of life in the latter sense, yet not alive
or capable of life in the sense implied in or by the expressions
mentioned above. What we mean by a full life, I take it, is one
full of significant experience and activity, and we apply it in the
first instance only to human beings. An acorn might realize all
its potentialities as a budding oak tree; yet we would not on that
account think of it as having lived a full life. Just the contrary:
the question of living or of having lived a full life doesn't arise
in discussing acorns and oak trees. The reason, plainly, is that,
as we normally conceive them, questions about the quality or
character of their experience, except in mythic contexts, make no
sense. Again, a person who is lively or full of life is one who is
vivacious, active, eager for experience and capable of participating in forms of activity which yield significant experience. Here
too, what we have in mind is the behavior of beings, conceived as
conscious, purposeful, concerned with and engaged in various human
activities. Life in this sense is a normative concept: it is
something to be cherished, worthy of nurture and concern in its own
right.

173

But there is another sense of the term "life," as employed in biology and the other so-called life sciences, which carries with it none of these connotations. In this sense, to be alive is simply to meet certain bio-physical conditions. So understood, something is alive if its behavior, as a phenomenon, is explainable and predictable in accordance with certain covering scientific laws together with accurate descriptions of certain antecedent conditions. The variables required in giving an account of it may be more complex than those required in giving an account of non-living chemical changes. But that fact, if such it is, carries with it no normative implications whatever. In this, the biological sense, "life," like "zinc" or "entropy," is intrinsically a neutral descriptive term. Accordingly, no one has any intrinsic obligations with respect to it, save perhaps to observe it accurately and to explain its changes as best one can. No one, that is to say, has any obligations to it, to preserve it in being, to nurture it, to help it to realize its potentialities. In this sense, the right to life is entirely contingent. Its application depends entirely upon its bearing upon possibilities of life in the other, human and normative sense of the term.

Now a word must be said about the concept of a right. This concept involves, on the one side, the idea of a rightful claim, made in behalf of someone or another and, correlatively, that of responsible persons to whom alone such claims may be addressed and who are presumed to be held liable for their respect or fulfillment. Normally, rights are claimed only within contexts of developing social practices, and the same holds, whether the rights in question are legal or moral rights. A right does not exist merely because of someone's wish or aspiration. Commonly legal rights, in a society such as ours, are presumed to rest upon and to be justified in terms of more fundamental rights which we call "moral." And a legal right which has no independent moral justification is one which can be defended, if at all, only on the ground that its persistent violation would undermine the legal system to which, as a whole, we have some obligation to sustain. However, as in societies whose legal systems permit, say, the institution of slavery, it is plain that the legal rights of masters ought systematically to be reprobated and/or violated.

Why? Surely the reason is that such rights, or their observation, do violence to our notions of humanity and of the rights pertaining to a human being.

The adequacy of this answer turns, of course, upon our understanding of what it means to be a human being, a question to which I shall turn shortly. But before doing so, let me make a few additional remarks in defense of the preceeding sketch of the notion of a right itself against certain objections to it which were made, explicitly or implicitly by certain other authors of this volume. According to them, a right amounts merely to an expectation and, hence, that X has a right if, and only if, he can expect society or a social group or another person to do something. This will not

do. The society we live in creates many expectations which entail
no corresponding right. Conversely, rights may be justly claimed,
even when, alas, there is all too little reason to expect that the
claims in question will generally be honored. The defeat of an
expectation does not entail the defeat of a right or a claim
regarding it; nor does the defeat of a right turn merely on the
defeat of any accompanying expectations.

What is missing in the expectation theory of rights is precisely the notion of responsibility or obligation which, as I
contend, that of a right essentially involves. When I make you a
promise, for example, it does not suffice that you expect me to
keep it. What is required is that you are entitled, ceterus
paribus, to hold me liable for keeping it. And when I fail to keep
it, you are entitled to demand an excuse or justification and, if
none can be provided, then I must make amends in some appropriate
way. Similarly, one may expect that people in a particular society
will behave, or are likely to behave in certain ways toward living
things without in the least being justified in inferring that they
have, or consider themselves to have, any corresponding responsibilities or that the living things in question have any right or
rights to live.

From a moral point of view, then, rights pertain primarily,
although perhaps not exclusively, to human beings. Now it is true
that we frequently use the term "man" as a virtual synonym for
"human being." Thus, when the 18th century philosophers and publi-
cists spoke of the "rights of man," it is evident that they were
thinking of man as a human being, as a person entitled, as such, to
realize certain potentialities and to exercise certain powers and,
correspondingly, obliged, as a member of the human race, to respect
(at the least of it) the rights of other human beings. But there
is another use of the term "man" which carries with it no such
implication. It does not follow from the fact that X meets the
conditions required of anything which may be truly said to be a
man, as the zoologist employs the term, that a claim is thereby
established that X is a human being, entitled to the prerogatives
and required to meet the obligations which our common humanity may
entail.

Thus, we must distinguish between man conceived simply as a
biological or bio-physical phenomenon and man conceived as a human
being. The former sense of the term "man" is no less neutral than
that of the terms "rock" and "pine tree;" the latter is not. The
Greeks, for example, were not unaware that barbarians were, like
themselves, featherless bipeds; they simply did not regard barbarians as fully human. Similarly, racists may be excellent biologists
who can recognize a black man in the neutral biological sense as a
member of a certain species just as accurately as an anti-racist.
The racist's difficulty is that he does not recognize the black man
to be a full-fledged human being who ought therefore to be accorded
all the rights which pertain to our common humanity. The question
for the racists as well as for the humanists, in short, cannot be

settled in purely empirical terms; for both it is a question of who or what must be or deserves to be treated as a human being. And in sum, man as human, is essentially and saliently a distinctive normative concept, whereas man, as the natural scientist employs the term, is not a normative concept at all.

This is not to deny, of course, that our conceptions of humanity--what is involved in the notion of being human and what is required of human beings in their dealings with one another--are capable of enlargement or diminution. Owing in part to our developing anthropological knowledge of the behavior of men in so-called primitive societies, to our grasp of the fact that primitive societies, like other societies, have histories, to our understanding that man's psychological and social endowments do not vary significantly with his color, that his capacities for human development are profoundly affected by his physical and social environments, and, more ominously, that scientific technological skills make it possible to reduce any individual to a condition little different from that of a plant, our notions of man's human possibilities and of their fragility are subject to a radical change.

Indeed, precisely because man, the organism, is so variously subject to manipulation, a good many pundits such as B. F. Skinner, now argue in effect that such concepts as human dignity and autonomy or agency should be consigned to the semantical wastebasket into which many others have already been thrown, including such notions as soul and spirit. In this connection it is also worth recalling that prescient technocrat, Jeremy Bentham, contended nearly two centuries ago that the same should also be the fate of such "fictitious entities" as moral, as distinct from legal, rights and responsibilities themselves. Were Bentham and Skinner to have their way, in fact, the whole problem of the right to live, in the moral and human sense, would disappear from discussions of public policies along with, whether they realize it or not, the entire system of practices comprehended under the heading of personal and/or human relations. In that case, however, the primary issues with which we are here concerned would simply disappear.

It is not for me to deny that such issues could disappear or that in certain quarters they may already be in the process of disappearing. No doubt, we might reach a situation in which the only essential relations in which we stand to others are relations of scientific observer to neutral object. However, even in that case, honest observers would still have obligations and rights in their scientific undertakings which make it difficult, if not impossible, to understand how they could conceive one another as mere input-output systems. Science itself is an essentially human activity which precludes the scientist from treating his fellow scientist merely as an object. For an object or phenomenon has no obligation to tell the truth, not to mention a right to tell it. If an Einstein regarded a Niels Bohr as nothing more than a rather subtle bio-physical entity and vice versa, their putative "disagreements," from their own points of view, would degenerate by stages into minor collisions with respect to which questions of truth and validity, of honesty and perfidy, would be reduced to the same order as that of falling bodies which happen to get into one another's way. In fact, were an Einstein really to treat a Bohr as a system of inputs and outputs, he would eventually come so to regard himself. To that extent the self-corrective enterprise of scientific inquiry, with all the characteristic responsibilities and rights pertaining thereto, would lose its own integral meaning for the individuals involved.

Now the right to a human life--that is, to the life we call "human"--is of course fundamental, since it encompasses the whole life of the mind, intellectual, artistic, religious, moral and communal. It includes also the various forms of bodily gratification too often ignored by ascetic moralities which, mistakenly, assume that intellectual and other spiritual activities can go it on their own, regardless of our bodily needs and wants. As here understood, then, the right to life is the great encompassing right of which all other human rights are aspects. And even if the former is conceived, again mistakenly, as unconditional, the latter plainly are not. Their limitations are set by the other forms of being which belong, no less essentially, to an acceptable human existence.

The right to a human life, most certainly, is nullified unless there is also a right to life in the biological sense of the term. But this does not mean that the right to life in the latter sense is unconditional. Just the contrary. From a human point of view, the preservation of life, biologically, is at once conditional and contingent, like the right to fresh air. Other rights, such as the right to the liberties essential to a developed human existence, are also conditional, since their exercise affects other inherent dimensions of human beings. But they are plainly not merely contingent. For they are aspects of human life itself.

The significance of this point may be seen in the following way. In earlier times, men normally conceived themselves as belonging to a continuous cycle or (later) a progressive development of human existence. Their forbearers and successors were virtually as actual to them as their own contemporaries. In such circumstances the rights of the unborn, the dying, or even the dead were scarcely distinguishable from those of the living.

For better or worse, such assumptions can no longer be taken for granted. Nowadays, owing in part to our increasing mobility, physically and (at least, in Western countries) economically and socially, and hence owing to a new nomadism not contemplated in previous ages, men frequently have little or no sense of belonging to an enduring family or local community, let alone a nation or state. Our anonymous forefathers are homogenized, along with the traditions they represented, into a great semi-alien and pre-human past. And our successors, whose lives we can scarcely envisage, have become part of a largely problematic future which, if not tomorrow, then a few decades (or centuries) hence, may contain no human beings whatever.

The consequence is a conception of human existence in which, by stages, generalized potentialities are themselves reduced to mere possibilities and present actualities become overwhelmingly precious. Thus, whereas it appeared to our predecessors that the right of the fetus to continuing life was not less, or possibly even more, compelling than the right of its mother to hers, and the right of one's as yet unconceived successors was no less exigent than one's own, the presumptions of continuous human being and of the rights pertaining thereto are now radically foreshortened. For us, accordingly, the rights of man are the rights, in the first instance, of existing human beings. And it is their lives which, in the biological sense, are now objects of central moral concern. Indeed, it is a cruel joke to require that a fully living mother sacrifice her being for the sake of an unborn fetus whose continuing existence, not to say its promise of human life, remains problematic. Justice, in the modern world, does not command it; on the contrary, it is revolted at the prospect. Let it be shown that the unborn sons and daughters of woman will be capable of guaranteeing her rights to human being, and then we shall see what to make of their own. Let us make sure that the potentialities of the born stand a chance of realization before we commit ourselves to the putative rights of the unborn or unconceived.

Now I believe three interlocking and overlapping sets of rights are essential to our modern conception of human being. The first may be called rights to the forms of enlightenment essential to free agency. A free agent, however, is not simply one who is at liberty to do as he pleases, for a man may do as he likes and not be a fully free human being. A fully free human being is one who is able to distinguish between what he pleases and what his obligations commit him to and who realizes accordingly that those to whom he is obligated have rights to which his own pleasures or interests should, on occasion, be sacrificed. Accordingly, the rights necessary to the exercise of free agency include rights to participation in all of the human practices essential to the development and exercise of considered moral judgment and deliberation; rights to instruction in the main historical conceptions of human society, personal development, and of a good, or tolerable, life; rights to unimpeded analysis and criticism and hence to free inquiry and speculation; rights to the acquisition of all available knowledge concerning matters of fact indispensable to the formation of sound judgment; and, accordingly, rights to free speech, press, and use of all media whereby such knowledge is acquired and disseminated.

A second main group of rights are those pertaining to what J. S. Mill called "the inner life," for example, rights to artistic creation and appreciation, and rights to the formation of religious sensibilities, attitudes, and criticism, and to the foundation of associations for the cultivation of artistic and religious concerns; and, not least, rights to the formation of friendships and comradeships without which the life of the mind loses its substance.

But there is also a third group of rights, which I call "material rights," without whose enjoyment rights pertaining to free agency and the inner life become merely formal and claims concerning them bare pieces of rhetoric. Under this head are included rights pertaining to self-maintenance, to adequate food and shelter and, not least, fear from radical material deprivation or want. However, private philanthropy, as the whole history of the race demonstrates, never suffices to ensure such rights. Hence, we must include among the material rights of human beings, rights to the formation of political and social institutions designed to ensure human beings from material deprivation.

Minimal guarantees, however, are not enough, so long as there exist radical material inequalities among the members of society. Rich and poor can rarely meet as equal human beings, any more than great nations can meet with client states save on terms analogous to those of master and servant or slave. Accordingly, it is essential not only that individual men but also that political institutions, whether at the national or international level, acknowledge, in principle, that all human beings are entitled to roughly equivalent shares of the world's material goods and powers. And this, I take it, is an essential part of the indwelling meaning of the right to democracy or a democratic way of life.

Analytically, such rights of human beings are distinguishable, but in practice they cannot be sharply separated. They form natural Gestalts such that the diminution or abrogation of rights in one domain will normally result in corresponding diminutions and abrogations of rights elsewhere. To give absolute priority to material rights in a particular society aborts the lives of the human beings whose full stomachs are paid for at the expense of their inner lives. And the converse, generally speaking, is no less true.

By the same token, we can establish no platonic hierarchy of human rights, nor any principles which give invariant preference, in situations of conflict, to one right, or set of rights, in relation to another. In one society, at a particular time, the overwhelming obstacle to the common exercise of rights pertaining to enlightenment or to the inner life is widespread poverty and insecurity. In another, there may be widespread but mindless guarantees of material rights that leave the individuals involved spiritually and hence humanly inert.

Now, in barest outline, we have provided a context within which we may seriously begin to discuss the right to life for man in the bio-physical sense which concerns this conference. As I have already suggested, this right is not only conditional but contingent. For even though biological life is a _sine qua non_ for human life, it is not, as such, a part of human life. A man may live, or have promise of continuing to live, as an organism, yet in so doing lose, or else be devoid of, all promise of genuine human being. But the promise, or possibility, of human life depends not only on biological but also on social conditions of survival. Where such conditions are absent, the contingent right to biological life has a decreasing claim upon the consciences of enlightened men.

Already, even in Catholic countries, contraception is widely tolerated, or even encouraged, by enlightened persons on the ground that unrestricted conception itself aborts, or tends to abort, the human rights of the living. And the right to abortion of the fetus, although more problematic, is accepted on the grounds that the realization of its putative potentialities for human life preclude fulfillment of the rights of already living human beings. Actual human beings, and the rights pertaining thereto, come first. The alternative, which places no limitation whatever on the right of man to biological life, would be inevitably a counter-ideology of dispair which regards life as an abomination and its destruction a consummation devoutly to be wished: in short, nihilism. Such a counter-human ideology, pressed to its extreme, would lead to the position that either there are no human rights or else that the only human right is a right to immediate self-destruction or suicide.

I conclude first that claims regarding the right to biological survival are entirely contingent upon the ability of the individual in question to make, with the help of others, a human life for himself. This means that in circumstances where there exists no possibility of anything approaching a truly human life, the right to biological or physical survival loses its own raison d'etre and, hence, that the merciful termination of life, in the bio-physical sense, is acceptable or perhaps even obligatory. Other things equal (which they rarely are), the rights of parents to accept the onus of caring for a radically defective child which has no capacity for enjoying a human life may be acknowledged. But then this is owing not to the child's right but to the human rights of its parents. And when the care of such a child seriously endangers the well-being of others, including in particular the members of its own family, parental rights (which are themselves, of course, always conditional) must give way to other, more exigent claims. The same holds true in the case of the lives of older individuals who, for one reason or another, can no longer function as human beings. But here, even more clearly than in the case of a radically defective fetus, it is the rights of others, including also members of society who have no familial relations to the individual in question, which must decide the issue.

Who shall be entitled to make decisions in such cases is of course a question of fundamental importance. But it is a different question, and until this fact is recognized, it cannot be rationally answered. With all respect, it seems to me that the state is usually far too coarse an institution to be entrusted with such decisions. At best, it may enact laws which make mercy killings legally permissible when conducted under proper auspices by just and competent persons, usually with the consent of other human beings whose own rights are directly involved.

Such an answer, I freely admit, is inadequate. This much, however, does seem certain--the consent of members of the individual's own family is never absolutely decisive. Indeed, in societies where overpopulation reduces most of its human inhabitants to a condition of perpetual misery, the consent of the family seems to me a matter of secondary importance.

In this connection, I would be less than candid if I did not at least raise the question of justifiable infanticide, even in circumstances where no genetic defect is discernible. Now the primary argument against such a practice has always been that healthy new-born infants have the capacity of developing into full-fledged human beings. And the right of the infant to life is based largely or entirely upon such presumptive potentialities. However, potentialities are not actualities, and where the rights of actual human beings are (for example) widely jeopardized by otherwise uncontrolled exponential population increases, then the above-mentioned argument loses much of its force. And in circumstances in which the potentialities of the infants in question promise only lives of endless misery and frustration for themselves, then the force of the arguments is further, if tragically, reduced. Human potentialities, in short, presuppose certain actual conditions of fulfillment. When such conditions cannot be met, the potentiality in question reverts to the status of a bare possibility, and bare possibilities afford no secure basis for a doctrine of human rights. But in candor I should also add that I have no clear notion of how a practice of justifiable infanticide might be properly implemented. And so I must leave the issue here unhappily unresolved. It is enough, at this stage, merely to raise it for your consideration.

It is time, however, to reverse the preceding line of argument. Granted that the right to life is conditional, many men are pointlessly denied their rights as human beings for indefensible reasons. And many are murdered daily for bad reasons or else for no reason at all.

Not only Nazi Germany but also every great nation-state in modern times has become involved in wholesale murder: that is, the extreme violation of the right to human life. And the more powerful the nation-state, the more is it in danger of becoming involved in wholesale murder.

What conclusion can we draw from this? For one thing, either that the concept of the sovereign nation-state is obsolete, or that nation-states and their putative legitimate rulers are subject to continual moral critique. The "national interest" is no longer acceptable, if it ever was, as a basic category of practical, not to say moral, reasoning. Nations, like individuals, are as they do, and deserve to be judged and treated accordingly. And their rulers, no less than their ordinary citizens, have, or should have, moral responsibilities not to their subjects or fellow-citizens only but to all humankind. There are such things as crimes against humanity. The essential trouble with the Nurenburg trials (for example) is not that they occured but that they were administered exclusively by the victorious nations.

Nation-states, as such, have at best only a contingent and derivative moral authority. Accordingly, the contention that their subjects are always obliged to obey their de facto rulers is indefensible. The rights of considered dissent, disobedience, rebellion, and revolution are also indispensable, if derivative, human rights. Nor are they suspendable, as Justice Holmes emphasized, even in the presence of a "clear and present danger" to the nation-state itself. In short, neither citizens nor their rulers (including members of the judiciary and the military) are ever exempt from moral criticism and punishment when they engage in wholesale violations of human rights.

If the right to a human life is, as it should be, the object of our primary moral concern, then the major threat to it is not the conscienceless abortionist or the fetishist for whom every fetus is already a full-fledged human being, but the rulers of nation-states and their military and industrial auxiliaries for whom unlimited warfare, or the threat thereof, are acceptable conditions of national survival. National survival is in itself at most a contingent right which is limited by the human rights not only of the citizens of the nation in question but of all other human beings. The profound horror of modern war is not simply that it involves inescapably the large-scale killing of innocents, but that it destroys systematically the whole form of life we call human, and in so doing violates or degrades the humanity of the guilty as well as innocent.

In fairness, it should be asked whether the same thesis, consistently maintained, does not equally prohibit violent forms of resistance, rebellion, and in extremity, revolution. I shall not deny that revolution, like war, is frequently murderous. However, it rarely happens in our time that those who perform acts of revolutionary intent, not to mention those who are engaged in acts of resistance or rebellion, are in a position to destroy, in effect, an entire civilization and hence to negate all the conditions of meaningful human being. More saliently, their aim, when justified, is not the defense of a particular national interest or the interests of a particular social class, but rather the recognition and protection of human rights which have hitherto been ignored by the rulers of nation-states and their auxiliaries.

This in no way condones or excuses rebels and revolutionists who terrorize or degrade their oppressors, when they make them more beastly than they were before by acts of torture, by random assassinations, etc.--just the contrary. Fanon and his admirers to the contrary, there is no right to terrorize one's oppressors, if this means treating them simply as objects or things. For in doing so, the terrorist places himself automatically in a situation of terror which debases him no less than those he terrorizes.

I realize that the issues here are complex and that this brief excursion has done them scant justice. Thus, let me return to my

main theme. We do not live in a paradise in which every featherless
biped or proto-biped is or is automatically to be viewed and treated as human. The right to human life is part of the more inclusive
right to a human life, a pattern of being which includes all the
rights I have mentioned above. Abstracted from this context, I
fail to see why the right to life among featherless bipeds is any
more sacred than the right, if right there be, to life on the part
of mosses, insects, or cancer cells.

As matters stand, we all move, unreasonably, between the
fetishism of life and the fetishism of self-interest, whether it be
the interest of the individual, the class, the nation, or the race,
in both cases ignoring the arduous task of trying to be a human
being.

IMPLICATIONS OF PRENATAL DIAGNOSIS FOR THE HUMAN RIGHT TO LIFE

Leon R. Kass

It is especially fitting on this occasion to begin by acknowledging how privileged I feel and how pleased I am to be a participant in this symposium. I suspect that I am not alone among the assembled in considering myself fortunate to be here. For I was conceived after antibiotics yet before amniocentesis, late enough to have benefited from medicine's ability to prevent and control fatal infectious diseases, yet early enough to have escaped from medicine's ability to prevent me from living to suffer from my genetic diseases. To be sure, my genetic vices are, as far as I know them, rather modest, taken individually--myopia, asthma and other allergies, bilateral forefoot adduction, bowleggedness, loquaciousness, and pessimism, plus some four to eight as yet undiagnosed recessive lethal genes in the heterozygous condition-- but, taken together, and if diagnosable prenatally, I might never have made it.

Just as I am happy to be here, so am I unhappy with what I shall have to say. Little did I realize when I first conceived the topic, "Implications of Prenatal Diagnosis for the Human Right to Life," what a painful and difficult labor it would lead to. More than once while this paper was gestating, I considered obtaining permission to abort it, on the grounds that, by prenatal diagnosis, I knew it to be defective. My lawyer told me that I was legally in the clear, but my conscience reminded me that I had made a commitment to deliver myself of this paper, flawed or not. Next time, I shall practice better contraception.

Any discussion of the ethical issues of genetic counseling and prenatal diagnosis is unavoidably haunted by a ghost called the morality of abortion. This ghost I shall not vex. More precisely, I shall not vex the reader by telling ghost stories. However, I would be neither surprised nor disappointed if my discussion of an admittedly related matter, the ethics of aborting the genetically defective, summons that hovering spirit to the reader's mind. For the morality of abortion is a matter not easily laid to rest, recent efforts to do so notwithstanding. A vote by the legislature

185

of the State of New York can indeed legitimatize the disposal of
fetuses, but not of the moral questions. But though the questions
remain, there is likely to be little new that can be said about
them, and certainly not by me.

Yet before leaving the general question of abortion, let me
pause to drop some anchors for the discussion that follows. Despite
great differences of opinion both as to what to think and how to
reason about abortion, nearly everyone agrees that abortion is a
moral issue (1). What does this mean? Formally, it means that a
woman seeking or refusing an abortion can expect to be asked to
justify her action. And we can expect that she should be able to
give reasons for her choice other than "I like it" or "I don't like
it." Substantively, it means that, in the absence of good reasons
for intervention, there is some presumption in favor of allowing
the pregnancy to continue once it has begun. A common way of
expressing this presumption is to say that "the fetus has a right
to continued life" (2). In this context, disagreement concerning
the moral permissibility of abortion concerns what rights (or
interests or needs), and whose, override (take precedence over, or
outweigh) this fetal "right." Even most of the "opponents" of
abortion agree that the mother's right to live takes precedence,
and that abortion to save her life is permissible, perhaps obligatory. Some believe that a woman's right to determine the number
and spacing of her children takes precedence, while yet others
argue that the need to curb population growth is, at least at this
time, overriding.

Hopefully, this brief analysis of what it means to say that
abortion is a moral issue is sufficient to establish two points.
First, that the fetus is a living thing with some moral claim on us
not to do it violence, and therefore, second, that justification
must be given for destroying it.

Turning now from the general questions of the ethics of abortion, I wish to focus on the special ethical issues raised by the
abortion of "defective" fetuses (so-called "abortion for fetal
indications"). I shall consider only the cleanest cases, those
cases where well-characterized genetic diseases are diagnosed with
a high degree of certainty by means of amniocentesis, in order to
sidestep the added moral dilemmas posed when the diagnosis is
suspected or possible, but unconfirmed. However, many of the
questions I shall discuss could also be raised about cases where
genetic analysis gives only a statistical prediction about the
genotype of the fetus, and also about cases where the defect has an
infectious or chemical rather than a genetic cause (e.g., rubella,
thalidomide).

My first and possibly most difficult task is to show that
there is anything left to discuss once we have agreed not to
discuss the morality of abortion in general. There is a sense in
which abortion for genetic defect is, after abortion to save the
life of the mother, perhaps the most defensible kind of abortion.
Certainly, it is a serious and not a frivolous reason for abortion,

defended by its proponents in sober and rational speech--unlike justifications based upon the false notion that a fetus is a mere part of a woman's body, to be used and abused at her pleasure. Standing behind genetic abortion are serious and well-intentioned people, with reasonable ends in view: the prevention of genetic diseases, the elimination of suffering in families, the preservation of precious financial and medical resources, the protection of our genetic heritage. No profiteers, no sex-ploiters, no racists. No arguments about the connection of abortion with promiscuity and licentiousness, no perjured testimony about the mental health of the mother, no arguments about the seriousness of the population problem. In short, clear objective data, a worthy cause, decent men and women. If abortion, what better reason for it?

Yet if genetic abortion is but a happily wagging tail on the dog of abortion, it is simultaneously the nose of a camel protruding under a rather different tent. Precisely because the quality of the fetus is central to the decision to abort, the practice of genetic abortion has implications which go beyond those raised by abortion in general. What may be at stake here is the belief in the radical moral equality of all human beings, the belief that all human beings possess equally and independent of merit certain fundamental rights, one among which is, of course, the right to life.

To be sure, the belief that fundamental human rights belong equally to all human beings has been but an ideal, never realized, often ignored, sometimes shamelessly. Yet it has been perhaps the most powerful moral idea at work in the world for at least two centuries. It is this idea and ideal that animates most of the current political and social criticism around the globe. It is ironic that we should acquire the power to detect and eliminate the genetically unequal at a time when we have finally succeeded in removing much of the stigma and disgrace previously attached to victims of congenital illness, in providing them with improved care and support, and in preventing, by means of education, feelings of guilt on the part of their parents. One might even wonder whether the development of amniocentesis and prenatal diagnosis may represent a backlash against these same humanitarian and egalitarian tendencies in the practice of medicine, which, by helping to sustain to the age of reproduction persons with genetic disease has itself contributed to the increasing incidence of genetic disease, and with it, to increased pressures for genetic screening, genetic counseling, and genetic abortion.

No doubt our humanitarian and egalitarian principles and practices have caused us some new difficulties, but if we mean to weaken or turn our backs on them, we should do so consciously and thoughtfully. If, as I believe, the idea and practice of genetic abortion points in that direction, we should make ourselves aware of it. And if, as I believe, the way in which genetic abortion is described, discussed, and justified is perhaps of even greater consequence than its practice for our notions of human rights and of their equal possession by all human beings, we should pay special attention to questions of language and in particular, to the question of justification. Before turning full attention to these matters, two points should be clarified.

First, my question "What decision, and why?" is to be distinguished from the question "Who decides, and why?" There is a tendency to blur this distinction and to discuss only the latter, and with it, the underlying question of private freedom versus public good. I will say nothing about this, since I am more interested in exploring what constitutes "good," both public and private. Accordingly, I would emphasize that the moral question--What decision and why?--does not disappear simply because the decision is left in the hands of each pregnant woman. It is the moral question she faces. I would add that the moral health of the community and of each of its members is as likely to be affected by the aggregate of purely private and voluntary decisions on genetic abortion as by a uniform policy imposed by statute. We physicians and scientists especially should refuse to finesse the moral question of genetic abortion and its implications and to take refuge behind the issue, "Who decides?" For it is we who are responsible for choosing to develop the technology of prenatal diagnosis, for informing and promoting this technology among the public, and for the actual counseling of patients.

Second, I wish to distinguish my discussion of what ought to be done from a descriptive account of what in fact is being done, and especially from a consideration of what I myself might do, faced with the difficult decision. I cannot know with certainty what I would think, feel, do, or want done, faced with the knowledge that my wife was carrying a child branded with Down's syndrome or Tay-Sachs disease. But an understanding of the issues is not advanced by personal anecdote or confession. We all know that what we and others actually do is often done out of weakness, rather than conviction. It is all-too-human to make an exception in one's own case (consider, e.g., the extra car, the "extra" child, income tax, the draft, the flight from the cities). For what it is worth, I confess to feeling more than a little sympathy with parents who choose abortions for severe genetic defect. Nevertheless, as I shall indicate later, in seeking for reasons to justify this practice, I can find none that are in themselves fully satisfactory and none that do not simultaneously justify the killing of "defective" infants, children and adults. I am mindful that my arguments will fall far from the middle of the stream, yet I hope that the oarsmen of the flagship will pause and row more slowly, while we all consider whither we are going.

GENETIC ABORTION AND THE LIVING DEFECTIVE

The practice of abortion of the genetically defective will no doubt affect our view of and our behavior toward those abnormals who escape the net of detection and abortion. A child with Down's syndrome or with hemophilia or with muscular dystrophy born at a time when most of his (potential) fellow sufferers were destroyed prenatally is liable to be looked upon by the community as one unfit to be alive, as a second class (or even lower) human type. He may be seen as a person who need not have been, and who would not have been, if only someone had gotten to him in time.

The parents of such children are also likely to treat them differently, especially if the mother would have wished but failed to get an amniocentesis because of ignorance, poverty, or distance from the testing station, or if the prenatal diagnosis was in error. In such cases, parents are especially likely to resent the child. They may be disinclined to give it the kind of care they might have before the advent of amniocentesis and genetic abortion, rationalizing that a second-class specimen is not entitled to first-class treatment. If pressed to do so, say by physicians, the parents might refuse, and the courts may become involved. This has already begun to happen.

In Maryland, parents of a child with Down's syndrome refused permission to have the child operated on for an intestinal obstruc-tion present at birth. The physicians and the hospital sought an injunction to require the parents to allow surgery. The judge ruled in favor of the parents, despite what I understand to be the weight of precedent to the contrary, on the grounds that the child was Mongoloid, that is, had the child been "normal," the decision would have gone the other way. Although the decision was not appealed to and hence not affirmed by a higher court, we can see through the prism of this case the possibility that the new powers of human genetics will strip the blindfold from the lady of justice and will make official the dangerous doctrine that some men are more equal than others.

The abnormal child may also feel resentful. A child with Down's syndrome or Tay-Sachs disease will probably never know or care, but what about a child with hemophilia or with Turner's syndrome? In the past decade, with medical knowledge and power over the prenatal child increasing and with parental authority over the postnatal child decreasing, we have seen the appearance of a new type of legal action, suits for wrongful life. Children have brought suit against their parents (and others) seeking to recover damages for physical and social handicaps inextricably tied to their birth (e.g., congenital deformities, congenital syphilis, illegitimacy). In some of the American cases, the courts have recognized the justice of the child's claim (that he was injured due to parental negligence), although they have so far refused to award damages, due to policy considerations. In other countries, e.g., in Germany, judgments with compensation have gone for the plaintiffs. With the spread of amniocentesis and genetic abortion, we can only expect such cases to increase. And here it will be the soft-hearted rather than the hard-hearted judges who will establish the doctrine of second-class human beings, out of compassion for the mutants who escaped the traps set out for them.

It may be argued that I am dealing with a problem which, even if it is real, will affect very few people. It may be suggested that very few will escape the traps once we have set them properly and widely, once people are informed about amniocentesis, once the power to detect prenatally grows to its full capacity, and once our "superstitious" opposition to abortion dies out or is extirpated. But in order even to come close to this vision of success, amniocentesis will have to become part of every pregnancy--either by making it mandatory, like the test for syphilis, or by making it "routine medical practice," like the Pap smear. Leaving aside the other problems with universal amniocentesis, we could expect that the problem for the few who escape is likely to be even worse precisely because they will be few.

The point, however, should be generalized. How will we come to view and act toward the many "abnormals" that will remain among us--the retarded, the crippled, the senile, the deformed, and the true mutants--once we embark on a program to root out genetic abnormality? For it must be remembered that we shall always have abnormals--some who escape detection or whose disease is undetectable in utero, others as a result of new mutations, birth injuries, accidents, maltreatment, or disease--who will require our care and protection. The existence of "defectives" cannot be fully prevented, not even by totalitarian breeding and weeding programs. Is it not likely that our principle with respect to these people will change from "We try harder" to "Why accept second best?" The idea of "the unwanted because abnormal child" may become a self-fulfilling prophecy, whose consequences may be worse than those of the abnormality itself.

GENETIC AND OTHER DEFECTIVES

The mention of other abnormals points to a second danger of the practice of genetic abortion. Genetic abortion may come to be seen not so much as the prevention of genetic disease, but as the prevention of birth of defective or abnormal children--and, in a way, understandably so. For in the case of what other diseases does preventive medicine consist in the elimination of the patient-at-risk? Moreover, the very language used to discuss genetic disease leads us to the easy but wrong conclusion that the afflicted fetus or person is rather than has a disease. True, one is partly defined by his genotype, but only partly. A person is more than his disease. And yet we slide easily from the language of possession to the language of identity, from "He has hemophilia" to "He is a hemophiliac," from "She has diabetes" through "She is diabetic" to "She is a diabetic," from "The fetus has Down's syndrome" to "The fetus is a Down's." This way of speaking supports the belief that it is defective persons (or potential persons) that are being eliminated, rather than diseases.

If this is so, then it becomes simply accidental that the defect has a genetic cause. Surely, it is only because of the high regard for medicine and science, and for the accuracy of genetic diagnosis, that genotypic defectives are likely to be the first to go. But once the principle, "Defectives should not be born," is established, grounds other than cytological and biochemical may very well be sought. Even ignoring racialists and others equally misguided--of course, they cannot be ignored--we should know that there are social scientists, for example, who believe that one can predict with a high degree of accuracy how a child will turn out from a careful, systematic study of the socio-economic and psycho-dynamic environment into which he is born and in which he grows up. They might press for the prevention of socio-psychological disease, even of "criminality," by means of prenatal environmental diagnosis and abortion. I have heard rumor that a crude, unscientific form of eliminating potential "phenotypic defectives" is already being practiced in some cities, in that submission to abortion is alleg-edly being made a condition for the receipt of welfare payments. "Defectives should not be born" is a principle without limits. We can ill-afford to have it established.

Up to this point, I have been discussing the possible implica-tions of the practice of genetic abortion for our belief in and adherence to the idea that, at least in fundamental human matters such as life and liberty, all men are to be considered as equals, that for these matters we should ignore as irrelevant the real qualitative differences amongst men, however important these differences may be for other purposes. Those who are concerned about abortion fear that the permissible time of eliminating the unwanted will be moved forward along the time continuum, against newborns, infants, and children. Similarly, I suggest that we should be concerned lest the attack on gross genetic inequality in fetuses be advanced along the continuum of quality and into the later stages of life.

I am not engaged in predicting the future; I am not saying that amniocentesis and genetic abortion will lead down the road to Nazi Germany. Rather, I am suggesting that the principles under-lying genetic abortion simultaneously justify many further steps down that road. The point was very well made by Abraham Lincoln (1854):

"If A can prove, however conclusively, that he may, of right, enslave B--Why may not B snatch the same argument and prove equally, that he may enslave A?

"You say A is white, and B is black. It is color, then; the lighter having the right to enslave the darker? Take care. By this rule, you are to be slave to the first man you meet with a fairer skin than your own.

"You do not mean color exactly? You mean the whites are intellectually the superiors of the blacks, and, there-fore have the right to enslave them? Take care again. By this rule, you are to be slave to the first man you meet with an intellect superior to your own.

"But, say you, it is a question of interest; and, if you
can make it your interest, you have the right to enslave
another. Very well. And if he can make it his interest,
he has the right to enslave you."

Perhaps I have exaggerated the dangers; perhaps we will not
abandon our inexplicable preference for generous humanitarianism
over consistency. But we should indeed be cautious and move slowly
as we give serious consideration to the question "What price the
perfect baby? (3).

STANDARDS FOR JUSTIFYING GENETIC ABORTION

The rest of this paper deals with the problem of justification. What would constitute an adequate justification of the
decision to abort a genetically-defective fetus? Let me suggest the
following formal characteristics, each of which still begs many
questions. (1) The reasons given should be logically consistent,
and should lead to relatively unambiguous guidelines--note that I
do not say "rules"--for action in most cases. (2) The justification
should make evident to a reasonable person that the interest or
need or right being served by abortion is sufficient to override
the otherwise presumptive claim on us to protect and preserve the
life of the fetus. (3) Hopefully, the justification would be such
as to help provide intellectual support for drawing distinctions
between acceptable and unacceptable kinds of genetic abortion and
between genetic abortion itself and the further practices we would
all find abhorrent. (4) The justification ought to be capable of
generalization to all persons in identical circumstances. (5) The
justification should not lead to different actions from month to
month or from year to year. (6) The justification should be
grounded on standards that can, both in principle and in fact,
sustain and support our actions in the case of genetic abortion and
our notions of human rights in general.

Though I would ask the reader to consider all these criteria,
I shall focus primarily on the last. According to what standards
can and should we judge a fetus with genetic abnormalities unfit to
live, i.e., abortable? It seems to me that there are at least three
dominant standards to which we are likely to repair.

The first is societal good. The needs and interests of society
are often invoked to justify the practices of prenatal diagnosis
and abortion of the genetically abnormal. The argument, full blown,
runs something like this. Society has an interest in the genetic
fitness of its members. It is foolish for society to squander its
precious resources ministering to and caring for the unfit, especially for those who will never become "productive," or who will
never in any way "benefit" society. Therefore, the interests of
society are best served by the elimination of the genetically
defective prior to their birth.

The societal standard is all-too-often reduced to its lowest common denominator: money. Thus one physician, claiming that he has "made a cost-benefit analysis of Tay-Sachs disease," notes that "the total cost of carrier detection, prenatal diagnosis and termination of at-risk pregnancies for all Jewish individuals in the United States under 30 who will marry is $5,730,281. If the program is set up to screen only one married partner, the cost is $3,122,695. The hospital costs for the 990 cases of Tay-Sachs disease these individuals would produce over a thirty-year period in the United States is $34,650,000 (4). Another physician, apparently less interested or able to make such a precise audit has written: "Cost-benefit analyses have been made for the total prospective detection and monitoring of Tay-Sachs disease, cystic fibrosis (when prenatal detection becomes available for cystic fibrosis) and other disorders, and in most cases, the expenditures for hospitalization and medical care far exceed the cost of prenatal detection in properly selected risk populations, followed by selective abortion." Yet a third physician has calculated that the costs to the state of caring for children with Down's syndrome is more than three times that of detecting and aborting them. (These authors all acknowledge the additional non-societal "costs" of personal suffering, but insofar as they consider society, the costs are purely economic.)

There are many questions that can be raised about this approach. First, there are questions about the accuracy of the calculations. Not all the costs have been reckoned. The aborted defective child will be "replaced" by a "normal" child. In keeping the ledger, the "costs" to society of his care and maintenance cannot be ignored—costs of educating him, or removing his wastes and pollutions, not to mention the "costs" in non-replaceable natural resources that he consumes. Who is a greater drain on society's precious resources, the average inmate of a home for the retarded or the average graduate of Harvard College? I am not sure we know or can even find out. Then there are the costs of training the physician, and genetic counselors, equipping their laboratories, supporting their research, and sending them and us to conferences to worry about what they are doing. An accurate economic analysis seems to me to be impossible, even in principle. And even if it were possible, one could fall back on the words of that ordinary language philosopher, Andy Capp, who, when his wife said that she was getting really worried about the cost of living, replied: "Sweet'eart, name me one person who wants t'stop livin' on account of the cost."

A second defect of the economic analysis is that there are matters of social importance that are not reducible to financial costs, and others that may not be quantifiable at all. How does one quantitate the costs of real and potential social conflict, either between children and parents, or between the community and the "deviants" who refuse amniocentesis and continue to bear abnormal children? Can one measure the effect on racial tensions

of attempting to screen for and prevent the birth of children homozygous (or heterozygous) for sickle cell anemia? What numbers does
one attach to any decreased willingness or ability to take care of
the less fortunate, or to cope with difficult problems? And what
about the "costs" of rising expectations? Will we become increasingly dissatisfied with anything short of the "optimum baby?" How
does one quantify anxiety? humiliation? guilt? Finally, might not
the medical profession pay an unmeasurable price if genetic
abortion and other revolutionary activities bring about changes in
medical ethics and medical practice that lead to the further
erosion of trust in the physician?

An appeal to social worthiness or usefulness is a less vulgar
form of the standard of societal good. It is true that great social
contributions are unlikely to be forthcoming from persons who
suffer from most serious genetic diseases, especially since many of
them die in childhood. Yet consider the following remarks of Pearl
Buck (1968) on the subject of being a mother of a child retarded
from phenylketonuria:

> "My child's life has not been meaningless. She has
> indeed brought comfort and practical help to many people
> who are parents of retarded children or are themselves
> handicapped. True, she has done it through me, yet
> without her I would not have had the means of learning
> how to accept the inevitable sorrow, and how to make that
> acceptance useful to others. Would I be so heartless as
> to say that it has been worthwhile for my child to be
> born retarded? Certainly not, but I am saying that even
> though gravely retarded it has been worthwhile for her to
> have lived.
>
> "It can be summed up, perhaps, by saying that in this
> world, where cruelty prevails in so many aspects of our
> life, I would not add the weight of choice to kill rather
> than to let live. A retarded child, a handicapped
> person, brings its own gift to life, even to the life of
> normal human beings. That gift is comprehended in the
> lessons of patience, understanding, and mercy, lessons
> which we all need to receive and to practice with one
> another, whatever we are."

The standard of potential social worthiness is little better
in deciding about abortion in particular cases than is the standard
of economic cost. To drive the point home, each of us might consider retrospectively whether he would have been willing to stand
trial for his life while a fetus, pleading only his worth to
society as he now can evaluate it. How many of us are not socially
"defective" and with none of the excuses possible for a child with
phenylketonuria? If there is to be human life at all, potential
social worthiness cannot be its entitlement.

Finally, we should take note of the ambiguities in the very notion of societal good. Some use the term "society" to mean their own particular political community, others to mean the whole human race, and still others speak as if they mean both simultaneously, following that all-too-human belief that what is good for me and mine is good for mankind. Who knows what is genetically best for mankind, even with respect to Down's syndrome? I would submit that the genetic heritage of the human species is largely in the care of persons who do not live along the amniocentesis frontier. If we in the industrialized West wish to be really serious about the genetic future of the species, we would concentrate our attack on mutagenesis, and especially on our large contribution to the pool of environmental mutagens.

But even the more narrow use of society is ambiguous. Do we mean our "society" as it is today? Or do we mean our "society" as it ought to be? If the former, our standards will be ephemeral, for ours is a faddish "society." (By far the most worrisome feature of the changing attitudes on abortion is the suddenness with which they changed.) Any such socially determined standards are likely to provide too precarious a foundation for decisions about genetic abortion, let alone for our notions of human rights. If we mean the latter, then we have transcended the societal standard, since the "good society" is not to be found in "society" itself, nor is it likely to be discovered by taking a vote. In sum, societal good as a standard for justifying genetic abortion seems to be unsatisfactory. It is hard to define in general, difficult to apply clearly to particular cases, susceptible to overreaching and abuse (hence, very dangerous), and not sufficient unto itself if considerations of the good community are held to be automatically implied.

A second major alternative is the standard of parental or familial good. Here the argument of justification might run as follows. Parents have a right to determine, according to their own wishes and based upon their own notions of what is good for them, the qualitative as well as the quantitative character of their families. If they believe that the birth of a seriously deformed child will be the cause of great sorrow and suffering to themselves and to their other children and a drain on their time and resources, then they may ethically decide to prevent the birth of such a child, even by abortion.

This argument I would expect to be more attractive to most people than the argument appealing to the good of society. For one thing, we are more likely to trust a person's conception of what is good for him than his notion of what is good for society. Also, the number of persons involved is small, making it seem less impossible to weigh all the relevant factors in determining the good of the family. Most powerfully, one can see and appreciate the possible harm done to healthy children if the parents are obliged to devote most of their energies to caring for the afflicted child.

Yet there are ambiguities and difficulties perhaps as great as with the standard of societal good. In the first place, it is not entirely clear what would be good for the other children. In a strong family, the experience with a suffering and dying child might help the healthy siblings learn to face and cope with adversity. Some have even speculated that the lack of experience with death and serious illness in our affluent young people is an important element in their difficulty in trying to find a way of life and in responding patiently yet steadily to the serious problems of our society (Cassell, 1969). I suspect that one cannot generalize. In some children and in some families, experience with suffering may be strengthening, and in others, disabling. My point here is that the matter is uncertain, and that parents deciding on this basis are as likely as not to be mistaken.

The family or parental standard, like the societal standard, is unavoidably elastic because "suffering" does not come in discontinuous units, and because parental wishes and desires know no limits. Both are utterly subjective, relative, and notoriously subject to change. Some parents claim that they could not tolerate having to raise a child of the undesired sex; I know of one case where the woman in the delivery room, on being informed that her child was a son, told the physician that she did not even wish to see it and that he should get rid of it. We may judge her attitude to be pathological, but even pathological suffering is suffering. Would such suffering justify aborting her normal male fetus?

Or take the converse case of two parents, who for their own very peculiar reasons, wish to have an abnormal child, say a child who will suffer from the same disease as grandfather or a child whose arrested development would preclude the threat of adolescent rebellion and separation. Are these acceptable grounds for the abortion of "normals"?

Granted, such cases will be rare. But they serve to show the dangers inherent in talking about the parental right to determine, according to their wishes, the quality of their children. Indeed, the whole idea of parental rights with respect to children strikes me as problematic. It suggests that children are like property, that they exist for the parents. One need only look around to see some of the results of this notion of parenthood. The language of duties to children would be more in keeping with the heavy responsibility we bear in affirming the continuity of life with life and in trying to transmit what wisdom we have acquired to the next generation. Our children are not our children. Hopefully, reflection on these matters could lead to a greater appreciation of why it is people do and should have children. No better consequence can be hoped for from the advent of amniocentesis and other technologies for controlling human reproduction.

If one speaks of familial good in terms of parental duty, one could argue that parents have an obligation to do what they can to insure that their children are born healthy and sound. But this formulation transcends the limitation of parental wishes and desires.   As in the case of the good society, the idea of "healthy and sound" requires an objective standard, a standard   in   reality. Hard   as   it   may   be   to   uncover   it,   this   is   what   we   are   seeking. Nature as a standard is the third alternative.

The justification according to the natural standard might   run like   this.   As   a result of our knowledge of genetic diseases, we know that persons afflicted with certain   diseases   will   never   be capable   of   living   the full life of a human being.   Just as a no-necked giraffe could never live a giraffe's life, or a   needle-less porcupine   would   not   attain true "porcupine- hood," so a child or fetus with Tay-Sachs disease or Down's syndrome, for example,   will never   be   truly   human.   They will never be able to care for them-selves,   nor   have   they   even   the   potential   for   developing   the distinctively   human   capacities for thought or self-consciousness. Nature herself has aborted many similar cases, and has provided for the early death of many who happen to get born.   There is no reason to keep them alive; instead,   we   should   prevent   their   birth   by contraception   or   sterilization   if   possible,   and   abortion   if necessary.

The advantages of this approach are clear.   The standards   are objective and in the fetus itself, thus avoiding the relativity and ambiguity in societal and parental good. The standard can be easily generalized   to   cover   all such cases and will be resistant to the shifting sands of public opinion.

This standard, I would suggest, is the one which   most   physi-cians and genetic counselors appeal to in their heart of hearts, no matter   what   they say or do about letting the parents choose.   Why else would they have developed   genetic   counseling   and   amniocen-tesis?   Indeed, the notions of disease, of abnormal, of defective, make no sense at all in the absence of a natural   norm   of   health. This   norm is the foundation of the art of the physician and of the inquiry of the health scientist.   Yet, as Motulsky   and   others   in this volume have pointed out, the standard is elusive.   Ironically, we   are   gaining increasing power to manipulate and control our own nature at a time in which we are increasingly confused   about   what is normal, healthy, and fit.

Although possibly acceptable in principle, the   natural   stan-dard   runs   into   problems in application when attempts are made to fix the boundary between   potentially   human   and   potentially   not human.   Professor   Lejeune   (1970)   has   clearly   demonstrated the difficulty, if not the impossibility, of setting   clear   molecular, cytological, or developmental signposts for this boundary. Attempts to   induce   signposts   by   considering   the phenotypes of the worst cases is equally difficult.   Which features would we take to be the most relevant in, say, Tay-Sachs disease, Lesch-Nyhan syndrome, Cri du chat, Down's syndrome?   Certainly,   severe   mental   retardation. But   how   "severe"   is   "severe"?   As Abraham Lincoln and I argued earlier, mental retardation admits of degree.   It too is   relative. Moreover it is not clear that certain other defects and deformities might   not   equally   foreclose   the possibility of a truly or fully

human life.   What   about   blindness   or   deafness?   Quadriplegia?
Aphasia? Several of these in combination? Not only does each kind
of defect admit of a continuous scale of severity, but it also
merges with other defects on a continuous scale of defectiveness.
Where on this scale is the line to be drawn: after mental retardation? blindness? muscular dystrophy? cystic fibrosis? hemophilia?
diabetes? galactosemia? Turner's syndrome? XYY? club foot?   Moreover, the identical two continuous scales--kind and severity--are
found also among the living.   In fact, it is the natural standard
which may be the most dangerous one in that it leads most directly
to the idea that there are second-class human beings and sub-human
human beings.

But the story is not complete. The very idea of nature is
ambiguous.   According to one view, the one I have been using,
nature points to or implies a peak, a perfection.   According to
this view, human rights depend upon attaining the status of human-
ness. The fetus is only potential; it has no rights, according to
this view.   But all kinds of people fall short of the norm:
children, idiots, some adults. This understanding of nature has
been used to justify not only abortion and infanticide, but also
slavery.

There is another notion of nature, less splendid, more humane
and, though less able to sustain a notion of health, more acceptable to the findings of modern science. Animal nature is characterized by impulses of self-preservation and by the capacity to
feel pleasure and to suffer pain. Man and other animals are alike
on this understanding of nature. And the right to life is ascribed
to all such self-preserving and suffering creatures. Yet on this
understanding of nature, the fetus--even a defective fetus--is not
potential, but actual. The right to life belongs to him. But for
this reason, this understanding of nature does not provide and may
even deny what it is we are seeking, namely, a justification for
genetic abortion, adequate unto itself, which does not simultaneously justify infanticide, homicide and enslavement of the genetically abnormal.

There is a third understanding of nature, akin to the second,
nature as sacrosanct, nature as created by a Creator. Indeed, to
speak about this reminds us that there is a fourth possible standard for judgments about genetic abortion: the religious standard.
I shall leave the discussion of this standard to those who are able
to speak of it in better faith.

Now that I am at the end, the reader can better share my sense
of frustration. I have failed to provide myself with a satisfactory intellectual and moral justification for the practice of
genetic abortion. Perhaps others more able than I can supply one.
Perhaps the pragmatists can persuade me that we should abandon the
search for principled justification, that if we just trust people's
situational decisions or their gut reactions, everything will turn
out fine. Maybe they are right. But we should not forget the sage
observation of Bertrand Russell: "Pragmatism is like a warm bath

that heats up so imperceptibly that you don't know when to scream."
I would add that before we submerge ourselves irrevocably in
amniotic fluid, we take note of the connection to our own baths,
into which we have started the hot water running.

NOTES AND REFERENCES

*1. This strikes me as by far the most important inference to be drawn from
the fact that men in different times and cultures have answered the abortion question differently. Seen in this light, the differing and changing
answers themselves suggest that it is a question not easily put under, at
least not for very long.*

*2. Other ways include: one should not do violence to living or growing
things; life is sacred; respect nature; fetal life has value; refrain from
taking innocent life; protect and preserve life. As some have pointed
out, the terms chosen are of different weight, and would require reasons
of different weight to tip the balance in favor of abortion. My choice of
the "rights" terminology is not meant to beg the questions of whether such
rights really exist, or of where they come from. However, the notion of a
"fetal right to life" presents only a little more difficulty in this
regard than does the notion of a "human right to life," since the former
does not depend on a claim that the human fetus is already "human." In my
sense of the terms "right" and "life," we might even say that a dog or a
fetal dog has a "right to life," and that it would be cruel and immoral
for a man to go around performing abortions even on dogs for no good
reason.*

*3. For a discussion of the possible biological rather than moral price of
attempts to prevent the birth of defective children see Neel (1970) and
Motulsky, Fraser, and Felsenstein (1971).*

*4. I assume this calculation ignores the possibilities of inflation,
devaluation, and revolution.*

*Buck, P. S. (1968). Foreward to The Terrible Choice: The Abortion
    Dilemma, New York, Bantam Books, pp. ix-xi.*
*Cassell, E. (1969). Death and the Physician, Commentary, (June) pp.
    73-79.*
Lejeune, J. (1970). American Journal of Human Genetics, 22, 121.
*Lincoln, A. (1854). In The Collected Works of Abraham Lincoln, R. P.
    Basler, editor. New Brunswick, New Jersey, Rutgers University Press,
    Vol. II, p. 222.*
*Motulsky, A. G., G. R. Fraser, and J. Felsenstein (1971). In Symposium on
    Intrauterine Diagnosis, D. Bergsma, editor. Birth Defects: Original
    Article Series, Vol. 7, No. 5.*
*Neel, J. (1972). In Early Diagnosis of Human Genetic Defects: Scientific
    and Ethical Considerations, M. Harris, editor. Washington, D. C.
    U.S. Government Printing Office, pp. 366-380.*

IMPLICATIONS OF PRENATAL DIAGNOSIS FOR THE QUALITY OF, AND RIGHT TO, HUMAN LIFE: SOCIETY AS A STANDARD

Robert S. Morison

My framework will be one, as Dr. Kass has already predicted, of a rather crass pragmatist. I have no expertise such as is represented by the other contributors, but I once had a fairly close association with public health. And since I was given the topic of talking about amniocentesis from the standpoint of the social standard, I have drawn a little bit on my past public health experience.

Actually, I want to ally myself with the very thoughtful presentation of Professor Gustafson and that ethical attitude which relies principally on a careful weighing of the probable practical consequences of a given choice of alternatives.

In doing this, I withdraw in horror from the tendency exhibited, I am sorry to say, not only by Dr. Kass but also by Dr. Callahan and others, to reduce this utilitarian procedure to a cheap matter of dollars, cents, and simple linear equations. It clearly is a much more complicated matter than that and involves judgment of all kinds of values, as Dr. Kass hinted as he went through this. But he would like you to remember that it is really dollars that we use. And I don't believe that is really the case.

I am also relatively unimpressed with the camel's head argument. I don't think that looking at an ethical viewpoint from the standpoint of--"You do this and inevitably this terrible thing is going to happen later on"--is an acceptable way of going about it.

I have noticed, as Dr. Callahan on other occasions has observed, that principles, whatever their logical base, are valid only over a certain limited range; when pushed toward their limit, they tend to conflict with one another or become absurd. Even Oliver Wendell Holmes could not extend the principle of free speech to those who falsely cried "fire" in a crowded theatre. Even the most concerned believers in the sanctity of life do not always equate the life of a four-day-old, yet-to-be-implanted egg with the life of a Mahatma Ghandi.

Again, I follow Dr. Callahan in his view that modern ethical decision-making should be guided by what I think he calls moral policies rather than by principles. As he points out, policies are--and indeed usually should be--developed in relation to principles, but they need not be completely bound by them. Policies do not determine decisions by themselves. There must always be a decision-maker in the background, or a group of decision-makers.

Fortunately, the decision-makers in the abortion case are already in the process of being identified for us, and we need not spend time on this problem. A steadily-increasing proportion of the developed world is deciding that the principal decision-maker should be the woman carrying the fetus--assisted, perhaps, by her physician. This primacy of the prospective mother cannot be based only or even primarily on the feminist assertion of the woman's right to do what she wants with her own body. As many people have pointed out here, the biological evidence is conclusively that a fetus is something quite different from a right hand or even an eye, which even the Bible urges us to extirpate or pluck out if they are offensive. I realize the Bible is equivocal on this point, and one can quote other passages against self-mutilation. The woman in the case, however much she would like to, cannot help participating as a trustee or guardian of the developing human being. The fact that the fetus is so primitive and so helpless, far from justifying a ruthlessly destructive attitude, should be added reason for compassionate concern.

It seems to me, therefore, that society, in its capacity as protector of the weak and moderator of differences between individuals, should not become indifferent to the welfare of the fetus or to the effect that the continuance or discontinuance of its life will have on the fabric of society as a whole.

The recent worldwide move towards liberalizing the abortion laws should not be construed as reflecting the belief that such laws have no constitutional standing. The change in attitude is so sweeping and so recent, especially in this country, that it is difficult to assess all the reasons that have influenced so many different people to change their minds--including me. But it appears that the majority finally concluded that the old rules were simply not working as acceptable policies.

One way of describing what we have done with our recent legislation is to say we have converted a matter of principle into a series of individual problems in situational ethics. This by no means implies, however, that society should relinquish all interest in the question. In place of the previous formal and legal restraints, it must find informal ways of impressing the decision-makers with the gravity of the situation in which they find themselves. And--here again, I think I agree with Kass--pointing out the numerous issues which must be weighed before arriving at a decision.

In reviewing the legislative history of the new arrangements, it appears that principal attention has centered on allowing the mother to base her decision on the effect of another child on her own health, on the welfare of the other children, and on the standard of living of the entire family unit. The particular qualities of the particular fetus to be destroyed were not at issue, in part because they seemed destined to remain unknown.

It may be worthwhile to pause and note that the presumptive unknowness of the individual characteristics of the fetus may have contributed to the lack of concern that some people have felt for the right of the fetus as an individual. As long as it remained in the darkness of the womb, it could be safely dismissed as in limbo, a subhuman entity, a thing rather than a person.

What amniocentesis may have done for us, among other things, is to make it clear that the fetus is an individual with definite, identifiable characteristics. In considering whether or not to abort a fetus because of certain such characteristics we don't happen to like, we recognize her or his individuality in a way we could avoid when we talked simply about the addition of any new member, or an essentially unknown "X," to the family circle.

However much considerations of personal identity will heighten our awareness of what we are doing and increase our sense of what I have called the gravity of the situation--and here I think I really agree in large part with Professor Lejeune, although I don't believe in his final conclusion--I believe these considerations will not keep us from weighing the finding of amniocentesis in the balance when it comes to deciding on particular abortions.

This conference is based on the assumption that we will indeed use such findings, and I understand my task to be to discuss if and how the interests of society as a whole are to be taken into account.

I will, in fact, argue that society does have substantial interest in both the quantity and quality of the children to be born into its midst, and that it is already expressing this interest in numerous ways. These ways provide a precedent and at least partial justification for expressing an interest in the results of amniocentesis and in the way these findings are used in arriving at individual abortion decisions.

I should explain that I am using the word "society" in a flexible and--you may think--ambiguous way. Part of the time I am thinking of society as what the mathematicians refer to as a "set" or collection of individuals with needs, interests, and rights. More often I include with this notion the formal and informal organizations and institutions through which people express, satisfy, and protect their collective interests and rights.

Any suggestion that society may have some sort of stake in the proceedings may be greeted with the prediction that such ideas lead directly and immediately to the worst abuses of Nazi Germany. Let me say at once, then, that in trying to analyze the interest of society in unborn babies, I am not for a moment suggesting that legislation be passed forcing people to have abortions or to be surgically sterilized. If it turns out that society does have defensible interests in the number and condition of the infants to be born, it can express these interests in ways that fall far short of totalitarian compulsion.

It can, for example, facilitate or ban abortion. It can develop or not develop genetic counseling and contraceptive services. It may offer bounties or impose taxes on parents for having or not having children. Purists may object to such procedures as invasions of personal liberty, as perhaps they are, but they are the kind of invasions which all societies find necessary for survival.

No modern society could long endure without making it as easy as possible for parents to send children to school. But expressions of interest in individual education do not stop there. Most societies require that children be sent to school for some years under penalty of the law. In most countries the courts have the right to protect children from physical abuse, to order ordinary medical care in opposition to the parent's wishes, and even to remove them entirely from a family environment that appears to be inadequate.

Such protection and fostering of infants and children by the state can be explained wholly in terms of an obligation to protect the child's right to life, liberty, and the pursuit of happiness. But in point of fact, this is not the only consideration. Society is also protecting its own safety and welfare by ensuring that there will be maximal numbers of people capable of protecting the goods and services and composing the the songs necessary for a good society. Note that "composing songs." It is not purely a matter of dollars and cents. We want people who are able to contribute at every level. At the same time, society is minimizing the number likely to become public charges or public enemies.

Similarly, the provision of maternal and child clinics and the requiring of vaccination against disease can be explained in part as an expression of society's interest in controlling the spread of disease to third parties, and in part by the desire to ensure that each individual citizen be as healthy as possible. Part of this concern is altruistic, but public health officials can also argue that such preventive measures help society avoid the cost of caring for the incapacitated and handicapped later on.

These social concerns about individual health are not limited to persons already born. They extend back to the period of pregnancy and fetal life. Perhaps one of the earliest legal expressions of society's concern for the unborn infant was the dramatic requirement by the ancient Romans that Cesarean section be performed on all women who died while carrying a viable fetus. Less dramatic perhaps, but far more important quantitatively, are our present procedures for encouraging prospective mothers to eat the right foods, have their blood tested for syphilis and Rh antibodies, and even to give up smoking.

This concern for the unborn extends back into time before the new individual is even conceived. Mothers are urged to check their health and to undergo such procedures as vaccination against German measles before becoming pregnant. Vaccination of young women against German measles is now so fully accepted that we may overlook how sophisticated a procedure it really is. It is not proposed as a protection of the woman, herself, against what is usually a scarcely noticeable illness; its purpose is purely and simply that of protecting an unborn, unknown individual against a small but identifiable probability that it may be born with a congenital defect.

Perhaps the foregoing examples are sufficient to establish the following points:

(1) Society has an interest in the welfare of children and fetuses.

(2) This interest is recognized by the general public as legitimate, and various expressions of it have the sanction of tradition and current practice.

(3) In several important cases, the interest is thought to justify not only the use of educational persuasion, but even the force of law to control or shape the behavior of mothers and prospective mothers.

It is highly probable that different people have different reasons for supporting these policies, and of course there is a minority which has reasons for opposing them. Some will talk of the right of the infant to be born healthy as a part of a more general right to health, which some enthusiasts regard as having been established by the World Health Organization shortly after the close of World War II. Other more utilitarian types will simply point out that the results for both mother and child are usually "better"--and that the cost to society is less.

Still others will maintain that the Christian commandment to love everyone requires society to analyze all the angles in each particular case and that, by and large, love will be maximized if society takes an intelligent interest in the welfare of infants and fetuses.

The important thing to note is not the variety of reasons, but the general agreement on the conclusions. In a pluralistic society one must never lose sight of the fact that it is much more important that people agree on a policy rather than that they agree on the reasons for agreeing.

We must now move from this all too brief discussion of how society is currently expressing its interest in the yet-unborn, to how we can build on this experience to formulate policies to guide mothers and their counselors in adding the facts revealed by amniocentesis to all the other matters in their minds and hearts as they decide whether to continue or interrupt a pregnancy.

In the first place, I will assume that a prospective mother has a right to consider the specific characteristics of a specific fetus as she weighs the probable results of carrying a given pregnancy to term. If so, it follows that a society like ours has an obligation to provide, either through public or private means, facilities for amniocentesis in the same way as it customarily provides diagnostic facilities in other areas of medicine and public health.

So far, everything seems to be in accord with normal public health practice. But as we look a little further we encounter perplexities. The major difficulty is that the facts revealed by amniocentesis do not tell us what to do as clearly as many other laboratory tests do.

When a laboratory test reveals the presence of a streptococcus or a treponema, there is not much doubt in anyone's mind that the thing to do is to get rid of it.

When amniocentesis reveals an hereditary or a congenital defect, the situation is rather different. In the first place, the object to be got rid of is not a bacterium but an incipient human being. In the second place, it is not always immediately clear what the results will be if the defective fetus is allowed to go to term. Who is to say whether a child with Downs' syndrome is more or less happy than the child with an IQ of 150 who spends the first 16 years of his life competing with his peers for admission to an ivy league college? Who is to assess the complex effects on parents of coping with a handicapped child?

Most troublesome is the recognition that the interest of the individuals directly concerned may be more often at variance with those of society than is the case in most public health procedures. For example, most public health officials have little difficulty in urging or even requiring people to be vaccinated, since the risk is very small and the benefits appear to accrue more or less equally to society and to the individual concerned.

The interests of parents and the interests of society in the birth of children, however, may often be quite at odds with one another. In some rapidly growing societies, for example, the birth of additional children of any description may be looked upon with dismay by society as a whole, however much the new citizens may be welcomed by their parents. In societies where the over-all rate of growth is under better control, society may properly still have an interest in maximizing the proportion of new members who can at least take care of themselves, and if possible return some net benefit. Some parents, however, may long for any child to love and to cherish. They may regard any talk of social costs and benefits as shockingly utilitarian.

Even more difficult situations could arise when the prospective child may, himself, be quite normal, a joy to his parents, and a net asset to society—except for the fact that he is a heterozygous carrier of a serious defect who would, as a matter of fact, not have been started at all had the way not been made clear for him by aborting one or more homozygous siblings.

The more one thinks of these problems in abstract, philosophical terms, the more appalled he becomes, and this is one of the reasons for meetings like this. I am beginning to suspect, however, that the situation will turn out to be less serious in practice than it is in theory.

In the first place, it seems highly improbable that the wishes of parents and the interests of society will really be at odds in cases of severe defects like Downs' syndrome or Tay-Sach's disease. In other words, if the parents' views are such that abortion is an acceptable option on general grounds, they are likely to exercise it for their own reasons in the kinds of cases in which carrying the fetus to term would also be most costly and least beneficial to society. In cases where the option is unacceptable to the individual for religious or similar reasons, society, under existing and generally agreed upon policies, has no business interfering anyway.

At the other end of the spectrum, relatively mild defects which may alter only slightly the subject's chances of becoming a useful citizen, like six fingers, may be safely left to the parents to decide without comment from outside since the social costs of either outcome are likely to be negligible. There may be a number of areas where the net cost to society may be appreciable but hard to quantify and where family attitudes may be quite variable. It would seem unwise to emphasize the possible conflicts between individuals and society in these gray areas until we know a lot more about them.

Particularly troublesome, of course, are those genetic conditions in which the homozygotes suffer a severe disorder while the heterozygotes show little or no deficit. There may come a day when the question of what to do about such heterozygous fetuses may indeed involve ethical problems between the long-run interest of society in its gene pool and the short-run interest of the individual in family life. At present, however, the technical difficulties of identifying heterozygotes in many conditions and especially of evaluating the possibly unusual "fitness" of the latter may excuse us from taking any firm position which might breathe life into a latent conflict between individuals and society.

To point out that the number of potential conflicts is probably not so large as some people have feared is not to say that there is no problem. But the realization may be of some comfort to prudent men as they start to formulate policies.

It is also true that the above analysis depends very largely on the assumption that the general public knows as much about the disorders in question as the representatives of society do and that decisions will be arrived at more or less autonomously. This, of course, is not the case, and we are thus brought to the heart of the problem that worries many moralists and men of good will.

In most instances the facts revealed by amniocentesis must be interpreted to the prospective parents. In advanced countries these interpretative services are likely to be at least partially supported by society. How are we--and perhaps equally important, how is the counselor--to be sure that he is providing the interpretation in the best interests of the patient? Alternatively, how far is he justified in presenting the interests of society, especially if these may appear from some angles to be in conflict with those of the parents? These are indeed difficult questions. But I am not persuaded that they are so difficult as some people think they are.

Some commentators appear to feel that society is making an unjustifiable invasion of personal liberties if it undertakes to persuade an individual to make any decision in the reproductive sphere other than that suggested by his uninstructed instincts. The criticism is particularly severe if the proposed learning experience is coupled with rewards and penalties. It is hard to understand this squeamishness, since societies have been rewarding people from time immemorial for doing things which benefited society and even more enthusiastically penalized its citizens for actions against the public interest.

Even without this background, it is hard to see how offering a man a transistor radio if he refrains from having a child is interfering with his personal freedom. Indeed, one would ordinarily suppose that by increasing the number of options open to him, we increase rather than restrict his freedom. Furthermore, transistor radios may be looked upon primarily as educational devices, a way of making real to a not very sophisticated mind that children impose costs on society--and that society can in turn use its resources to benefit existing individuals if they cooperate in reducing the potential competition.

Again, this increase in understanding should be considered liberating rather than confining.

If society has a definable and legitimate interest in the number of children to be born, then it is clear that it also may have an interest in their quality. This is especially true in a period of sharply reduced birth and death rates. In an earlier day when both were high, normal attrition worked differentially to eliminate the unfit. A much smaller proportion of society's resources was devoted to keeping the unfit alive. Now, when a defective child may cost the society many thousands of dollars a year for a whole lifetime without returning any benefit, it would appear inevitable that society should do what it reasonably can to assure that those children who are born can lead normal and reasonably independent lives. It goes without saying that if the model couple is to be restricted to 2.1 children, it is also more important to them that all their children be normal than it was when an abnormal child was, in effect, diluted by a large number of normal siblings. And the over-all point here again is that the interests of society and the interests of the family become coincident at this stage, when they both realize that there are a limited number of slots to be filled.

That is really the situation that we are approaching in many countries. There is a limited number of slots that human beings can occupy, and there do seem to be both social and family reasons to see that those increasingly rare slots are occupied by people with the greatest possible potential for themselves and for others.

What then can society reasonably do to work with potential parents to insure as high quality a product as possible? It certainly can encourage and support the development of research in genetics and the physiology of fetal life. It can certainly support, in the same way, work on the technique of amniocentesis. It can make abortion available under appropriate auspices and regulations. Many societies are doing some or all of these things right now.

Our problem, if there is one, centers on what society can and should do in helping the individual mother to use the available information not only in her own best interests, but also in those of the society of which she is a part. And the whole assumption here is that we are not going to require any behavior. We seem to be working toward a position which gives to the mother's physician or genetic counselor the greatest possible influence. Sometimes the two functions may be discharged by the same individual. In either case, the relationship is a professional one, with the individuals giving the advice owing primary responsibility to their patient or client. I think all of us with medical training feel our first obligation in any such situation is to the patient before us.

Just what the amniocentesis counselor will say to a given client is likely to remain a professional matter, biased in favor of the client when her interests and those of society conflict. On the other hand, there seems no good reason to discourage the advisor from pointing out to the client what the interests of society are. Indeed, there seem to be several good reasons for encouraging him to do so.

In the first place it seems proper, even if it is not always precisely true, to assume that the client wishes to be a good citizen as well as a good parent. Thus, it is in some sense an insult to her intelligence and good will to withhold information about social repercussions on the grounds that such advice might curtail her Anglo-Saxon freedom to act ignorantly in her own selfish interest.

It may also be remembered that every professional man is an officer of society--although I realize not everybody agrees with this--as well as an individual counselor. True, most lawyers, clergymen and physicians like to think of themselves as owing a paramount obligation to their patients, clients, and parishioners. But the clergyman has at least a nominal interest in the diety, the lawyer in justice, and the physician in the health of the community.

Fortunately, in medicine at least, the welfare of the patient usually coincides reasonably closely with the welfare of society. But there are well-known cases of conflicts in which the physician is supposed to act in the best interest of society even at some cost to his patients, and sometimes he does.

Thus, the conscientious physician reports his cases of venereal infection and T.B. in order to protect society, even at the risk of embarrassment and inconvenience to his patient. In a

similar vein he urges his epileptic patients and those with seriously defective vision not to drive automobiles. These and other
examples provide ample precedent for injecting the interests of
society into a counseling situation.

I hope it is obvious that when he does so, the counselor will
wish to make clear exactly what he is doing and why. It would of
course be totally inadmissible for a professional counselor of any
kind to deceive his patient or client, in order to gain what he
thinks of as a socially desirable end.

We have heard of cases where it may be necessary to deceive a
patient for his own good (or what is thought to be his own good),
but I don't think any of us would countenance deceiving a patient
for society's good.

On the other hand, it would be almost equally reprehensible to
conceal the long-term effects on the gene pool of substituting a
heterozygous carrier for a homozygote of limited life expectancy,
or to fail to mention social dislocations which might follow from a
decision to use abortion as a method of sex determination.

In summary, the position I have described is a simple and
straightforward one. Many people are likely to feel it is too
simple. It is based on the fact that society has placed or is in
the process of placing the burden of decision as to whether or not
to have an abortion in the hands of the woman carrying the fetus.

It accepts the proposition that in arriving at that decision,
she will be allowed to add to a number of already stated
considerations, evidence on the probable characteristics of the
child.

It does not accept the inference that society no longer has
interest in the matter simply because it has released the formal
decision-making power.

It suggests that the best way of expressing its interest is
through the counselor-physician, who in effect has a dual
responsibility to the individual whom he serves and to the society
of which he and she are parts.

Finally, it holds out the hope that instances in which the
interests of the individual woman are clearly seen to conflict with
the interests of society will be less numerous than might be
feared.

In review, I find that I must add one point. Just as I
believe there are no simple principles which take precedence over
all others, I believe that everything one does affects everything
else. We are now all so interdependent that there are no such
things as purely private acts.

There is a danger that the present effort to make abortion a
crime without a victim will obscure the seriousness of all such
decisions.

As Dr. Kass has pointed out, we will all certainly be
diminished as human beings, if not in great moral peril, if we
allow ourselves to accept abortion for what are essentially trivial
reasons. On the other hand we will, I fear, be in equal danger if

we don't accept abortion as one means of ensuring that both the quantity and quality of the human race are kept within reasonable limits.

DISCUSSION

FRIED: Dr. Kass is clearly ambivalent on the subject. I take his statement that he is ambivalent at face value, and that he finds it agonizing; that is how I feel about it. I think, in part, his very strong statement is a cry for help at some kind of resolution.

Let me suggest something that came to mind as I tried to put together what I heard in the course of this session and particularly what I heard from Dr. Kaback and Dr. Murray.

Take the case of the woman who discovers she is pregnant with a Tay-Sachs or a Down's fetus. She is by no means saying, "This infant does not have a right to live, is worse than me, is inferior," or anything of that sort. But rather the mother is saying, "This involves a pain I cannot bear."

Obviously, this is how the doctors view the matter. Dr. Murray's perspective is clearly not eugenic. He is responding to that claim of the mother that, really, bearing this child involves a pain she cannot bear. She is not judging that child and not involving herself in the kind of judgments that you were concerned with. She is saying, "Look, this child has a right to live, is as good as anybody else, is as deserving of love. But the sorrow this child will bring into the world will fall on me. It will not really be shared by anybody else."

Now, if that is the case, let me invite your attention, then, to a parable. It is the invention of Professor Judith Thompson of MIT, and it is relevant to this view of the claim.

Imagine that you wake up one morning to find that strapped to your back is a fully-grown concert violinist who is plugged in to all your vital organs, and you are told that, "Yes, it is true, he is plugged into you. If he is unplugged, he will die. But don't worry, it will only be for nine months, and after that time he will be on his own."

Surely the question will arise--"But why me? True, going around with this person strapped to me for nine months is as nothing compared to his death, which is what would ensue if he were unplugged, but why me?"

And I think that really is the claim, perhaps, of the mother. She is not saying that this death is an inconsequential event, but-- "Why am I the one who must bear all this pain and sorrow unaided?"

HIMSWORTH: Are you trying to raise the question of whether the mother has the right to say she will not have a defective fetus?

FRIED: I am trying to do more than that. I am trying to suggest that in making that claim, the mother (and in responding to it, the doctor) may be making a judgment which is not to the effect that this individual is less worthy, less human, substandard, or anything of the sort.

KASS: Though I indicated my concern over the elastic, relativistic, and limitless character of suffering, I would hope with Dr. Fried that, if such decisions are to be made, they would be discussed and justified in the terms he suggests. I have been both moved and impressed at this meeting by the understanding and compassionate way in which the people who practice counseling have talked about their patients and their work. I have seen very much evidence of the kind of sensitivity that Dr. Fried mentioned.

On the other hand, the concern about labeling and inequality is not necessarily dispelled even if the decision is discussed and justified in the way Dr. Fried suggests. If one were to ask--"Why would this child have caused you so much suffering?"--the answer would have to return to the "defectiveness" of the child, and hence to a consideration of normal and subnormal.

The problem comes up not only in the matter of abortion, but also with screening. That is, if the medical profession says, "There are certain kinds of disease for which we will provide fetal screening." it is in effect saying, "These are the conditions which we think make a fetus abortable." The problem of the implications for those who have these conditions and who make it through the screen, remains.

FRIED: I'd like to respond to that briefly. You say that you learned something from listening to Drs. Kaback and Murray, and you heard much the same that I did. Why not see in the screening an anticipatory version of that same care, instead of seeing it as a eugenic judgment? I really have not seen that in evidence.

KASS: I agree that we have here little or no talk about eugenics. But my point has nothing to do with intention. A prenatal screening program, undertaken and practiced because of a compassionate regard for the women, might have exactly the same discriminatory consequences for the offspring as if its intent were eugenic.

STETTEN: I would like to add to Dr. Fried's point. We have heard repeatedly that the fetus is a human or prospective human. The fetus is also something else, and it might simplify our thinking if we recognize what else it is.

It is a tumor. It is a tumor whose etiology we know a good deal about. We know the causative agent to be a protozoan flagellate. We know the route of infection to be venereal. Pregnancy is, if you please, a venereal disease. It is a tumor which often normally is self-terminating. However, it is not always self-terminating, and it can, as we all know, undergo frank malignant degeneration to a condition which will kill the mother. Fortunately, this happens very rarely.

However, there is another kind of malignancy and this is the malignancy which was brought home to me by Dr. Kaback with his story of a child with Tay-Sachs disease. Malignancy does not to me necessarily mean invasion or metastases. It does necessarily mean misery. And that was a miserably unhappy mother.

I suggest that when a tumor causes misery, the mother, with the advice of her physician, has every right in the world to eliminate it. And the process of elimination is a familiar one. It is a good, well-established, scientific one, and it starts with a biopsy which we call amniocentesis. The real reason we do an amniocentesis is not to fortify our justification for an abortion, any more than the real reason we do a biopsy on a lump in the breast is to justify a radical mastectomy. On the contrary, the purpose of the biopsy is to find out what breasts do not have to be removed. The purpose of the amniocentesis that Dr. Kaback and his associates perform is to establish the appropriateness of not doing an abortion.

It seems to me that viewed in this light, there is very little doubt that a proper procedure in the presence of high risk, as in the situation with Tay-Sachs heterozygote parents, is that described by Dr. Kaback.

LEJEUNE: There was a debate on the French television about amniocentesis, and I was in that debate. There were people arguing that when an extra chromosome was found in the amniotic fluid, the child should be removed--that we had to change the law in France.

I received a letter two days later from the mother of one of my patients. The patient is a 16-year-old trisomic. She has an IQ of 40. And she was watching the television with her mother because she knew I was on TV and she wanted to see me. When she heard what was said, she suddenly said, "What is this imbecile man saying? He is going to kill the Mongol?"

With the letter from the mother telling this, I received a very badly written letter from the girl, and the letter said in those bad letters that she could draw, "I like you because you love the Mongol."

I think it is relevant to compare these facts with the idea of removing a tumor after a biopsy.

AIKEN: Something I said this afternoon may have some bearing upon this discussion. Genetic matters affecting abortion were discussed in a context of either the right to life or something else called "the interest of society," whatever that might be.

It seems to me that abortion ought not to be considered from the standpoint only of the quality of the individual who might result if the abortion were not performed. But one must consider, it seems to me, the question of abortion generally, with a view of the "right to live" within a wider context, which I called the right of a human being, the right to human being.

Now, I thoroughly agree with Dr. Kass that there is a problem of justification here. But I suggest that if you follow my line you might be able not only to bring into better focus the particular forms of abortion that were being discussed here, but the wider problem of abortion where there is no presumption of genetic defect at all.

I want to invite your consideration of the idea that life is a part of human being or a condition of it, but that it is not in itself human being. That is, it isn't synonomous with it. Any deep and reflective discussion of this topic ought to focus upon this. The task of justifying or not justifying abortions of one sort or another ought to be made in the light of these larger considerations.

There are, of course, no rights where there are no practices. But if you have a society that has nothing but ad hoc policies without any practices, and where there are no responsibilities that are derived from these practices, it seems to me you have a society which, however well intentioned in a pragmatic or utilitarian sense, will do profound and continuing injustice to its citizens. This is not simply because in such a society you don't know what to count on, but because the whole notion of human dignity tends to go down the drain. I think you have to talk about the rights pertaining to the idea of a human being.

I also want to suggest that our task here is not one of finding out what is the good of society. Our task instead is essentially one of distributive justice.

CONDLIFFE: As I look at the panel before me, I am struck again by the lack of women on our program committees and the paucity of women at this conference and at similar meetings where human reproduction, abortion and related issues are discussed.

Here we are discussing abortion without a single woman on the panel. I have noticed that it happens all the time. Men discuss abortion. Most professors of obstetrics in the United States are men, with only one or two exceptions. There are over a hundred medical schools in the United States. It is incumbent upon those of us who are men to remember this. I have tried to remember it in this meeting but without too much success.

While women are perhaps not the only actors on the stage when it comes to abortion, they nevertheless have the star role. The leading man is the physician and the supporting actors are the family, the lawyers, sometimes the police, and the members of the courts. But it is the woman who stars. Those of us who are in the majority in the intellectual professions ought to remember this point.

That is all I have to say. I couldn't help being struck by the row of distinguished gentlemen before me this evening.

CAPRON: My question to Dr. Kass is: If, as I take you to be saying, you do not propose an absolute right to life on the part of the fetus, at least in practical terms, would you favor what would amount to a random selection, the same as a random selection in other situations? That is to say, that mothers can abort but only if they have no reason other than their own suffering? In other words, if they give no explanation of their suffering and do not say this child is unwanted for reasons that he is unwanted. That is an extension, I think, of Dr. Fried's borrowed example.

KASS: Yes.

SINGER: Not only are we sorely lacking in women participants in this discussion, but we have simply not heard from or plugged into this discussion that portion of the population that is immediately affected and will be in the position to make the choices we are opening or foreclosing to them.

GRIFFO: We have repetitively discussed the rights of the individual, the rights of society, and the mother-child-doctor relationship with regard to who should make the decision about abortion of a potentially defective child. We have frequently heard the view that it might be solely the mother's "privilege" to sit in judgment over her future offspring's "to be or not to be." One person shockingly conspicuous by his absence from all these discussions is the father. It required a father and a mother to create life. Therefore, a so-called mother-child-doctor relationship is rather inconsequential, and a mother-child relationship incomplete. Only a family, where a family exists, is responsible for the future welfare of its offspring. Husband and wife should therefore jointly share the grave responsibility to terminate an undesirable child's life.

HOTCHKISS: There has been a lot said about "probable bad consequences" of action, and argument that abortions should not be performed. Actually there exists another very real "consequence of inaction," and that is human suffering. First, there is the suffering of the child doomed to be inadequate to the human activities around him; second, there is the suffering of the mother and father, looking upon the kind of "life" their child is subject to.

This is very different from the amusing parable of a person having to live for nine months with the violinist fastened to his back. To be sure every mother goes through those difficult months, but with the optimistic belief that it will finally be over and a normal baby will be born. The tragedy starts when at the end of that time, it is discovered that a new, indefinitely prolonged period of profound dependence and misery is to begin.

Even graver is the situation when a potential mother does know in advance that her child is not going to become a fully expressed human being. It won't be able to become conscious of itself, communicate its feelings, respond to outside stimulus. In that particular case, I don't see the purpose of this future suffering. Should we really claim that suffering is "ennobling life" and therefore should be obligatory? Should we add suffering knowingly to our lives, as if there were not enough of it already? I don't see the logic of it.

Let me put it this way: Would we give up or stop developing preventive medicine because the danger "could" arise that actually sick people would therefore not be taken care of in the hospitals? Everybody seems to favor preventive medicine, with the implicit understanding that if a person actually does get sick, we and society fully intend to take care of him or her in the hospital.

It isn't clear why one thing should exclude the other: why an abortion of a responsibly diagnosed defective embryo should lead to the neglect of human beings already born and suffering--either in hospitals or at home. I think both exist in our life--abortion and humane care. We should take them as facts of life, and not go into what seems abstract and fruitless reappraisal of already accepted and tested "ifs" and "hows" and "whys" and "probable consequences." In my opinion these have become empty concepts and abstract words. Meanwhile, human beings are suffering--children and parents. Why should they be penalized? Why should children knowingly be allowed to enter upon a vegetative existence for a shorter or longer time, and die a slow death? Why be brave--or weak, maybe--and admit: "I cannot face this suffering; I will prevent it if I can; I choose abortion as the lesser sacrifice."

MACINTYRE: Following this same point, Dr. Kass emphasized his concern about our potential lack of ability or lack of desire to have compassion for the defective child already born. Philosophically the point is an interesting one, but I agree with Madame Hotchkiss that it is not likely to emerge as a problem. Furthermore, if we feel that such a danger exists, the proper preventive measure would be through public education rather than by ceasing our efforts to minimize the number of defective children.

Along the same line of thought, I take issue with my good friend Jerome Lejeune. I too have letters from mongoloid children whom I love with compassion, and who react to me with love. The fact that a mentally defective child, once born, can develop a personality to which we can reach with warmth and compassion is not, I suggest, the point at issue. The point is that we are able to give a choice to a family in which there is already a defective child; a child whom they may love in their way and by whom they may have been destroyed in certain ways. If the question is asked, "Would you, if given the choice, choose to have another defective child?"--I don't believe in criticizing a family for answering, "No!" At the same time, I would not fail to consider the already-born, tragically retarded child with warmth and compassion. I don't believe that these two attitudes are incompatible. I think it is immoral to neglect the retarded child, and I think it is immoral to force a family to have one.

CROW: My topic is a little different from the rest. I am bothered by the fact that eugenics has become a dirty word. Everybody says it is all right to do this or that because there is no eugenic motive involved. A concern for the future is highly ethical. In my discussion yesterday, I went through some calculations and decided that some of these procedures were quite wise things to do this generation because they were not going to have a large impact on the next generation. My conclusion would have been quite different had the calculations been quite different.

I am an ardent conservationist. I am concerned with the future. I am quite willing to put severe restrictions on this generation in order to have a better environment next generation. I am quite willing to put restrictions on individual freedoms this generation in order to have a lower mutation rate for the benefit of our posterity. Perhaps we should consider other ways in which the gene pool is influenced.

I want eugenics to be a good word rather than a bad word; or if the word is bad, find another word that means the same thing and start thinking about it.

HOTCHKISS: We are accustomed to saying that our world has been changed so rapidly by technology and acculturation that our biological evolution cannot keep up with it. There is one way in which our biologic evolution may have had a great deal to do with what we are trying to formulate here today.

I should take it to be essentially clear and probable that one of the survival traits most built into us, almost incontrovertibly built into us, is the care of our young; that is, the tendency to look upon a small embodiment of our species as something precious, deserving sentiment, care and attention, both from the mothers and the fathers.

This may of course also be embellished with a cultural overlay of self-identification, self-preservation and so on. We seem to be struggling very hard now in our cultural evolution to overcome some of these built-in imprints, which make it very hard for us to accept the things that our biological and social sciences are beginning to tell us: that some survival factors which have enormous value in a primitive world may actually be working against our civilization. We may, therefore, sometimes find it necessary to resolve against these "instincts" as we have had to do against other "self-evident" instincts (such as shrinking from the pain of surgery or dental work, for example) wherever they are no longer truly self-evident, but seem to act against our best interests.

LUDMERER: I would like to comment on the point Dr. Kass made as the main message of his talk. It seems to me that we can pursue our efforts to treat or prevent genetic diseases without making those afflicted with such conditions feel guilty or stigmatized.

This is certainly true in the case of infectious diseases. The stigma once attached to having syphilis or venereal disease has vanished, despite our continuing efforts to eliminate these conditions. And it seems to me the same will be true of genetic diseases. The fact that we screen to try to prevent them does not mean that there will be a stigma attached to those who nevertheless are born genetically defective.

KASS: I did not mean to suggest that I thought anyone present, or the medical profession at large, would do anything other than give the best medical treatment to the abnormals who continue to be born. My concern over stigmatization and over a decreased willingness to care pertains to the wider general public. It has to do with a society which recognizes that certain kinds of individuals are largely being aborted as unfit to live. I am not predicting the future, nor am I insisting that there is a necessary connection between this practice and an erosion of public compassion. However, there is at least a logical connection, and the erosion is a real possibility. For the moment, I am content to have this possibility in mind, to be guarded against and grappled with if it begins to occur.

LUDMERER: The question here illustrates one of the difficulties when we discuss some of the ethical aspects of scientific problems: namely, that in certain instances we have a great gap between principle and fact, between theory and practice. So far as I know, there is absolutely no indication at present that there is going to be any stigma to a person suffering from a genetic disease any more than an increased stigma to sufferers from syphilis today.

Another question in which there could be a great theoretical problem but which in fact does not seem to be a problem is the motive of genetic counselors today. Similarly, in theory there are great ethical problems when you consider positive eugenics, certainly many more problems than there are when you discuss negative eugenics. Yet in practice, positive eugenics is not much of a problem, because when you look at Victor McKusick's list, about 800 traits are now known to follow Mendelian patterns of inheritance in man, and there are another thousand or so in which the possibility is likely. Almost all of these are diseases. Very few, if any, positive traits follow simple Mendelian patterns of inheritance and it makes the question of breeding for positive eugenics an issue. Here we have something which is not an issue which theoretically could be very, very touchy.

WEISIGER: Since the consumers of our sperms are essentially not represented, I think we need two kinds of statistical information. First, we should ask the mothers of mongoloid children if they would have preferred to have a normal child if they could have chosen to. Secondly, we should ask those people who do suffer from hereditary diseases but are mentally normal, whether they would prefer if a normal child would have been born instead of them. I think the answers would be very illuminating.

LITTLEFIELD: Dr. Kass, when you related the case of parents who didn't want surgery done on their Mongoloid infant, you seemed to feel that of course it should be done. This is a not uncommon problem in pediatrics which has no absolute answer. In a recent discussion about a Mongoloid infant with a cardiac defect, I heard a house officer insist the infant must have his heart fixed, while a clinical fellow from India felt we were quite foolish to give so much attention to an infant with limited potential.

You put it in absolute terms which I think unfair, and perhaps you would clarify your point of view.

KASS: No, what ought to be done there is a difficult question, and I don't have a firm conclusion (although the case mentioned involved not cardiac surgery but correction of duodenal atresia at birth). But the point I was making was not whether or not the surgery ought to have been done. Rather, I was commenting on what is the insidious character of the judge's opinion. He could have said, "Look that infant is dying anyhow. Why prolong his dying?" The case could have been considered as a case of death with dignity. But, instead, what he said was, "The reason you are not forced to operate is because the child is a Mongol." And that has very different implications.

MORISON: I have been trying to think how I could possibly reply to Professor Aiken's question in relation to rights. I prefer not to talk about rights because they are something I don't know very much about, and I left them out of my talk on purpose because of this.

But from what little reading and thinking I have been able to do, I have found two sorts of difficulties with the concept of rights. The first one is that I just don't know what the philosophical base really is. Rights are not self-evident to me the way they presumably were to Franklin. Actually, I think that Franklin, being the pragmatist he was, put the statement about "self-evident" in the Declaration for pragmatic reasons. He knew perfectly well there was no other way to determine their existence.

AIKEN: He was a rhetorician.

MORISON: That is right. Rights are not self-evident to me, and I doubt if they really were to him. I do not believe in something being revealed by some higher power, so I am handicapped in that respect also. I have tried to follow the natural law arguments as set forth by Aristotle, Aquinas and others, but the arguments are not convincing.

If I look at another side of the matter, the practical, empirical question of the use of rights in ordering society, I run into another type of difficulty. Perhaps I have over-interpreted Dr. Callahan, but if I recall his book correctly, he found it very difficult to resolve the abortion issue either on the right of the mother to do what she wants to do with her body or, conversely, on the absolute right of the fetus to exist as a human being. He thus came up with a policy that placed the decision in the hands of the mother but surrounded her with a great deal of information, advice and feelings about the sanctity of life so that she would make a decision that would best fit the circumstances.

What seems to me important in the world is to make decisions to do something. It turns out that it is usually possible to get a group to decide to do a particular thing, even though, as I said in the paper, each may have a different reason for doing it.

As a practical decision-maker, it seems to me far more important to formulate a policy that people can agree on than to try to reach agreement on why they agree.

Dr. Kass and I, for example, would agree much oftener on what to do about a particular patient than we would agree on our reasons for doing it. When the chips are down, Dr. Kass is not going to oppose doing an amniocentesis on a person with a high risk for Tay-Sachs disease. He is going to feel uncomfortable about it; I am going to feel uncomfortable about it, but we are both going to do it. That's what is important to the patient and to society, and neither of them is going to be particularly interested in following the mixture of logic and feeling which brought us to the decision.

LEGAL RIGHTS AND MORAL RIGHTS

Alex M. Capron

The relationship of a genetic counselor and his patients is a delicate, complex and important one. Treating as it does subjects of great moment--the prevention of crippling diseases, even life and death themselves--it commands growing public interest and scrutiny, especially as the counselor's predictive skills increase. It involves not only parents but geneticists, physicians, ministers and others, in more lengthy and careful contemplation of the conception and birth of a child than occurs in any other type of "planned parenthood." Its highly charged subject matter and deeply involved participants open it to the internal and external pressures which encumber all significant decisions. Yet when we look at the moral and legal rights of the participants in genetic counseling, the picture before us begins to grow less distinct, and we inevitably see only the sharp features, outlined in black and white and not the interesting shadings of gray.

While this difficulty is inherent in any attempt to state general rules about complicated and varied relationships, it will be particularly pronounced in what follows. There are any number of rights which could be asserted on behalf of those who play a role in the relationship--genetic counselor, parents, unborn child, other family members, and even professional and public institutions. But I have chosen, not too arbitrarily I hope you will agree, to focus on the two sets of immediate participants, counselors and parents, and on only the one right which I believe ought to be of central concern to us.

Before we get to that right, perhaps we should pause to ask: What do we mean when we say a person has a right? The term "right" is customarily used when a person has a claim on the way another person or group behaves, especially toward himself. The concept is often defined by its reciprocal: to say that A has a right is to say that B has a duty to do, or abstain from doing, something at A's prompting. Sometimes "right" and "privilege" are used interchangeably, but "right" is by far the stronger term, suggesting that B's duty is not subject to recall without A's approval. If A has a "legal right," he can compel B to perform his duty by calling on the organized power of the state; if his right is a "moral" one, he has to rely on B's conscience (abetted perhaps by persons or groups possessing "moral authority") to compel B to fulfill his duty.

It is perhaps only a reflection of my lawyerly literalness, but I find the term "moral right" to be something of an anomaly. While we speak easily of a "moral duty," the legal unenforceability of that duty makes strained any reference to a corresponding "right." In this sense of the word, we usually say a person has a "moral right" precisely when we believe that he ought to be able to compel another's behavior (or whatever) but legally cannot. You may, for example, have no legal right to collect on a debt which you foolishly and unnecessarily forgave me, but--perhaps to make you feel better if not richer--we might say you had a "moral right" to collect, particularly if I used the loan to get rich and you are now destitute. A desire to reduce this category of "moral right" (and the perceived injustice with which it may be associated), partly explains the development of courts of equity in the English (and by transplantation, the American) legal system; such courts sat only where the plaintiff was without "legal remedy" (legal in this case being distinguished from equitable).

My premise is that in genetic counseling the parents (1) have a legal right to be fully informed decision-makers about whether to have a child; or in the terms just discussed, the genetic counselor has the duty to convey to those he advises as clear and comprehensible a picture of the options open to them, and the relative risks, benefits, and foreseeable consequences of each option, as he can. This formulation is basically a legal one, and it suggests that the parents have recourse to the authority of the state, should the counselor breach his duty by negligently or intentionally withholding options or misdescribing their risks, benefits, etc. This right can also be seen from a "moral" vantage point, however. A dominant ethic in Western culture is the importance and inviolability of each individual human being; from this derives a right to make decisions about one's life, to be "master of one's fate" (2).

Despite the broad way in which this right to be an "informed decision-maker" can be stated, it is certainly narrower than many rights which might be (and have been) asserted to arise in genetic counseling. I would defend the primacy of this right for a number of reasons. First, it is as good a reflection of the underlying moral and legal principles (the sanctity of life; the protection of each member of the community) as any other, such as "the right of every child to be born with a sound physical and mental constitution, based on a sound genotype" (3). Second, it avoids, at least on the legal side, the ticklish problems which other such formulations of rights raise concerning "the quality of life." Third, it limits the issues under review to those which are comprehensible given the present state of genetic knowledge.

I anticipate that this limitation on the definition of the right which should concern us will meet with some objection, since our past discussions of genetics have ranged over a host of moral principles, which I would exclude from consideration. At the risk of stirring up the hornets' nest further, then, I will challenge a premise on which those discussions sometimes proceeded: that the moral conclusions reached were necessarily translatable into legal conclusions. My purpose in doing so is to try to demonstrate two things about the legal right set forth previously: (a) that it operates in the genetic counseling situation independently of any "moral" conclusions, and (b) that, for the time being at least, it is not only a necessary, but sufficient, legal right to regulate the participants in genetic counseling.

A CONNECTION BETWEEN LAW AND MORALITY

I would like to endorse the hypothesis that "there is no necessary connection between law and morality" as the starting point for my discussion of "Moral Rights and Legal Rights." I embark on this course with some trepidation. First, not being a moral philosopher, there is danger in my saying anything about "moral rights," and I might be better advised simply to speak only of legal rights in genetic counseling. Second, by taking on the "no necessary connection" hypothesis, I run the risk of spawning a positivist-natural law debate. Moreover, there is a great deal of evidence that suggests this position is untenable. And finally, there is a part of me which wants to reject this premise and to assert rather that law not only must but should enact a set of morals -- my set, of course. Nevertheless, I shall proceed on the premise of "no necessary connection," not merely to be provocative but because I believe it is useful to see the need for building separate, albeit related, lines of argument when we discourse in the moral and legal spheres, and because I hope to demonstrate that courts in disposing of the legal issues in genetic counseling cases need not venture into the "moral thicket," to paraphrase Justice Frankfurter.

Let us begin our discussion by exploring the different meanings which attach to the words "connection," "law," and "morality."

1. Connection

The term "connection" can imply an historical relationship, a chance overlap, or a strict cause-and-effect nexus. In an historical sense, there can be no denying that our system of laws has been closely related to morality, particularly that body of conventional morality known as religion. Even when a link is not provable as a matter of historical fact, the occurence of similar rules in the legal and moral domains suggests the existence of a connection, perhaps one with an anthropological explanation. Yet neither of these meanings, nor even that of cause-and-effect, is adequate once "connection" is modified by "necessary," for we are then referring to a "but for" relationship. In this sense, to speak of a necessary "connection" between a moral right and a legal right is to argue that the ultimate rationale for the existence and validity of the legal right is to be found in the moral one (4). Any less rigorous meaning of "necessary connection" raises the danger of post hoc reasoning. For even without a knowledge of the moral views of a society, one can from a careful examination of its legal system derive a statement of that system's view of man, which could be cast in moral (or psychological or political) terms; but this falls far short of demonstrating the necessity of the connection, or even of showing which way it runs.

2. Morality

There are two ways in which "morals" might be said to be related to the law. The first--the one which people most often have in mind when they speak of law enacting morality--is illustrated by the set of criminal laws which punish abortion, prostitution, homosexual activities and the like. As an historical matter, it is undeniable that the felt immorality of feticide and of variant sexual practices accounts for their prohibition by statute; however since an examination of such relationships (whether perceived as what I term "codification" or "replacement") shows them to be merely historical, the definition of "connection" previously set out has not been satisfied.

a. Law as Codified Morals. Over the years, ethical thinkers have contributed to the growth of society's legal system as well as having guided its conscience. Most prominently, organized religion has had profound direct and indirect impact, through ecclesiastical law and general religious precepts, on legal rules not only on the Continent but also in the common law and in our own constitutional system (5). This influence is even reflected in the language and customs of the law: for example, the "repentence" for which a judge looks in setting the sentence of a convicted man, or the oath on the Bible by which witnesses affirm that they will tell the truth.

During the period when the Anglo-American legal system was molded by the common law judges, legal rules represented what the courts took to be the community's view of the proper relationship of moral men. In these circumstances, "the law" was merely a formal endorsement by the community of views which its members (or most of them) already held. Once legislation came to play an important, or predominant, role in the legal system however, the more complex and less simply "moral" drives of law-makers became apparent (6). It became more difficult simply to assert that since the people (directly or through their judges and legislators) create the law and the people (judges, legislators) hold moral views, therefore the law enacts morality (7). This syllogism fails because under it we could as well say that law enacts biology, economics, psychology, astrology, or any other set of views which people hold and often believe in strongly.

   b. Law in Place of Morals. There is another sense in which law and morals might be said to be connected--a sense in which a law-biology connection would not be even facetiously asserted. This relates to the role law has as a replacement for morality. Usually, in peaceful, smoothly-functioning relationships and stable societies, there is little need for "the law" to play an active role in many areas, such as the family, education, or the like. The conduct of the individuals involved is guided by the commonly-accepted norms for these relationships: e.g., children obey their parents (teachers, etc.), achieving greater independence with their increased maturity; parents are responsible for the well-being of their children; old people can rely on their position within the family to provide respect and, if need be, sustenance. These norms are not only provided by custom but explicitly sanctioned by moral codes, enforced either by internally-assimilated standards or by outside forces operating with moral authority. Once this system breaks down, once the "commonly accepted" view of proper behavior is more widely questioned and less commonly accepted, however, people may turn instead to the law to restore relationships. In the process, law brings along new sanctions, new actors and new modes of action; in effect, it creates new relationships, although such relationships usually are presumed to be the heirs of the traditional ones and bear their names. While it is possible to see this as just another instance of law enforcing morality (akin to a common law judge creating the crime of "larceny by trick")(8), in fact, the operant fact here is the failure of the moral system to operate, so that the legal system's intrusion might more accurately be seen as a desertion of morals for law (seen as a set of regulations fashioned on the basis of the sciences of human behavior rather than on a _priori_ principles).

   c. Justice and Fairness. In neither of these senses ("codification" nor "replacement"), then, does it seem accurate to say there is any necessary link between law and that notion of morals with which it is commonly associated. Yet one principle is not so easily disposed of--the principle of fairness. To hold that a law does not comport with a person's standards of sexual behavior is one thing, but to declare that it does not square with his standards of fairness or justice is quite another. The standard of fairness, like the standard of sexual behavior, can be seen as a moral one but unlike the latter, its connection to law seems almost indisputable. It provides the yardstick by which individual laws and decisions as well as whole legal systems are judged; its connection with "the very notion of proceeding by rule is obviously very close" (9). In deciding on the distribution of benefits and burdens or the compensation of injuries, it is the precept to which the law turns; as Professor Hart has formulated it: "Treat like cases alike, and treat different cases differently" (10).

All this does not, however, make out a necessary connection between law and morality. First, the "Treat like cases alike" precept is functionally incomplete; a definition of likeness must also be given, and this need not be in "moral" terms. Some would argue that other standards of judgment (e.g., "rationality" or "reasonableness") are thereby simply made part of the concept of justice and that the overall concept remains a moral one. Under this view, to state that it is unreasonable to punish blue-eyed thiefs but not brown-eyed ones is to make a moral statement (11). It can equally well be argued that the non-moral judgment (i.e., the "rational" definition of where lines are drawn for "like" classes) is the determinative one and the principle of fairness and justice only secondary. Moreover, even the fairness principle itself can have an amoral rationale: a legal system, or a judge deciding a case, might employ the principle because to do so decreases the costs of the system or increases subjects' allegiance to their sovereign, or whatever. These rationales might in turn reduce to a utilitarian calculus on closer inspection; while as such they would be part of a moral system this is a long way from what is usually taken to be the morality with which law is assertedly connected.

3. Law

In order to develop the distinction between two meanings of the third word--law--which concerns us, I should like to offer some definitions, albeit tentative ones, of morality and law. A moral system serves as a guide to conduct which is considered "good" in itself or which will lead to "the good" (variously defined as happiness, holiness, etc.). The system may be seen as a discoverable natural pattern or as a strictly human creation, or somewhere in between; that does not alter the basic definition. Law can be seen as the collection of enforceable rights and responsibilities through which the members of a society relate to one another and to their society as well as the system by which the society assigns these rights and responsibilities and resolves asserted conflicts among its members (12).

Law and morality are similar in that both attempt to prescribe human behavior according to a set of rights and duties. If one adheres to a moral or legal system, he does nothing more than it gives him the right to do and nothing less than it makes it his duty to do. But these definitions also suggest some differences between morals and law. First, the definition of morality includes on its face a normative element and that of law does not. This is more than a matter of chance or of arbitrary definition--the heart of a moral system is its judgments of right and wrong, in an outward-referring sense, while the heart of the legal system is the ordering of relationships, in which only consistency with the system's own rules need be sought.

A second difference arises from this matter of "reference." If you found yourself alone on the proverbial desert island, you might find cause to employ a moral system, but you would have no use in any reasonable sense for a legal system. If, however, I were then to be washed ashore on your island, a need for laws would arise. (We might decide not to have any "laws" as such but to talk through each matter on its own merits; that decision, however, would in it-self create a legal system, one of negotiation without precedent.) If I decided that I did not like a law, you would then have to make reference to some "justification" which demonstrated my obligation to obey the law (13).

To do this, you would make reference to some principle (that I acknowledged as binding) which either justified the particular dis-puted rule or established my general obligation to obey all valid rules, including the one in question. Law, in other words, has two meanings: that of individual rule and that of a system of rules. The Positivists argue, convincingly I believe, that law in the narrower sense can find its justification by reference to law in the broader sense; that is, a law need not rest on moral principles to have force. In the modern formulation of Professor Hart, binding legal duties (or, more generally, legal rules) are those which meet the criteria of what Hart calls "the rule of recognition" (e.g., "a law adopted by majority vote of the legislature and signed by the chief executive"), which in turn rests on its acceptance by members of the society (14). Thus, neither individual rules nor the system as a whole need be traced back to a "moral" wellspring (15). The role of morality in this system is to supply a standard of judgment or criticism.

In sum, the thesis of "no necessary connection between law and morality" is valid to a limited extent. If we adopt the positivist view, reference need not be made to moral rights or duties to justify either individual legal rights or duties or the aggregate legal system. We may sometimes invoke the moral judgment that "This law is unjust," but this is only a criticism of the law and does not reduce the law's binding force on its addressees, provided its valid pedigree is established. (Our discussion of this point would have to go into much greater detail if we were faced with deciding whether to punish a person who engages in civil disobedi-ence against a law he believes is unjust, or conversely a person who committed what is now regarded as an unjust act in compliance with an apparently valid law which he believed was binding on him. The questions raised by our topic, while complex, are less knotty.)

INFORMED DECISION-MAKING: A LEGAL RIGHT?

1. The Legal Pedigree

Does the "informed decision-maker" rule I have suggested,then, state a legal right? There are two aspects to the right--information and decision--and both of them have been recognized by the law. The information component is of recent origin; it was developed out of recognition that knowledge is necessary to make meaningful the power to decide (16). The doctrine of "informed consent" has been developed in cases involving malpractice claims arising out of the physician-patient relationship, which is basic-ally the same as the relationship of genetic counselor and parents (if we assume that genetic counselors are either physicians or fall into a special professional class of their own). The second right --the right to self-determination--has a fundamental place in Anglo-American law; its pedigree is indisputable, as reflected in the rules of consensual agreements in contracts law and consent as a defense to assault and battery in torts law. As previously suggested the two rights have come together in "the obligation of a physician to disclose and explain to the patient as simply as necessary the nature of the ailment, the nature of the proposed treatment, the probability of success or of alternatives, and perhaps the risks of unfortunate results and unforeseen conditions" (17) before obtaining the patient's consent.

Despite this rather clear rule, physicians often withhold information from their patients. Usually this reflects only an understandable desire to "keep things simple" and "move patients along" and if challenged in such a case, a physician would probably admit that he hadn't adhered to the standard of full disclosure but argue that no harm was done thereby. (If harm did occur, however, the physician would be in an unenviable position defending a mal-practice or battery action.) In some instances, however, failure to disclose is based on intention rather than inadvertance. When he believes his patients' "best interests" would be served by ignorance, a physician may decide to withhold diagnosis, prognosis, or information about an impending medical intervention, as where a patient is found to have a malignant tumor but is told that the growth is benign so that "his final days can be happy ones." All the problems raised by this "therapeutic privilege," and few of its justifications, seem to be present in genetic counseling, although it is apparent that most counselors presently believe they have an unqualified right to withhold information from their patients. While the question is surely a ticklish one (and the examples given by Drs. Murray, Motulsky and Kaback in this volume illustrate well the complexity and fragility of the counseling interaction which I mentioned at the outset), I do not agree that a "therapeutic privilege" is wise or proper in this setting. I would rather that counselors proceeded on the premise, as the court said in a leading case, that "the law does not permit (the physician) to substitute his own judgment for that of the patient by any form of artifice or deception" (18).

The theoretical problems involved are highlighted by Dr. Murray's statement that a patient's freedom is limited if knowledge (specifically, that he carries the sickle cell trait) is communi-cated without treatment being possible. Yet, as is so often the case, under the flag of "enhancing freedom," freedom (in Professor Berlin's "positive" sense, of being able to make choices for oneself) has been severely limited--we deny the person before us freedom of choice (by depriving him of the knowledge which would inform, or even prompt, his choice) in order to increase his "true freedom" as we perceive it. Substituting our view of what should be done for that of the persons affected is always a dangerous course, and it is particularly so in the case of genetic counseling because of the great risk that counselors will not choose as their patients would--or even in their patients' "best interests."

Briefly, my practical objections to the modus operandi adopted by genetic counselors are as follows. First, genetic counselors, unlike the family doctors of yore, are not intimately acquainted with their patients, their families, communities, etc. I have been impressed by the time and effort that we have heard the genetic counselors here devote to their clients, but I think this reflects qualities one would expect in men and women who are willing to come to such a conference and expose their practices to ethical and legal scrutiny. Similar sensitivity--and time--cannot be expected on the part of all counselors, particularly once the demands on counseling facilities increase substantially, as they are bound to. When counseling becomes much more routine, part of accepted practice should not be the routine withholding of information from the counselees on the spurious grounds that the counselors know what is best for patients they hardly know at all.

A second reason derives from the innumerable internal and external pressures operating on counselors which will interfere with an accurate assessment of their patient's "best interests." In Dr. Brock's efficiency/humanity terms (this volume), the really "efficient" course for most counselors is not full disclosure on a computer print-out, but the withholding of information which if disclosed would involve the counselor in a long and arduous process of truly "counseling" his patients. In short, it is more "efficient" (and certainly easier) for him to make the choices himself rather than to bring into open discussion facts (about carrier status, etc.) which are difficult to contemplate or discuss. This points toward another pressure which operates here: physicians' well-known tendency to overreact to disease. The phenomenon of regarding disease as an "enemy" to be "conquered" (noted by Drs. Murray and Callahan, this volume) has its origins, I suspect, in the medical fraternity itself. As Professor Renee Fox has observed, this frame of mind may be quite necessary for physicians, particularly those working on the frontiers of medical science (19). Whether it is necessary, or merely a reflection of doctors' training or the pre-existing psychological makeup which brought them into the profession, this attitude is hardly conducive to a counselor's making a good choice for his patient. As Dr. Kaback commented yesterday, he is much more upset and distressed by the diagnosis of the Tay-Sachs trait than are the carriers to whom he communicates this fact.

Third, a physician's judgment may also be clouded by his own set of values, which will not necessarily correspond to his patient's. The potential for conflict is especially great in genetic counseling in which the options elected depend on one's opinions about such controversial matters as the importance of the traditional concept of family, the morality of divorce and of abortion, etc. Finally, the physician's map of social goals may differ markedly from the one held by the patient. A counselor who, for example, strongly believes in the elimination of a genetic disease for eugenic reasons, ought to convey his eugenic premises to any woman to whom he suggests an abortion for that disease, lest her choice be uninformed (20).

To conclude this aside on "therapeutic privilege," not only do I think that withholding information is theoretically and practically unwise, but I find it unjustified in that the opposite course is perfectly acceptable. The terms in which the alternatives have been posed at this conference—revealing the "brutal truth" or keeping the patient in "benign ignorance"-- give a false impression of the courses open to the counselor. They are reminiscent of the early discussions of how much dying patients should be told, discussions which also obscured much through the blinding dichotomies they employed. Only slowly did a few practicing physicians, and some enlightened sociologists, suggest that the question was not whether to tell but how to tell and how fast to tell (21). Dr. Lejeune's description of his method of informing couples which of the marriage partners is a trait carrier illustrates the advantages of beginning with the assumption that the information should be conveyed and then applying one's creativity to devising a sensitive humane means of conveying it (22).

Since its articulation by the courts establishes the "informed decision-maker" right as valid law (by reason of the "rule of recognition"), no moral justification for it need be given for its application to the participants before us. We may wish, however, to ask "Is it just?" In legal terms, as we have already noted, the right in question is an application of the same rule as that which is applied in torts and contracts law: that each person is free to govern his life as he chooses subject only to those constraints or interferences which have his voluntary assent. This principle also has its reciprocal: that each person is responsible for the consequences (sometimes limited to the foreseeable consequences) of his choices. A statement of rights in genetic counseling which denied parents "informed decision-maker" status would run afoul of the "like cases" precept on both points; the right is therefore necessary to a "just" treatment of counseling.

To conclude that the "informed decision-maker" right states a just principle of law in no wise denies that it also has moral equivalents (23). Indeed, the very concept of man as a "moral being" is closely linked with this principle. In the view of many philosophers, as well as biologists and anthropologists, man's distinctive characteristics are his abilities to communicate, to reason, to imagine alternative possibilities so as to anticipate future events, and to act so as to alter them. Given his faculties, if man is to act morally he must take responsibility that each of his acts comports with moral rules (however conceived, i.e., "do no harm," "help thy neighbor," etc.). Giving each person power, as well as responsibility, for his own conduct also, in the view of some philosophers, assures that the good of the whole community is maximized.

2. The Question of Liberty

This raises a question which I have skirted. My primary interest in the "informed decision-maker" right is to identify its allocation of authority and responsibility between parents and counselor. Thus far, the state has entered the picture only as the enforcer of the right (through its courts). One implication of the right, however, is that the parents' decision takes precedence not only against the counselor's wishes but also against those of the state. I raise this point not to discuss it at any length (24), but because it reflects one of the major forms of the law-morality debate. The view that one should have free choice about his own conduct is, of course, identified with John Stuart Mill. His critics argue that Mill's concept of liberty is not (25) and should not be accepted by society, for each member of a society owes the collectivity a duty to keep himself "physically, mentally and morally fit" (26). This argument provides another perspective on, or way into, the question of a necessary connection between law and morality. Rather than asking whether it is possible to view the legal system as a useful, justified entity, independent of moral-ity, it asks whether one can conceive of a society operating suc-cessfully without imposing its moral views on its members. While this debate, between libertarians on the one hand and paternalists and collectivists on the other, is as fascinating as that between positivists and naturalists, I don't think we need go into it here. Suffice it to say that I defend the full implications of the "in-formed decision-maker" right, even against the state's authority.

Having concluded that genetic counselees do have a legal right to act on full information about the options open to them and their risks, I should like now to apply this analysis to a hypothetical situation presenting some of the potential conflicts among the rights and obligations of the participants in genetic counseling.

RIGHTS AND DUTIES IN GENETIC COUNSELING: A CASE ANALYSIS

Suppose that a couple who believe their potential offspring to be "at risk" for a genetically-linked disorder consult a physician who specializes in genetics. The stage of the unborn child's devel-

opment at the time of consultation, the type of advice, and the
sorts of data used might vary greatly.   Let us assume that the
parents seek out the counselor after the child has been conceived
but in time to terminate pregnancy safely; further assume that the
data is restricted to family histories (the probabilities of the
disease being calculable on that basis, but the disease not being
amenable to diagnosis by amniocentesis, etc.); and finally assume
that the advice given is a straightforward assertion that there is
no known risk of the disease occurring. On this assumed set of
facts, what consequences follow if the counselor intentionally
withholds information or makes a negligent mistake in his advice
and a child with the feared genetic disorder is born?

Although no such case has arisen to the best of my knowledge,
analogies are available.   Perhaps the closest of these is the
decision of the Supreme Court of New Jersey in Gleitman v. Cosgrove
(27), which provides us with a useful vehicle for analysis, not the
least because Lord Kilbrandon takes a rather different view of the
result reached from that which I take. I believe it will be worth
our while to examine Gleitman in some detail, both because it is
the leading case on this subject, and also because I believe both
the New Jersey court and its critics have mistaken the rights and
duties involved.   Using the analysis we have developed, I believe
we come inescapably to a different, and better, resolution of the
contentions raised by the case.

The Gleitman court held that there was no cognizable claim
against a physician who erroneously advised a woman that the German
measles she suffered during the first month of pregnancy "would
have no effect at all on her child" (28). Apparently Dr. Cosgrove
knew the risk of rubella damage to be about 25 percent, but he
withheld this information because he believed it unfair to abort
three healthy fetuses to avoid one diseased one. By a divided vote,
the justices ruled that neither parents nor child could sue for the
child's substantial birth defects, because the mother had testified
that if she had been properly warned of the risks she would have
sought an abortion; the parents were foreclosed because an abortion
even if legal (which the court assumed)(29), would have violated
"the preciousness of human life," and the child was foreclosed because he would "not have been born at all" had his parents carried
out the abortion. While it is not difficult to understand why the
New Jersey court reached the conclusion it did, I believe its
opinion rests on a misunderstanding of legal principles, a mis-
application of precedent, and a misapprehension of the consequences
of the result it reached as compared with the contrary result (30).

1. Misunderstood Principles

The first question which arises is whether the legal rule
established in this case is a just one. The reason it seems unjust
is that the general rule -- that (a) a person (b) who suffers

injuries (c) will be made whole by (d) the person who caused the
injuries--was not applied here. In consequence the court is open
to criticism for not treating like cases alike.

As my statement of this tort rule suggests, in determining
whether justice was done in the _Gleitman_ case, we first inquire
into the infant plaintiff's standing to sue. Is Jeffrey Gleitman,
the defective child, "a person" in the eyes of the law? This question did not detain Justice Proctor of New Jersey for long. Looking
to _Smith_ _v._ _Brennan_ (31), in which the court upheld the right of
a child to sue for injuries sustained _in_ _utero_, he quoted that
"justice requires that the principle be recognized that a child has
a legal right to begin life with a sound mind and body" (32). In
other words, the court relied on the principle of fairness to reach
the conclusion that the protection of, and redress for, postnatal
harm to "mind and body" should likewise be available to persons
alleging prenatal injuries.

As to the second element of the rule--injuries--no question
arose: the judges all agreed that Jeffrey suffered severe impairment. If we skip momentarily over the third element--compensation--
the fourth element poses the question whether Dr. Cosgrove was "the
person who caused (Jeffrey's) injuries." The physician did not
cause the impairment in the sense of having given Mrs. Gleitman
rubella; however, in torts parlance he was the proximate cause of
the impairment because his mistaken advice prevented the Gleitmans
from avoiding the manifestation of injuries. Had Jeffrey been a
grown man who received negligently inaccurate advice from Dr.
Cosgrove about a neurological disorder which thereafter, in absence
of treatment, rendered him blind and deaf, the legal rules governing the doctor-patient relationship would require Dr. Cosgrove to
compensate Jeffrey for his impairment (33). The court's contrary
conclusion that Dr. Cosgrove's conduct "was not the cause of infant
plaintiff's condition" (34) is nonsensical--as the court itself
recognizes, the plaintiff would not have been in that condition had
Dr. Cosgrove told the Gleitmans of the risk of impairment.

The reason why the New Jersey court felt constrained to deny
Jeffrey a "just" application of the usual rule of recovery is not
that Dr. Cosgrove did not cause the injuries, but its conclusion
that there was no way to calculate how to make Jeffrey "whole"
again. This aspect of _Gleitman_ is very pertinent for us; given the
present state of genetic counseling, the only "treatment" available
in most cases is to abort the fetus.

There are two grounds on which the court's holding is open to
criticism. First, the conclusion that a court "cannot weigh the
value of life with impairments against the nonexistence of life
itself"(34) is contradicted by courts making similar subjective
calculations (the value of lives cut short, of pain and suffering,
and other intangibles) every day. Second, if the New Jersey court
intended a broader point, that life with any handicap is _per_ _se_
better than no life at all, it cited no authority for this conclusion. What it did cite is Professor Tedeschi's argument that "no

comparison is possible since were it not for the act of birth the
infant would not exist" (35). But this adds nothing to the court's
own a priori judgment in favor of impaired life versus abortion; it
only serves to create confusion over the act for which plaintiff is
suing. Jeffrey did not sue Dr. Cosgrove "for his life," although
such a suit is not as illogical as Justice Proctor, relying on Professor Tedeschi, suggests (36). Rather, Jeffrey sued the physician
for his failure to give accurate advice on which a decision could
be made by Jeffrey's parents, acting in their child's behalf, that
for him not to be born would be preferable to being born deformed.
If one objects to awarding damages for the violation of this right,
it seems to me that the objection goes either to the policy of
allowing abortions (the court assumed one could have been legally
obtained) or to giving parents, who may have conflicting motivations, the authority to make this decision (as the law now does).
The fact remains that the Gleitman court departed from the rule
that the choice in this matter lies with the patient, not the
physician (37), and its action is no more defensible than that of a
court which, faced with a patient who was ravaged by an untreated
disease, were to dismiss the suit on the grounds that the standard
treatment (about which the physician negligently failed to inform
the patient) is highly dangerous and nearly always fatal.

2. Misapplied Precedent

If the New Jersey court's failure to heed prevailing legal
doctrines led it into one sort of error, its application of prior
cases led it into other errors, although certainly not all of its
own making. The Gleitman court relied on "two cases from other
states which have considered the theory of action for 'wrongful
life'" (38), Zepeda v. Zepeda (39), an Illinois case, and Williams
v. New York (40).
The New Jersey court's reliance on these cases is misplaced
because, as the court observed, they "were brought by illegitimate
children for damages caused by their birth out of wedlock, and in
both cases policy reasons were found to deny recovery" (41).
Policies relevant to illegitimacy clearly have limited, if any,
application to a suit by a child made deaf and blind by rubella.
Moreover, the opinions of the New York and Illinois courts are
unsatisfactory on their own facts. In Williams, for example, the
plaintiff was an infant who had been conceived when her mother, a
mental defective in the custody of a state hospital, was raped by
another patient. The child claimed that the state's negligence in
protecting her mother had caused her (the child) to be deprived of
a normal childhood and rearing and "to bear the stigma of illegitimacy" (42). The New York Court of Appeals recognized the "unfair
burdens" the plaintiff would bear, as do "many other sons and
daughters of shame and sorrow" (43). But, it concluded, "the law
knows no cure or compensation for it, and the policy and social

reasons against providing such compensation are at least as strong
as those which might be thought to favor it" (43). If "the policy
and social reasons" against making illegitimacy a "suable wrong"
are of no assistance to the Gleitman court, perhaps it had in mind
the arguments presented by Judge Keating's concurring opinion in
Williams (44). These concerned the "logico-legal" difficulty
(derived by Judge Keating from Tedeschi's article) "of permitting
recovery when the very act which caused the plaintiff's birth was
the same one responsible for whatever damage she has suffered or
will suffer" (43). We have already seen the error in the "same
act" approach, which by characterizing the claim as one for "wrongful life" fails to distinguish between the act of conception and
the circumstances under which it is done. Having intercourse is
not a crime, but having it when unmarried is, and in this case that
was the state's fault. Of course, "had the State acted responsibly," as Judge Keating noted, the plaintiff "would not have been
born at all" (45). Yet the state's failure to do so created not
only the infant plaintiff but also her cause of action.

In Williams not only were the act (conception) and the tort
(negligence in failing to protect the mother from men to whom she
was not married) separable, but the latter was even partly remedi-
able without abortion, since the illegitimacy could have been
"cured" by subsequent marriage, adoption, etc. This is not so in
the genetic counseling situation nor in the Zepeda case, where the
defendant father was already married when he fraudulently induced
the plaintiff's mother to have sexual relations with him by promis-
ing to marry her. Yet the Zepeda case is also of little comfort to
the Gleitman court because the Illinois court agreed with plaintiff
Zepeda "that the elements of a wilful tort are presented by the
allegations of the complaint" (46). The Zepeda court saw no barrier
to the suit in the tortious act or omission having occurred at, or
even before, the plaintiff's conception; nor was the suit barred by
the nature of the injury, which "is not as tangible as a physical
defect but...is as real" (47). Yet the "radical" nature of the
injury alleged--loosely, "bad" parentage--was the factor which led
the court to deny recovery for the tort. If the Gleitman court
relied at all on the "policy" set by Zepeda, it must be on that
aspect of the opinion which held that recovery should be permitted
only after the legislature had undertaken a "thorough study of the
consequences."

3. Misapprehended Consequences

The Illinois court was not merely worried that entertaining
Zepeda's suit would open the floodgates of litigation, leaving the
courts inundated by the claims of the quarter million illegitimate
children born each year in the United States, but also that damages
would soon be sought "for being born of a certain color (or) race;
...for being born with a hereditary disease,...for inheriting

unfortunate family characteristics; (or) for being born into a large and destitute family, (or to) a parent (who) has an unsavory reputation" (48). There is a surface appeal to the court's reasoning.   Being born into a minority group or a "disadvantaged" family may subject a child to burdens similar to those of illegitimacy, and hereditary disease may cause greater suffering still.

But opening the court to the infant Zepeda would not necessarily open it to the others cited by the court, for poverty, race and genetic makeup do not constitute "moral wrongs(s) and..criminal act(s)"(49) which the court held Mr. Zepeda's sexual relations with the plaintiff's mother to be. Being poor or carrying an hereditary disease are not crimes; procreating in these circumstances violates no legal right of the child conceived.

Nevertheless, although nothing in the "policy reasons" of Williams or Zepeda is either convincing or applicable to Gleitman, we owe it to the New Jersey court to puzzle through the consequences of the result we believe it should have reached before criticizing as unjust the one that it did reach. Can it be said of the Gleitman decision "that, regrettable though it is, the demands of justice... must be overriden in order to preserve something held to be of greater value, which would be jeopardized if...discriminations (between Jeffrey Gleitman and other plaintiffs injured by a negligent failure to give complete medical advice) were not made" (50)?

To bring one possible countervailing value into view, let us alter the facts of the Gleitman case. Suppose the child alleged that the physician gave accurate advice to the parents but that the parents disregarded the risks and did not abort, resulting in his being born deformed.   If the claim against Dr. Cosgrove is good, must not that against the parents also succeed? If we assume that there is no longer intrafamilial immunity in the jurisdiction (51), there remains the simple fact that such suits are unlikely because the child's parents, as his guardians or "next friends," actually instigate suits on the child's behalf, and it is unlikely that they would, in effect, sue themselves. Yet even if the state routinely appointed special guardians for all defective children (or all children for that matter), with instructions to bring any necessary lawsuits, such suits would be of little practical value. Parents are already legally obliged to support their children, and most do so to the limits of their ability whether the child is "normal" or not. Consequently, unlike a recovery against an outside party like Dr. Cosgrove, a recovery against the parents would just shift family funds (less lawyers' fees and court costs) from one pocket to another (52).

While there is at least some merit to these practical reasons why a suit against parents would be unlikely to follow had Gleitman been differently decided, the really persuasive argument denies that there is any claim against the parents at all. For there to be a recovery, the defendant must have breached a duty legally owed the plaintiff. Dr. Cosgrove violated such a legal (and moral) duty when he failed to give competent medical adivce; by contrast, parents, in choosing not to abort, have exercised their legal right to make this choice. This right of the parents has two sources: (a) one derived from the child's own right, in which case the parents are considered to be making their decision on behalf of their offspring, in what they judge to be his "best interests"; and (b) one which focuses on the parents' own right to exercise control over an event which is of major importance to their lives (directly so in the mother's case, and indirectly in the father's). The second rationale is of more recent vintage and more narrow in scope, being applicable, so far as I know, only in the choice to have an abortion to safeguard the mother's life or health or, in a few jurisdictions, for any reason the parents may have prior to 24 weeks of gestation (53). Since the decision not to have an abortion would probably be viewed by the courts as being based on both rationales, absent proof of intentional disregard of their child's interests or gross negligence in the exercise of their discretion, such an exercise of judgment would not subject the couple to liability. In the view of the law, it is up to them to weigh the probabilities and risks and to decide whether life with any defects is better than abortion or whether in some cases life with defects is "a fate worse than death."

CONCLUSION

From this discussion, I would conclude that our hypothetical genetic counselor has a legal duty to give competent advice so as to place the parents into the position of informed decision-makers (54), and that if by his negligent or intentional breach of this duty a defective child is born, the child (and its parents) have a valid claim for damages against him. This is true whether the parents come to him for advice on whether to abort or on whether to conceive in the first place. (I take the latter situation to be an easier case to establish liability for medical advice and, consequently, have addressed myself only to the former).

Unless we accept as a valid legal rule the Gleitman court's dictum that every child has "a legal right to begin life with a sound mind and body" (55), however, a child who suffers a genetic disease does not have a claim against its parents because they decided to give it birth despite the risks of the disease. The Gleitman court did not accept this principle at face value, and neither should we. As a moral precept it states an admirable guide for conduct and aspiration; as a legal rule it is too far-reaching. The legal rule which I have suggested should be applied protects courts from the nearly impossible task of reviewing the parents' good faith judgment about the "quality of life" which a child will experience; the child is protected against intentional harm by the parents, as he would be after birth; and the parents are protected in the prudent use of the capabilities with which nature endowed them. This comports with our moral sense that it is unjust to blame someone for something (such as his genetic makeup) which he cannot (presently) control. It would be cruel to add to the injury of a defective gene (and the undeserved self-blame which is felt when the disease manifests itself in an offspring) the insult of a suit by the offspring. On the other hand, parents who knowingly and recklessly took a drug with a substantial teratogenic risk would be liable if their offspring were deformed. Similarly, major manipulations of the birth process, done in the face of adverse or incalculable risks, would expose their creators to liability for injuries suffered.

None of these eventualities are pleasant to contemplate, and one can hope that they never pass from the hypothetical to the real. But if they do, I am confident that the courts, and in some instances the legislatures, will make clear the right of children to recover for their injuries. Gleitman v. Cosgrove neither will, nor should be, the final word on the subject.

ACKNOWLEDGEMENT

The author is grateful to Dr. Jay Katz and Miss Barbara A. Brown for their comments on this paper, which also profited from work done on a related subject under grant HSM 110-69-213, Health Services and Mental Health Administration, DHEW.

NOTES AND REFERENCES

1. *For the moment, I shall use the phrase "parents' rights" to include both those they assert on their own behalf and those they assert as the representatives of others, particularly their unborn child. This point is discussed infra in "Rights and Duties in Genetic Counseling."*

2. *Berlin, I. (1969). "Two Concepts of Liberty," in Four Essays on Liberty. Oxford: Clarendon Press.*

3. *Glass, B. (1971), Science: Endless Horizons or Golden Age?, Science, 171, 38. See also Smith v. Brennan, 31 N.J. 353, 364 (1960), ("the right to begin life with a sound mind and body") quoted in Gleitman v. Cosgrove, 49 N.J. 22, 28 (1967), which is discussed extensively in "Rights and Duties in Genetic Counseling" in this paper.*

4. *It is often assumed that the asserted "connection between law and morality" refers to law incorporating, or resting on, morality. The opposite meaning is equally plausible, but the interesting questions it raises go beyond the scope of this paper. What is at issue is whether the Old Testament view of the law as "a lamp unto the feet and a light unto the path" should be taken as a description of law's effect on morality or merely on conduct.*

5. *Under our constitution, the historical connection between a statute and that body of morality known as religion can present some intrigu-*

ing questions of legislative intent and legal effect, but these need not detain us now. See generally John Hart Ely, "Legislative and Administrative Motivation in Constitutional Law," 79 *Yale Law Journal* 1205 (1970).

6. Even when the framers of a law speak in moral terms ("equality," "social justice"), the law-morality connection is not patent. Take, for example, Workmen's Compensation, which makes an employer liable for job-related injuries without a showing that he is at fault for their occurrence. There was much opposition to these statutes in the early years of this century, and for a while the courts held them unconstitutional on the grounds that they deprived the employer of his property without due process of law in violation of the fourteenth amendment. See, e.g., *Ives v. South Buffalo Railway Co.*, 201 N.Y. 271, 94 N.E. 431 (1911). (To do this, the courts found the doctrines of the fault system of liability, which along with numerous exceptions they had themselves created over the preceding centuries, to be an immutable part of the concept of "due process.") But while a "moral" rationale can be thought of for or against these statutes, the basis on which they were enacted by the legislatures and eventually accepted by the courts (as a valid exercise of the "police power" of the state) was, in the words of the draftsmen of the 1910 New York law, that the existing negligence system was "economically unwise...wasteful, uncertain and productive of antagonism between workmen and employers." The legislators concluded (1) that if employers, particularly in "dangerous trades," had to bear at least some of the cost of injuries, they would be more likely to improve the safety of working conditions, and (2) that both the costs of the accidents and of their prevention are costs of doing business, which ought to be reflected in the price of the goods produced.

7. Cahn, E. (1955). *The Moral Decision*. Bloomington and London: Indiana University Press.

8. *King v. Pear*, 168 Eng. Rep. 208 (1779).

9. Hart, H. L. A. (1961). *The Concept of Law*. Oxford: Clarendon Press.

10. Id. at 155.

11. See id. at 156. Professor Hart identifies the "moral outlook" of equality as the principle underlying justice and fairness, but he acknowledges that other bases for a "just" system are possible. Id. at 160-161.

12. Some of these rules or arrangements are described as "customs" by anthropologists. Similarly, Prof. Hart argues that primitive societies which lack "secondary rules" (roughly, procedural rules) cannot be said to have law at all. (Unlike his fellow positivist John Austin, however, Hart holds that some customs count as law even before a law-making institution recognizes them.) I would argue further that those rules at the edge of the legal system, which enjoy their non-legal status primarily because the law has foreborne incorporating them for the present, ought to be regarded as part of our concept of law. What is said hereafter is not affected by these distinctions, however.

13. *The question of justification is what really lies behind most discussions of the connection between law and morality. The question underlying such discussions is whether one need obey a law for which the
connection is missing.*

14. *In addition, some rules--or customs, really--are binding in Hart's
scheme because they too are "accepted" rather than achieving their
validity by means of the master rule.*

15. *Extra-legal (possibly "moral") principles do have a place in Hart's
system. When a "hard case" is not decided by an existing rule, or
when an existing rule leads to a harsh result, the "rule of recognition" gives certain people (typically judges) discretion to fashion a
new rule. In the exercise of their discretion, the judges may rely on
extra-legal standards; consequently, some individual laws may (but
need not) be grounded in moral principles. This explains the connection between morals and certain laws which was discussed under the
previous heading. Critics of the positivist model insist that the
legal system is more than just a collection of individual laws. For
example, Prof. Ronald Dworkin's contextualist approach attempts to
supply a theory of legal obligation that squares with our social
practices; particularly, he is concerned to avoid the positivists' use
of "discretion" which leads to ex post facto results inconsistent with
our social practice of blaming someone only for the breach of an
existing social obligation. Unlike the positivist judge who may refer
to standards outside the law as a guide to decision-making, a Dworkin-
ian judge is bound by certain principles which as such are part of the
law. In other words, Dworkin denies the dichotomy between law and
morals and locates the notion of legal duty in the general practice of
social obligation.*

16. *See Natanson v. Kline, 186 Kan. 383, 350 P.2d 1093, clarified, 187
Kan. 186, 354 P.2d 670 (1960); Salgo v. Leland Stanford, etc., Bd. of
Trustees, 154 Cal.App.2d 560, 317 P.2d 170 (1957). Cf. Miranda v.
Arizona, 384 U.S. 436 (1966) (prescribing information about rights to
remain silent and to confer with counsel which must be communicated to
criminal suspect prior to interrogation); Banzhaf v. F.C.C., 405 F.2d
1082 (D.C. Cir. 1968), cert. denied 396 U.S. 842 (1969) (broadcasters
required to air anti-smoking information.)*

17. *Natanson v. Kline, 186 Kan. at 417, 350 P.2d at 1106.*

18. *Id. at 407, 350 P.2d at 1104.*

19. *Fox, R. C. (1959). Experiment Perilous: Physicians and Patients
Facing the Unknown. Glencoe, Ill.: The Free Press.*

20. *This formulation highlights the question of what "facts" must be disclosed. Ordinarily, this question may not be an easy one (how much of
a diagnosis or description of risks, side-effects, etc., is "fact"?)
but at least it is limited to "facts" about the patient (the results
of his lab tests, etc.). But what of further information about the
significance of the diagnosis, risks, etc., or about the physician's
premises, etc. I believe that these too must be included in the information required to be disclosed, but while I may for economy's sake*

refer to "disclosing facts," I recognize that this phrase encompasses
hard, factual data as well as opinions, beliefs and interpretations.
Indeed, the very "non-factual" nature of the latter category suggests
the great need that it be disclosed and that the disclosure include as
full a statement of the competing opinions, beliefs, and interpreta-
tions as is possible.

21. *See, e.g., Glaser, B. G. and A. L. Strauss (1965), Awareness of Dying,*
    Chicago: Aldine Publishing Co.; Weisman, A. D. (1967), "The Patient
    With a Fatal Illness: To Tell or Not to Tell," J. Am. Med. Assn., 201,
    153.

22. *Another way of stating my thesis is that the "best interests" doctrine*
    is acceptable to the extent it mirrors the physician's Hippocratic
    duty to "do no harm," but that it should be abandoned to the extent it
    would permit a physician to substitute his judgment for his patient's.
    Thus, this modified "best interests" would place a floor under the
    standard of acceptable conduct by physicians, by refusing to excuse
    intentional or reckless harm to patients, without allowing this pro-
    tection against potential harm to swallow up the patient's whole right
    to information and consent.

23. *One moralist's approach to informed consent is found in Prof. Paul*
    Ramsey's description of the deontological dimension of consent: "The
    principle of an informed consent is a statement of fidelity between
    the man who performs medical procedures and the man on whom they are
    performed." Fidelity is thus an aspect of "the faithfulness that is
    normative for all the covenants or moral bonds of life with life."
    Ramsey, P. (1970), The Patient as Person, New Haven and London: Yale
    University Press.

24. *The issues involved would require lengthy treatment in a separate*
    paper. The state's right to act against the parents' wishes would
    probably depend on such issues as: (a) in whose behalf is the state
    acting, that of the unborn child, the community, future generations,
    or science; (b) is its action premised on paternalism, the "common
    good," or the limitations which it places on the exercise of certain
    privileges it grants; and (c) how does it enforce its decisions, (by
    prohibiting abortions or commanding them, or by compulsory amniocen-
    tesis, contraception, sterilization, etc.).

25. *As Lord Devlin has observed: "Mill's doctrine has existed for over a*
    century and no one has ever attempted to put it into practice."
    Devlin, P. (1965), The Enforcement of Morals, Oxford: Oxford Univer-
    sity Press.

26. *Id. at 104.*

27. *49 N.J. 22, 227 A.2d 689 (1967).*

28. *Gleitman v. Cosgrove, 49 N.J. 22, 24 (1967).*

29. *The court's assumption accords with one of the grounds for abortion*
    proposed by American Law Institute (and now accepted in a dozen
    states): that a licensed physician believes there is substantial risk

the child will be born with grave physical or mental defects. Model Penal Code Section 230.3.

30. *The discussion herein is limited to the child's right to recover, since the parents' claim is either derivative, dependent on the same theory, or governed by whether abortion is legal. The court assumed that the Gleitmans could theoretically have obtained an abortion, but cited "policy reasons" why recovery should be denied. If an abortion had been actually as well as theoretically, possible on a legal basis, the court would not have been able to rely on these policies.*

31. *31 N.J. 353 (1960).*

32. *Id. at 364.*

33. *Jeffrey's legal right to competent advice from an expert, and Dr. Cosgrove's duty to provide it, are paralleled by the moral rights and duties set forth in the Principles of Medical Ethics which state that physicians should render "to each (patient) a full measure of service and devotion."*

34. *49 N.J. at 28.*

35. *Tedeschi, G. (1966). "On Tort Liability for 'Wrongful Life'", Israel Law Review, 1, 529.*

36. *Would a court throw out a suit brought by a patient who had contracted a disabling injury through a physician's negligence in administering transfusions, simply because the physician proved that but for the transfusions the patient would have died? Although the plaintiff would "owe his life" to the physician, he could, of course, still sue him.*

37. *This choice may even extend to a patient's refusing "life-saving" therapy. See In re Brooks Estate, 32 Ill. 2d 361, 205 N.E.2d 435 (1965). The imposition of such therapy against the patient's wishes in Application of the President and Directors of Georgetown College, Inc., 331 F.2d 1010 (D.C. Cir.) cert. denied 377 U.S. 978 (1964), was defended by the judge there because the patient had shifted the "legal responsibility" for the choice over to the hospital. Moreover, cases involving adult patients turn on the applicability and interpretation of the policy against suicide which does not apply to cases involving fetuses under a "liberal" abortion law. And both the Brooks Estate and Georgetown lines of cases start from the position that if the patient's choice is overriden it can only be done by someone (usually a judge) officially enpowered to act as his guardian, and not by the physician alone, as in Gleitman.*

38. *49 N.J. at 29.*

39. *41 Ill.App.2d 240, 190 N.E.2d 849 (App. Ct. 1963), cert. denied 379 U.S. 945 (1964).*

40. *18 N.Y.2d 481, 223 N.E.2d 343 (1966).*

41. *49 N.J. at 29.*

42. *18 N.Y.2d at 482.*

43. *Id. at 484.*

44. *The Appellate Division, whose decision was being reviewed, had based its decision in part on the Keating line of reasoning (that damages cannot be ascertained because they rest "upon the very fact of conception"). 25 App.Div.2d 907 (1966).*

45. *18 N.Y.2d at 485.*

46. *41 Ill.App.2d at 259.*

47. *The court built its theory of injury on a detailed review of the "lot of a child born out of wedlock." It contrasted the ignominy and hardships of illegitimacy in the past with the enlightened attitude of modern statutes, which do much to equalize the rights of bastards with those of legitimate offspring. It concluded, nonetheless, that:*
        Praiseworthy as they are, they do not, and no law can,
        make these children whole. Children born illegitimate
        have suffered an injury. (Id. at 258.)
    Earlier in the case the court had concluded that three more specific types of injury were not made out by the complaint--mental suffering was not properly averred; defamation requires communication to third persons, which was not alleged; and no child, legitimate or illegitimate, has a legal right to love or a happy home. Id. at 253-255.

48. *Id. at 260.*

49. *Id. at 253.*

50. *Hart (1961), 158.*

51. *English common law permitted tort actions as well as those involving property and contracts between children and parents. "But beginning in 1891 with Hewlett v. George (68 Miss. 703, 9 So. 885 (1891)), a Mississippi case of false imprisonment which cited no authorities, the American courts adopted a general rule refusing to allow actions between parent and minor child for personal torts, whether they are intentional or negligent in character." Prosser, W. L. (1971), Handbook of The Law of Torts, Section 122, 865. This result was justified as necessary to avoid introducing "discord and contention where the laws of nature have established peace and obedience." Wick v. Wick, 192 Wis. 260, 262, 212 N.W., 787, 789 (1927); the danger of "fraud" has also been stressed. The "retreat" from this rule is now "under way," as Prof. Prosser notes, and parent-child immunity for personal torts may soon be a thing of the past. See, e.g., Gibson v. Gibson, 92 Cal. Rptr. 288 (1971); Gelbman v. Gelbman, 23 N.Y.2d 434, 245 N.E.2d 192 (1969): and Coller v. White 20 Wis.2d 402, 122 N.W.2d 193 (1963). The courts continue immunity, however, for matters subject to "parental discretion" over the care, etc. of children, and this would serve as a further bar to suits for inherited diseases, unless they involved wanton disregard of or intentional injury to the child's health.*

52. *Additional funds would be injected only in the unlikely event that an insurance policy held by the parents covered this situation.*

53. *Act 1, Hawaii Sessions Laws of 1970; N.Y. Penal Law Section 125.05 (McKinney 1970).*

54. *Our discussion has focused solely on the rights and duties relating to liability for negligent advice. Time does not permit an exploration of the myriad other rights and duties which arise from the geneticist-patient relationship or of the limitations (and their remedies, if any) which are placed on the exercise of these rights and duties by internal and external constraints. Some exploration of these problems especially concerning informed consent, appears in my "Law of Genetic Therapy" in The New Genetics and the Future of Man, M. Hamilton, editor, Grand Rapids, Eerdmans (1972), and see Hans Jonas, "Philosophical Reflections on Experimenting with Human Subjects," 98 Daedalus 219 (1969); Henry K. Beecher, "Consent in Clinical Experimentation: Myth and Reality," 195 J. Am. Med. Assn. 124 (1966).*

55. *49 N.J. at 28, quoting 31 N.J. at 364.*

THE COMPARATIVE LAW OF GENETIC COUNSELING

Lord Kilbrandon

Although this is a paper on comparative law, it is necessary that I begin by saying something about my own native system. The law of Scotland may be placed, owing to its processes of development, in the common-law stream, although in its principles it can be fundamentally different from the law of England. Our roots are in the law of Rome; they were established from contacts, before the Reformation, with the centers of canon law learning, and, after the Reformation, in the 17th and 18th centuries, from a close liaison between the Scottish legal profession and the great schools of the Netherlands. I believe that even today, for this reason, the Scottish lawyer may find himself less at home in London than in South Africa, Ceylon, the Province of Quebec, or the State of Louisiana.

One thing which we have in common with the English is our system of government. In this sense, England and Scotland ceased to exist in 1707, when the State of Great Britain was born. This may be relevant to the topic under discussion. For example, to an American a great part of the instant problem may be: How far would enabling legislation in a new field such as this, in which human rights are so vitally concerned, be vulnerable to a plea of unconstitutionality (1)? In Britain, by contrast, the expression "unconstitutional legislation" is without meaning. There is no authority in Britain, superior to Parliament, by whom Parliament's laws can be struck down as offending against entrenched and inviolable provisions. On the other hand, I am not sure that this theoretical and technical difference is quite as important as it is sometimes made out to be. There are in Britain, as elsewhere, informal agencies, individuals, organizations, and media of communication which in combination make up what is known as "public opinion." This can be nearly as formidable as a written constitution; the promoters of legislation which steps over the boundaries of what is considered permissible by the average man of goodwill would find themselves up against a preventive barrier which is almost as powerful as formal rejection by the United States Supreme Court. We may take this as a specimen of the first lesson which the comparative lawyer has to learn. It is possible, by much reading, to acquire a comparative knowledge of the statutory law, decisions, and learned writings of many a foreign legal system. (I may say in parenthesis that this is not a knowledge to which I have any pretensions.) But unless the student is more or less acquainted with the way in which a system actually works in practice, including all the unpublished and almost anonymous influences which affect the operation of the code he has gone to such pains to acquire, he may very well mislead himself and others. This admonition I am, of course, primarily concerned to address to myself.

As a further preliminary discipline, I would wish to impose on myself the warning not to be too impressed, when it comes to legal analysis, by the glare and wonder of new things. The universe is rushing very fast, in some direction or another, as speed is measured by physical progress. The mind of man, his intellectual appreciations, and the technology of his reasoning have, at first sight, changed so fundamentally that he is in a sense a being differing in kind from his grandfather. But I doubt whether there is much of a spiritual metamorphosis to be discerned. I do not use the word in a religious sense; I mean that the essential man is the same as he was yesterday. Give or take some peripheral variations, for example in the sexual field, he has the same behavioural code, the same attitude to personal relationships, and the same knowledge of good and evil that he acquired so long ago. And, surprisingly, his social organization is still fairly conventional. The communal units are the family, the neighborhood, the township, and the nation. And this organization is held together, as in times past, by some social principles which we call laws. These principles do not greatly alter; much of the private law contained in the Institutes of Justinian would be workable in an American city today. The relevance of that proposition is that, even when we are faced by a development so sudden and, perhaps, so destructive of our previously formed assumptions, such as genetic counseling, we must not be surprised if, by and large, existing legal doctrines are adequate to contain and regulate it.

It has been said that genetic counseling "is concerned with advising parents on the risks of recurrence of hereditary disorders and therefore indirectly with the prevention of these disorders. The purpose of genetic counseling is four-fold. First, to explain as simply as possible the nature of the disorder and what is meant by saying it is 'genetic.' Second, to dispel feelings of guilt which parents often have who have borne a child with such a disorder. Third, to explain the risks of recurrence and, finally, to give appropriate advice when this is requested" (2). Before passing to more revolutionary matters, let us pause to observe that according to this definition, our problem seems to present itself, from the point of view of personal and legal relationships, in a quite old-fashioned setting. First, a man and a woman are planning to have a child, so they are in the relationship of marriage or something analogous thereto. Second, they are concerned about the quality of that child, so presumably they mean to bring it up in a family, with all the social complexities which that association implies. Third, they have consulted a professional person, possibly a scientist but more probably a doctor. By this act, the doctor and the parents have placed themselves in a position in which well-known legal rights and obligations can be identified. In this last relationship, which we will proceed to examine, the state also takes an interest, which it may exercise, in certain circumstances, through the operation of the criminal law.

There can hardly be a civilized legal system in which, once a patient has consulted a doctor, that doctor does not come under the obligation, whether by virtue of an implied contract or as part of his duty to take reasonable care for the safety of his neighbor, to make reparation for the consequences of his negligent advice or treatment. To select from the bookshelf at random, this is the law of France (3), Germany (4), Greece (5), Ethiopia (6), and Malaysia (7), as well as being the common law in America and in England and Scotland. That law has been stated as follows: "If a medical man holds himself out as a person who undertakes the care or treatment of human ailments, there is on his part an implied warranty that he is of a skill reasonably competent to the task he undertakes-- spondet peritiam artis. The public profession of an art is a representation and undertaking to all the world that the professor possesses the requisite ability and skill. The amount of skill which must be displayed depends on the extent of the profession of the person employed. A specialist, for example, is one from whom, in a case of contract, more skill can be demanded than from a general practitioner" (8). The principle seems to be the same everywhere, though the standards of skill called for by the law may differ in different countries, and actions of damages against medical persons may succeed more often in one country than in another (9).

Genetic counseling, as we have seen from our definition, is simply medical advice on a rather new, rapidly developing, and highly specialized topic. There is, therefore, here an impact with the law as it is everywhere understood; if the counselor exhibits, in his practice, less than a reasonable standard of competence and diligence, so that his advice is unreliable, he is liable to compensate persons upon whom that bad advice has caused loss to fall. He must exhibit the skill of a specialist in his field; if a general practitioner undertakes work which is only appropriate to a consultant, he cannot defend himself by saying he did not have a consultant's experience--except perhaps in a grave emergency. But the comparatively rapid developments in the science of genetic counseling themselves might give rise to a defense, since the standard attained must be tested by the state of knowledge in the specialty at the time of the treatment, not by that later acquired by the profession (10).

I have said that an action will lie against a negligent doctor at the suit of any persons who have suffered loss by that negligence. The question of who are included among those persons was debated in a leading case from the State of New Jersey (11) and

requires careful examination. Mrs. Gleitman, being two months
pregnant, consulted her doctor, the defendant. (The legal issue
was, for technical reasons, decided on the basis of assuming that
her account of the facts was true, though not necessarily proved.)
She told him that one month earlier she had had an attack of
rubella (German measles). The defendant advised her this would
have no effect on her child. Three months later, in consequence of
some prenatal advice she had received, she saw the defendant again
and got the same advice. In due time her son Jeffrey was born; he
suffers grave physical and mental defects. Mr. Gleitman, Mrs.
Gleitman, and Jeffrey brought suit against the defendant on the
ground that the defendant's failure to advise the mother of the
probable, or at least posssible, consequences to her child of her
attack of rubella, as to which there was no dispute, constituted
professional negligence. If he had given the advice he should have
given, she would have obtained other medical advice with a view to
obtaining an abortion. The father claimed damages representing the
extra costs he had incurred in caring for Jeffrey. The mother
based her claim on the effects of the child's defects on her
emotional state. Jeffrey claimed damage with respect to his birth
defects. It is this last claim which I propose to examine first.

Now plainly the medical service which the defendant was employed to give to Mrs. Gleitman was not genetic counseling, because
the damage done by an attack of rubella to the child in utero is
not a consequence of any transmissible genetic defect in either
parent. Although no prenatal or postnatal treatment will avail the
child, the mother suffers no permanent injury, and her subsequent
children will be at no risk from her temporary illness. But clearly
we have here a very close analogy. If a doctor, after conception,
were negligently to give advice which overlooked a strong probability of a damaged child arising from genetic defect in the parents,
the law applicable would be the same as that canvassed in the
Gleitman case.

We may first dispose of an argument that prenatal injuries,
injuries to a person not yet born, do not give a ground of action
against the perpetrator; an injury to a fetus, it is said, is an
injury to a non-existent person. This is not convincing; a fetus
is not an inanimate object without independent legal rights of its
own. For example, in most legal systems a legacy "to the children
of A who are alive at the time of my death" will include a child of
A in utero at the death of the testator (12). Furthermore, as Professor Tedeschi points out, the wrong done is a continuing wrong;
the damage derives from a prenatal act, but continues throughout
the child's life (13). There could be no doubt that the negligent
automobile driver who injures, whether physically or mentally, both
a mother and her unborn child is liable in damages to both.

In a case before the Bundesgericht in 1952 (14), a pregnant
married woman was given a blood transfusion in the hospital; by the
negligence of the hospital, she received it from a donor who was
infected with syphilis, and she gave birth to a syphilitic girl.

On the principle I have just stated, it was held that the girl had an action of damages against the hospital. It is thought, however, that a different result would follow if the birth defect were attributable to the act of conception itself. So, although an Italian court (15) had held that a child had an action of damages against its parents for transmitting a venereal disease, and the Oberlandesgericht at Schleswig had come to a similar conclusion (16), the Bundesgericht took a contrary view (17), expressing it in terms which are directly relevant to our assessment of the Gleitman case. They pointed out that the plaintiff child could not succeed because, had it not been for the sexual act complained of, the plaintiff would have had no existence at all. It was on this ground--namely, that if Mrs. Gleitman had been, as she claimed, properly advised, and had obtained an abortion, Jeffrey would have been, not a healthy child, but non-existent--that the New Jersey Court decided in favour of the defendant. The action was dismissed on the ground that the pleadings disclosed no cause of action: that is why the court accepted, arguendo, for purposes of the decision, the statement of the facts presented by the plaintiffs. The defendant doctor, of course, had filed a very different version. The ground of the decision was stated by Justice Proctor as follows: "The infant plaintiff .... is required to say not that he should have been born without defects but that he should not have been born at all. In the language of tort law he says: but for the negligence of defendants, he would not have been born to suffer with an impaired body. In other words, he claims that the conduct of defendants prevented his mother from obtaining an abortion which would have terminated his existence, and that his very life is "wrongful." The normal measure of damages in tort actions is compensatory. Damages are measured by comparing the condition the plaintiff would have been in, if the defendants had not been negligent, with plaintiff's impaired condition as a result of the negligence. The infant plaintiff would have to measure the difference between his life with defects against the utter void of nonexistence, but it is impossible to make such a determination. This Court cannot weigh the value of life with impairments against the nonexistence of life itself. By asserting that he should not have been born, the infant plaintiff makes it logically impossible to measure his alleged damages because of the impossibility of making the comparison required by compensatory remedies" (18).

I find myself in respectful agreement with this judgment. It is supported by the decision of the Bundesgericht to which I have referred and also by Professor Tedeschi (19). It has been followed by the Supreme Court of the State of New York (20). However, it has been criticized by at least one commentator (21); he challenges the view taken by the courts, which he states in diagrammatic form as

Life	=	a plus value (+)
Life with defects	=	a plus-minus value ($\pm$)
Non-existence	=	a minus value (-)

He would prefer to substitute

Life without defects	=	a plus value (+)
Non-existence	=	0
Life with defects	=	a minus value (-)

There are two objections to the latter diagram. First, if you delete, as you are entitled to do in comparing values, a term which has been described by a mere cipher, you are left with exactly the plus against minus situation which you find in all accident cases and which the German Court in the syphilitic blood transfusion case (14) had no difficulty in translating into an award of damages. So the instant problem has been shelved. Second, when the author attempts to express his diagram in words, he is forced into the use of an indefinite pronoun which conceals a semantic vacuum. "Such an analysis," he says, "assumes that life without defects is to be desired most, but that in certain situations it would be preferable not to exist rather than to endure life incapacitated by severe physical and mental defects." But if for the words "it would be preferable not to exist" you substitute, as a plaintiff must do, the words "I would prefer not to exist," the fallacy is plain; the "I", which is the subject, being ex hypothesi non-existent in one alternative, cannot predicate his preference for another alternative. It would be like saying, "I am glad I do not exist, because if I did I would be mentally and physically handicapped." This is non-language. Or, as Chief Justice Weintraub put it, "Ultimately, the infant's complaint is that he would be better off not to have been born. Man, who knows nothing of death or nothingness, cannot possibly know whether that is so" (22).

The Court also found support for its decision from two cases, one from Illinois (23) and the other from New York (24); in each of these cases a bastard child had unsuccessfully sued his parents for damages arising from his illegitimate birth. The cases are not particularly relevant in our present field, but they illustrate a divergence in attitude between American and British courts which may well be a consequence of the differing constitutional backgrounds to which I have alluded. In the first of these cases, at least, the court recognized in its judgment the plaintiff's cause of action; "the judgment repeatedly stresses that the child suffered a wrong, but because of the far-ranging consequences, which would result in many other cases, of his right to compensation, it concludes that the matter was better left to legislative action" (25). A British court would have decided conversely; if it had come to the conclusion that the child's claim was well-founded in law, it would have replied to anyone who argued the far-ranging social or political consequences, "It is for the legislature, if you are right, to take away such grounds of action. We must administer the law as we find it, regardless of consequences."

The claims by Mr. and Mrs. Gleitman, on the bases respectively of out-of-pocket expenses and emotional injury, stood on rather a different footing. They were both dismissed, first on the ground that, for the same reasons as we expounded in Jeffrey's claim, you cannot know that you would rather have no child than a defective child. I need not go into this reasoning again; it seems less convincing on this branch of the case. Another ground of decision, which was elaborated especially by Justice Francis is important to our subject, because it deals with legal consequences arising not so much from genetic counseling itself, as from the secondary advice as to treatment, which may follow the primary counsel given. The whole basis of all three claims was that Mrs. Gleitman had, by the defendant's negligence, lost her opportunity for having an abortion. But such an abortion would have been contrary to the criminal law. In the State of New Jersey, it was at that time a crime to terminate a pregnancy "without lawful justification;" the majority decided that potential defects in the child did not supply such justification. As I read the judgments, there was, in fact, at that time no state in the United States in which such an operation would have been legal (26). Under these circumstances, it is hard to see how the failure to render advice as to the desirability of such an operation which would not have been legally available, could be an actionable wrong.

In Great Britain, the situation might have been different. The Abortion Act of 1967 provides that a doctor who terminates a pregnancy is not guilty of an offense if two doctors are of opinion either that the continuance of the pregnancy would involve risk to the life or health of the woman or her family, greater than if the pregnancy were terminated, or that there is a substantial risk that if the child were born, it would be seriously handicapped. What is meant by "substantial risk" may be, as the saying goes, anyone's guess. There is a striking passage in the judgment of Justice Francis, which bears that out: "We have Dr. Cosgrove's testimony that when Mrs. Gleitman informed him of the rubella, he advised her that the incidence of damage to babies of mothers who had the disease in the early stages of their pregnancy was about 20 percent. He said also that he told her there were places where abortions were performed for this reason, but that he did not consider it proper to handle obstetric cases in that way; he did not think that in order to eliminate one baby who might be deformed, the destruction of four more babies who might be perfectly normal was a very reasonable way to conduct the practice of medicine" (27). This argument, of course, would apply only in a case in which a uterine examination capable of disclosing fetal defects was impossible. If such an examination were possible, then the "substantial risk" test demanded by British law might be satisfied, and the controversy would be confined to the question whether the anticipated handicap to the child was "serious." This seems to be the legal significance of the development of amniocentesis; the destruction of a fetus which can be shown to be actually defective (even as a potential "carrier" of a genetic fault) may be justified where such an act done on purely statistical grounds cannot.

I think it is important that as far as possible a legal paper should avoid making value judgments; the whole question of abortion is highly controversial and emotive, as a study of the British Parliamentary Debates at the time of the passing of the 1967 Act would demonstrate. The nature of the argument which was then used against the introduction of what has been called "eugenic abortion" can be deduced from a definition, modestly nestling in a footnote to the article in the Minnesota Law Review to which I have referred --"An eugenic abortion is one which is performed to preserve the integrity, well-being and physical perfection of the human race" (28). The constituting of a competent authority qualified to exercise the coercive measures which would be necessary to achieve this social utopia would present, fortunately, a political and not a legal problem.

For the purposes of an exploration of comparative doctrines, it is clearly important to have some knowledge of which states tolerate abortions carried out for purposes other than saving the life or health of the mother, because if the aborting of a fetus on the ground of its genetic or other defects is anywhere prohibited by the criminal law, then much of the discussion on counseling becomes, for such countries, irrelevant. And it will be important to see whether the law of a particular state permits termination when the fetus will, at birth and during its life, exhibit no perceptible defect but is nevertheless a carrier of genes which may be expected to give rise to defects in its descendants. A comprehensive study of the statutory law on this topic has been carried out by the World Health Organization.

The state, accordingly, has an interest in, and may be expected to pursue, methods of preventing the transmission of genetic defects; one method will be the discouraging, preventing or punishing of such sexual congress as might be expected, for genetic reasons, to give rise to defective progeny. An obvious precaution would be to insist on premarital medical examination of the parties. This is compulsory in France. "Each party must...produce a certificate from a doctor testifying that he has had a premarital medical examination. The examination includes an X-ray and blood-test, but the results are made known only to the person examined; they are not revealed to the other spouse or the registrar of civil status" (29).   It appears that this examination is directed mainly towards venereal disease and tuberculosis, and it may be that it would be unlikely to disclose genetic defects. But the system is there and could be expanded and adapted. The aspect of confidentiality is very marked; the examining doctor is in a professional relationship with the examinee, with all the consequences which follow from the adherence to Hippocratic ideals. But if the examinee were a public servant, owing his duty to the state which employed him, would he have any duty not to disclose? And surely, to be effective, there would have to be a prohibition which could be enforced when a certificate was unfavorable. This, however, might only result in concubinage becoming more popular than marriage. The constitutional validity of such a proposal in countries where this was relevant would also have to be examined.

The risks which are run when sexual partners have mutant genes in common have not been only recently discovered; even the framers of the Mosaic law were aware of them, though they could not have assigned a scientific cause. To this day, in Scotland, the criminal law of incest and the permissible degrees of marriage are regulated by a statute (30) of King James VI which forbade, on pain of death, congress within the degrees set out in the 18th chapter of the Book Leviticus. As Dr. Clive observes, "Some minimal rules of this sort are practically universal in human societies. Even the free and easy Kaingang of the Brazilian highlands, who recognized monogamous, polyandrous, polygynous, and joint marriages and also quite regularly married their nieces, step-mothers and mothers-in-law, either alone or in combination, drew the line at marriage between parents and children and between full brothers and sisters" (31). It is true that the prohibited degrees in marriage are to some extent maintained in order to preserve order and decency within the family; for example, by British Law, for the purposes of marriage an adopter and his adopted child "are deemed to be within the prohibited degrees of consanguinity" (32), which in very many cases they are not. Nevertheless, the universal enforcement of incest laws demonstrates that in every country at all times the state has claimed the right to interfere, by prohibition or punishment or both, with the liberty of its subjects to join together sexually, whether in marriage or not, and to do so with the object of protecting the health of unborn generations. This is done for genetic reasons which can only have been guessed at as a result of empirical reasoning; if by actual examination, rather than on a balancing of probabilities based on past experiences, it were to be possible to predict more or less accurately that the consequences would be disastrous, it does not seem to be more than a step forward on a well-trod path to prohibit and punish unions with such potentialities.

But prohibition may be ineffective, and punishment will probably be too late; sterilization, either voluntary or compulsory, has the element of certainty. Voluntary sterilization, it is understood, is more commonly undergone for family limitation reasons than for the purpose of removing from the breeding stock a person likely to transmit defects. But in either case, few legal problems are involved where a true consent has been given. The lawful limitations of consent have sometimes been debated (33), and there are dicta to the effect that, as it is not possible validly to consent to bodily maiming, the operation of sterilization, even with ostensible consent, is unlawful (34). This may be the rule in countries in which all forms of contraception are forbidden, but since we are here rather in the realm of private law as between husband and wife, it is not necessary to go further. I will only say that I do not personally agree with that legal opinion.

Compulsory sterilization raises quite a different question,

being one of public law, that is, the rights of the state in
relation to the citizen. In many countries the legislature is not
all-powerful in this field, as I have already pointed out. In the
United States, for example, according to Professor Gard, "there is
no doubt that...compulsory eugenic controls of a 'positive' nature
would violate the due process clause of the fifth and fourteenth
amendments, as well as the ninth amendment of the Federal constitution as most recently interpreted" (35). The case of <u>Griswold</u> <u>v.</u>
<u>Connecticut</u> (36) is thus interpreted by the same learned author:
"The decision by a husband and wife to have children, or not to
have children, or how many children to have, is one in which the
state may not interfere, whether the purpose be to limit the
population or to improve it genetically."

I have already alluded to a further control, i.e., that of
public opinion, and in European countries, even those like Britain
that have no entrenched constitutional guarantees, there is also an
international legal obstacle to the unlimited exercise of national
legislative power. Article 12 of the European Convention on Human
Rights provides: "Men and women of marriageable age have the right
to marry and to found a family, according to the national laws
governing the exercise of this right," and Article 14 declares that
"the enjoyment of the rights and freedoms as set forth in this
Convention shall be secured without discrimination on any ground
such as sex, race, color, language, religion, political or other
opinion, national or social origin, association with a national
minority, property, birth or other status." This Convention has
been ratified by Belgium, Denmark, France, West Germany, Iceland,
the Irish Republic, Italy, Luxembourg, the Netherlands, Norway,
Turkey, Great Britain, Greece, and Sweden. Persons whose rights
under the Convention have been denied have a right of appeal to the
European Court. It seems certain that compulsory sterilization
would be unlawful under the Article quoted if it were sought to be
imposed on racial grounds, and it is probable that the same result
would attend an attempt to sterilize, for example, habitual criminals, a practice which has been condemned as unconstitutional by
the United States Supreme Court (38); it could be held that that
amounted to discrimination against persons on the ground of status.
It might well be, however, that the European Court would not condemn "national laws governing the exercise of" the right to found a
family if those laws were designed to prohibit the willful transmitting of genetic defects. Such laws would stand on exactly the
same footing as those which, for genetic reasons, forbid marriage
and punish sexual intercourse between persons of particular degrees
of consanguinity (39).

Reverting to Professor Emery's definition in which he includes
in genetic counseling the giving of appropriate advice when requested, one of the situations in which such advice is likely to be
called for is where the genetic make-up of a husband and wife
renders it most unwise for them to have children, yet they have the

natural longing to bring up a family. One of the possibilities is
artificial insemination from a donor who, in conjunction with the
mother, will make a safe parent. The only legal point arising out
of artificial insemination by a donor(A.I.D.) is when it is without
the husband's consent, and whether that constitutes a matrimonial
offense, and if so, what. There is some English authority (40) that
it amounts to adultery, and some Scottish authority (41) to the
effect that it does not; certainly under English law, as recently
changed, it would be a sufficient ground for divorce (42).

     The legal difficulties in the way of A.I.D. probably spring
from religious objections to it; it is prohibited by the Roman
Catholic, Lutheran and Orthodox Jewish religions (43), whereas the
attitude of the Anglican Church is not hostile in principle.
Leaving aside moral considerations, the legal position seems to be
fairly simple, at least in those countries in which the influence
of religious bodies is not decisive in the process of law-making.
No public considerations seem to be against A.I.D., unless it were
the fact that a child so conceived is probably not a legitimate
child (44).   For example, a legacy from A to "the lawful children
of B" would not benefit an A.I.D. child of B's lawful wife.   This
matter is, at least in Britain, not so serious as once it was. The
practical distinction, in the matter of social status, between a
legitimate and illegitimate child has been largely swept away (45).
In any case it is most probable that parents in these circumstances
would adopt the child; the legal rights and capacity of an adopted
child are now very much the same as that of a natural child (46).
It is, however, a topic for discussion whether the law should not
be changed, so that an A.I.D. child, the husband consenting, is to
be deemed for all purposes to be legitimate (47).   This raises
social, not legal, questions.   One result would be to make the
benefits of A.I.D. available to those members of the British
peerage who enjoy hereditary titles. It may be presumed that the
companion technique, namely the implanting in an infertile woman of
an ovum from a donor, for subsequent fertilization by intercourse
with her husband, will, when it is established, have similar legal
consequences.

     It would be possible--but I must resist the temptation--to
attempt an application of legal principles to other facets of the
accelerating development of genetic research, experiment, and therapy. This would be outside the fairly limited terms of my subject.
In some cases we would find ourselves again discussing problems of
status; an example would be found in the question: What relation
do the products of clonal reproduction bear to their fellow-clones
and to the parent stock? I assume that they would be conceded the
status of human beings. Other controversies might be of a more
far-reaching character, for example, whether there are not some
directions in which the law should prohibit even research, at least
upon human material. It is possible that the right of the free man
to acquire and transmit knowledge must at some stage give place to

the concept of the dignity and integrity of the human being, looked at as a fundamental requirement taking precedence of all law, learning, and ethical analyses.

A final instance of the confrontation between the relevant medical procedures and the law may perhaps be of more interest to lawyers than to others. I have been given to understand (48) that research into the virological aspects of cancer causation is now being undertaken, and that this work carries a serious risk of injury to the laboratory staff concerned. In the event of such damage taking place, what legal remedies would be open to the victim? At present it would seem that, at least in the common law and civil law systems, the right of a plaintiff to recover damages would be conditional on his establishing causative negligence on the part of the institution or of those in charge. It may be questionable whether this is satisfactory. Modern legal systems are beginning to give effect to what is almost an ethical consideration, namely, that he who for his own purposes exposes others to a serious risk of a kind that they may be unable by their own precautions to avoid, must himself accept the role of insurer, so that he is liable to make reparation whether or not his operations have been conducted by him with due care. In Britain, the use of atomic energy has been put into this class (49), and perhaps the process to which I have referred should be so classified. There are, in fact, some who go as far as to say that many years ago we should have insisted on this doctrine accompanying the introduction of the automobile to our public highways (50).

ACKNOWLEDGEMENTS

I should like to express my thanks to those who have been generous with their professional advice, especially Professor A.E.H. Emery and Dr. Anne McLaren, both of the University of Edinburgh, and Mr. Willi Steiner, of the Institute of Advanced Legal Studies in the University of London.

NOTES AND REFERENCES

1. See F.P. Grad, *Legislative Responses to the New Biology*, 1967-8, 15 UCLA L. Rev. 480. W. Carey Parker, *Some Legal Aspects of Genetic Counselling, Progress in Medical Genetics*, Vol. 7, 1970, p. 217.

2. Emery, *Genetic Counselling*, (1969) 14 *Scottish Medical Journal* 335.

3. Amos & Walton, *Introduction to French Law*; 3rd Ed. p. 218.

4. *B.G.B.* 823 (1).

5. *Code Civil Hellenique* Art, 914.

6. *Code Civil* Art 2031, 2059.

7. See *Chin Keow v. Government of Malaysia* (1967) 1 WLR 813.

8. *Charlesworth on Negligence* 4th Ed. at para 1013, quoting Willes J. in *Harmer v. Cornelius* (1858) 5 C.B. (N S) 236.

9. I was informed in conversation with a Dutch surgeon and one from California that the premium for insuring against medical negligence was 100 times higher for the latter than for the former. In *Hunter v. Hanley* 1955 SC 200, an action in Scotland against a doctor for professional negligence, it was observed by the Court "that there are practically no decisions on this question in the reported cases." The Court was therefore obliged to proceed largely upon precedents relating to the analogous relationship between attorney and client.

10. See *Roe v. Minister of Health* (1954) 2 Q.B. 66.

11. *Gleitman v. Cosgrove,* 49 N.J. 22, 227 A. 2d 689 (1967).

12. "Qui in utero est, pro jam nato habetur."

13. Tedeschi, *On Tort Liability for 'Wrongful Life',* 1966, 1 Israel L.R. 513, 525.

14. 20 XII 1952, *Juristenzeitung* 1953, 307. The *Bundesgericht* is the German Federal Supreme Court.

15. *Foro it.* 1951, I 981.

16. *Neue jur. Woch,* 1950, 388. The *Oberlandesgericht* is a Provincial Court of Appeal.

17. *Juristenzeitung* 1951, 758.

18. 227 A. 2d, at 692.

19. See notes 17 and 13, supra.

20. *Stewart v. Long Island College Hospital.* 58 Misc. 2d 432 (1968). The Supreme Court is not the highest appeals court in New York, but the highest trial court.

21. 55 *Minn. L. Rev.* 58 (1970).

22. 227 A. 2d, 711.

23. *Zepeda v. Zepeda,* 41 Ill. App. 2d 240 (1963).

24. *Williams v. State of New York,* 18 N.Y. 2d 481 (1966).

25. Tedeschi, supra, N. 13, at 520.

26. Parker, op.cit, supra, N. 1 writing in 1970, says, at p. 229, that "in the United States, Canada and England the prevailing legal pattern is

an absolute prohibition of abortion, except to save the mother's life". This has not been the case in England for many years--see R. v. Newton *(1958)* Crim. L.R. *469; or Scotland--see Gordon,* Criminal Law, *p. 381-2.*

27. *227 A. 2d, at 694.*

28. *Op.cit., supra, N. 21, at 61.*

29. *E.M. Clive, Reform of the Scottish Marriage Law. Thesis submitted to the University of Virginia School of Law, 1967, p. 111.*

30. *1567 cap. 14.*

31. *Clive, supra, N. 29, p. 141.*

32. *Adoption Act, 1958 sec. 13.*

33. *See, e.g.,* R. v. Donovan *(1934) 2 KB 493, a case of sexual flagellation.*

34. *See the dissenting judgment of Denning L.J. in* Bravery v. Bravery *(1954) 1 W.L.R. 1169.*

35. *Grad, supra, N. 1, at 486.*

36. *381 U.S. 479 (1965).*

37. *Grad, supra, N. 1, at 488.*

38. Skinner v. Oklahoma, *316 U.S. 535 (1942).*

39. *It is, however, interesting to note that incest became a crime in England, rather than an ecclesiastical offense, as recently as by the Punishment of Incest Act, 1908.*

40. *Russell v. Russell (1924) A.C. 687, 721.*

41. MacLennan v. MacLennan *1958 S.C. 105. This has been questioned; see Walker,* Principles of Scottish Private Law *I, 237.*

42. *Divorce Reform Act, 1969. "The respondent has behaved in such a way that the petitioner cannot reasonably be expected to live with the respondent."*

43. *See Leach,* The Biocrats, *Cape 1970, p. 72.*

44. *Smith,* Law, Professional Ethics, and the Human Body, *1959 SLT (N) 245.*

45. *See Legitimation (Scotland) Act, 1968.*

46. *See Adoption Act, 1958.*

47. *Walker, op. cit. supra, N. 41, at 163, suggests that in Scotland this*
    may already be so, since A.I.D. has been held not to be adultery. At
    least the law requires clarification.

48. *Conversations with Dr. Peter G. Condliffe, Fogarty International*
    Center, National Institutes of Health.

49. *See Nuclear Installations Act, 1965.*

50. *Kilbrandon, Other People's Law (Hamlyn Lectures).*

THE NEED FOR A PHILOSOPHICAL ANTHROPOLOGY

Charles Fried

Lord Kilbrandon's paper, on which I have been asked to comment, requires no detailed exegesis. With his characteristic lucidity, he has laid before us the legal issues relating to genetic counseling and given us as well a sense of the range of solutions implicit in existing law. What I wish to do is to set out the difficulties that beset the attempts to resolve the full range of questions raised by this and other techniques growing out of the "new biology." Perhaps the rights and obligations involved in genetic counseling (as opposed to some kind of therapy or other intervention) seem relatively straightforward. Thomas Reed Powell once said that if you can think about a thing that is inextricably related to another thing, without thinking about the thing to which it is related, you have the legal mind. Lord Kilbrandon, distinguished jurist though he is, does not display this quality of the legal mentality. For he sees that the practice, indeed the profession, of giving advice about genetic disorders is related to the practice of doing something about such disorders. Today that means avoiding conception, perhaps deciding not to marry, or preventing the birth of a fetus at risk. But it could mean other things. It could mean state intervention to prevent the birth of genetically defective individuals. And, through the extension of the techniques of prenatal analysis--amniocentesis--it could lead to parental choice of the sex of the children they would allow to be born. So here, as everywhere in this area, we are right in the middle of the whole congerie of ethical and political problems raised by the new biology.

In general it is my belief that very little truly illuminating or, therefore, useful has been written by way of solution, although much has been produced to show the implications of the existing and potential techniques of the new biology. These--ranging from the imminent to the remote--are probably quite familiar to this audience. I will not rehearse them. What I would like to do is to indicate the general categories of ethical questions that these possibilities raise. These categories are frequently ignored, to the added confusion of an often confused subject.

DISTRIBUTIVE JUSTICE

The definition of distributive justice given by Aristotle is the one I have in mind for this first category. Distributive justice relates to the distribution of undoubted goods in circumstances of scarcity. Thus (1) what constitutes a value is not in dispute. All would choose the goods involved. And (2) the problem therefore arises out of the scarcity, because there is not enough to go around. Thus the issues are easier, because we do not have to worry in this instance what our definition of values is, only how we distribute them.

Applied to the area of our concern, the problem is who is to benefit from scarce medical resources. This is hardly a new question. It obtains as well in respect to housing, education, or money in general. One special feature is the immediacy and sharpness of some of the distributive choices. Who gets access to an artificial kidney or who gets the organ transplant determines directly and immediately who shall live or die. Whether the choice should be made in terms of deserts--the worthier person or need--or on some random and thus equal basis--poses the traditional dilemma of distributive justice. And, of course, to pass the buck to boards of clergymen, citizens or whoever, is not to resolve the issue, only to leave it to others to resolve. I shall say more of this institutionalized evasion of intellectual responsibility later.

At a more remote and probably more practical level are questions relating to the allocation of resources between the fancy techniques of modern medicine and the new biology and humbler measures like vaccination, improved diets and the like. Who are the beneficiaries of each kind of expenditure? Are we not perhaps fooling ourselves when we say that future generations in large numbers will benefit by today's exotic research? Is it not more the case that some things are of greater interest to the scientist? Or worse still, is it not possible that those who make the distributional decision know that the humbler measures of public wealth will not benefit them, while they and their loved ones will be the beneficiaries of wonder cures?

On this question we need not only understand what our distributional norm is, but we also need to work out who, in fact, the beneficiaries of alternative choices may be. Vague references to the welfare of future generations certainly are not enough. Applied to genetic counseling, for instance, we need to know who the beneficiaries of the services provided are, what good is done, and what the alternative uses of resources might be--for instance, improved family planning information generally.

THE PROBLEM OF RIGHTS

The problem of rights--rights of individuals against each other, against the collectivity, even against the public good--is a modern problem. The modern liberal or individualistic concept of personality presupposes a concept of rights which the individual can claim against the socially defined good. This concept of right is heavily involved in the issues which concern us here. Even as to the special question of genetic counseling, we ask whether a person has the right to certain kinds of information, such as the right to have his case treated confidentially, the right to an abortion, or, conversely, the right to marry and have children. From a different angle, we ask whether it is a right to be born, once conceived. In other areas of the new biology, there has been talk of the right to die, the right to be genetically unique, and the right to be the product of normal sexual intercouse and pregnancy.

Two things are striking about such assertion of right. First, rights are usually asserted, so it follows that their possessor can waive their assertion. This is a corollary of the concept of rights as belonging to the individual. Second, if they are worth anything, the rights must be assertable as against the claims of the collectivity. And this is how they are characteristically used. The right to marry and have children need only be asserted if society is claiming that the common good, for eugenic reasons, requires that certain persons not reproduce. The right to confidentiality is asserted in the face of a public need to know. And the mother's right to an abortion is asserted against the unborn child's right to live. This last claim of right must be made on behalf of the unborn child, and for that reason some have thought it an invalid claim. It is made as well against the possible claim of the public good that unwanted children represent a public liability.

What we are far from having is a comprehensive theory of rights, much less a unified theory which shows how rights and the notion of the public good are functions of some over-all scheme. It is, however, a subject that is occupying the thought of some of the best modern philosophers. And, although there are no break-throughs in philosphy in the same sense as there are in science, we can expect increasing understanding.

THE FRANKENSTEIN PROBLEM

The issues which the new biology has raised more strikingly than any others have not been the foregoing, since they have always been clearly present in much that we do as individuals and as a society. The striking problem is that raised by our growing capacity to affect who we will become, to affect what the nature of man will be. Both distributive justice and the question of rights proceed from the assumption that we know what we want, and the question is which of our values will be realized. But eugenics, whether as a result of genetic counseling or of more arcane methods, as well as chemical and electrical intervention with mental processes, may allow us to determine what wants we or our children will have.

These capacities raise different questions. If we can ensure that we or some future person will have certain values, a particular constellation of appetites and preferences, how shall we choose? We are not cut adrift completely from the notion that we must try to realize the desires of existing and future beings. We must decide instead what should those desires be.

This requires a deeper conception of value, of the good. Education is the social process most nearly akin to the Frankensteinian possibilities of the new biology. But even there we have always been able to finesse--if we wished--the deep problems, by assuming an innate human nature whose potentialities education was designed to bring to realization. Here we can manipulate human nature itself. But for that we need unavoidably a normative concept of human nature. And, of course, to change nothing is to assume that the status quo is itself normative--an implausible suggestion in light of the evidence of anthropology that man's intelligence, capacities and temperament have themselves been subject to evolutionary forces throughout the millenia.

THE RESPONSES

What I have seen of the attempts to deal with these problems has been only occasionally encouraging. Perhaps the patent need to arrive at what I shall call a philosophical anthropology, i.e., a normative concept of human nature, has naturally suggested the intervention of theologians. Professor Paul Ramsey of Princeton has certainly grasped this kind of problem, although I must confess I have failed to grasp the structure of his analyses and solutions.

The dominant current of secular Anglo-American ethical philosophy is, I believe, a mixture of utilitarianism and Kantian humanism. Both of these provide only limited help in solving the Frankensteinian problem. The deeper philosophy, that derived from Kant, places a primary emphasis on respect for man's rationality and autonomy. This rational freedom, freedom even from determination by one's own psychological drives, is for Kant the defining feature of man's nature. Clearly this is a normative concept of human nature.

Unfortunately, the applicability of the Kantian ethic to these issues is problematic. Since morals are autonomous from man's contingent nature--his psychological makeup--it would seem that the content of that contingent nature is of no interest to moral philosphy. Perhaps, however, if we could get a better understanding than we now have--or than that which Kant gives us--of freedom of choice and its preconditions, we might discover what developments of the person are most conducive to moral freedom.

The distinguished French biochemist, Jacques Monod, has taken what seems to me to be the other leg on which Kantian ethics stand--rationality--and fashioned from it a criterion for value. In his "Ethique de la Connaissance," he proposes as distinctly human whatever enhances man's capacity to understand, truly and objectively, the structure of the universe. My difficulty with this standard is that it is incomplete. It gives no way of evaluating the relations persons may have to each other or the kinds of feelings they might have, except as these affect their capacity to obtain scientific knowledge.

Clearly the development of intellectually satisfactory and satisfying value criteria for the development of man's future is a remote and arduous task. It may involve the development of related epistemological and metaphysical structures. All this is a daunting prospect: no immediate results, no resolutions approved by international congresses. Partly out of the anti-intellectualism of modern science and scientists--many of whom are both unconcerned with and impatient of the great philosophical traditions--and partly out of an impatient desire to attain some results, to reach some conclusions, there has grown up what I would call a cult of second-orderism. Rather than try to develop systems of thought about these questions of value, thought is channeled into the fashioning of institutions in which these value choices would be made. In the corrupt version of this, which I shall call conferencism, groups of distinguished persons state their strongly held views, and then the effort is expanded in maneuvering for a group consensus. Of course, reasons for the strongly held views are only sketchily presented, if at all, and the task of dissecting the reasoning behind and the evidence for the views is quite out of order.

A more valid version of second-orderism is the design of institutional structures such that wide sectors of the public might be involved in the decisions that affect their future and that of coming generations. I say this is more valid because there are well-established norms that affirm the value of wide public involvement in the future of the commonweal. But this only takes us part of the way. Although the power of decision should be widely shared, this says nothing at all about the validity of the decision reached. It is a mindless fallacy to pass from the proposition that the majority should rule to the proposition that what the majority rules is right. We still have the responsibility, as responsible men of intellect, to conclude what we think is right on the merits, and to try to persuade our fellow citizens in the appropriate councils.

Thus, as in the example of genetic counseling, what the rights and obligations are to be should in the end be established by democratic institutions, but surely those institutions must be informed by the understanding of specialists such as ourselves. The development of that understanding, however, is a task for arduous, patient effort, and it is no more easily or casually attained than are the scientific discoveries which opened up these issues.

PRIVACY AND GENETIC INFORMATION

Herbert A. Lubs

INTRODUCTION

Privacy is a hot topic!
Invasion of privacy is decried on the streets and discussed in academic halls. The preservation of privacy is almost a holy cause in the United States and, indeed, it is somewhat un-American not to come to the vigorous defense of privacy. The other side of the coin, namely, the possible harmful effects of maintaining privacy, is less often displayed.

In this paper, I hope to provoke thought about what test cases might be most suitable to clarify the issues of medical ethics in relation to human genetics and what new laws might be desirable. However, one might ask whether we really would like to bring legal clarification to these issues. Perhaps instead a set of ethics for the medical geneticist would be more appropriate for handling this rapidly changing situation in human genetics.

One of the theses I submit is that over the next 10 to 20 years we must re-examine and possibly modify attitudes towards privacy. The geneticist must work in this sensitive area and it is critical for the future practice of medical genetics that questions of privacy be resolved. Stated succinctly, "How can optimal use of genetic data best be coupled with the maintenance of privacy?"

Genetic information may be used in three ways. A "good use" might be prevention of mental retardation by early treatment of a genetic disorder in a child known to be at risk. A "misuse" might be release of a report of an individual's abnormal chromosome complement in a way which would hinder his employment. "Nonuse," or complete privacy, would be a lost opportunity to use genetic information for the benefit of other family members.

The considerations must be made slightly more complex, however. Two levels of privacy are implicit even in these simple examples: (1) the patient's own privacy and (2) that of other family members, including future offspring. There are also two general routes by which an individual's privacy may be invaded.

The first is through the proband (or propositus), who is the individual through whom a family comes to medical attention. This

267

may occur in several ways.   An individual with a genetic disorder
may   seek   medical   attention and the medical geneticist may subsequently seek information from or provide genetic counseling to
other family members of the proband. Their privacy is therefore
invaded. Similarly, geneticists interested in research may begin
their clinical investigations with a group of individuals ascertained from clinics and hospital records and proceed to their
families.   If the investigation is on a larger scale, the genetics
investigator might search health insurance records of major insuring agencies for patients with Tay-Sachs disease, for example.
This would certainly be part of the "Big Brother" concern.

     The second route is the identification of individuals with
genetic disorders through surveys or screening programs. These may
be either legally required, such as the PKU screening program, or
for the purpose of medical research. The cytogenetic surveys of
consecutive newborn infants are examples.   In the future, medical
screening of individuals in health plans will likely include
certain genetic tests, such as tests for sickle and other abnormal
hemoglobins.   I emphasize this second route of invasion of privacy
because here the individual does not come to the doctor with a
medical problem. The relationship between the doctor and the
patient is thus different, and he is an unusual proband. We are
going to the patient and asking to help him.

PRACTICAL PROBLEMS

     The majority of our work in the last 5 years in the Department
of Pediatrics, University of Colorado Medical Center, has begun
with cytogenetic studies of relatively large unselected populations
of newborns or children, and we have become experts in how people
react to having their privacy invaded.   The range of reactions
displayed by these children's mothers was enormous: from interest
manifested by a letter every six months inquiring about the program
of the study, to refusal to participate in the study because the
mother was convinced my research nurse was really a commercial
photographer. We have ventured out into several hundred of these
thousands of families for more information and have experienced a
wide range of reactions, often from the same person in a family.
One hostile aunt of a child with a translocation, who initially
resisted being studied, finally cooperated, but later again became
hostile because more family studies had not been done sooner.
Perhaps I oversold. Most people have been extremely cooperative
and interested. Several examples will serve to illustrate certain
of the problems we encountered. The names and precise pedigrees
are hypothetical, but each situation has actually occurred.

     Jack was found to have an XYY karyotype in a survey of newborn
infants (Figure 1). Generally, the occurrence of an XYY karyotype
is a sporadic event, and we are not greatly concerned with its
transmission to offspring. We are concerned with the effect the

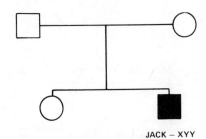

JACK — XYY

FIGURE 1. <u>Ascertainment Through Screening Programs:</u>
<u>Problems for the Individual</u>

XYY karyotype, as well as knowledge of this karyotype, on Jack's development and progress in life. The stereotype of the XYY "syndrome" has passed too quickly into the public domain, and the concern is what teachers, neighbors, and employers will think if they know that he is XYY. It is difficult to envision any benefit to his image, except in the eyes of an interested genetics investigator. Because of our knowledge of his karyotype, his development will be watched closely. Perhaps early referral for psychiatric help might help to prevent some of the potential psychological and social problems that appear to be associated with an XYY karyotype in some individuals. It is not known, however, that psychiatric intervention would be effective. Much has been written about the unproven association of the XYY karyotype with prisoner status, and I believe there is a real associated risk, since all surveys show a manyfold increase in frequency of the XYY karyotype in prisoners over that in newborn infants. Many XYY men, however, are normal, and the real problem is our ignorance. Jack may be the victim of this ignorance, and the question is how to safeguard him and protect society. My own temporary solution to this problem is to stall until we know more. The safest thing seems to be to withhold the information from everyone and to follow Jack closely. Ultimately, when perspective returns, society and physicians and the patient can handle the situation as it should be handled: by evaluating the particular person's performance and behavior. Privacy, ultimately, will not be so important in such cases.

What sort of informed consent should be obtained in studies such as this, which led to the detection of Jack's XYY karyotype? First, it should contain an assurance that the information will remain private. It should also include a statement that if important medical information is found, the investigator will inform the patient and his physician if it is felt to be helpful information. It should probably not include very much more. I do not see how we can discuss, when doing such surveys, all the possible disorders we may find and all of the implications. There are hundreds of abnormalities and we cannot possibly inform someone of each one.

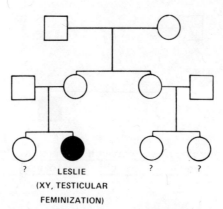

FIGURE 2 . <u>Ascertainment Through Screening Programs:</u>
<u>Problems for Other Family Members</u>

        Leslie was a normal appearing baby girl who showed evidence of
a Y chromosome in a survey of amnions (Figure 2).   This test was
being done on each infant at the hospital where she was born.
Further tests showed that she had an XY karyotype and the testicular feminization syndrome.   She will develop as a girl and have
normal intelligence, but she will have no uterus and a real risk
that a tumor will develop in her abnormal gonads. Her older sister
and two first cousins, all under 10 years of age, are at risk for
the same problems. How are we to proceed? We do not wish to   tell
the whole truth (that Leslie is a chromosomal male), but we do wish
to provide the best medical care for the family. Generally, we
explain the risks and offer both prophylactic surgery and hormonal
treatment, without being specific about the chromosomal information, and often we do not put the chromosome or pathology reports
in the medical chart. The most difficult question arises when the
family pursues the etiology of the problems and wants to know the
results of the chromosome studies. Privacy may be essential to
Leslie's psychological development and the geneticist for each
family must decide how to proceed. It is a case of her privacy (on
a very personal matter) versus her own and her relatives medical
well being.
        I believe we are obligated to offer similar chromosomal
studies to others at risk in the family, and therefore to invade
their privacy. Both real and imagined concerns will be introduced,
but we hope we will do more good than harm.   Once the issue is
raised, it is critical to proceed with dispatch and return answers
about the normality or abnormality of each person in question.   An
approach might be to wait until those at risk are age 5 or 10 and
then carry out the studies. Americans are a mobile population,
however, and we worry that the family will be lost to followup in
the interval and that a tumor might develop in a family member. We

do not have a nationwide medical data bank and it is likely that a relative will be lost to followup. Here, privacy is likely to be detrimental.

Who is the proper person to investigate, or at least to offer the possibilities of investigation, to the other family members? Is it the state, the geneticist, or the family? There is no current answer to these questions.

I believe that telling people the full truth is good and that this should be our goal, but I think it is too soon for this. People cannot yet cope with too much genetic knowledge about themselves.

The next case is presented as a complex situation involving an additional dimension, time, and should serve to caution us about rigid thinking and premature institution of laws. Hope was found to have 45 chromosomes and a D/G translocation in a survey of newborn infants five years ago (Figure 3). Her mother, grandmother, and aunt had the same translocation. No abnormal family members were found, yet it was felt at the time that a D/G translocation carrier had a significant risk of having a child with an unbalanced karyotype. The benefit from invading this family's privacy was the chance to have subsequent pregnancies monitored by amniocentesis and cytogenetic study, with therapeutic abortion of fetuses with an unbalanced translocation, as suggested by the question marks. The risk figure originally discussed with the parents was in fact a mean of several risk figures, since at least six possible combinations between D and G chromosomes were possible and at that time we could not determine which combination was present. The family was restudied this fall with the more precise new techniques and the translocation was found to involve chromosomes 14 and 22. It is likely that there is little or no risk associated with this particular translocation and that we have caused five years of worry. We hope that by having offered amniocentesis to the involved parents

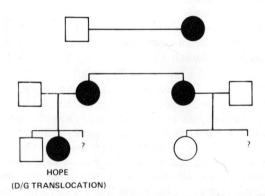

HOPE
(D/G TRANSLOCATION)

FIGURE 3. <u>Ascertainment Through Screening Programs:</u>
<u>Problems Created by Imprecise Methodology</u>

that at least the worry was minimal. The point I want to illustrate here is the hazard of incomplete knowledge. The five year interval between the initial ascertainment, nevertheless, provides an important perspective to the impact of such information on the involved families. Both the passage of time and precise information ultimately may produce a realistic acceptance and utilization of initially disturbing information. When first told that his daughter and wife had a translocation, the father responded half jokingly: "Is that grounds for divorce, Doctor?" Five years later he wrote a grateful letter, saying that they had given copies of my letters to their family physicians and were keeping a folder for each child with appropriate information to be given to them later. Lastly, he even referred to our "humane approach to research." Certain families, at least, are grateful for the invasion of privacy, even in the face of the uncertainties that may be raised in their minds.

Peter was brought to a hemophilia clinic at three months with severe bleeding and the diagnosis of hemophilia A was established (Figure 4). The family was shocked, disbelieving, and rejected the doctor's explanation of X-linked inheritance. No amount of persuasion would change their minds and they refused permission for the medical geneticist to contact relatives, even when it was explained that, by determining the sex of subsequent pregnancies in relatives at risk, it would be possible to prevent other cases of hemophilia in the family. The risks for having an affected male child are as follows (given only one affected male in the family):

Female Relatives	Risk of Having an Affected Male Child
	%
Mother	25.0
Sister	12.5
Niece	6.3
Grand niece	3.2
Maternal grandmother	25.0
Maternal grand aunt	12.5
Maternal first cousin	6.3
Maternal first cousin once removed	3.2
Maternal second cousin	1.6

Many family members have a significant risk. How then are we to proceed? To my knowledge, this situation has not been tested in court and the usual procedure is to respect the privacy of Peter and his parents and hope that other family members at risk will hear of the problem and seek genetic counseling. They seldom do. This, then, is a case of nonuse. No study has been made to determine how many relatives are aware of their risks (or lack of risks) in similar situations. When such a case does come to court, the legal case would seem to rest on how far two laws are extended: the first being the 4th Amendment which covers invasion of privacy,

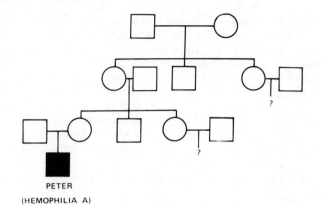

PETER

(HEMOPHILIA A)

FIGURE 4 . Ascertainment Through a Proband:
Refusal of Permission to See Other Family Members

and the second being the State's traditional right to control transmissable disease (e.g., infectious disease). We are on the horns of a dilemma. I can envision being sued by the mother if I went to other family members or by other family members if I did not.

THE DATA BANK AND BIG BROTHER

What has been discussed above are my concerns as a medical geneticist. Most people's concerns, I suspect, are about other possible misuses of computerized genetic data. Will "Big Brother" decide that certain parents cannot reproduce? How can we prevent computerized control of human behavior?

Are these real concerns? At the moment there is no prospect of a nationwide genetic data bank, but a number of genetic registries are being developed. Dr. William Kimberling has a very large family registry in Oregon, and the aim is to record in the computer registry all the families in Oregon with genetic disorders. Dr. Marie-Louise Lubs in our laboratory is beginning a similar registry for Colorado. One of our specific aims in computerizing the data is to make it relatively easy to contact each family once a year, both to provide them with information about newly available treatments and to update our records. In addition, we hope it will be a resource to which the families can continue to turn for help and information over the years as they move about the country. We proceed, I might add, only on a voluntary basis and one of our first projects will be to determine the families' reactions to this intrusion into their privacy.

There are a number of ways of maintaining the privacy of information on tapes and discs. The primary one is to code each person's data and identification, and to keep names and addresses on separate tapes. It is also possible to garble the coded information on the tape or disc in a number of ways, but this seems to me unnecessary. It would take a rather sophisticated intruder to find the number of the desired tape (there are thousands in the computer center), the format, and the coding system, hire a programmer and have access to a computer. The hazard is not the computerized data, no matter how extensive, but the people around it. I don't see any safeguard from an underpaid programmer who might be bought, or a crusading geneticist who wished to prove how dangerous this approach was by exposing all data to the public. Basically, we have to depend on the integrity of scientists for the maintenance of privacy.

Let us assume, for the sake of discussion, that there is a nationwide data bank and that a request for names and addresses of all individuals with hemophilia is made by an insurance company who wished to offer special high risk policies to families with hemophilia. Should this information be released? Who should decide on the "goodness" of such a request? We can get some information about this by looking at other parts of the world. In Sweden such a data bank for certain diseases does exist and is workable. Information is released to bona fide investigators and no one seems troubled by it. I mention this simply to show that we should at least consider the benefits from such an approach as well as the hazards. Perhaps a board of medical geneticists, laymen, and social scientists would be helpful in the future if such a data bank even comes to pass in the United States. It is the history of science that, if something can be done, it will be done. Our role, I believe, is to see that something is done well, not to prevent its being done at all.

SUMMARY AND CONCLUSIONS

A simple balance sheet can serve to summarize what has been presented:

Potential Hazards of Loss of Privacy

Loss of feeling of "privacy," per se.
Prejudicial use of genetic information by other persons.
Disastrous effects on the patient of "loaded" information such
    as chromosomal sex.
Creation of unnecessary concerns in other family members.
Control of reproduction in a biased or unsound fashion by
    society.

Potential Benefits of Loss of Privacy

Opportunity of realistically dealing with a high reproductive
    risk.
Opportunity to alleviate unnecessary fears in relatives at
    complications of genetic disease in relatives.
Opportunity to offer selective reproduction via therapeutic
    abortion to relatives at risk.
Opportunity to offer benefits of research to affected families,
    without the usual 5-10 year delay.

How can these problems be resolved? Time, I believe, is the
most important factor. The combination of better genetic information and better education of the public about genetics will resolve
most of them. Examples of abnormal human karyotypes and biochemical
disorders are now in many high school biology books, and sickle
cell disease is becoming a household word, albeit for the wrong
reasons. Privacy need not be such a hot topic. In the interim,
however, we must proceed cautiously.

DISCUSSION

SINGER: Dr. Lubs makes a point that is important for lawyers,
physicians, and philosophers to remember--facts always seem to
get in the way of our nice, theoretical analyses. They resist
getting shoved comfortably into the pigeonholes we design for
them. For example, one who is committed to full disclosure of
information cannot but be made uncomfortable by the example of the
XY female.

In analyzing issues of privacy we must ask to what extent and
under what circumstances is it appropriate to invade the privacy of
another? This question has two parts: the acquisition of information and the disclosure of information. It is one thing to
acquire genetic data from A, about A; a different question is
raised when we acquire data from A about B. On the disclosure
side, should disclosure be made to the donor of the information or
to some related party for whom the genetic information may be relevant? Perhaps the most difficult problem is disclosure of
information to an unrelated person. Whose privacy is being
invaded, by whom is it being invaded, and for what purposes is the
invasion made?

We may also come to the point where we ask whether there are
some types of information that we do not want to have acquired.
For the research community, are there some types of experiments or
information that you simply do not want to get into? One example
is the relationship, if any, between race and intelligence. I am
not anxious to acquire that information because I think it is

irrelevant to current social issues. Thus for the issue of mass screening, we must balance the need to know and the right to maintain privacy among human beings who live very closely in one society.

CAPRON: The primary harm to a patient arises in the screening process when information which was never sought by the patient is found out. Giving this information to the patient is the second point at which he is harmed. If, however, a patient comes to you asking for information about himself, this information should be conveyed to him, although in a proper psychological setting. But it does not seem to me that there are any grounds, other than a misimpression of what is in the patient's best interest, which would lead to withholding information which is sought.

MURRAY: You have exaggerated the situation. It is the exceptional case in which one withholds information, and it is certainly not routine medical practice. The kinds of cases in which I would do that are those involving emotional stability. Lawyers ought to know that you can get some of the biggest verdicts in suits relating to emotional distress. You are trying to ignore the emotions in your rule that knowledge should always be transmitted. Also, you are guessing, just as the physician is guessing, that the patient will be able to deal with the information, no matter how it is conveyed. All you need is one person who takes an overdose of barbiturates or jumps off a bridge, and the lawyers have a case against the physician or counselor. You can get in trouble whether you give the information, and a patient kills himself, or whether you withhold the information. I prefer to commit a sin of omission rather than take the chance of committing a sin of commission.

CAPRON: I have stated a rule, which I defended on both theoretical and practical grounds, and yet I admit that you may present a case to me which I will find very difficult to insist should be guided by the principle of full disclosure. I don't pretend to say that these choices are easy or that they should always be decided according to that principle.

MCLAREN: Mr. Capron has raised the problem of withholding information in the interests of the patient. This is really an example of the more general category of paternalism which is, of course, traditional to the medical profession. Medical practitioners should remember that if they do err, they are likely to err in that direction.

FRIED: Several non-physicians and I share Dr. McLaren's notion that the medical profession is indeed very paternalistic. Surely, if a physician has some findings, perhaps broad, inconclusive, or even incorrect, it would be very wrong to withhold this information on the mistakenly paternalistic notion that the people involved couldn't take it.

HIMSWORTH: Lord Kilbrandon made the point that a special relationship exists between a doctor and a patient, a relationship based on the expectation that the doctor will do the best for the patient that it is possible to do. The ultimate responsibility is on the physician to decide what information to give to the patient. If you get information that a fetus is abnormal, you have got to ask yourself what will be the effect of disclosing this, however tactfully and carefully, to the mother? Can she face bringing up this child? Or when she gets away from my persuasion and smoothness of talking, will she go take an overdose of barbiturates?

CAPRON: There seems to be no question that the relationship is a complex one, and there may be many doctors who believe, as Sir Harold does, that the doctor should make many choices for his patient. However, if doctors find themselves making choices not about the medical facts, but about future psychological factors of the child and the parents, then I think doctors have overstepped their role. This is not the role of the doctor; the doctor has the responsibility of conveying the medical import of the diagnosis.

MURRAY: Mr. Capron, in your analysis of one case you considered legal justification for performing abortion, and you supported the parents' right to decide to abort a fetus based on what they thought was in the best interests of the unborn child. I know a great deal more about a patient, even though I have only talked to him for a brief time, than those parents know about an unborn fetus. Therefore, I don't see how you can justify the rights of a parent to make a decision about a fetus, and say that the physician, who knows at least what the patient looks like, has no right to decide what is in the patient's best interests.

CAPRON: I am criticizing the substitution of judgment of best interests by one person for another. The person sitting across the table from you is able to make judgments for himself, whereas the fetus is not. Traditionally the role of making substitute judgment for children in our society has been given to the parents. If we were to conclude that the parent is no more able to make an accurate or an informed judgment for a fetus than a doctor is able to make for a patient, then we ought to find someone else to do it.

KILBRANDON: It may be a very serious question for the doctor whether he tells the truth or whether he gives the information which he judges to be most beneficial to his patient. If these two are in conflict, there is no doubt at all which he has to do. He has to give the information which is most beneficial to his patient. This may be a very difficult decision, and I really was quite horrified when Dr. Murray expressed the view that you can't win, because they will get you either way. If that were so, the law would be in a very shocking state. As I understand the law, a suit brought against a doctor raises the question of whether or not he has been negligent, not whether he has offered some treatment which another doctor would not have offered, or he has taken a view of the case which might not appeal to some of his other colleagues.

Whether you offer the truth or some modified part of the truth, or whether you offer beneficial information, is a very tricky question on which there is ample room for bona fide difference of opinion. If the law says that, having come down on one side in good faith, with adequate skill, and perhaps having discussed it with your colleagues, you are liable for damages, then the law ought to be changed.

HAVIGHURST: I pose the possibility that we litigate the matter. I will present some 20 expert witnesses drawn from this audience to indicate that the custom and practice in the profession of genetic counseling is to the effect that some information may be withheld. They would agree that in a particular case, it was professionally appropriate to withhold the information. Now, who would win, if that evidence were presented and not seriously challenged?

What I am asking is a clearer statement of what the law in fact is. I suggest that, in some states at least, the law on informed consent is that the doctor is obligated to inform his patient only to the extent that other practitioners in the area would inform the patient in similar circumstances.

CAPRON: Your premise is one which Lord Kilbrandon has already highlighted in that there is a great deal of "ought" as opposed to "is." Doctors have asked me exactly that question, and my answer has been that the prevailing law in judging the disclosure of information is, indeed, the standard which has always applied in malpractice, which is "the reasonable medical practitioner."

I suggest that some of the informed consent cases, for example, Salgo v. Stanford University Board of Trustees (154 Cal. App. 2d 560, 317 P 2d 170 (1957)) have conceived of the doctor's action not so much as a violation of the old standards of negligence, but under another tort standard whereby an intentional withholding of information or a deception would be judged by a reasonable man standard, so that the jury would be asked to decide whether it was reasonable to withhold information, and expert testimony as such would not be pertinent. Experts might persuade a jury that this was a reasonable course, but they would not be bound by that testimony under the instructions of the judge. An example of this approach in a therapeutic setting is Berkey v. Anderson (1 Cal. App. 3d 790, 805, 82 Cal. Rptr. 67, 78 (1969)) where the court stated:

> We cannot agree that the matter of informed consent must
> be determined on the basis of medical testimony...a phy-

sician's duty to disclose is not governed by the standard practice of the physician's community, but is a duty imposed by law which governs his conduct in the same manner as others in a similar fiduciary relationship. To hold otherwise would permit the medical profession to determine its own responsibilities...

For all the reasons I gave that is the rule that should be adopted in these circumstances because the old idea of the family physician knowing so well his patient and his family and the conditions of the community is no longer an accurate one, particularly vis-a-vis consultants, such as genetic counselors, who see a family only briefly. For the theoretical reasons which prompt my "ought," the rule should be one of reasonableness and not of medical malpractice.

VEATCH: A dilemma arises when the norms of professional ethics conflict with the normative system operating more universally in society. Many medical professionals operate within the context of professional ethics which may be summarized as doing no harm or acting only for the benefit of the patient. However, it is not at all clear that that ethical principle is shared by the general public or by moral philosophers. Thus, a medical professional may be forced by the nature of his occupation to interact with a person who is not operating within the same ethical frame of reference. A very fundamental problem is created once one articulates moral responsibility in terms of a particular ethical system for the professional sphere.

MANGEL: There is a distinction between the information that you give a patient, depending on whether you are in a research situation or whether you are in a therapeutic situation. The test Mr. Capron enunciated is probably applicable to the pure clinical research situation, in which case it is difficult to justify the withholding of any relevant information. This position was held in the recent case of Halushka v. University of Saskatchewan (53 D. L. R. 2nd 436 (1965). I do not think that the case law in this country has yet taken the position that there must be full disclosure in a therapeutic situation. Courts always deal with the question of whether negligence existed in something done, and I haven't seen any case in which liability was based solely on a failure to disclose information in a therapeutic situation.

RAMSEY: Regardless of the law, the ethics of medical practice has to agree with the principle of full disclosure and must put upon itself the moral burden of justifying the withholding of information. This is not really out of accord with the ordinary man's understanding of truth-telling in his interpersonal relations.

FRIED: I want to remove any excessive sense of assurance that doctors may have about the state of the law, where it has been said that the standard is what do most reasonable practitioners do. There is clearly movement in the law, in respect to all experts and special professional groups, not to let their relations to persons outside of their group be determined by the judgments of a majority of their own fraternity. There is a growing realization in the law that what doctors decide is subject ultimately to legal scrutiny. I suspect the only reasons that that movement has not gone further with doctors is that it might, one day, be applied to lawyers.

MACINTYRE: Dr. Lubs mentioned the testicular feminization syndrome. In my judgment, this case is one in which it is not only undesirable but highly dangerous to divulge complete information. Such individuals are genetically males, but externally they develop as females. In our society I can think of no psychological framework which is more emotionally important and sensitive than that associated with one's sexual identification.

Let's assume a situation in which a patient, married for some time and apparently female, comes to you asking why she has never menstruated or been able to become pregnant, and you ascertain that this individual is genetically male and is a case of the testicular feminization syndrome. If you divulge your complete findings and thereby destroy the patient's sexual identification as a female, I don't believe anyone could prevent emotional catastrophe in this patient and in her husband. I see no possible benefit, immediate or potential, to be derived from divulging complete information. I am familiar with two cases in which the total information was given carefully and with understanding and compassion. Nevertheless, the emotional impact was such that both previously happy marriages ended in divorce because of the inability of the members of each couple to look upon each other as they previously had.

CAPRON: However, isn't there a risk of cancer for these patients?

MACINTYRE: It is true that the testes probably should be removed because of the risk of malignant growth, but that does not mean they have to be specifically described as testes. They could be described by the general term, "gonads," and it should be pointed out that there is a risk of their becoming malignant and it is recommended that they be removed. It should be noted also that because of the developmental problem, the gonads would never be functional in a reproductive sense anyway. Counseling in this fashion protects the individual's identification with femininity which is all important.

The question frequently will arise with respect to notifying the parents of a child with testicular feminization syndrome. Here, too, I think there is a potential danger. I have seen parents become terribly upset by such information to the extent that they are warped in their attitude toward the child thereafter. I believe that parents ought to know that the condition has a hereditary component but they don't have to find out that their "little girl" is really a "little boy."

It may be argued that by careful and lengthy counseling one could eliminate the dangers I have mentioned, but I don't think so. Regardless of how intelligent individuals may be, emotional stress and shock are a tremendous deterrent to clear understanding and full acceptance of a counselor's statements.

LEJEUNE: It is wrong to tell this woman she is a man, because she really is not. You may tell her that in general the chemical reactions which determine the male sex correspond to an XY chromosomal set, but that sometimes, as in her case, a special chemical change of the genes can produce a female with an XY chromosomal set. Thus there is no reason to conceal the truth. Do not tell her she is male, which she is not, but that she is an exceptional female with an XY chromosome complement.

LUBS: The only long-term answer is education. If students learn more genetics and biology, it is possible that they can handle information such as this. But it is not appropriate right now with every patient.

MOTULSKY: The public is learning more and more about science, medicine, and genetics and often understands intellectually many of the processes involved. Intellectual understanding, however, does not mean that the emotional resources to accept bad news are available. Most people want a medical adviser or genetic counselor who knows science, but who is also a sympathetic human being who can decide what information will be in the best interest of the patient. I, as a patient, want that kind of physician. I would not want the "health technician" or the "genetics technician" who tells me the cold facts in an objective manner and then brings in a psychiatrist to make me feel better.

SOCIOLOGICAL AND PSYCHOLOGICAL FACTORS
IN APPLIED HUMAN GENETICS

James R. Sorenson

INTRODUCTION

For most of human history, man's genetic endowment has been a given. The particular constellation of biological traits, abilities, and dispositions that he was endowed with constituted a largely unalterable set around which he had to mold his biological and social life.

The fact that his biological endowment was largely beyond rational control did not deter the imputation of various meanings to different biological conditions. Historically much significance has been attached to congenital abnormalities, genetic and otherwise. To the ancient Babylonians such an event was sometimes seen as a favorable act of the gods. At other times it was seen as an act of divine wrath (Reisman and Matheny, 1969). In Sparta, Rome, Greece, and even ancient Egypt, medical diviners and philosophers made much of birth anomalies.

Many things are altering contemporary responses to such events. While the occurrence of a birth anomoly is still a personal tragedy to the family involved, society does not attach as much significance. Social ostracism can be a community response, but such reactions have lessened as our interpretations of these events has shifted from animistic to naturalistic explanations.

Selection of the biological qualities of man is possible today, but in a very limited sense. In fact, direct active selection of biological constitutions is limited to the traditional parental act of simply having or not having a child. In this situation, man's intervention into his biogenetic future is achieved not by selecting desired traits, but by not reproducing people at high risk for undesirable somatic or genetic constitutions.

Little is known of the social and psychological forces shaping the use of this form of participation in our genetic future. Too often our knowledge and discussions about man's biogenetic future are presented in terms of what is or simply will be technologically feasible. A corollary consideration is concern with those social factors shaping the dissemination and utilization of technological advances. A combined analysis of technological possibilities as well as social and psychological constraints should enable us to better understand not only current uses of applied human genetics, but probable uses and problems in the future.

The purpose of this discussion is to outline what is presently known about some of the social and psychological factors shaping man's use of medical genetics and in particular his use of genetic counseling. This discussion will not attempt to specify when people ought to receive genetic counseling, but rather will describe when, in fact, most appear to receive it. Likewise I will not attempt to specify ethical or professional guidelines for parents and counselors, but will look instead at what decisions are made and how parents and genetic counselors arrive at these decisions.

In order to place the following discussion in perspective, it will be useful to introduce a definition of genetic intervention provided by Tatum. I will not be discussing euphenics or genetic engineering, but rather, in Tatum's words, eugenic engineering, which he defines as, "the selection and recombination of genes already existing in the 'gene pool' of a population . . . and (the combination of these in ways) advantageous to or desirable both for the individual and society" (Tatum, 1965).

In the discussion that follows I will focus on three separate social forces which are central to contemporary eugenic engineering. These are (1) family uses of medical genetics (2) the current state of the professional delivery of medical genetics and (3) society and how societal values, beliefs, and mores affect the family and medical profession in their use of medical genetics.

MEDICAL GENETICS AND THE FAMILY

A primary function and a basic right of the family universally is that of procreation. In recent decades, the right of the family to procreate as much as desired has come under attack through birth control campaigns and warnings about a population explosion. While much attention and information has been aimed at the family concerning its rights and duties in limiting the quality of human lives, much less attention has been given to the rights and duties of the family concerning the biological quality of its members, be it somatic or genetic quality.

In the past, and to a great extent today, the concern of the family itself with procreation has focused more on quantity and less on quality. This is due to a number of factors, not the least of which is that there simply were no reliable means available to the family for determining the biological quality of its members until recently.

The discovery of Mendelian ratios underlying the genetic transmission of specific characteristics marked the first discovery of scientific knowledge of inheritance. Much later, when specific diseases were linked with specific modes of inheritance, there resulted increased accuracy in predicting the occurrence of some diseases and biological conditions. The development of empiric ratios for genetic conditions not following classical Mendelian ratios broadened the scope of predictable biological conditions (Neel, 1958). This development, however, did not alter the kind of information available to families.

The recent application of amniocentesis and other intrauterine diagnostic procedures to the detection of fetal biologic states has altered the kind of actions open to the family. Through these procedures parents now can be assessed of the health of the fetus for more than a dozen abnormal genetic and most major abberant chromosome conditions (Miller, 1972). These diagnostic procedures, combined with abortion when a defect is diagnosed, permit the family for the first time to actively participate in determining some aspects of the biological quality of its progeny.

Two factors are operating in society which can translate this possibility into reality. The first factor is, of course, the increasing feasibility of medical science to accurately diagnose, predict, and intervene in the reproducing process. The second factor involves the changing attitudes--public, private, and legal --concerning abortion in general and abortion of defective fetuses in particular.

How is man, however, actually responding to and using these new opportunities? Examination of three steps in the utilization process of medical genetics will shed light on current practices. These are (1) an examination of factors shaping the distribution of knowledge about genetic disease in society and the resulting public awareness of genetic services (2) an analysis of the conditions under which families seek medical genetic services and (3) a review of the decisions families make when faced with medical genetic problems. The literature on these separate topics is limited, so the following discussion must necessarily be tentative.

THE SOCIAL DISTRIBUTION OF GENETIC DISEASE KNOWLEDGE

A wealth of sociological research suggests that there is an inverse correlation between knowledge about various infectious diseases and social class (Feldman, 1966; Mechanic, 1968). This research also suggests that patterns of knowledge dissemination vary among classes. The more educated classes seem to rely primarily on the mass media for health information, while classes with less education rely more on interpersonal modes of communication, such as close family and friends (Feldman, 1966).

One would suspect that public knowledge about genetic diseases would be distributed in society similarly to infectious disease knowledge. Research suggests that, in fact, higher social classes have more knowledge about some specific genetic diseases than lower classes (Feldman, 1966). Existing research is insufficient to draw definite conclusions about variations across social classes in sources of information about genetic disorders. What data there is suggests that, contrary to information sources for infectious disease knowledge, information about genetic disease appears to be communicated primarily through interpersonal channels in all social classes (Feldman, 1966).

There are interesting and important consequences of the variation across social classes in disease knowledge. First, one would rightly suspect that the variation in information of genetic disorders and problems would reveal itself in the pattern of people visiting genetic units. Numerous genetic counselors have indicated that the majority of people they see are of the middle class or higher (Reed, 1963; Juberg, 1966). A research program we are conducting at Princeton University on applied human genetics in the United States adds credence to this observation. While our research is not final, preliminary analysis of a representative sample of 30 medical units offering genetic counseling suggests that these units see mostly middle or upper class clients.

Historically in the United States, it appears that the role of private information has been one crucial element in acquiring medical genetic services. This situation is changing slowly. Various private foundations and some public agencies have recently begun to make public information about genetic diseases and services. For example, the Black Panther newspaper has recently carried a series of articles on the problem of sickle cell anemia, what it is, what is known about it, and what can be done at this time (Black Panther, 1971). While it appears that the Black Panther organization will not condone the use of birth control or selective abortion to control this genetic disorder, they are playing a significant role in educating the Black population about an important genetic problem.

Additional attempts to provide mass educational programs about genetic disorders and available services are limited. The role of private information continues to be crucial in linking clients and genetic services. In the past, genetic counselors report that many of their clients came to them out of their own volition. In our research at Princeton, we have found that on the average about 20 percent of clients receiving genetic services are still self-referred. This process of self-referral is probably in transition, as more genetic service units are being made available to the public and as the medical profession becomes more aware of the existence of such units and better skilled in their ability to diagnose genetic and chromosomal abnormalities.

An additional factor is operating which molds medical genetics utilization patterns. This factor is that the middle and upper social classes have both the economic means, as well as the sets of attitudes and beliefs about the efficacy of medical practice, to permit ready acceptance of medical service when needed. Historically in this country, lower income classes have been both more reluctant and less able to recognize the need for and seek the assistance of medical counsel when needed (Mechanic, 1968). This fact is not solely dependent on differences in economic capacity. In the case of genetic counseling, it is only recently that clients are being charged for this medical counsel. Rather, an important factor operating to reduce lower class recognition of abnormality and the seeking of medical assistance has been sets of attitudes and beliefs about the appropriate role of the family in treating illness, and the lack of complete faith in doctors and medical practice in terms of their motives and efficacy.

The different sources that various social classes go to for information about diseases also has important effects on utilization patterns. Since the middle class typically goes to the mass media, it is generally more accurately and more immediately informed about medical advances than the lower classes. At the same time, the lower classes rely primarily on family and friends for information, and hence they are not as likely to be as well informed and there is an increased chance they will receive incomplete and erroneous health information. This is especially true in the case of genetics, where the experience of severe guilt and shame are often associated with the presence of a genetic defect, and considerable psychological pressures can be mustered to ignore or rationalize these recriminations.

FAMILY USES OF MEDICAL GENETICS

There are presently three steps in the family reproductive career where genetic information and services can be of some use. These are (1) the pre-marital stage, where mate selection is of primary concern (2) the period prior to conceiving a child, when the timing and quantity of conceptions are of interest and (3) the pregnancy stage, when the health of the mother and the fetus are of central concern.

1. Pre-marital Interest

Marriage is a highly valued social state in this country. Approximately 94 percent of all women are married at least once (Davis, 1965). Many factors go into the process of mate selection and such social variables as values and attitudes exhibit high levels of correspondence between mates, as do such biological traits as age and height. When asked to specify the characteristics of an ideal mate, most Americans will list intelligence, good looks, health, honesty, and so forth. The list includes ideal social and biological attributes, both defined mostly in terms of broad categories. However, there is often considerable variance between ideals and reality. The important role of the romantic complex in mate selection in our culture operates to make congruent ideals and reality. The idea that one should not marry if one has

a health problem, somatic or genetic, is objectionable, especially
if one is really in love.

Because of these values, health considerations play a relatively minor role in mate selection. This propositon is supported
by a number of observations. Many genetic counselors have reported
that a very small proportion of their clients come for genetic
services prior to marriage. Of the small proportion of couples
seeking counsel prior to marriage, most seek information because of
known consanguinity (Reed, 1963). Very little is known of the
decisions of couples about marriage plans subsequent to premarital
counseling. A valid prediction would seem to be that such counseling probably seldom deters marriage, although it may
significantly alter reproductive decisions.

Our research at Princeton also suggests that the number of
premarital cases that counselors see constitutes a very small
segment of their caseload. Approximately seven percent of cases at
the 30 clinics we have surveyed are for premarital purposes, and
apparently these remain predominately counseling for cases of consanguinity. Given the high social value placed on marriage, and
the corollary emphasis on the romantic complex, it would appear
that the impact of the new genetics on mate selection practices has
been, and will continue to be, relatively small.

2. Decisions Regarding Conception

A second area where medical genetics can be used is in decisions about reproduction. A corollary value in American society to
marriage is that of parenthood. Attitudinal studies report that
more than 95 percent of men and women want to have at least one
child (Freedman, et al., 1959). About 90 percent of these couples
are successful. The impact of recent birth control programs has
not been to reduce the value of parenthood, but rather to reduce
the significance of having many children.

The use of human genetics by families at this stage of their
reproductive careers is perhaps the major means by which human
genetics has been applied to date, and it will probably continue to
be so for some time. Most genetic counselors report that the majority of people seeking counsel are those who have had a genetically
defective child and know they are at some risk for a recurrence.
Our research at Princeton supports this observation. Our data
suggests that fully 80 percent of all cases at the genetic centers
we surveyed are parents in this situation.

Genetic counseling at this stage in the reproductive cycle can
have a significant impact on reproductive decisions. A study by
Carter (1966) reports that of 169 parents in this siutation, facing
a risk of one in ten or greater, fully 67 percent opted against
having further children of their own. Parents facing a smaller
risk had children in about three-fourths of all cases. Obviously
the magnitude of the risk has a significant impact on parental
decisions. But other factors are also operating. As mentioned,

the nature of the potential genetic disorder is probably a critical factor, as are the values and attitudes of parents toward genetic disease and their beliefs about the right of man to interfere in biological destiny.

The meaning of a genetically defective child varies from family to family and this meaning will affect parental reproductive decisions. A study by Zuk (1959) reveals graphically the relationship between the occurrence of a congenital anomaly in a family and the family's response to it as shaped by their values. Zuk studied the degree of acceptance of anomalies in offspring by mothers of varying religious persuasion. He found that Catholic mothers more readily accepted a mentally defective child and could more adequately cope with the resulting problems than could mothers of other religious beliefs. Zuk suggested that this was possible because the Catholic mothers and families could fit the event into a religious context in which it made sense. A problem child was seen as a special test of their faith, in a kind of Jacobian sense. Other families saw the event less religiously and more as a personal tragedy. Correspondingly they had no readily available meaning to attach to the event and the consequences for familial social and psychological stability were more hazardous.

3. Post-conception Stage

While the primary use of medical genetics today is the counseling of parents with a defective child, post-conception and pre-birth counseling is increasing. This is due of course to the recent development of _in utero_ diagnostic procedures. This development changes rather dramatically the historical uses of applied human genetics. Whereas human genetics is only predictive when used in premarital and preconception stages, intra-uterine detection permits prediction as well as control of the genetic health of offspring, be it control in a classically negative eugenics sense.

There is little information available on the use of amniocentesis today or on the people who use it. The use of this procedure is probably more constrained by moral prohibitions than are the uses of medical genetics in the premarital and preconception stages. While moral perspectives on abortion are changing, they are doing so slowly.

Amniocentesis has been performed perhaps only several hundred times in the United States (Milunsky et al., this volume). This is due to a number of factors, a basic one being the still somewhat experimental nature of the procedure and uncertainty about the impact of the procedure on the long-range health of the mother and the fetus (Miller, 1972). Another factor is the constraints imposed by religious and legal prohibitions. Laws permit abortion on the grounds that the fetus is deformed, or runs a high risk of deformity, in only one-third of the states.

In addition to the impact of social and legal prohibitions,

there are psychological factors shaping acceptance of amniocentesis
that are not operating in the premarital and preconception stages.
Perhaps one of the most important is the fact that a woman is
pregnant. Her personal sense of identify with the fetus is
developing, as is that of her family. If pregnancy proceeds much
beyond the fourth or fifth month then, in addition to the woman's
own sense of identification with the fetus, a process of social
identification of the woman as a mother-to-be is set in motion.
Under these conditions the decision to abort a fetus, even if it is
defective, can be very difficult. More things come to be considered
in the decision to abort than the couple's desires for a healthy
child. At such times the impact of extended family members, especially parents and parents-in-law, can be great.

APPLIED HUMAN GENETICS AND THE MEDICAL PROFESSION

The factors shaping the acceptance and use of medical genetics
involve more than the family. One additional factor is the professional group or experts concerned with delivery and application.
In the case of medical genetics, and in particular genetic counseling, it is difficult to specify a single group that is responsible
for day-to-day delivery, since medical genetics today is practiced
by an array of specialists in a number of institutional settings.
Applied genetics is not yet well institutionalized into the
fabric of American medicine. This is due to a number of factors.
Among the more important is the fact that genetics is a relative
newcomer to medicine. As recently as 1953, only 55 percent of the
medical schools in this country were offering courses on human
genetics (Herndon, 1956). Most of the physicians receiving training during this period are now achieving the height of their medical practice and thus constitute a major segment of the physicians
delivering medical services. While there have been some changes in
the medical school curriculum, many schools still do not have
courses in human genetics beyond an elementary level.
Applied human genetics is undergoing a shift in the institutional base through which it is offered to the public. Historically, genetic counseling was delivered as a special service by
scientifically, not medically, trained personnel. Because of this,
the early institutional base of applied human genetics in this
country was primarily the university and most often departments of
genetics or zoology within the university departmental structure.
An examination of an early pamphlet on genetic counseling prepared
by Hammons (1957) listing available services reports only thirteen
centers in this country in 1957. Of these, ten were located in
academic departments in universities, while three were based in
medical schools.
The early affiliation of applied genetics with the university
and academically trained individuals probably had a significant
impact on delivery practices. First, because applied genetics was

so divorced from routine medicine, it was a hard service to obtain. This is consistent with our earlier observation that historically self-referral was a primary means by which people received genetic services. A second consequence was that the scope and content of counseling must have been very limited. Most academically trained individuals have little or no medical diagnostic capacities, so often the patient had to know his own disease.

The institutional base of applied genetics is changing. The 1969 National Foundation - March of Dimes International Directory of Genetic Units reveals many more agencies and institutions involved in the delivery of medical genetics today than was true only fifteen years ago. We have gathered information on some 250 genetic service units in this country in our study on applied human genetics at Princeton. Since 1957 the number of units has grown from about thirteen to almost 250. Not all of these provide genetic counseling. In fact, about 180 were providing this specific service in 1969. However, many of the remaining centers do perform genetic services of one form or another, and thus enter into the total picture of the delivery of medical genetics to the American population (Lynch and Bergsma, 1969).

Of the 250 units in our study, 59 or about 25 percent are located in hospitals. Academic departments in universities housed about 15 percent, medical schools about 14 percent, government agencies and voluntary organizations and institutes about 8 percent, and finally medical centers nearly 6 percent. The remaining units were scattered among a host of organizations.

Hospital based medical genetics will probably increase significantly as the impact of the various intra-uterine diagnostic procedures become more accepted. Heretofore, the procedures involved in the delivery of medical genetics seldom required hospital and laboratory facilities. The diagnosis of a disease and assessment of its mode of inheritance were the two basic procedures involved. Today, with various forms of heterozygosity detection possible, as well as amniocentesis, there is an increasing need for the delivery of medical genetics to be associated with the facilities of a hospital and laboratory.

This information also suggests that applied genetics still retains some foothold in the academic world. There are a number of factors linking the delivery of human genetics to such departments. First, there is a continuing need for very specialized knowledge of genetics, a need seldom met in the majority of genetic training programs provided in medical schools. A second factor is that often there are no genetic services available in an area unless a professor of genetics provides them.

Genetic counseling is, as indicated earlier, basically a preventive form of medicine. This suggests that, since it is associated with reproduction, a convenient place for it to be would be departments of obstetrics and gynecology. It would seem that the most efficacious time for genetic counseling and diagnosis would be before a woman has any children. A routine check of about to be or newly married women concerning their family and relatives could turn up reasons for concern, and possible further investigation could be pursued if it seemed warranted. An examination of our data suggests, however, that medical genetics and genetic counseling are located primarily in departments of pediatrics. Fully 24 percent of the genetic units are placed in such hospital and medical school departments.

Additional analysis of our Princeton data reveals that, geographically, almost every state has some limited form of genetic service. California alone has approximately 20 percent of all genetic service units in the nation. Over 70 percent of genetics units are located in cities with populations that exceed 100,000, and 20 percent are in cities with populations that exceed one million.

As pointed out earlier, many professionals are involved in the delivery of applied genetics. This includes not only those who actually perform genetic counseling and amniocentesis, but those professional personnel, medical and paramedical, who refer individuals and couples for such services. Examination of the information we have on professional and institutional referral patterns linking genetic services and clients reveals several facts of some importance in understanding current utilization patterns. In the units surveyed, we inquired about the proportion of clients referred by specific medical professionals. We included in this list general practitioners, pediatricians, gynecologists-obstetricians, public health nurses, psychologists, and others. We also asked the units to indicate the percent of their client load referred by various public agencies, including adoption agencies, family planning agencies, agencies for the handicapped, and the courts.

An examination of this information suggests that existing professional referral sources are many. More than a dozen sources have been given. Seldom does the number of referrals by any single source exceed 15 percent of the total patient load of a genetic center. The medical professionals making the largest number of referrals are pediatricians, general practitioners and obstetricians-gynecologists. On the average, pediatricians refer about 37 percent of the cases, while general practitioners refer about 14 percent and obstetricians-gynecologists 11 percent. The remaining 38 percent are referred by an array of other medical and paramedical personnel.

Several social agencies are also active in referring cases to genetic units. In the sample of units examined, it appears that agencies for the handicapped and maternal and child health care units are basic agency sources. About 23 percent of institutional referrals came through such sources. Other public agencies of some importance are adoption agencies, referring about 6 percent, crippled children's hospitals and family planning agencies, both referring about 8 percent of agency referrals.

The genetic units also make use of social service institutions. In our sample, clients were referred to family planning agencies, agencies for the handicapped, adoption agencies, crippled children's hospitals, and maternal and child care health units. However, fewer than 30 percent of the units made use of these social service agencies.

Numerous articles and books have appeared recently discussing the many facets of applied human genetics (Sorenson, 1972). This literature portrays a picture of diversity concerning which medical professionals should provide genetic service, what kind of training they should have, and what services they should provide. For example, while some feel that no less than a Ph.D. is required for effective counseling (Kloepfer, 1964), other writers feel that only a sound basic introduction to scientific genetics is required (Stevenson, 1970). Some writers argue that the delivery of medical genetics ought to be by the family doctor since he has sufficient experience and knowledge of each family to make the most effective use of the service (Fraser, 1968). Others claim that medical genetics is best delivered through a team approach, with particular emphasis given to the psychodynamic aspects of counseling (Lynch, 1969).

Regardless of the variety of counseling strategies, genetic diagnosis, prognosis, and treatment are being undertaken by a large array of professionals, mostly medical. How in fact do they appear to be delivering this knowledge, and what guidelines are they employing in their practice? An analysis of two topics in the delivery of medical genetics will provide us with some ideas. These topics are (1) the orientation of the genetic counselor to his patient and the orientation of the patient to the professional delivering genetic services and (2) the structure and nature of the counseling services.

1. Genetic Counselor Orientation to Patients

In discussing the relationship between genetic counselors and patients, it will be useful to discuss two types of role orientations which have suggested themselves through interviews and observations in our research program at Princeton. First, there is what we can call the doctor-client orientation. In this situation, the emphasis of the counselor is on the transmission of the factual information about the client's genetic or chromosomal problem. We have selected to designate the orientation as doctor-client because (1) most individuals probably orient themselves to genetic counselors as they do toward medical doctors, whether the counselor is a medical doctor or not, and (2) because in this case, the counselor orients himself toward the counselee in a manner which stresses the learning nature of the relationship for the counselee.

The second type of orientation we can label the doctor-patient relationship. Here, the counselee again orients himself to the counselor as he would toward a medical doctor. The counselor, however, perceives the role of the counselee as that of a patient, not a client. We will attempt to spell out the implications of these two basic orientations for the delivery of medical genetics below.

One of the reasons that it is critical to analyze the nature of the relationships between the counselor and counselee in applied genetics is that the ultimate role of who makes final decisions regarding the use of genetic knowledge is usually less ethically and morally neutral than is the situation in the delivery of more standard medical services. This fact is readily apparent in the published professional medical literature which attempts to outline the moral and ethical aspects of the relationship. A basic tenet of this literature is that decisions about the use of genetic knowledge and future reproductive behavior of counselees must be left to the counselees. It is not assumed that the counselor has knowledge superior to the counselee about who should reproduce and who should not, or what size risks on what types of diseases parents ought to take. This norm reflects society's earlier mentioned value of charging the family with ultimate and final decisions regarding the quality of its offspring.

a. The Doctor-Client Orientation: Some genetic counselors feel that their primary task is simply informing counselees of the risks involved for a given condition. In the opinion of the genetic counselor, clients are there to learn. Concern with the social and psychological aspects of genetic counsel are of secondary importance. The counselor feels that even though he may think that the risk involved is too large for the couple to take, he should not pass this opinion along to counselees.

The type of information this counselor is likely to pass on to his clients will be the nature of the risk and some very factual information about the particular disease involved. Often, if the client does not request information about the disease, the counselor will assume he understands the disease and needs no further counsel.

While this is the manner in which such counselors would perhaps like the genetic counseling sessions to proceed, it does not always do so. As we have said, the clients in this situation often orient themselves to the counselor as they do to medical doctors. This is not unusual, for many genetic counselors are in fact medical doctors. But, regardless of the training of the genetic counselor, the nature of his relationship to the counselee is different than is the medical doctor's relationship to his patients. In the latter situation it is assumed that the patient will provide the doctor with information, and the doctor will by and large make the decisions regarding the future health behavior of the patient. In genetic counseling we have the reverse situation. With the exception of intrauterine diagnosis, there is really little that the doctor can do to actively intervene in the genetic health of either the couple receiving counseling or the not yet conceived or unborn child. In this situation, ideally the

doctor or counselor gives information to the couple, and they make
the decisions regarding their future reproductive behavior.

        b. Counselor-Patient Orientation: The second type of
counselor-counselee   relationship is one we have labeled the
counselor-patient relationship. This is the situation where again
the counselee orients himself to the counselor in the traditional
doctor-patient manner.   Complementing this is the counselor's
orientation of seeing the counselee more as a patient than as a
client.   In this situation, the counselor will still follow the
dictum that final decisions regarding the future reproductive
behavior of the counselees resides rightfully with them, not with
the counselor. However, the counselor is concerned much more with
the social and psychological aspects and meaning of the disease for
the counselees than is the counselor in the doctor-client relationship.   For example, the counselor may discuss the impact that a
defective child can have on the marriage or on other family
members.   He may also discuss the reactions of friends and distant
family members to such an event.   Finally, he may graphically
describe for the couple the progressive developments of the
disorder and what they can expect as the disorder runs its natural
course.   In this situation the couple is receiving the basic
scientific information about the disease risk, as do couples in the
doctor-client relationship. However, the couple is also receiving
considerable additional information. They not only know the risk,
but they can begin to think about the impact of the possible
disorder on themselves, their family, and friends. They can begin
to consider the difficult future they might face when they are both
advanced in age and not capable of caring for the special needs of
an abnormal person. Certainly, factors such as these can become
major components shaping the decisions of genetic counseling
patients.

2. The Structure of the Counseling Situation

        While counselors may espouse the value of not making deci-
sions for their clients, in fact the professional medical literature suggests that some do. If the risk the couple is facing is
particularly small, say less than one in fifty, then some
counselors report they stress the fact that the average couple
faces this risk in any given pregnancy. Hence they would not pay
too much attention to it (Carter, 1969).   Also, when faced with
possible additional reproduction by a couple with a particularly
unfortunate disorder, counselors indicate that there are numerous
options open to them to influence the decision of the couple. For
example, if the couple is facing the risk for an autosomal
recessive disorder, the counselor can tell the couple that they
have a three in four chance of having a normal child. He might do

this if he thinks that the couple ought to have more children. On the other hand, if he is pessimistic and believes that the couple ought not to chance reproducing, he might say that they face a risk of one in four that the child will be abnormal. In both cases the same factual information is conveyed to the clients. In the first situation the counselor stresses normality, while in the second he stresses the potential abnormality. This variation is certain to have an impact on the decisions of the clients.

In addition to structuring the meaning of genetic risks for clients, counselors shape the significance of defects in other ways. A not uncommon problem faced by counselors is the realization that the knowledge they are imparting to a couple is having a serious impact on the marriage relationship. The recognition that one's spouse is the sole responsibility for the risk the couple faces, or for the defect their child has, can raise problems for a marriage. Some counselors have reported that if they sense that the information they ought to give to a couple might create such problems, they will often selectively present this information. For example, if one of the spouses happens to be the carrier of an X-linked dominant disorder, counselors report that they might tell the couple that their child has a genetic problem and that both parents contributed to the genetic make-up of the child. Such a presentation of facts is likely to diffuse parental responsibility. Also, such a presentation is more likely to arise when the counselor adopts the doctor-patient orientation than when he simply wants to give the facts to the clients.

APPLIED HUMAN GENETICS AND SOCIETY

We have given attention in our discussion so far to the two major institutions involved in the application of human genetics, the family and the medical profession. In this final section our attention turns to societal values and their significance for the application of human genetics.

1. Past Uses and Current Projections

There are many discussions of the uses of human genetics in various historical periods (Haller, 1968). We do not need to review this long and fascinating history here. We do need to note, however, historical precedents that have been of considerable import in shaping opinions and even projections about the future uses of human genetics.

For several decades it has been possible to exercise some control over the human biogenetic future, if not through direct genetic control at least through indirect means. As Crow (1961) has argued, man's genetic evolution is already under human control to some extent through environmental manipulation, medical advances, and contraceptives. The question to be asked now is what will be the direction of our biological evolution. The very early historical uses of genetics, as can be discerned in Plato's Republic, need not concern us here (Darlington, 1964). Nor are we going to trace the highly significant impact of Darwin's The Origin of Species (Wilson, 1967; Haller, 1963). Instead, our focus will be on the more recent uses of human genetics and specifically the eugenics movement of the late nineteenth and early twentieth century in the United States.

As Haller (1963) has documented, the many people involved in the eugenics movement were a mixed lot. Some were the leading scientists of the age, some religious leaders, many social workers, psychologists, sociologists, and other academicians. These people shared many things in common. Primary among these was the idea that man could be perfected through biological means, more so than social. The social reformers, racial purists, and even scientific researchers in their over-zealous attempt to improve mankind saw the systematic application of existing principles of genetics to human populations as the panacea for the many social ills that were besetting nations at that time.

The early attempts to translate genetic principles into social programs resulted in many legislative reforms and laws regulating migration (Haller, 1963). Perhaps the most infamous application came in Nazi Germany and attempts there to maintain what was thought to be racial purity through eugenic measures (Tenenbaum, 1956). The notion of race became central to the application of eugenic measures, and assumptions about the nature of race, biology, and social behavior became crucial but unexamined premises in the eugenic movement.

Obviously programs of such magnitude and little scientific basis soon began to be discredited. The highly political nature of such knowledge also gave rise to an increasing mistrust about the political motivations as well as the scientific objectivity of the eugenicists (Haller, 1963). These developments, combined with the slow erosion of the central eugenic organizations through co-optation of their leadership by fanatics and the defection of their more scientifically trained members, led to the rapid demise of the eugenics movement in this nation in the early 1930's. But demise of the organizational base, as well as legislative appeals to enforce eugenic measures, did not remove public and even scientific skepticism and fear aroused by the excesses and misuses of these early applications. Such beliefs and fears are still prevalent today. Some counselors have expressed concern that their practice might be conceived as eugenic. They stress the fact that their orientation in the delivery of medical genetics is to an individual couple. Ideally they do not view the problem of the client from the perspective of society. The fact that the family may have several children who transmit genetic problems to future generations is not a central consideration of genetic counseling.

If we turn our attention from the excesses of the past to an examination of discussions about our possible genetic future, several things become apparent. By and large these discussions are couched in terms of the more sensational aspects of applied genetics. One reads about the biological timebomb (Taylor, 1968), as well as that man is becoming transformed into superman (Time, 1971). Popular novels on our biological future portray societies premised on control of the genetic constitution of each member (Orwell, 1949). In short, the most popular discussions and views of man's intervention in his genetic future often translate technical possibilities into social realities. In so doing, they often portray situations not unlike those attempted during the height of the eugenics movement of the past, and they often arouse prejudices and fears similar to those aroused by our memory of these events.

Together these conditions have an impact on public receptiveness to genetic advances. But it is important to place these public concerns in perspective. Genetics today is being applied more and more through medicine. By and large, the medical profession does not see the necessity of instituting society-wide eugenic programs. In fact, as outlined above, final decisions about reproductive behavior are largely left to the family, with the doctor, the technical expert, assisting through provision of information requisite for an informed decision. The early eugenics movement was a movement of experts. Eugenics engineering as practiced today is by and large a movement of experts also, but experts in applied medicine, not social reform. The continuing redefinition of genetics as a proper concern of medicine and its delivery through the medical profession ought to serve to counter earlier developed negative opinions and evaluations.

A second factor shaping the acceptance of applied genetics has been its historical association with sickness and pathology (Scheinfeld, 1956). Genetics is seen as the concern of individuals who are diseased or ill. It is not perceived as the concern of most individuals. This attitude is reflected in contemporary uses. As discussed above, most people visiting genetic service units in this country are couples with at least one child suffering from a genetic problem. Applied genetics is used in response to a genetic problem, not in a fully preventative manner. Applied genetics will probably remain largely associated with disease and disorder for some time. However, the increasing preventative potential of applied genetics can give it a more positive appeal through the guarantee of genetically healthy offspring.

The final factor to be explored is what can be called the environmental images of man in our society. The desire of man to improve his condition is surely an admirable goal. Of necessity, this goal has the premise that man is a malleable creature. Given this premise, there are two sources that one can adopt to change man. The first is his biological state. The second is his environment. The first view has been the less accepted means of improving mankind and has seldom been turned to, except in various eugenic movements. The second means is by far the most frequent and most tried historically.

Davis (1965) has given three reasons why we have relied traditionally on social mechanisms. These include (1) the assumption that social changes can be wrought more rapidly than biological changes (2) the fact that we did not have requisite scientific knowledge to bring about desired biological changes, and (3) even if we did, there was not sufficient agreement on what we desired.

Davis argues that these assumptions are no longer tenable. First, he suggests that it might be possible to bring about biological changes more rapidly than social changes. Second, he indicates that we now do have the requisite scientific knowledge to begin undertaking such changes. Finally, he argues there is sufficient agreement on the biogenetic future we want to make such programs feasible. While one may not totally agree with all of these assertions, certainly the possibilities for improving man through biological and genetic mechanisms has significantly improved in the past decades.

The bias in our history toward viewing the human condition as primarily socially shaped, with biology of secondary importance and largely of no practical significance, is engrained in our value structure. Belief in free will, the dignity of the individual and, above all, equality, has of necessity forced us to assume a predominately environmentalistic posture toward the nature of man. These beliefs have guided us in our selection of means available to improve men and mankind.

An important point to be emphasized now is that man is increasing the potential for both social and biogenetic means of improvement. We need no longer partake one position or the other, as was done in the past, for either practical or ideological reasons. If this is the case, then we can agree with Davis that the potential inherent in recent biogenetic developments is truly great.

ACKNOWLEDGEMENT

The research for this paper was supported in part by a grant from the Russell Sage Foundation, 230 Park Avenue, New York, New York.

REFERENCES

Black Panther (1971). April 10, 6, 2, and May 22, 6, 17.
Carter, C. O. (1966). "Comments on Genetic Counseling," in Proceedings of the Third International Congress of Human Genetics, 97-100.

Carter, C. O. (1969). *An ABC of Medical Genetics*, Boston: Little Brown and Company.

Crow, J. F. (1961). "Mechanisms and Trends in Human Evolution," *Daedalus*, *90*, 416-431.

Darlington, C. D., *Genetics and Man*, New York, MacMillian Company, 1964.

Davis, Kingsley (1965). "Sociological Aspects of Genetic Control," in *Genetics and the Future of Man*, J. Roslansky, editor. New York: Appleton-Century-Crofts.

Feldman, Jacob J. (1966). *The Dissemination of Health Information*. Chicago: Aldine.

Fraser, F. C. (1968). *The Canadian Medical Association Journal*, *99*, 19.

Freedman, R., P. Whelpton, and A. Campbell (1959). *Family Planning, Sterility, and Population Growth*. New York: McGraw Hill.

Haller, Mark (1963). *Eugenics*. New Brunswick: Rutgers University Press.

Hammons, H. (1957). *Heredity Counseling: Its Services and Centers*. New York: American Eugenics Society.

Herndon, N. (1956). *American Journal of Human Genetics*, *8*, 1.

Juberg, Richard (1966). *Nurses Outlook*, *14*, 28.

Kloepfer, H. (2964). "Genetic Counseling," in *Human Genetics in Public Health*. Minneapolis: University of Minnesota.

Lynch, H. T. and D. Bergsma (1969). *Birth Defects Genetic Services*. New York: National Foundation-March of Dimes.

Lynch, H. T. (1969). *Dynamic Genetic Counseling for Clinicians*. Springfield, Illinois: Charles C. Thomas.

Mechanic, D. (1968). *Medical Sociology: A Selective View*. New York: Free Press.

Miller, O. J. (1972). "An Overview of Problems Arising from Amniocentesis," in *Early Diagnosis of Human Genetic Defects*, Maureen Harris, editor. Washington, D. C. : U. S. Government Printing Office.

Neel, James V. (1958). *Eugenics Quarterly*, *5*, 41.

Orwell, George (1949). *Nineteen Eighty-Four*. New York: Harcourt.

Reed, S. C. (1963). *Counseling in Medical Genetics*. Philadelphia: Saunders.

Reisman, Leonard E. and Adam P. Matheney (1969). *Genetics and Counseling in Medical Practice*. St. Louis: C. V. Mosby Company.

Scheinfeld, A. (1957). *Acta Genetica et Statistica Medica*, *7*, 487.

Sorenson, James R., with the assistance of K. Courant, N. Sorenson, and C. Yinger (1972). *Genetic Counseling Bibliography*, unpublished ms.

Stevenson, A. C., B. C. Davison, and M. Oakes (1970). *Genetic Counseling*. Philadelphia: J. B. Lippincott Company.

Tatum, Edward (1965). "The Possibility of Manipulating Genetic Change," *Genetics and the Future of Man*, J. Roslansky, editor. New York: Appleton-Century-Crofts.

Taylor, G. (2968). *The Biological Time Bomb*. New York: World Publishing Company.

Tenenbaum, Joseph (1956). *Race and Reich*. New York: Twayne Publishers, Inc.

Time (1971). "Man into Superman", April 19.

Wilson, R. J., editor (1967). *Darwinism and the American Intellectual*. Homewood, Illinois: The Dorsey Press.

Zuk, G. H. (1959). *American Journal of Mental Deficiency*, *64*, (1), 139.

PARENTS IN GENETIC COUNSELING:
THE MORAL SHAPE OF DECISION-MAKING

John Fletcher

INTRODUCTION

This paper is an attempt by a student of moral and ethical conflict to contribute to the discussion of the issues involved in the uses of genetic knowledge. My primary interest in research is the dependency relationship in all of its forms, especially where the dependent person relates to an "expert" who controls highly significant or risk-laden knowledge, technique or processes. In the field of biomedical investigation, my interest led me to study the dynamics of the moral agreement when a patient or volunteer consents to medical experimentation (Fletcher, 1967). Due to the great interest generated by rapid development in human genetics and the application of amniocentesis to cases of prenatal diagnosis (Harris, 1972), it seemed mandatory to investigate the actual shape of moral problems and social-ethical issues embedded in genetic counseling and its aftermath.

The study of morality and ethics must not be separated, even though in practice the human behaviors to which the terms refer are not identical. I owe it to the reader to explain how the terms morals and ethic are used in the context of this paper. In normal usage and especially in the biomedical community, the two terms are used interchangeably to refer to a wide range of personal and public issues concerning values, purposes, and legitimate means to ends (Gustafson, 1970). Because a distinction between morals and ethics is widely made in philosophical and theological literature, and since the discussion of value questions in biomedical science is interdisciplinary, a simple distinction here may prove useful.

The study of morals focuses upon the immediate decisions human beings make. The moralities to which men appeal in decision-making when confronting the immediate question--"What ought I or we to do in this situation?"--are those systems of norms, standards, and rules which exist for the purpose of guiding behavior and reducing conflict in everyday life. In this sense, the "morality" which regulates biomedical research refers to those standards and rules

301

to which investigators typically refer to guide their decisions. In practice this morality may be written in a code or expressed in the unspoken sanctions applied in the peer group itself. There is, however, an existential side to morals. I refer to the struggles of individuals making decisions in relative degrees of conflict with stated norms and codes for conduct. Their struggle may be of the intensity described as a "moral tension" (Callahan, 1970). At times persons experience such intense struggle between conflicting values and their own conscience that "moral suffering" is the most apt description of their condition. Moral suffering occurs most often in those situations in which any course of action will cost the decision-maker dearly in terms of compromised principles, values and aspirations. A study of morals is concerned with the continuing development of the systems of norms and rules within which human conduct occurs. Any study of morals should be concerned with refreshing those systems through the losses and victories of the human struggle of conscience. Thus, any study of morality should be situational and concrete.

Since the progress of biomedical techniques affects the moral life of man, we must take special care to analyze this interaction. We must show how men construct new solutions to moral conflicts, drawing in part on ancient wisdom and in part on peer-group consensus. At times neither of these sources relieves the dilemma and the risk of an entirely new action must be taken. The richest source of moral experience are the experiences of the actors involved in particular moral problems. The student of morality must organize his inquiry in their midst.

Ethics is to morality as theory is to practice. Ethics is the reflection which members of communities do when they hold up whole patterns of behavior and histories of decisions for critical examination in the light of their most cherished values and traditions. Most often ethics is concerned with the relevance and meaning of moral codes to particular decisions. For example, in times of rapid social change the conventional morality governing human sexuality, marriage and family life may not apply to new conflicts of conscience. How ought one behave in an unprecedented situation? From what baseline should we develop new moral strategies? New moral conflicts in the practice of human genetics make it necessary for physicians and their colleagues in other disciplines to meet for careful reflection on the reasons which may or may not justify wide application of techniques like amniocentesis or genetic screening programs. Ethics may involve a basic reconsideration of the moral code itself (Aiken, 1962). Ethics is informed by religion at the point at which human beings come to terms with the moral suffering they must bear and endure.

Further, a serious ethical inquiry searches for answers to the question of why we should be concerned to be moral in the application of scientific knowledge to society. Underlying every inquiry in ethics is a vision of the meaning of life and a set of claims and obligations proceeding forth from that vision. In our time many visions of life prevail. A pluralistic society awards no school of thought a monopoly on ethical wisdom or its application. For this reason, students of ethics must practice their profession increasingly in a commonwealth of inquiry and criticism. However, after a period of careful consideration of the strengths and weaknesses of each contributor to the debate, an ethicist should venture his own judgments on the direction of particular moral policies and the underlying justifications for his judgments. The basic purposes served by inquiry into ethics and morals are (1) the increase of self-knowledge and (2) concrete guidance in the problems of human life (Niebuhr, 1963).

This paper focuses upon the moral problems of parents who seek genetic counseling and amniocentesis as means to knowledge in their exercise of parental and social reponsibility. Through the generous cooperation of the Department of Obstetrics and Gynecology in the George Washington University Medical School, arrangements were made for periodic interviews with a series of 25 couples and their genetic counselor. Following a discussion of the results of this study, I shall offer my own arguments as to the morality applicable to the uses of knowledge obtained by amniocentesis. In conclusion, I shall offer a consideration of social-ethical issues posed by this procedure as a forerunner of new forms of genetic therapy. Amniocentesis is a stage upon which we may project some possibilities of the future.

PARENTS IN GENETIC COUNSELING

A study was designed to develop hypothesis about the structure of moral problems in one genetics counseling unit. As my interest was primarily in the moral problems of parents seeking genetic counseling and possibly amniocentesis, I interviewed a series of 25 couples and the counselor at crucial points in the counseling process:

(1) After their meeting with the counselor
(2) With the counselor after the initial counseling session
(3) With the couple after the report on amniocentesis results
(4) With the couple after birth or abortion.

In addition to these interviews, a number of discussions were held with staff members of the genetics counseling unit. The purposes of this study were:

(1) To investigate, identify, and classify moral problems emerging in the interactions of physician, staff and patients
(2) To describe the responses of the actors to specific problems

(3) To identify the reasons upon which resolutions of moral
    conflicts are based
(4) To study the effect on problem-solving of the presence
    of a paramedical person whose questions center on moral
    concerns
(5) To provide an empirical basis for discussion of more
    inclusive ethical issues about the use of genetic
    knowledge in medicine.

The informed consent of the couple to a series of interviews
was obtained by the counselor and the interviewer. Each couple was
told that the interviewer was interested in collecting data on the
"human side" of their experience in amniocentesis and in evaluating
the way their problems were met within the context of the genetics
counseling unit.

There are two types of situations most commonly identified as
"moral problems." The first is when a person or group is perceived
by others to be in fundamental violation of responsibilities to the
welfare of a significant human community. The important feature of
this situation is that the moral problem is defined in collective
terms. The collective poses the question of basic loyalty to the
decision-maker. "Are you with us or against us on this matter?"
(Parsons, 1951). An individual is judged by the norms of a community, in this case, whether he feels guilty or not. For example,
when medical investigators who have not obtained consent for experiments are punished for this lapse, even though they feel that they
were only doing what "everyone else" was doing, their standing in
the ethos of medical research has been violated.

The second situation finds a person confronting sharply conflicting responsibilities, divided within himself, and making a
decision which expresses the conflict. His subsequent behavior
will often show evidence of the conflict. This situation has been
described as "the conflict of rule situation" (Carney, 1968). For
example, some genetic counselors allow couples to believe that each
contribute to a particular genetic disease, when in fact one is the
carrier. Caught between a concern for the marriage and a concern
to give accurate information, the counselor may be untruthful and
hence suffer some remorse (Sorenson, 1972).

The most intense moral suffering may occur when these two
situations firmly coalesce into one. An analysis of moral problems
may be served by a distinction between individual and collective
aspects, but the formality of that distinction tends to remain.
Most "everyday" moral problems are situations which have elements
of (1) collectively defined loyalty, and (2) individuals confronting decisions which express conflicts of loyalty. This definition
of a moral problem guided our study of parents in genetic counseling. What the patient or the couple said about the experience of
violating standing in a significant community or an inner conflict
of loyalties was the datum to be studied.

The study was designed to search for answers to the following questions:

(1) What are the major moral problems parents in genetic counseling experience?
(2) Do these problems occur frequently? Is a pattern of problems recognizable?
(3) How are the problems resolved, if at all?
(4) What forms of help do parents seek, if any, in moral problem-solving? What role does the genetic counselor or members of the staff play in addressing moral problems?

The results of a study with this small sample of parents showed three major periods or phases of decision-making within which "clusters" of problems collected. The tape-recordings and notes found parents engaged in recognizing and solving of problems in these phases:

(1) Motivation to seek genetic counseling and a decision about amniocentesis
(2) Decision following amniocentesis and learning results
(3) Post-abortion and sterilization, post-birth.

Figure 1 outlines these phases. On the first line are listed the major events prior to, in, and after the genetic counseling relationship. On the second line are listed the major moral problems experienced by parents and the genetic counselor within the time frame of the events on the first line.

PHASE I: DECISION ABOUT AMNIOCENTESIS

The 25 couples' experience confirms many research findings about genetic counseling. At certain important points, however, their experience was divergent. All of the couples interviewed were expecting a new baby. All but one of the couples were from the middle-class or above, and the majority had graduated from a four-year college. Twenty-four couples were white (Sorenson, 1972).

The religious affiliation of the couples are as follows:

Protestant (both)	11
Jewish (both)	4
Catholic (both)	2
Mixed religious marriages	5
No religious affiliation	3

Figure 1.   Structure of Moral Problems of Parents in Genetic Counseling

I. DECISION ABOUT AMNIOCENTESIS

Events   genetic problem → information from ↗ consultation with ↗ genetic counseling
            arises   media, physician,   physician or spouse   amniocentesis
                                friend, etc.

Moral   unresolved guilt — how trustworthy? — abortion question;   impact of counselor's
Problems   questions from   conflict with physician values; risk vs.
            previous births or   and/or family;   benefits; informed
            abortions   autonomy; religious   consent; indications
                                                       conflict   for amniocentesis

II. DECISION FOLLOWING AMNIOCENTESIS

Events   post-amniocentesis → results reported ┤ negative → birth
                                                     └ positive → abortion/sterilization/
                                                                     birth

Moral   fidelity to family   decision on abortion
Problems   and marriage;   and sterilization;
            anxiety vastly   re-evaluation of child-
            heightened   bearing, marriage;
                                                        "rejection" of living
                                                        child or sib with same
                                                        genetic problem while
                                                        making abortion decision

III. POST ABORTION STERILIZATION BIRTH

Moral   justification of
Problems   decision; cosmic doubts;
            self-rejection; decision
            about future birth;
            fidelity to marriage

Thirteen couples came to the unit due to a previously defective child and were now pregnant again. Ten couples were motivated by the "age factor" and its relation to occurrence of Down's syndrome. These latter couples discovered the risk ratio largely through reading or the media. One couple sought counseling due to a sibling or twin who had a defective child; one requested counseling because her three brothers had a genetic disease, muscular dystrophy. Recent research done at Princeton on motivation for genetic counseling showed that 80 percent of all cases are parents with a defective child (Sorenson, 1972).

More **than half of the couples** (14) were self-referred to the center. Within this group four couples were "repeaters," having had amniocentesis previously. Three of the four repeating couples had chosen abortion and sterilization following positive diagnoses of Lesch-Nyhan syndrome, Patau syndrome, and sex factor related to **muscular dystrophy**. Twenty-two fetuses were negatively diagnosed and at the time of writing, 12 normal babies had been delivered. Eleven couples had been referred by either a gynecologist or through a program for parents of retarded children. Those who were motivated in part through reading articles about amniocentesis or hearing of it through live media presentations were sometimes disappointed to learn of discrepancies in fact. Especially was this true regarding the optimum time to perform amniocentesis. When told by the counselor that he would not perform the procedure, if indicated, until a fetal heartbeat had been detected and recorded, and that they would have to delay, they were very disappointed, though better informed. This raises the issue of accuracy and trustworthiness in science reporting. Many news stories and articles present this procedure only in terms of its being done, but rarely in terms of the details and ramifications.

The initial interview with these couples revealed several clusters of moral problems and provided the interviewer with evidence to hypothesize about the dominant values informing these parents as they sought assistance.

1. Unresolved Guilt

Parents with one defective child were quick to express their reasons for seeking counseling and amniocentesis when asked. Since the defect had been, for the most part, a shock to them, many acknowledged that though they had learned to live with it, the effect had not worn off. There is often an unusual sense of shame and guilt associated with genetic disease which I came to call a "cosmic guilt." Having no previous choice over being parents of a defective child, several parents voiced their gratitude at finally being able to do something about the new pregnancy. The sense of being isolated from the community of the "normal," evident in illness generally, is much more in evidence in these particular parents. "I don't know why fate singled me out, but it did," said

one mother. The great expense and personal difficulty in adjusting
to a defective child was often mentioned. Parents bring their
previous problems to the counseling situations in expectation of
the relief of information and the partial freedom that it brings.
The relief may stem from a sense of having conquered in part the
previously arbitrary fate assigned to them as carriers.

The couples, especially the wives, who were "repeaters" with
earlier abortions, still bore vivid memories of their disappointment and sense of failure. Later interviews with these couples
underlined their need for support and counseling at the time of
therapeutic abortion and the deep depression suffered at the time.
Each declared an intention to make this "the last time."

2. Conflicts with Physicians or Family Members

In five cases, serious conflicts with obstetrician-gynecolo-
gists or with family members had preceded their entering genetic
counseling. In the couples' opinion, the physicians had been
motivated by either a religious objection to the option of abortion
or by a poor opinion of the indication for amniocentesis. One 40
year-old mother of three reported that when she consulted her
obstetrician about her intention to seek amniocentesis because of
her age, he informed her that her "mental, not physical health,
needs attention," and strongly advised her against this course of
action. As he had delivered her three children, she felt his words
deeply, and she showed considerable ambivalence in counseling.   A
26—year-old Catholic mother, carrier of Lesch-Nyhan syndrome, with
one affected child, said that the physician she first consulted "as
much as called me a murderer when I said that I wanted a test."
Another couple reported opposition from their physician because he
thought this an "expensive, unnecessary gimmick which some people
are using to build up their reputation."

In 25 interviews I detected no substantial disagreement between spouses as to the justifications for seeking help in prenatal
diagnosis. Two women told of arguing with family members who
strongly disapproved of their actions. One told of her mother-in-
law, who herself had given birth to a defective child and kept him
at home, attempting to shame her for "taking the easy way out." To
the casual observer, such conflicts may seem easily dismissed as
projection and "sour grapes"; to those who are on the receiving end
of them, however, they assume serious proportions. Such is especially true of conflict with physicians.

3. Prior Consent to Abortion

When asked, each of the 25 couples answered that they were
agreeable to abortion, if indicated by diagnosis, as a morally
acceptable means of managing a genetic problem. Judging by content

analysis of tapes and notes, the abortion question was the prevailing moral problem faced by these parents during the process. More time, energy, and reasoning were expended on explaining their positions on this issue than on their reasons for seeking counseling. Why is this so? My hypothesis has two parts: (a) The structure of the situation calls for a readiness to be committed to abortion as the means of managing a positive diagnosis; (b) being parents strongly motivated to have children and to go to extraordinary lengths to exercise responsible parenthood, these parents are "sensitized" to the abortion question in considerably more depth than other parents. Therefore, wanting another child (sometimes desperately) and being explicitly committed to abortion constitute a tension of severely conflicting loyalties and is perceived as a moral problem.

In this genetics counseling center the policy was not to elicit a firm commitment of the couple to abortion as a prior condition for undergoing amniocentesis. Here we note a difference from what has been reported as the prevailing practice by counselors and physicians (Epstein, 1969). Such an opinion was emphatically offered by Littlefield (1970) when he stated: "Of course amniocentesis should not be undertaken unless the family is committed to subsequent intervention if appropriate." As the counseling relationship unfolded the couples' opinion on the acceptability of abortion was usually revealed, but the counselor was careful to point out that only the facts were relevant to the decision and deciding on subsequent action should be postponed until after the final report. When asked, all but one couple resisted the concept of signing a consent form accepting abortion prior to amniocentesis.

The guiding motives for abortion in these parents were largely between the "on demand" and "never" extremes. They explained their own views most often in terms of sufficient reasons for abortion: serious genetic defects, among other reasons, (rape, incest, injury to mother) justified abortion. There were many echoes of the theme struck by one mother. "I am nervous about abortion solely for psychiatric or economic reasons, but if my child is seriously affected, I would agree to it."

The parents were almost universally serious about the moral responsibility in being willing to opt for abortion. A father put it:

We have discussed it at length...we only want an abortion if we have to for medical reasons...it is not an easy decision to make, since you are talking about a life. It is a moral issue.

Only one couple approved "abortion on demand." Only one couple gave evidence of coming to genetic counseling on the pretext of having genetic problems but wishing for an abortion of an unwanted child. This couple was not accepted for amniocentesis.

The "moderate" position on abortion held by the great majority of these parents probably stems from their parental values as modified by the success of the technique of amniocentesis. They deeply desire children, but they are willing to allow an intervention to test for genetic defects and to act on the consequences. As a mother said, "These days you have a choice about having a healthy baby." While this statement is not exactly true, it reveals a willingness to employ the technical utility of prenatal diagnosis while holding firmly to a yearning for children. As the first generation of parents who have had an informed choice about abortion for genetic reasons, as indicated by amniocentesis, they did not suppress affection for the fetus or deny that there was a human life at stake. "When the baby is inside you, you start loving it," said a mother carrying Lesch-Nyhan Syndrome. "When you feel movement, you feel ashamed about contemplating abortion," said another mother. These statements appear to indicate a deep moral problem. Caught between a loyalty to the life of their child and a loyalty to the norm of "healthy" life (as expressed in children with no genetic defects)there was considerable suffering expressed. It is my hypothesis that two forces assisted these parents in justifying their decision to accept abortion: (1) experience with genetically defective children which led them to believe that the child's life would be unfulfilled, and (2) belief in the values of health and intelligence which their lifestyle requires for a sense of adequacy and success. Given the choice of accepting a genetically defective child or resorting to abortion, and being informed by their own largely middle-class values, they would choose the latter, even though they suffered from the thought of being responsible for ending the life of their child. Our culture and its preferences tend to reinforce each belief of these parents.

4. Reasons for Seeking Genetic Counseling

In seeking to identify the deeper reasons, a pattern of justification, for the need for genetic counseling, the parents most often offered an argument based on their understanding of parental responsibility to provide for the health of their children and the security of their families. The same mother who spoke of her resistance to abortion for strictly economic or psychiatric reasons said "It is not fair to it (the child), to the family, to society, or to me to bring another child like the one I have into the world." The concept of "fairness" was often used for justification. Parents with one defective child reasoned from their experiences or psychic and economic loss most often to reflect on their responsibility. The important note in their reasoning was that of a willing acceptance of parental and genetic responsibility. None of these parents could be described as proactive eugenicists, and only a tiny fraction reasoned solely on the basis of individual convenience. In extended conversation about the underlying justification for genetic counseling, it became readily apparent that population problems, genetic responsibility, and parental values were interwoven in the social ethics of the majority of couples. For example, a Catholic father said, "We have an obligation to our children before they are born; you can't turn your back on the future." Another father said, "I couldn't go through it again . . .it is not doing anything for the child or for society just to be born so sickly . . . it will not make society better for it to happen again."

Several parents, but not a majority, mentioned the concept of a "right to good mental life." In a discussion with one father about this concept, he said that "everyone has a right to live, but each should have a right to a good life, mentally." When I pressed him to try to take the concept to some logical conclusions as applied to society or individual cases, he admitted that he would not want to have rigid standards about "intelligence" or "mental ability" used in screening who would be born. Given the choice, however, between having a child retarded as his own and abortion, he would choose the latter. He realized that if the majority of people reasoned in a similar manner about all children, a "tyranny of the majority" could develop, aided by an exclusive value on "intelligence" and having little tolerance for weakness or sickness. He made a distinction between those whose mental potential had been drastically destroyed by genetic disease and those who did not have this particular problem, saying that abortion ought only be available on proof of the former. "Medical reasons for genetic betterment are safer than social reasons," he declared.

Parents who sought genetic counseling because of the "age factor" cited social and economic reasons for their inquiry just as did parents who had defective children. "I have two children and did not intend to get pregnant again," said a 42—year-old mother, "and I must do everything possible to see that my child is healthy. The world has enough problems, I don't want to add to them."

5. Autonomy

Throughout the counseling process, in all three of its phases, these couples showed a consistent reliance on their own authority in decision-making. Only two couples in the sample had consulted a nonmedical person for advice, and these advisers were personal friends, not a clergyman, counselor, or lawyer. Even though the majority perceived moral conflicts in the process of making up their minds, there was no sufficient cause for official moral "counsel," since they considered their own parental roles the source of moral authority for child-bearing and family matters. This finding is consistent with the attitude that the family is the seat of control in procreation. They sought medical advice freely, often consulting other physicaans. Parents saw no need to consult an authority or helper outside of the medical world for the problems they faced with amniocentesis. Yet there were signs of need for counsel in the normal dimension of their decisions.

At this point, I would hypothesize that the time and energy given by the vast majority of the parents to interviews and telephone discussions indicates a need for ventilating their concerns and receiving informed "moral counsel." Parents were extremely diligent in keeping appointments and giving time to the interviews. Several indicated that they enjoyed our discussions, and four relationships of "moral counseling" developed in which the interviewer --on the suggestion of the genetic counselor--invited couples to discuss their most difficult decisions with him. These discussions suggested to me that alongside an attitude of moral autonomy in these parents may lie a need to establish a sense of moral direction with the larger community. They are not "individualists" and as such found fulfillment in reflecting on their social commitments. I felt that it was striking that the two couples who consulted friends were Catholic, and that the two friends were cited as being very "religious" and knowledgeable about religious matters. Both Catholic couples also asked the genetic counselor about religious conflicts with their possible course of action. One would normally expect the greatest religious and moral conflict regarding abortion in Catholic couples, or where one spouse is Catholic. One Catholic father in a mixed marriage said, "All of my childhood training has suddenly come back to haunt me." He felt that he had achieved a high degree of autonomy in the development of his conscience, until this decision. At points such as these, the interviewer's own preferences about moral development would begin to intrude, and I delayed any further discussion of the meaning of the substitution of a lay moral counselor for a priest, planning to look back at the action following the conclusion of the process.

Summing up the discussion of the structure of the morality of the decision-making process to this point, the most important value informing decision-making appears to be parental protection extended to the child; because prenatal diagnosis carries with it an informed alternative for abortion, the ethical sensitivity of the parents is greatly heightened. They enter the counseling relationship, on the whole, ready to have their alternatives sharpened, but they are actually aware of the alternatives before they come to the counselor. Sorenson (1972) made a vital observation about the moral structure of the counseling relationship in applied genetics:

> One of the reasons that it is critical to analyze the
> nature of the relationships between the counselor and
> counselee in applied genetics is that the ultimate role
> of who makes final decisions regarding the use of the
> knowledge is usually more critical and less ethically and
> morally neutral here than is the situation in the normal
> delivery of medical services.

6. The Counselor's Values

Sorenson distinguishes between two types of orientations in the counseling relationship in applied genetics (1972). First, the "doctor-client" relationship, characterized by the doctor's strict adherence to supplying information and reluctance to enter into a determining role in decision-making. Second, the "doctor-patient" relationship, in which information is indeed supplied, but the doctor actively enters the scope of decision-making to the extent of making his own views clear, at times suggesting to the couple a course of action, and discussing his own views about the impact of a defective child on the family and society.

The style of the genetic counselor in this instance was almost uniformly in the second type. A young, active (34-year-old) pioneer in the use of amniocentesis for prenatal diagnosis, the counselor-physician was deeply involved in the decision-making and feelings of his patients. While making it clear from the outset that the "final decision" about the action taken on amniocentesis and its consequences belonged to the patient, he was proactive in his counseling. He did not hesitate to reveal his views on the social issues involved in genetics and retardation, population increase, and the problems of defective children in society. In addition to the exploration of the couple's immediate problem, he would often launch into related issues, such as the optimum time for conception, statistics on the number of defective children in general, and research into human genetics. A great deal of instruction went on in these counseling sessions.

The structure of the session was informed by six activities: (1) a genetic history of the families of both spouses, (2) an estimate of the indications for amniocentesis, (3) informing as to the risks and benefits of the procedure, (4) exploring the attitudes and feelings of the couple, including answering any question on moral or religious issues, (5) explaining the technical process of obtaining the products of amniocentesis and how they would be used, (6) general instruction on human genetics and social values.

As the reader may imagine, a great deal of time went into these sessions. The average length of one session was well over an hour. The more complex the moral and personal issues in a case, the more time he spent in counseling in person and over the telephone.

The counselor's impact on parents with defective children or a history of abortions was especially significant, and there was considerable difference between the manner in which these children responded to him and those whose "age factor" had caused them to enter counseling. Again, the distinction between the two types of counseling relations sheds light on the intensity of the response. The perception of need and degree of anxiety present is considerably greater in the case of parents with defective children. They came to hold the counselor in high esteem as a physician and helper. Only one couple in the sample came away from the process "badly

disappointed" in the counselor and the help they had received.   In
this case, following four spontaneous abortions, a positive diagnosis of D/G translocation led to abortion and sterilization.   The
couple seized upon the counselor's mannerisms and a delay in
reporting the results of amniocentesis to "blame" the counselor for
much of their misfortune.

When asked about the counselor's style of working, the responses grouped in four categories: (1) an appreciation for his
time, effort, and concern invested, (2) a feeling of the counselor's
"selling" the test, but not a "hard sell," (3) a consciousness of
having been helped personally by the counselor in a psychological
or personal sense, and (4) an awareness of the counselor revealing
his position on abortion.   The only negative response frequently
mentioned was a tendency to use too complex terms and intricate
explanations.   "At the end I wish he had given me a pamphlet or a
diagram to see what he had been talking about," one mother said.

Some of the comments of patients about the counseling experience follow:

.. He goes through a meticulous process...he reinforces
you...he makes you conscious of what you are doing, and
he showed me a picture of a fetus so that I would be sure
that I knew what was at stake.

.. He is great...I learned so much and enjoyed it. He
buoyed me up.

.. He is so enthusiastic. He takes his time, and spent
an awful long time telling us about it.

.. He gives you plenty of details, and at times it was
too complex; I didn't think he was trying to do that
deliberately to confuse us, but we were somewhat confused
at the end and had some questions we didn't ask till
later.

.. He leaves it up to you, of course, but you know what
he thinks of it by the time it is over.

The impact of the physician's style and values, which I came
to call "interventionist," is shown in a report written by a husband about the experience. A graduate student, he wrote an account
for a course he was taking in counseling at a university; excerpts
are presented here.

My daughter is mongoloid. Because of this, my wife and I
were recently counseled by Dr._____. Dr._____ was
counseling because my wife is pregnant and we are
concerned about our next child.

Our experience with Dr.____ is almost too much to be expressed. He took an entire morning to talk to us. And the point of it all was that this man was open, honest, and perhaps brutally frank with us about our child and the problems we will have to face.

It may seem improbable that one meeting with a person can open your mind to what you have closed it to. But I feel this happened. I had been trying in vain to compartmentalize my life as far as my daughter and her problem were concerned. I had sealed it off and had done so by not bothering anybody about it, discussing it, or getting involved in it with the other parents in the Washington area who are deeply entangled in the world of retardation through their children. I have been so afraid of the idea of having a retarded child that it was only through great effort that I could even associate myself with the other parents or look at their children. All the time I was unconsciously thinking that my child was different.

What I am trying to tell you is that because one man was open and exposed his real self to me honestly, I have begun to shed my unhealthy and unrealistic position. I have been in conflict for the last two days but I feel some realization of first, what I had been denying, and second, the tasks and realities that I must now meet.

It seems clear to me now that being open or transparent to others is not only a healthy approach for the individual's health and integrity but can inspire others to become healthy or at least promote growth in some way. Dr.____'s transparency toward me ... was very threatening for it put me in a position of either re-evaluating my stance as regards my child or trying to defend it. I was fortunate to be able to recognize that my ideas about our problem were indefensible. But, although, others have tried to help my wife and me, Dr.____ was the only one who, through his honesty, hurt us enough so that we could begin to help ourselves, our child, and hopefully, others.

The danger in an "interventionist" approach to genetic counseling is that it may obscure the very real moral responsibility of the parents to make decisions with more independence than the typical patient. By spending large amounts of time with patients and earning their gratitude, the counselor may likewise "earn" the responsibility of "taking care" of the patients' decision-making as well. Hypothetically, the more acute the problem, the more ready

the patient is to deliver his moral authority to the physician.
While spending long periods of time in technical discussion, other
processes may be at work "behind the eyes" of physician and
patient. Both may be trying to find the other's real point of view
about the issues. Even though the couples in this sample felt that
they had control of the decision to take amniocentesis, they were
quite aware of the counselor's opinions. While never overtly instructing the actions of parents, the counselor would nevertheless
communicate his views through informing them as to the risks of
amniocentesis and the benefits to be derived. In interviews the
counselor said that he preferred an open, interventionist style to
guard against the possibility of his being manipulated by the
patient. He agreed that it could also be a problem for the
patient, but he made no substantial changes.

The counselor had well-formulated views about religion and the
social impact of genetic disease. He favored abortion in most
serious genetic disease, but he would also respect a parent's decision not to choose abortion even after knowing a child would be
defective. While this experience had not happened in over 500
cases, he remains open to the possibility. He was most conservative
in agreeing to sterilization and counseled the three mothers who
requested sterilization to consider other options, presenting a
cautious approach. He expressed hope to these patients that new
methods of sex selection and perhaps egg implantation may give them
new options for childbirth. In each case the patients chose
sterilization, but the counselor's position was clear to them.

This discussion of the impact of the counselor's values should
not imply that his patients perceived him as a moral problem to
them. This was not the case. On the contrary, several patients
stated that he was of great assistance to them in working through
their moral concerns. Hypothetically, a counselor who adopts the
interventionist style without being conscious of a motivation to
take care of his patients could present a substantial moral problem
for them. In like manner, there is a moral problem related to a
too strict adherence to the "doctor-client" relationship, since the
patient assumes that the physician has opinions and values. To
refuse to give support for the decision-making of the parents or to
fail to point out a real moral conflict dehumanizes the counseling
relationship and reduces it to a mechanical process.

7. Medical Reasoning and Morality

A small cluster of problems centered around the issues of
risks and benefits of amniocentesis, informed consent, and deciding
on the indications for amniocentesis. The counselor always stated
that amniocentesis carries a very small risk of infection, damage
to the fetus, or bleeding in the mother. No bad effect on the living fetus had been detected in well over 400 cases when the series
began. He also frequently spoke of heightened anxiety between the

time of the tap and learning the results. When asked to feed back their understanding of the risks, most couples would name one or two, but hardly ever repeat the entire list of risks the counselor had covered in the session. He had communicated that the risk was minimal, but the details remained remote. Like other patients who are being informed by physicians, these patients do not recall the details of risk and frequently deny that there are any risks at all (Fletcher, 1967).

Every couple felt "well informed" immediately prior to amnio-centesis, when asked by the interviewer. In subsequent interviews, however, it became clear that they did have second thoughts as well as questions which had not been answered. Many of these questions were about technical matters. Exactly why must there be a heartbeat in the fetus before the tap can be done? Is the use of an ultra-sound absolutely necessary? Why is there a three-week delay in learning the results of the tap? Will there be enough information for a decision to be really informed? Whenever the interviewer found second-thought questions he related them back to the physi-cian for more complete informed consent.

Only two cases in the entire sample were defined by the coun-selor as truly "borderline" with reference to indications for amniocentesis. In one case the age of a woman (38) who sought counseling, combined with the spouses' pedigrees did not indicate as high a risk as women over 40, but he nevertheless allowed amnio-centesis. The second case involved a couple whose last child was born ten months prior to a new pregnancy. The wife had been a dental assistant and feared she had been exposed to radiation, but this job had been prior to her first pregnancy. They readily admitted that their real worry was the close proximity of births. When the counselor was firmly assured of their commitment to have a child if the diagnosis was negative, he admitted the wife to amniocentesis. In a subsequent interview, he reasoned that the anxiety of the mother and father over the pregnancy was sufficient to warrant a tap, and the diagnosis proved negative. This couple also told of having visited a distant medical center seeking amniocentesis under "false colors," having concocted a story about genetic problems in their family. They were "repentant" and honest about their deceptions and sought assistance on the basis of their worries about having children very close together. In my opinion, the physician admitted them to amniocentesis for psychological reasons, which is not a strictly medical indication for the procedure.

PHASE II: DECISION FOLLOWING AMNIOCENTESIS

1. Anxiety Before the Diagnosis Report

The period following amniocentesis to the report on the results of the tap found the parents in considerable anxiety and

whatever problems existed in their marriage or family relationships
were exacerbated. The average time between test and reporting in
25 cases was 20.9 days. The physician told each couple that normally the time lapse was three weeks. Telephone calls to the
physician by parents were numerous, and his staff often counseled a
spouse over the telephone to tell them of the status of their case.

On looking back at process with the couples, they described
"toughest" time as the anxiety in waiting for a report on amniocentesis. "We shouted at each other and fought like tigers," said
one husband. Another husband who sought marriage counseling in
this period stated that the long wait had made him angrier at his
wife for being a carrier, and that he wanted more than ever out of
the relationship. Several couples testified to the fact that only
their strong marriage relationship sustained them and that without
it they would be without support and comfort. "I don't know what I
would do without his being with me, since I get so depressed," said
a mother carrying Down's syndrome.

If a marriage is troubled, the strains will most likely break
forth in this period, testing to the limits the capacity of the
couple to face their problem and make plans. I saw this trouble
more often in younger couples than in the older parents. One husband in particular acted out his feeling trapped in a marriage to a
carrier partner by making homosexual liaisons. After intensive
counseling and some psychotherapy more realistic assessments were
made by the parents.

As the techniques of culturing the amniotic fluid are refined
and the time period shortened, some of the anxiety should be
relieved. Nevertheless, counselors should be particularly atten-
tive to the deeper personal problems which emerge in this period.
The genetic counselor in this instance sought outside help for the
marital problems which came to his attention. Having chosen to
rely primarily on the sinews in the marriage for the strength to
make decisions in this process, the parents who had previous
marital problems were considerably troubled and unreliable to one
another during this "waiting period."

2. Decisions Following Positive Diagnosis

The most acute moral suffering, in the opinion of the interviewer, followed a positive diagnosis. In each of three cases the
couples decided for abortion and sterilization by hysterotomy. A
great deal of grief and self-condemnation followed these procedures. Following the report it was as if the whole decision had to
be made anew. One might expect that significant preparation had
been made which would lessen the burden. Possibly because the
couple had so hoped for a normal child, a set of expectations
heavily weighed in that direction formed and were shattered.

The reasons offered for the step to be taken were uniformly
personal and related to the emotional strain the parents had been
under. "I just can't go through this again," said a mother. "If

they can't tell me that my child is normal, I don't want to try again. I have three brothers with muscular dystrophy, and I am not going to take a chance on it." "No one who knows me would say that I don't want children, but I have had enough," said the third mother. The counselor, sensitive to the profound disappointment of the parents, advised caution in their decision, especially towards sterilization, but none preferred to remain able to bear children.

The three mothers who elected sterilization, and the fathers as well, suffered deeply from guilt and a sense of failure. Added to the guilt associated with being a carrier of genetic disease was their realization that their experiment to get a whole child had failed, and there would be no more children of their own. I was particularly interested in the plight of the women. One of them stated:

> I am just crushed and disappointed. I had so hoped to
> give my husband a healthy baby, and now I know that I
> will not. You spend all your life looking at pictures of
> pretty babies and their mothers and growing up thinking
> that will be you. It is pretty gruesome when you are the
> one who is different.

When asked about vasectomy as one option open to them, each mother rejected it vehemently. "It is my fault, why should he have to pay for it?" said one. "He may want to marry again, if anything happens to me, and he should be able to have his own children," said another.

One couple had never been able to have children successfully; four early natural abortions had preceded their attempt at prenatal diagnosis. Their reaction at the positive diagnosis of Patau syndrome was rage towards the physician-counselor. They seized on some of his mannerisms and the fact that their report was delayed for a short period to express their disappointment. He received their barbs and accusations without making any interpretation. In their interview prior to hysterotomy, I attempted to ask them to assess just where striking out against the physician would get them in the end. The husband was preoccupied with finding fault with the physician. I had the distinct impression that he was beating the physician verbally rather than his wife.

Two mothers electing hysterotomy had living children or family members suffering from genetic disease. They were acutely aware that aborting a fetus affected by the same problem amounted to a type of "rejection" of the relative. One mother talked of her child:

> He knows what's going on. I wonder what he thinks about
> the baby. He could think . . . they want to put me out
> of the way, too. And he could think, no one should have
> to suffer the way I do. I suppose it would be more the
> second.

Neither mother felt strongly enough about the meaning of abortion
to a living person suffering the same disease to choose against it.
Several parents with living children remarked that one of the
forces driving them against amniocentesis itself was the effect an
abortion might have on the security of a child at home with the
same problem.

PHASE III: POST ABORTION, STERILIZATION, BIRTH

   1. Reflection After Action

      An interview was held with parents following childbirth or the
the termination of pregnancy. No parent regretted using amniocentesis.   Parents who could look forward to having a "normal" child
said they were greatly eased by the knowledge and that the latter
part of pregnancy was easy.
      Parents who elected abortion and sterilization were still
troubled, but they were also taking other steps to help themselves.
Two couples made plans for adoption and a third decided to move to
a farm.
      Parents electing abortion and sterilization took particular
pains to justify their decision and to put the decision into a
framework which made sense to them. A Catholic couple alone attempted to place the event in a religious framework, but one which
no longer satisfied them morally or intellectually. "Why does God
give so many terrible things to children?" queried the mother. She
then told of several years of religious doubts due to the birth of
a previous child and her rejection by a priest when she earlier
sought amniocentesis. "I have a very hard time believing in God
anymore. I have prayed to God this time for his protection and for
a normal baby, and you see nothing has happened." As she talked she
cried openly. Feeling that she was reaching for a form of faith
which would help interpret suffering without condoning magic, I
offered her help in examining the religious views she had been
holding. First, she made no distinction between nature and God.
"God" was the source of good and bad genes. Secondly, she lived in
a universe with a very small margin of moral freedom, if any at
all. God determined everything, including one's choices. Thirdly,
her anger and cosmic resentment were clearly unacceptable in the
eyes of such a God. I reasoned that God was at least as gracious
to us as we are to our own children. "Would you always keep your
child penned up in the backyard, even when he was older?" I asked.
She got the point quickly and began to talk more about her unsatisfactory religious beliefs and fear of the church.

   2. Following Abortion

      Each mother revealed an element of "cosmic doubt," even though
the Catholic mother alone cast her doubt in a strictly religious

perspective. "You try to understand how things like this happen," said a Jewish mother, "and there is a scientific explanation... but...I feel the fickle finger of fate pointed at me."

"I lie awake nights damning God, even though I don't believe in a God," a third mother with no particular religious persuasions stated. The experience of genetic disease and ending a pregnancy may lead people to the "borderline" question about the meaning of human existence. These questions are of their nature religious questions, since people attempt to come to terms with their fate and a profound sense of isolation from the roles of parenthood. Even if religion is not used as a last line of defense against the arbitrariness of life, parents probably will seek to make some ultimate sense out of these events, and seek some ultimate security in their insecurity.

Following the birth of children, couples who had undergone genetic counseling re-examined their role as parents thoroughly. It was as if the process made them evermore serious about child-bearing and parental responsibility. Parents who knew that their children were carriers of a defective gene resolved to instruct them about their problem and to do everything possible to assist them in controlling their marital future. No parent even considered seriously the eugenic possibility of aborting a child who was a carrier. Amniocentesis or another technique would be open to them in the future.

3. Additional Reflections

Discussions with parents at the conclusion of the process provided a good format for inquiry into their attitudes about sex determination and genetic surgery. Only one of the 25 couples preferred not to learn the sex of their child. Those who preferred to know gave pragmatic reasons for wanting to know. "It takes some of the mystery out of it, but it helps to prepare us," said a father. Only the parents with sex-linked genetic diseases felt that sex determination was advisable. None of these couples felt that it was wrong to predetermine that a male or female be born if genetic disease could be avoided. Medical indication for sex predetermination was the predominant justification for this step when it becomes feasible. One mother stated:

> It wouldn't be a good idea to let everyone select the sex
> of their children. There would be too many problems.
> But in our case...Fabry's disease...it would be a
> blessing.

In discussing concepts of genetic surgery these parents were wary of prenatal interventions. None preferred to be the first to allow genetic surgery unless there were good reasons to hope for success. Attitudes of these parents were distinctly conservative in this regard. Yet the same parents had no doubts about the technique they were using. After the birth of a child, I asked parents if the possibility of "technical failure" (false negative) had worried them prior to birth. With one exception, a dental surgeon, the answer was "It crossed my mind but I did not seriously consider it." The exceptional person said that he was not truly at ease until the baby had been examined by a pediatrician. Thus, the power of technology and the credibility of physicians combine to reduce doubt in the average couple using amniocentesis.

None of the mothers who were in a position to discuss "surrogate parenthood" would have chosen this alternative of having a child rather than adoption. Each mother was a carrier of a deleterious gene and would (in surrogate parenthood) have to be the recipient of a donated ovum fertilized by her husband. The husbands preferred to have children either by adoption or when "it is my sperm and her egg."

Two areas for improvement in the genetic counseling process were mentioned frequently. First, there is a need for abortion counseling and support during the period around an abortion. "There should be someone like a psychiatrist to tell you what it is and how you are going to feel," said one repeating mother. Secondly, there was a felt need for more careful explanation of some of the adjunct techniques used with amniocentesis: ultrasound and fetal electrocardiogram. One couple commented that the adjunct staff in the genetics counseling unit played an important role in keeping them abreast of the facts. Communication is a vital avenue for allaying anxiety and supporting the parents during the waiting period.

My presence as an interviewer probably had more effect on the physician-counselor than anyone else. He "tightened up" his punctuality and reduced the number of conflicts in his schedules so as to be more available to patients. He was open and communicative with me about his career goals and directions in research he would like to take. As I provided a feedback loop of some importance to him, he sought information about positive and negative aspects of his effect on patients. The couples were quite open and eager to solve problems. The counselor asked me to meet in special sessions with several couples with difficult problems or troubled marriages. In his opinion, these counseling sessions were effective. My presence did not cause the counselor to change his style or content in counseling. Interviews with other staff members showed that he quickly included me as a member of the staff and related to me in much the same way as to the others. Our association was a perfect vantage point to study human genetics in the present and future.

SUMMARY OF HYPOTHESES:

1. Consideration of abortion is the major moral problem of parents in genetic counseling.

2. Parents are inclined to favor abortion in case of a positive diagnosis, and they have reached this position prior to counseling.

3. Parents in genetic counseling do not favor abortion "on demand" but only for specific, medically indicated reasons.

4. Parents feel morally competent to make decisions in genetic counseling without seeking any non-medical advice.

5. More moral suffering occurs when parents are faced with choices including sterilization as well as abortion.

6. The counselor's wishes for outcomes in a case will be conveyed directly or indirectly to the patient.

7. Although Catholic mothers are more ready to accept a genetically defective child, there will be more Catholics seeking prenatal diagnosis due to the autonomy of the family in issues of reproduction.

ETHICS AND HUMAN GENETICS

1. Amniocentesis and the Morality of Abortion

There is no compelling reason why prenatal diagnosis and abortion should not be one viable option (among others) in managing genetic disease. I want to argue that there are a number of reasons to support its use until treatment of genetic disease replaces abortion as a solution. Abortion of a genetically defective fetus is not the same as treatment. One should face the issues in abortion squarely and not rationalize genetically indicated abortions as "therapeutic" (Ramsey, 1970). Abortion is never therapeutic for the fetus. Abortion of a fetus with serious disease will most likely be a decision based on reasoning that it is more just and causes least suffering to the parents to proceed to other options in child-bearing without the burden of one or more than one defective child. One could argue that it is more just and causes least suffering to the fetus to abort it, rather than allowing it to suffer pain and illness, or to endure injustices inflicted on the mentally retarded. This latter argument is vulnerable because of the problem of paternalism. Whenever a strong group argues on behalf of a weaker group that their removal would be better than their survival, we should not be duly impressed. As Callahan argued (1970), it is not inevitable that every severely handicapped person can expect little or no fulfillment in life. One could also hold that it is unjust to society to allow more defective children to be born. This argument is especially vulnerable to the charge of intolerance. By and large the families of genetically defective children must bear the weight of their care and nurture. Consideration of the family's situation and values should be the fulcrum upon which the morality of the uses of genetic knowledge in amniocentesis turns. Given the choice of an abortion in the first half of pregnancy for a genetic disease that would so cripple the the infant that one could say that it will not have a capacity to respond to its environment, parents may prefer abortion. Among the indications for abortion terrible deformities must be included. Abortion is a serious and life-changing event, as these interviews with parents showed. Some genetic diseases are even more serious and lifechanging events. It can be responsible, under certain circumstances, to prevent the birth of a deformed child. We are under obligations to reduce suffering and to do justice. We shall never eliminate suffering or the sources of injustice, but we must not fail to take steps to reduce these conditions when faced with certain choices.

The first criterion for decision about aborting a defective fetus should be the severity of the disease. There are degrees of severity in genetic disease which must be taken into account as genetic knowledge becomes applicable to decisions about abortion. For example, within the three general types of mongolism, two are considerably more serious in effects and inheritability than tri-somy 21. It is not unusual for a person with this genotype to learn a useful occupation. There are genetic diseases so painful in their consequences (e.g., Lesch-Nyhan) that one can imagine no circumstances under which life could be preferred to the disease for oneself. Again, it is dangerous to put one's self in the place of a fetus and reason that the fetus should want death rather than life under certain circumstances. Abortion is a consequence of what adults want. But it is useful to know how painful certain diseases can be and to be aware of the difficulty in finding solutions to pain.

The second criterion is the availability of treatment for the genetic condition. The best argument against abortion as a mass solution to genetic disease would be the fact that new treatments are in different stages of development. Where no treatment to a severe and crippling disease was available, the logic of abortion may make more sense. There will be many parents whom physicians will meet on the "borderline" between the experimental stage of a new genetic therapy and the stage when it can justly be called a therapy. The stakes in these experiments will be very high indeed, but the opportunities must not be shunted aside. Medical research-ers in human genetics should begin now to consider the rights of their subjects in genetic therapy experiments where failure could prove very costly.

The third criterion is the family situation of the couple. Are there other children to consider? Other obligations? Finally, the values and beliefs of the family about procreation must be clearly respected. The decision-making authority on matters of procreation should reside with the family, in consultation with medical-moral counselors.

As long as this last value obtains, moral doubts about the use of genetic knowledge which are born in the fear of state-enforced eugenic regulations should be allayed. The primary enforcers of the morality of the applications of genetic knowledge are at present the family and their physician. The practice of experimental human genetics should be regulated by the same restrictions as presently apply to experimental therapeutics, but no extraordinary regulations are called for.

2. The Social Consequences of Genetic Intervention

To argue as I have done opens one to the criticism that if these directions are followed there will be less tolerance in society for the weak, the imperfect, the unlovely, and the unacceptable. To suggest that we ought to act to reduce pain seems to some to deny the good purposes to which pain can be turned. To others, my arguments reinforce the economic and social dominance of the middle and upper classes, since they tend to act upon genetic knowledge much more frequently than minority or lower class groups. I do not deny any of these possibilities as consequences of prenatal intervention. Yet I do not understand how the reduction of disease, under voluntary methods, harms a democratic society and its purposes. Put another way, the avoidance of responsibility in treating genetic disease and acting upon its presence in the unborn undercuts one of the central social values, to reduce suffering in all of its forms. One does not have to hold the position that parents are required to agree to abortion of every defective fetus. I hold that genetic counseling centers ought not to compel parents to agree to abortion prior to amniocentesis, for this position works against the voluntarism inherent in present practice. Furthermore, since the range of diseases and disfigurations caused by genetic problems is practically limitless, the argument against genetically indicated abortion based upon intolerance for weakness appears time-bound and finite. Will we not discover just as many medical problems to beset us in ages to come? Finally, there should be extraordinary efforts to extend genetic medicine to those groups in society who have been discriminated against economically and medically. Unless the benefits of medicine are distributed equally among groups in society, the people will not perceive "benefits" as being in their interest. For practical purposes, medical policy towards genetic treatment should be directed towards those diseases which are catastrophic in their personal and physical consequences. We should be aware of those who plan to engineer vast social changes through genetic engineering, such as raising the level of intelligence or reducing aggression in mankind.

3. New Steps in Genetic Medicine

I chose to follow the progress of couples in amniocentesis because this procedure appears to occupy the center stage of the application of human genetics to practical problems at the present time. It is as if amniocentesis is a "forerunner" of solutions to future problems. I found that the "consumers" of genetic progress (parents) were conservative in their consideration of proposals for sex determination, implantation, and genetic surgery. Their baseline for decision on genetic progress was related to serious genetic disease rather than to whole upgrading populations. They realized that they were the first generation of parents to benefit from information gained from prenatal diagnosis, and they were eager that its benefits be extended widely. Their views, on the whole, coincide with mine as to the ethical parameters of progress in genetic medicine. Theological tradition tends to support man's intervention into natural processes to improve his physical and social environment. This is not to say that an unlimited blessing is extended to technical progress. Theologians must beware of providing "cover" for medical progress or codes of behavior which are derived entirely apart from faith. Each proposal in genetics must be evaluated for the benefits and risks to human beings contained in it. Moreover, risks must be assumed by informed human beings who are agreed as to the terms of their experiment. To this theologian, human genetics at present does not violate anything inherently "human," for the most characteristic act of man is to attempt to change himself and his condition. Human freedom is an experiment in itself, conducted within the limits of human finitude and self-interest. The most authentic Western religious visions prompt interventions into our condition as long as we do not expect to seize eternity or ultimate security through any one or several of these man-made plans. We must not deceive ourselves: human genetics will create as many problems as it solves. Nevertheless, when one has unleased the full force of theological self-criticism upon a therapeutic direction in genetics, he emerges with no compelling reasons to cry "stop it." Indeed, one can imagine therapeutic uses for the newest projections for human genetics, including implantation and sex selection. It is the task of the nonmedical professions aligned with physicians to call to them to adhere to their therapeutic calling and resist any attempt to hasten the "kingdom of God" through technical progress.

4. A New Stage of Life

Others have discussed the development of new "stages of life" in the context of the development of modern culture (Keniston, 1968; Erikson, 1970). It is plausible that the demands of an advanced industrial society create a set of needs plus the means for the appearance of a new stage of life: prenatal. Given the means to study and monitor the development of the fetus, and given the recognition of the complex demands in the environment the fetus will enter, it stands to reason that adults in this period will surround the fetus with whatever supports or interventions they hope will better equip its development. Before this period in history human beings reckoned that the first stage of life began at birth. Judged by our own actions and inventions we are assisting in the birth pangs of a new stage of life prior to the birth of the child. One of the consequences of this development will be the assignment of developing human status to the fetus from conception forward. There is no way to avoid regarding the embryo as human, although the stages of development through which the fetus passes towards birth will carry decisive weight in defining its identity. The more the unknowns of human development prior to birth are exposed to light, possibly the more care can be extended to unborn children. But because care is never "pure" and is mingled with self-interest and ideology, the unprotected fetus is more than ever exposed to the wish fulfillments of adults. One of the primary tasks of ethical inquiry for the generation to come will be defining the limits and possibilities of intervention into the newest human stage of life.

REFERENCES

Aiken, Henry D. (1962). *Reason and Conduct*, New York, Alfred A. Knopf, Inc.
Carney, Fredrick S. (1968). *Norm and Context in Christian Ethics*, Outka, G. S. and Ramsey, P. (editors), New York: Charles Scribner's Sons, 3-36.
Callahan, Daniel (1970). *Abortion: Law, Choice and Morality*, London, The Macmillan Company.
Epstein, Charles J. (1969). *The Hastings Law Journal 21*, 1, 35-49.
Erikson, Erik (1953). *Childhood and Society*. New York, W. W. Norton and Co.
Keniston, Kenneth (1968). *Young Radicals*. New York: Harcourt, Brace, and World, Inc.
Fletcher, John C. (1967). *Law and Contemporary Problems, 32*, 620-629.
Gustafson, James M. (1970). *Soundings, 53*, 141-180.
Harris, Maureen, editor, (1972). *Early Diagnosis of Human Genetic Defects*. Washington, U.S. Government Printing Office.
Littlefield, J. W. (1970). *New England Journal of Medicine, 282*, 627-628.
Niebuhr, H. R. (1963). *The Responsible Self*, New York, Harper and Bros.
Parsons, Talcott (1951). *The Social System*, New York, The Free Press.
Ramsey, Paul (1970). *Fabricated Man*, New Haven: Yale University Press.
Sorenson, Jr. R. (1972). *Decision-Making in Applied Human Genetics: Individual and Societal Perspectives (this volume)*.

DECISION-MAKING AND THE INTERESTS
OF MINORITY GROUPS

Reverend David Eaton

It is paradoxical, bordering on hypocrisy, that we are here discussing under what conditions, principles, and policies a fetus should be aborted. At this very moment, thousands of normal fetuses in this country are suffering growth deficiencies and probably brain damage--not through any genetic disease, but simply due to malnutrition. And I am wondering whether, as geneticists, you have marshalled your concern for these potential individuals also. I wonder whether geneticists and genetic counselors really concern themselves with the real problems of the poor. In respect to your professional training and political influence upon the medical profession, are you equally concerned with the continued development of the fetus, both prior to and after birth as the child?

I have been asked to comment on decision-making in genetic counseling as it relates to minority groups. In fulfilling my assignment, I will share with you some of the reasons why many non-white minority groups in general and the Afro-American minority in particular do not really care what you decide in respect to genetic counseling.

In order for you not to receive my message in a harsh light, I think it is necessary for you to understand the level of awareness that is present in non-white communities in respect to white/non-white relationships. First, white racism is viewed as the number one deterrent to non-white advancement in America's society.* Because of this, increasingly, non-white groups do not trust white groups, or groups whose leadership is dominated by whites, to make decisions affecting them.

Second, it has become apparent that white racism is a result of the justification of slavery in this country, in particular, and

---

*The White House conference on Youth's Task Force on Race and Minority Relationships stated that "White racism is the cancer of American socity." Report of the White House Conference on Youth, April 18-22, 1971, Estes Park, Colorado.

exploitation over non-white minorities, in general. In 1619, when
the first man-of-war deposited the first slaves in Jamestown Col-
ony, slavery was not a new phenomenon in the history of man. But
at no previous time in history was the term "slave" associated with
mere skin color. At no time in history had skin color been made
synonymous with non-human. The economic act of slavery had to be
justified. The beginning of racism in this country was a process
to justify slavery; the moralist had to justify it.

The Christian Church was quite influential with the scholars
of the day as well as with the criminals, prostitutes, pimps and
other dredges of Europe who occupied the southern part of the
United States. These Christians could not rationalize putting a
fellow human being into captivity; therefore, the rationalization
that the Black man was not fully human became the justification for
his being a slave. This justification had to be distributed
throughout society; therefore, the institutions assumed the responsibility. The family, church, business, schools, and all the
institutions of the society began to teach that the white man was
superior and the Black man was non-human, and therefore inferior.
This was the beginning of white racism and institutional racism.

The third level of awareness which you should know exists in
non-white communities in general and the Afro-American community in
particular has to do with how we preserve institutional racism.
Due to the history and nature of racism in this country, we believe
that it has become the very fabric of American institutions. No
matter how sincere a few whites may be, no matter how non-racist a
few whites may think and behave within a particular institution,
the institution will still exhibit racism unless a massive effort
is made to rid the institution of its "cancer." Those of you who
would like to explore this issue in greater depth are invited to
read The Choice, the issue of Black survival in the United States,
by Samuel Yette. Mr. Yette was a counsel for the Office of Economic
Opportunity and is now a reporter for Newsweek magazine.

Due to the historical and contemporary realities of the Afro-
American men and women in this country and the historical and contemporary realities of other non-white minority groups, the issue
of survival is, for many of us, a real issue. This is why I say
that whatever decisions made here, in isolation from non-white
minority groups, will have little or no meaning in connection with
the minority groups.

When I referred to your possible political strength within the
American Medical Association, I was in fact suggesting that because
of the way "morality" has been used as a weapon of oppression in
this country, I would prefer that "men of good will," as opposed to
"men," be concerned with the political and economic thrusts necessary in bringing about a just society.

The Afro-American in particular and non-whites in general are
increasingly rejecting the concept, the myth, of America being a
melting pot for us, for them. Increasingly, non-whites are talking
and living "self-determination." The concept of integration has

failed. It failed not because of the theory of the idea. It failed because of the way it was being implemented by the liberal white community--a way in which the white man planned the menu and invited the non-white community to dinner. So integrationists went, and we ate dinner together, but we did not plan the menu together. For an example, how many of you hear the phrase, "Well, we passed the Civil Rights Bill for you," (meaning me)? And my comeback is, "No, you did not pass the Civil Rights Bill for me." When I went to the library in Chattanooga, Tennessee in 1950, I knew I was a human being. I knew that my parents paid taxes. I knew that Black workers had helped build the building. And I knew that I should have gotten into that building. But the guard did not know it. And he threw me out.

I knew I could go in. The Civil Rights legislation was written for whites, because the whites in Congress sent a note to the guard and said, "Yes, David is supposed to be in the building, white guard; admit him."

But the attitude is -- and you have heard this at cocktail parties--Why are they still pushing? Haven't we given them enough? With minority groups understanding this attitude, with minority groups understanding that the majority group in this country historically has never done anything out of "moral suasion," then why should the minority groups now think that something called genetic counseling is of real and intensive concern? We want to know how much money has been set aside for research into sickle-cell anemia and who controls the money.

I share all of this with you so you will know of the type of sensitivity that has developed in the non-white community.

The types of exploitation -- even the subtle psychological exploitation that has been going on in nearly all non-white communities--somehow affects the fetus. I wish there were some way you could find it necessary to add to your agenda other concerns like malnutrition in terms of the fetus. Maybe you will have to expand the meaning of the word "disease." However, if you still want to help the minority communities, the best way would be to involve the counselors who are already in the minority communities. Enable the appropriate amount of money to go to the training of these persons in the subject matter necessary for genetic counseling. Most of the persons to whom I refer already know enough about counseling techniques; all that would be necessary would be the relevant data and understanding.

We are living and moving and having our being in America today amidst an attitude of group self-determination. No longer can we play God with the lives of other groups of people.

Dr. Morison gave a reason for aborting the fetus with genetic disease, and he said, "Because of the problems of over-population creeping upon us, there are only so many slots, and we need the best people to fill them." I am concerned about who defines best. Dr. Morison is not a racist, but he is a product, as all of us are, of racist institutions. He does not understand the very subtle implications that hit me directly between the eyes, when he says, "There are only so many slots, and we need the best people to fill them."

Also, my concern is--Who defines what a disease is and how is that definition reached? We have already had a few presentations that have alluded to the fact that maybe we can get some really good people if we mate people who have the same or similar intelligence and set some intelligence criteria. This has been suggested in some papers. We heard it. I watched the smiles. Your smiles were not those of approval, but those of--Oh, oh, somebody is about to open up Pandora's box. So I would just say, if my interpretation of your sincerity is in fact true, that the only politically permissible way that geneticists and genetic counselors can express their human concern for human personality is to work through the established organizations, especially in minority communities.

There is a sense of arrogance which you do not mean to have, and I am not talking about you in particular; I am talking about the white population in general. Since you know the "truth," you will dispense it. You will help those people. A very paternal feeling. Understand, "those people" are turned off by this type of attitude. I would never go to an Indian reservation to help the Indians. I would go to work with the Indian people. A different attitude. With this attitude, one will learn as well as teach.

DISCUSSION

SEEGMILLER: Dr. Fletcher has pointed out one of the areas of weakness in the success of our prenatal programs--the realm of education of the general physician. I certainly think that in order to have such programs succeed, we need to devote considerably more attention to making the concepts readily available so the average physician is aware of the potentials. Then their patients can get over this first hurdle which Dr. Fletcher pointed out.

CHEZ: I found what Dr. Fletcher talked about very moving. It pertains not only to genetic counseling but also to counseling of the dying patient or counseling of the cancer patient. In fact, his quotations from patients were exactly those that we have recorded when we did research on the dying patient and the patient with cancer. That is the general response of patients to stress.

It seems to me that the way that we can help our peers and ourselves learn about the care of patients is to include in the educational process, in the medical schools and in residency, the concept of communication in the doctor-patient relationship.

I would also like to expand on Rev. Eaton's comments because I think there are subtleties that we are coming to in pregnancy research that are not as overt, in my estimation, as chromosome analysis.

There are some of us in this room who spend our full time in research in trying to determine placental function, the adequacy of the placenta in providing the growing fetus with the proper supplies of nutrients, humoral substances and oxygen, and then we spend time in the research which surrounds labor and delivery.

As we develop diagnostic procedures whereby we can determine when the fetus is existing in a suboptimal environment secondary to inadequate exchange from its mother, we may still remain unable to therapeutically change this environment. We will then be in the same position as we are today in genetic counseling, and that is: What decisions can parents make about this? What controls or options should they have in deciding whether they should continue with a pregnancy in which a suboptimal environment exists for the fetus? And what happens when we finally do know with more precision than we do now what effect the nature of the parturition will have on that individual's eventual growth development, what will then happen at delivery?

Now I am not talking about a selective kind of disease state which only affects a small percentage of all pregnant patients, but rather situations that will permit us to test every pregnancy. The deliberations that we are having will be very important foundations for those future times.

CONDLIFFE: When Rev. Eaton raised the question of malnutrition, I remembered the debate within NIH over the changing nature of nutrition research.

Some years ago it was obvious that nutrition was altering its nature as a scientific discipline. It was expanding far beyond the confines of the research laboratory. By 1955 we all felt that it was really time to take the research results in nutrition, which we had from great pioneers in nutrition and biochemistry, such as Elmer McCallum, and apply this. Adequate scientific information was available by 1955 that, if applied, could greatly improve the nutritional state of any population group. The reason geneticists do not work on nutrition, as scientists, is that nutrition is not an exciting research problem. It is an economic problem, a political problem, a social problem, but it is not particularly a scientific problem. There is no dearth of knowledge about what could be done were the political-economic distributive mechanisms functioning better than they seem to be.

EATON: Let me react to that very briefly. Since you are concerned with the fetus as a part of your intellectual and medical discipline, then why aren't you concerned with all fetuses in terms of their living to age of developing into a personality? Where is the political thrust within the American Medical Association to make the appropriate changes, to bring about the political clout so a normal fetus is not damaged because of malnutrition--which happens all over the country.

I see enthusiasm here. It is like the man who loves humanity but hates people. Where is your concern, you know, collectively, for any fetus in this country having the appropriate conditions--to use that behavioral psychologist's term--medical conditions to survive and grow up to be a healthy being? I am wondering how you draw the line on where you protect the fetus. Are only diseased fetuses your concern? Or are all fetuses medicine's concern?

CARMODY: I think, Rev. Eaton, you answered your own question in your paper. The clout has to come from the Black community to take care of their own people. I think you know that reality. The whole question of morality without power to back it up is, as you know, just words. And it has always been that way. I don't know if you wanted someone of us to say it also.

EATON: I used the term "role" earlier, but when the Black community moves to protect its own fetuses, especially in the delta area of the South, then persons--not you, but your brothers--label those Black leaders--militants, violents. And we don't get the support from you to protect our own fetuses.
So, even though the role may not be the frontline role, I don't see the support through the AMA for those fellows down there who are insisting upon the type of programs and insisting on the type of medical care and food that are needed for a healthy fetus.

JACOBSON: The leading thrust of the new change is a very acute awareness that perhaps 3 percent of the retardation we deal with in America is genetic in origin and probably 10 percent is caused by socioeconomic deprivation. Nutritional deficiency is one of the major aspects of this. But this is not restricted to minority groups on the mainland: in fact, it exists also in Pacific Trust Territories and tribal reservations.
It is not that the members of this council are not aware of this, but we have come here for a small, isolated program, and we can't attack a technical one. But we certainly are missing a very easy place to prevent severe damage to man via mental retardation. And these are genetically normal individuals. They recur at a much higher frequency in the pregnancy at risk than any genetic condition that we have discussed today. With the poor family planning, the severe malnutrition, and the very poor obstetrical care, this is affecting sequential fetuses.

LUDMERER: Two thoughts occurred to me concerning your remarks about malnutrition in infants.
First, medicine is a very broad discipline. The fact that a group of doctors might meet to discuss one problem does not mean that they are unsympathetic to other problems. An interest in alleviating genetic disease does not preclude a concern with malnutrition and conditions caused by environmental deprivation.

Second, it seems to me that the question of malnutrition related to race is a matter somewhat apart from the other racist institutions which you mentioned. Though I agree with you that malnutrition cannot be totally separated from racial issues, neither can malnutrition be separated from the development of public health measures. It seems to me that malnutrition is really a public health question. In the twentieth century improved public hygiene has saved more lives than all the antibiotics and miracle drugs combined. Nevertheless, public health is a very recent development in the history of medicine, and in all countries it still requires more effort and more interest.

CAPRON: Two situations have been described to us. One described by Dr. Fletcher involves, I presume, family doctors telling their patients factual information about genetic counseling which misleads the patients--in the view of Dr. Fletcher and, I would gather, in the eyes of this group as well. I presume that those doctors acted in what they regarded as the patients' "best interests." Since they were fairly open about their prejudices, the patients were able to detect quite easily that these doctors were acting from premises with which the patient did not necessarily agree.

But, of course, there are many times when this revelation will not be detected by a patient, and a doctor--such as the one the Gleitmans had, in the example I gave this morning--will give information based on hidden premises. Yet, I presume that that doctor will be thought of as serving his patients' "best interests."

FLETCHER: I see no formal distinction. One thing I omitted--it is a very primitive hypothesis of mine that obstetricians who deliver babies for the same woman may tend to develop a sense of proprietorship of that woman and her babies. I've had some substantiation of this. None of the 25 couples were sorry that they knew the sex of their child prior to birth. But two of them reported that the obstetrician attending the wife when she delivered showed signs of jealousy that she knew it and he did not.

AIKEN: Dr. Carmody, in his remarks to Rev. Eaton, said two or three things that simply astonished me. I wonder if they astonished you? And if they didn't, why not?

He said that Rev. Eaton had qualified the answer to his own question. And in the course of your remarks, you stated that morality, in effect, has no clout.

While I want to recognize a logical distinction, to be sure, between the concept of power and the concept of moral responsibility and moral conviction, nevertheless, it does seem to me that it is quite unfounded and, indeed, is a prejudice that I would wish to challenge, that moral conviction and the sense of moral responsibility does not carry a power of its own. Why should we suppose that all power is either merely political, or merely economic, or merely X, or merely Y?

One of the things we have observed in the last decade is that the moral passion and the moral outrage of Black people, for example, have been powerful sources of their ability to make such changes as indeed have occurred, small though they may be. The moral passion and conviction of many young people on our campuses have, indeed, brought people to awareness of problems of a political and economic sort that might not otherwise have occurred to them.

I am not saying that there is not such a thing as political clout or economic clout. But I do think that behind these forms of clout, there may be moral and, indeed, religious clout, a sense of the sacred, a sense of the holy. I want to suggest that a main reason why what appears to be moral conviction carries so little clout is that most of us are bloody hypocrites--that we, indeed, make formal professions of moral responsibility but in our behavior we belie these.

EATON: I have a very difficult time breaking reality up into segments. I very seldom, for example, use the words liberal and conservative, in talking about people. I didn't even learn these terms in the sense of public speaking until I got up to All Souls Church and began to deal with a group of intellectuals. Then I found out that I had to earmark everything. I find it very difficult, Professor, to do this. Jesus of Nazareth was asked, "How do we know that this guy is really on the ball, how do we know he really is with us, how do we know that he is thinking correctly?" And He said, "By their fruits you shall know them."

I have a feeling of the holy, of the sacredness of personality. I do distinguish--though it was not my job to do it in the paper, so I didn't--between human personality and biological existence. But it is very difficult for me to understand this gentleman here. In terms of logic, certainly I know a geneticist is supposed to be primarily concerned with genetics. But that type of gross compartmentalization--does that mean he does not use his influence in the AMA on anything other than genetic issues? I can't divide things up that clearly.

I am aware that the phenomenon is no more important than how the phenomenon is perceived. You are perceived by the Black community as a physician who is not concerned with certain very real things that are happening in our intimate community.

You are not perceived as a geneticist or a genetic counselor: that is your bag. Therefore, we don't have anything to say about these other things. So mere moral suasion, moral consciousness has to be demonstrated. We are in an isolated, ethereal ivory tower here fed by the ozone of existence. It is something that is alive; it is vibrant; one can detect movement and concern.

Now, how do we translate these concerns for fetuses into something that has much more social consequence, not only for 1971, but beyond? Some of those guys who really are not as concerned as you are will use your data to continue the systematic annihilation of human beings, probably in the fetus. And you will have unwittingly furnished the data and information where people can do this justifiably without your knowledge. You will not be doing it with any cognitive awareness. You will be doing it because you are a good scientist, furnishing facts.

But when you get the overview that Samuel Yette puts out in his book, and if your moral integrity is still intact, you may decide that you have to do something political or something described as political, before you take another step in genetics.

You may have to share some of this data and say, "Before this is published, certain things will have to occur in society: Can you help us so that our data is not used in a way that we don't want it to be used?"

Those are the types of moral questions and those are the types of things I am concerned with. So I quite agree that I can understand the moral right only in terms of the fruits.

With regard to population growth, I think statistics show—and, again, since I am not sure of my facts—I will use the words "I think," and those of you who know can correct me. I think that since 1935, the largest extent of growth has occurred in the white community as opposed to the Black community in terms of the numbers of people being added to the census.

NEEL: I happen to have here the cold dope with which to answer this question. I expected to introduce it tomorrow morning in talking about the priorities we face. Population control is a priority which bristles with genetic issues. There are good reasons why it is resisted by the so-called minority groups.

A UN publication of 1953 attempts to reconstruct the growth of the world's population since 1650. Population has increased by an estimated factor of 5. By reference to geographic areas of the world, and with some oversimplifications, one can consider the increase of various ethnic groups. If we equate Northern and Latin America and Oceana with the American Indian, Polynesians, Australian aborigines, then even with a generous allowance for hybridization, this part of the world's gene pool has increased by a factor of about 2.

If we equate Africa with Negro, and one-sixth of America's gene pool is of Negro origin, then the gene pool of this ethnic group has increased by 2.5.

Equating Asia with Mongoloids and East Indians, that gene pool has increased by a factor of 5.

By the same reckoning, the Causcasoid pool has increased in the last 300 years, from an estimated 113 million persons to an estimated 935, a factor of 8.

Now, it is very easy to see why some minority groups say—all right, this is the time you Caucasoids may want to stabilize, but is this the time we want to stabilize?

HIMSWORTH: My point is to Dr. Fletcher and to Mr. Capron. All this morning we were discussing this question of giving full information, and how the genetic counselor should not intrude his personality or seek to influence the decision of the person to whom he is giving counsel.

I can see various theoretical points of view there. But all the time, I felt the situation was unreal. There was one thing missing from it. And that was the patient.

Therefore, this afternoon, I think we heard from Dr. Fletcher a very important point to keep in mind. If I am correct, you said, sir, that the people you were watching were striving to find out what the doctor's attitude was. And my experience of dealing with patients is that we can pretend as much as we want that we won't influence them. We may fool ourselves into thinking we are not doing this. But the patient will get his teeth into us, and he won't rest until he has found out what we really think about the situation in which we are advising him.

It is not confined to genetic counseling. If you advise a patient to have an operation, he will find out whether you would have it if you were in his position. And he does not feel secure until he has found out what the person to whom he has come for advice really thinks about a situation from his own personal point of view. Am I correct in thinking that your observation of the natural situation was that the majority of the people there wished to know what the assessment of the counselor himself was, however much he tried to keep detached from the situation.

FLETCHER: That is correct. They not only wished to know, but they found out, either directly or indirectly. That is, they asked, or they surmised. The counselor in this case would not give his views freely. But he would, if asked, and if the time was appropriate in his opinion. The patients were grateful for not having to do much jousting or speculating.

KABACK: I would agree with many of the sentiments in Dr. Fletcher's paper and certainly with the comments made by Sir Harold. Doctor Fletcher, I would like to look at the issues in terms of your study in some greater detail.

Twenty-five couples came for amniocentesis and, as you correctly pointed out, they came because they wanted to have amniocentesis. To some degree, therefore, their seeking the support of the counselor was to support psychologically and reinforce the decision they had already made. One has to emphasize in this context that these couples were really seeking corroboration and not a decision from the counselor.

Perhaps the most interesting part of the presentation was the very small sample of three couples who actually terminated their pregnancies. This sample is quite small, as I believe Dr. Fletcher mentioned, but it is here that the most critical data concerning the role of the counselor can be gathered.

Most people in my experience who have come for amniocentesis have some real concern about possible risks, but I do not believe they think that it is going to happen to them. The amniocentesis is really a precautionary measure. The issue really comes to a head when, based on the results of amniocentesis analysis, a positive diagnosis is made and the pregnancy might now be terminated. Now, a real decision has to be made. This is the decision that counts--not the one that is speculative and "unlikely to affect me."

Therefore, I would contend that the analyses that you have done on the role of the genetic counselor are going to be most vital in terms of the responses of those couples who, in fact, actually terminate the pregnancy. In these cases the role of the counselor may be most critical.

As you pointed out, one might find different reactions in different genetic units. This might be true also for the attitudes of families which have terminated pregnancies. I was interested in the fact that in each of the families that terminated their pregnancies, the women were sterilized after the procedure. This is quite different from our experience. All of the families which have terminated pregnancies are anxious to have subsequent pregnancies.

STETTEN: Would you venture to guess, Dr. Fletcher, that the election to sterilization may have been conditioned by your counselor?

FLETCHER: No. He was very conservative about it. In four of the sixteen pregnancies that were terminated, the sterilization procedure was done. In this regard, counsel was to use the lowest morbidity procedure to terminate pregnancy, which would be saline at this stage. This counsel was overridden by the obstetrician, who wanted to do a surgical procedure, because he wanted to combine the sterilization with the abortion. This was counseled against, because it was felt that sterilization could be done very effectively under a laparoscope, which is a minor procedure, so that there would be a three to six months period for the patients to really overcome what their feelings were about the abortion and not mix this in with the sterilization. This counsel was valid because two of the cases are now showing considerable guilt regarding the sterilization procedure, which was rather forced on them by a reaction of their obstetrician to the genetic risk.

Over 300 of these procedures have been done, and it is not typical that they, in fact, are sterilized. Many of them come back for as high as three taps.

STEINBERG: In effect, he has answered the question I had,

except that I would like to direct a complement to that question to Dr. Kaback.

How many of your patients have had an abnormal child and are coming for a second or third abortion, or being aborted after an abnormal child? My impression from your survey is that you are detecting people before they have had an abnormal baby.

KABACK: This is correct, Doctor Steinberg. As yet, we have not done an amniocentesis on a couple identified as at-risk for Tay-Sachs disease prior to the previous birth of an affected child. A number of couples have been so identified, but none have as yet become pregnant.

What I am referring to is that in our Prenatal Diagnostic Clinic at Hopkins, we evaluate families with various indications for intrauterine diagnosis, both chromosomal and metabolic. Although our experience is not as large as Doctor Jacobson's, I would say that several families have come back for second amniocenteses and, in those pregnancies that have been terminated, none of the women have elected to become sterilized.

CROW: I, too, was bothered by so much generalization from three cases. But I want to ask a question of the man with so much data whether you had any insights as to why it is that Japanese behavior in this regard is so different?

SORENSON: I talked to Dr. Inouye in Paris about this, and he suggested that it was a result of the fact that the parents have been so much more involved in the mate selection process there than here.

But he has observed that this tradition in Japan is changing. With this change, most people now going for counseling are young people, after marriage rather than before. Thus, it is becoming more like the pattern of counseling in this country.

PROSPECTS FOR FUTURE SCIENTIFIC DEVELOPMENTS: AMBUSH OR OPPORTUNITY

Robert L. Sinsheimer

Ours is a time of intense self-doubt, corroding confidence, and crippling resolve; a time of troubled present and ominous future; a time of strange clouds and sudden shadows seen in a fading light with cracking nerve. And hence it is not surprising that so great a triumph as man's discovery of the molecular basis of inheritance should provoke fear instead of joy, breed suspicion instead of zest, and spawn the troubled anguish of indecision instead of the proud relief of understanding.

Thus we read in an article by George Steiner (1971): "It is as if the biochemical and bio-genetic facts and potentialities we are beginning to elucidate were waiting in ambush for man. It may prove to be that the dilemmas and possibilities of action they will pose are outside morality and beyond the ordinary grasp of the human intellect."

Or Sir MacFarlane Burnet, the noted immunologist, has written (1969): "Man, that dominant mammal, evolved in a middle-sized world: his curiosity has led him into two universes which are totally irrelevant to his evolution from mammal to man. The first which concerns both the cosmic universe of the astrophysicists and the infinitely small world of the fundamental physical particles, is the process by which elements evolve in stars. The second is the chemical basis of life, the coded nucleic acid polymers that we call DNA and RNA. There is a third forbidden universe still to be effectively explored, the nature of what we call thought or consciousness and its relation to brain structure and function. It also is not relevant to human evolution, and its partial understanding may present us with even greater perils than have come from our intrusion into the other two."

Do we face an ambush--or an epic opportunity? A forbidden universe--or the long-sought land, the goal toward which evolution has been striving for five billion years--to be, in its product, aware of its essence, and thus to rise above chance? To continue, from this time on, the exploration of the potential of life, by means less harsh, in directions more varied. To begin--slowly,

341

with this imperfect instrument, homo sapiens--the application of forethought to evolution. And with forethought, conscience.

These are most certainly profound questions, and they merit both our deepest thought and our highest motive. We have over the past few centuries achieved a very considerable mastery over our physical world--and many are less than pleased with the results. We can now foresee--through our new insight into the bases of life --a growing mastery over our biological world-- and that includes us--and many are terrified at the prospect.

They are not without reason. Much of the despair of our time stems from the realization that--at last--after all the toil and all the invention, all the savagery and all the genius--the enemy is "us." Our deepest problems are now "made by man." Their origin lies in the inherent innate corrosion of imperfect man. Should we then arm this creature with vast new powers?

I expect that it is not the prospect of the application of the new knowledge to the biological world in general that frightens thoughtful men. If we can clone prize cattle to improve our food supply; if through designed genetic change we can produce more nutritious crops which make more effective use of sun and water; if we could, for instance, greatly expand the range of plants with the capacity to serve as hosts for nitrogen-fixing bacteria; if we can engineer viruses or microbes to curb pests or to destroy cancer; these innovations might produce ecological concern, but not dire doubt. It is the possible application of genetic intervention to man that generates the shock wave. For this possibility--remote as it may yet be--illuminates from a new direction all that is encompassed in the word "human", and thereby challenges traditional concepts in every area of human activity. And much of the alarm is that we scientists--with our clever new tools--could crudely disrupt much of our social order, imperfect as it may be, with scant regard for its replacement. It has happened.

What, in logic, may we today reasonably expect or foresee in consequence of our new knowledge and insight? Out of the vast range of possibilities, I would like to discuss a small but important and interrelated set. These derive from our growing understanding of genetics, of development, of cell biology and biochemistry, and they involve appreciation of the nature of the genome, the means of its variation, and the control of its expression. The practical application of these potentials may take the form of improved genetic counseling, cloning, extrauterine gestation and chimeras, genetic therapy, and designed genetic change.

Genetic counseling is a new profession based upon our increasing understanding of the genetic origin of human disorders (McKusick, 1966) and our increasing ability to recognize the genetic or chromosomal bases for these disorders--either in a prospective parent or in the developing fetus (Nadler, 1971; Milunsky et al., 1970). The techniques for the discovery and analysis of simple single gene defects that obey Mendelian rules are well established; in an increasing number of these the biochemical defect is known and can be assayed, even in heterozygotes. Of course, the known existence of the defective gene in the parent only conveys a certain probability of the appearance of the disorder in the fetus. The detection of such a defect in the fetal cells derived from amniotic fluid is more certain. Such detection may not always be straightforward, but it is plausible to suggest that means can most often be developed to cause cultures of such cells to display the enzymatic potential in question (or more importantly, the lack thereof) by exposure to appropriate circumstances.

The most urgent field for further advance in genetic counseling concerns those conditions which, while subject to evident genetic influence, cannot be attributed to simple single gene defects. In my view the evidence for a major genetic component in such widespread disorders as schizophrenia (Koch, 1966), diabetes (Neel, 1970), certain forms of cancer (Knudson, 1971), susceptibility to heart disease, even rate of aging (if that is properly a disease) is unarguable. The indications for a major genetic influence upon such psychological traits as intelligence or artistic ability are again, in my view, convincing. In all these instances the inheritance is complex, and we have as yet little concept of the associated biochemistry.

One important possibility for further empirical advance in the field of genetics lies in the potential for more detailed chromosomal analysis. The recent development in the use of fluorescent stains (Casperson et al., 1969; Sumner et al., 1971; Laberge and Gagne, 1971) or Giesma stain (Patil et al., 1971) have indicated the existence of marked differentiations along individual chromosomes, and thereby the existence of previously unknown variations among the human population. It seems to me not unlikely that such variations may be correlated with some of the genetically complex disorders mentioned above.

Further, it is at least possible that the differentiation along the individual chromosomes may by appropriate techniques be carried to much finer levels than are revealed by the light microscope. Although visualization of individual nucleotide base pairs is still a remote and perhaps unobtainable possibility, the visualization of less fine, but submicroscopic differentiation along human chromosomes--if such exist--is certainly within our reach and is most worthy of exploration.

Of course, the implications of such possible advances for genetic counseling are scientifically evident--and ethically confounding. For what conditions will one counsel genetic restraint, or abortion?

Such a prospect of detailed genetic premonition has many philosophic implications. A partial consequence of the explicit realization of our genetic constraints and inequalities may be an increased impetus toward a more active, a more eugenic attitude toward our collective biological inheritance. Two technical developments which seem likely could significantly increase the feasibility of a potential eugenic program: cloning and extrauter-

ine gestation. Cloning, or vegetative reproduction, in principle
removes the element of chance from the game of heredity. It
replaces the genetic lottery with selection--based, however, it
must be remembered, upon one initial phenotype. The technology of
cloning is derived from the concept that the nuclei of all cells of
an organism contain its entire genome. Different portions of the
genome are in use in the cells of different tissues. This being
so, it should in principle be possible to reproduce the entire
organism manyfold by use of the genetic information replicated
manyfold in its many cellular nuclei.

Such cloning has in fact been accomplished by nuclear transplantation in amphibia (Gurdon, 1968). Nuclei extracted from cells
in young amphibia can be transplanted into previously enucleated
eggs of the same species. Such eggs then develop, with a small but
real percentage of success, into mature amphibia. Obviously the
process can be performed with a considerable number of nuclei and
eggs to produce a clone of genetically identical individuals. And
it can be carried on through successive generations.

Cloning by nuclear transplantation has not yet been accomplished in mammals, but as far as is known only technical problems
intervene. If a nucleus could be successfully transferred into
an activated egg cell, the remaining steps are virtually in hand.
In mice, for instance, in vitro fertilization of egg cells by
sperm, followed by blastocyst development, implantation into
prepared female mice, followed by normal gestation and birth has
already been accomplished with a respectable percentage of success
(Mukherjee, 1970; Hsu, 1971). The possible extension of such
techniques to the human species seems very plausible and indeed
initial experimentation is in progress (Steptoe et al., 1971).

Cloning would permit the preservation and perpetuation of the
finest genotypes that arise in our species--just as the invention
of writing has enabled us to preserve the fruits of their life's
work.

But man is certainly not an amphibian, nor even a mouse. The
relation of phenotype--the basis of selection--to genotype, which
is selected, may be much less direct. I think there are profound
questions to be asked before one can advocate this seemingly
attractive shortcut to human genetic improvement. The first cloned
man, the new Adam (or Eve), will be an orphan in a new and potentially poignant sense. He will be truly a child of the race,
selected and produced by its collective wisdom. But how will he
fit into our ongoing society? How will he be received by his
genetic relations--by his fellow clonees? The special psychological problems of twins have been extensively studied (Koch, 1966).
(It is an interesting fact that in many of the African tribes, it
was the custom to allow one of a pair of twins to perish soon after
birth.)

Assuming the phenotype reproduced as hoped, how would this
Adam be received by his professional colleagues--as a superior but
a fellow--or as an alien to be outcast? And how would he react to

his special status in the world? Would he accept and enjoy it or would he be likely to rebel against his predestination?

I hope these question will be given serious thought before cloning--which may well be soon upon us--is attempted in a casual manner. It may well be that some of these matters can only be resolved by the experiment--but if so, I hope such experimentation can be confined at first to a very small scale. A half-step toward cloning would be in vitro fertilization, using eggs and sperm from donors selected for specific qualities, followed by implantation and normal gestation. While improving the odds, such a process, of course, cannot circumvent the chromosomal lottery.

In one sense the concept of extrauterine gestation--the test tube babies of a Brave New World--has always appeared to me to be a technological gimmick, a complex means to accomplish what nature has equipped our species to do very well--too well if one considers population trends--in a natural way. But if one is seriously committed to human genetic improvement, then the banks of artificial uteri appear in a different light. The practice of routine amniocentesis and frequent abortion as a means toward genetic change would be complex and dangerous and even repugnant. A technology of extrauterine gestation would certainly simplify the problems of analysis and selection--if not necessarily the problem of repugnance, to which I will return.

In contrast to cloning, the technological status of extrauterine gestation is at present essentially undeveloped. Eggs fertilized in vitro can be successfully cultured to the blastocyst stage at which they would normally implant into the uterine wall. No adequate uterine equivalent exists and blastocysts cultured beyond this stage degenerate. That a substitute for the uterine wall and thereby an artical placenta could be developed is by no means inconceivable--but it will require a far deeper understanding of the physiology and biochemistry of placental development and function than we now have.

All these approaches toward even partial control of our collective inheritance--amniocentesis and abortion, cloning, in vitro fertilization and implantation, extrauterine gestation--all impinge to a greater or lesser degree upon the concept of the sanctity of human life. They do so both explicitly and implicitly because some of the experiments, however well planned and intentioned, will fail.

This topic has been discussed earlier in this volume. I will only add here that the sanctity of human life is a concept which however admired in the abstract has never been truly implemented. It has been violated innumerable times for the base purposes of war, by the hangman's rope, by local abundance in a world always pocked by famine, etc. For humanity, I prefer the concept of reverence for life--for this will, to my view, include a global comprehension of the deep impact of external circumstance and social interaction upon the quality of individual life and thus its value. Indeed, philosophically, nature knows no absolutes--and I expect neither can man, except in his impotence. Man is a finite creature, and I would suggest that values, extrapolated to absolute infinity, become inhuman.

I think it is very likely that we will for some generations to come be faced with a situation in which we have increasing knowledge of individual genetic predestination, with limited means and probably limited will to eradicate the less adequate genes from the population--and therefore with a rapidly increasing demand for techniques of somatic genetic therapy.

Varied approaches to this end can be envisioned, dependent upon the particular condition and the stage in life at which therapy can or must be applied. If we consider a single gene defect, the most evident therapy would be to supply a valid copy of the defective gene, incrementally. For a disease such as galactosemia or phenylketonuria, provision of the gene after birth might be adequate. For a disease such as Tay-Sachs, therapy to a much earlier stage--perhaps the blastocyst stage--following in vitro fertilization and prior to implantation might be essential.

Therapy at the blastocyst stage would of course require means of diagnosis at this state. It might be argued that if a defect were thus discovered, it would be the simplest course to discard the small clump of cells. However, I would like to consider the possibilities for genetic intervention at this stage, for they obviously extend beyond limited therapy.

At the stage of the blastocyst, at least three means of genetic intervention might be considered: DNA transformation, the uptake of a specific DNA by the exposed cells (there is increasing evidence that this process, well known in bacteria, can occur in eukaryotic cells); DNA transduction via a temperate virus (Sinsheimer, 1969); and chimera formation (Mintz, 1971). The first two, which involve incremental addition of small amounts of DNA, presumably designed to alleviate the specific condition, have been discussed rather widely and I do not think I need elaborate here. The third, chimera production, is based upon the dramatic experiments performed successfully in mice, initially by Dr. Beatrice Mintz.

An obvious solution to certain genetic diseases would be to transplant appropriately functioning cells to the patient from a donor. As is well known this general approach is presently stymied by the process of immune rejection. Conceivably, solutions may be found for that problem. However, one evident solution would be to provide the functional cells or tissue prior to the appearance of the immune rejection mechanism, which develops shortly before birth in humans.

What Dr. Mintz has accomplished in mice has been to dissociate the cells of blastocysts of two mouse species at the eight cell stage, and then to reassemble an eight cell blastocyst, composed of mixed cells of the two species--and subsequently to allow this to develop, implant it in a prepared female mouse, and achieve at term a live mouse chimera--composed of cells of two distinct genotypes, dispersed clonally throughout the animal. There is, of course, no immune rejection here because all the cellular antigens are recognized as indigenous. Such a mouse is tetraparental--a form previously unknown to life. Could such a human chimera be made? What would be his characteristics, especially psychological and behavioral? No one knows. Even more exotic is the concept of interspecies chimeras.

From the aspect of therapy, if an enzyme or hormone provided systemically is adequate, introduction of one or a few cells carrying a valid gene into a blastocyst might be adequate. If, however, the defective product must function intracellularly, then a mechanism such as transformation or viral transduction, which can alter all of the exposed cells may be necessary. Obviously transformation and transduction are, in principle, applicable also to those diseases which may be treated after birth.

Those diseases that may be the consequence of a defect involving a significant portion of a chromosome, or a whole chromosome, offer a more difficult problem. I fear there may be little we can do for these--that we may learn to cope with disease involving two or three or four genetic defects but that there may well be practical limits.*

Alternative modes of genetic therapy for specific diseases might involve the activation of specific genes, in cells in which they are normally inert, through understanding and control of the developmental programs in these cells--or the transplantation of cells antigenically identical to those of the patient but bearing an appropriate chromosomal (or extrachromosomal) fragment selected after cell hybridization and induced somatic recombination. None of this is more than an extension--admittedly into the unknown--of techniques already partially developed.

Beyond gene therapy, I would like very briefly to discuss the possibility for true genetic change--that is, for the advance of our species beyond anything now known. All that I have discussed so far are means for potentially alleviating the effects of defective genes, for forming new combinations with genes or cells, or for increasing the proportion in the population of favorable combinations of genes and chromosomes.

Now it can be argued--and indeed demonstrated--that given the apparently wide diversity of the human gene pool, we have not begun to exhaust the possible favorable combinations in human inheritance. And it is also undeniably true that we should foster and preserve human diversity. It is the interaction of different human talents and points of view, as in this conference, that most stimulates human progress.

---

*If conceivably we could learn how to inactivate an entire specific chromosome--as in the Lyon effect on the X-chromosomes--such a technique might afford hope for treatment of diseases such as Down's, involving supernumerary chromosome.

But nevertheless, from an evolutionary point of view, it seems certain that there are limits to human capability-- both physical, which most will concede, and intellectual. Indeed, many who are most opposed to human genetic intervention argue that we lack the intellect and wisdom adequate to assume such a responsibility.

They question our intellectual capacity to foresee the probable results--and if we could, they question our moral ability to define and choose the better. As implied by MacFarlane Burnet, this point of view would question whether anything in the evolutionary history of our species had prepared us for this godlike role.

In one sense the only candid answer must be negative. It is, in my view, a miracle that the neuronal circuitry developed to cope with predators and permit adaptation to climatic shifts should also be able to comprehend the universe, to unravel the secrets of life and its own origin.

But, here we are--at this juncture in our evolution. And we have really only two choices--to proceed with all the wisdom we can develop--or to stagnate in fear and in doubt. The choice seems to me to be--Are we as a species to lead a furtive, timorous existence, in terror of our brute past--oppressed and confined by our finite vision and our unfinished state--or using all that evolution has given us, do we seek to find the way to a higher state?

Now by a higher state I mean--I think most mean--a higher form of intellectual and emotional and moral existence. But, specifically, I would argue that we are--in those terms--on a higher plane than the other primates, and so I can believe that higher states than ours may indeed be possible.

We are of course grossly ignorant of the genetic factors that underlie intelligence or emotion or conscience. We will need intense study of the physiology and biochemistry of the mind, its ontogeny, and its development before we are equipped to attempt to enlarge its capacity. In this regard the application of some of the genetic techniques to other primates to attempt to achieve some understanding of the evident changes that have led to us--to man-- might be of considerable value.

As to the means to introduce such change we really cannot yet say. In part this is because we know so little of what is required genetically to influence such a quality as intelligence. And as yet we know so little of the detailed processes underlying the evolution of the eukaryotic genome, which will surely provide clues toward a technology of genomic alteration. We do not understand the mechanism of gene duplication, of chromosomal recombination, of chromosomal inactivation as in the Lyon effect, of chromosomal elimination as in hybridized cells, of the selective control of transcription achieved by differentiation. But I have confidence we do have the intellectual capacity to elucidate these processes, and then the means will become apparent.

I have been talking rather coldly, reasonably factually, I hope, but I am aware of the dangers in these concepts--practical as well as ethical. For what purposes should we alter our genes? To whom should we give this power? To those who have already perverted physics into atomic weapons, chemistry into poison gas, or electronics into guided missiles? If we make men gods, are they to be gods of war?

One of the greatest threats to the rational development of genetic modification will appear if it should become captive to irrational, nationalist purposes. For this reason I think it is imperative that we begin now to establish international cooperation in, and regulation of, this entire enterprise. I suggest that we should resurrect the plan for an international atomic energy authority that this country proposed in 1946 (Baruch, 1946; Lillienthal, 1947 Bull. Atomic Scientists 3, 1947); that we begin now to apply those principles to the development of an international authority for human genetic research; and that we hope the world may have profited enough from the grim experience of the past 25 years that it may this time be more willing to act with reason.

I know that some here regard all of this as a malignant human vanity. I would challenge this view. Vanity is one of the seven deadly sins, but I wish to suggest that vanity properly directed is not altogether evil. Vanity in an individual, be it in his possessions, his accomplishments, or his genes, is odious. But vanity, or sober pride, in a self-aware species may indeed be a virtue. It is of course vain to think that we, man, should play a pivotal role in evolution. What gives us this role? Circumstance perhaps. But in truth, here we are.

And, I believe, we need a further goal for man as a species. For I expect there is another latent cause for our current despair. Science has done much to make man proud, but curiously and profoundly it is not enough. It is not enough to tame the rivers and water the deserts, to control the climate or extinguish plague; it is not enough to diminish distance and condense time, to project sound and image across a continent, to journey to the moon, to explore the atom and the cell and the galaxy. These are glorious achievements, but they are not enough. In a deep sense they torment man for they make his own mortality, the brevity of his span and all its kinship, all the more senseless, frustrating and unbearable. Man needs a sense of the enduring, and I wish to suggest that he can find this in a proud role for his species. For although each of us is and must be only a brief flare of consciousness, our species is potentially immortal and, as we now see, potentially crucial in evolution.

An ancient and valuable question has been—What does it mean to be human? I believe the answer to that has changed as we have added our growing cultural inheritance to our biological inheritance. If these now interact, the answer will change still more. And that is in itself an important part of the answer which can only be—in a Delphic fashion—that to be human is simply to partake in an endless experiment to resolve that very question.

What, in an evolutionary sense, are the distinctive characteristics of humanity which--as we seize our destiny--we may wish to enhance? I might suggest a few, with no conceit that this is a complete list but rather with the intent to commence an inquiry:

(1) Our self-awareness
(2) Our perception of past, present, and future
(3) Our capacities for hope, faith, charity and love
(4) Our enlarged ability to communicate and thereby to create a collective consciousness
(5) Our ability to achieve a rational understanding of Nature
(6) Our drive to reduce the role of Fate in human affairs
(7) Our vision of man as unfinished.

This is clearly a complex of characteristics; it is incomplete--and worse for as of now we simply do not know to what extent these features of man are inherently coupled, one to another--or may be intrinsically hierarchical. I would hope that we might begin to explore these questions.

Who can know what man may become as we choose our way across the endless future? In homo sapiens--self-aware, endlessly curious, endowed with a capacity for logic, gifted with the opportunity for choice and thus the burden of decision--something new appeared on this small globe. The next step for evolution is ours.

We must devise that once again on this sweet planet a fairer species will arise--a being new and finer to expand the meaning of life.

REFERENCES

Burnet, MacFarlane (1969). *Changing Patterns*, New York, American Elsevier Publishing Company.
Baruch, Bernard M. (1946). *The American Proposal for International Control*, *Atomic Scientists*, 2, pp. 3-5, 10 (July 1).
Bulletin Atomic Scientists, 3, 253-265 (1947). *Operation and Developmental Functions of the International Agency*.
Caspersson, T., L. Zech, E. J. Modest, G. E. Foley, O. Wagh, and E. Simonsson (1969). *DNA-Binding Fluorochromes for the Study of the Organization of the Metaphase Nucleus*, *Exptl*. *Cell Res.*, 58, 141.
Gurdon, J. B. (1968). *Transplanted Nuclei and Cell Differentiation*, *Scientific American*, 219, 24-35.
Hsu, Y. (1971). *Post Blastocyst Differentiation in vitro*, *Nature*, 231, 100-102.
Knudson, Alfred G., Jr. (1971). *Mutation and Cancer*, *Proc*. *Natl*. *Acad*. *Sci*. 68, 820-823.
Koch, Helen (1966). *Twins and Twin Relations*, Chicago, University of Chicago Press.
Laberge, C. and R. Gagne (1971). *Quinacrine Mustard Staining Solves the Length Variations of the Human Y Chromosome*, *Johns Hopkins Medical Journal*, 128, 79-83.

Lillienthal, David E. (1947). Organization and Administration of the International Agency, *Bull. Atomic Scientists, 2*, 203-206; 231-231.

McKusick, V. A. (1966). *Mendelian Inheritance in Man*. Baltimore, Johns Hopkins Press.

Milunsky, A., J. W. Littlefield, J. N. Kanfer, E. H. Kolodny, V. E. Shih, and L. Atkins (1970). Prenatal Genetic Diagnosis, *New England Journal of Medicine, 283*, 1370-1381, 1441-1447, 1498-1504.

Mintz, B. (1971). Genetic Mosaicism in vivo: Development and Disease in Allophenic Mice, *Fed. Proc., 30*, 935-943.

Mukherjee, A. B. and M. M. Cohen (1970). Development of Normal Mice by in vitro Fertilization, *Nature, 228*, 472-473.

Nadler, H. (1972). Risks in Amniocentesis. In *Early Diagnosis of Human Genetic Defects: Scientific and Ethical Considerations*, M. Harris, editor. Washington, U. S. Government Printing Office.

Neel, J. V. (1970). The Genetics of Diabetes Mellitus. In *Advances in Metabolic Disorders*, Suppl. 1, R. A. Camerini-Davalos and H. S. Cole, editors. New York, Academic Press.

Patil, S. R., S. Merrick, and H. A. Lubs (1971). Identification of Each Human Chromosome with a Modified Giemsa Stain, *Science, 173*, 821-822.

Rosenthal, David (1971). A Program of Research on Heredity in Schizophrenia, *Behavioral Science, 16*, 191-201.

Sinsheimer, R. L. (1969). The Prospect of Designed Genetic Change, *American Scientist, 57*, 134-142.

Steiner, George (1971). *New Yorker* (March 6).

Steptoe, P. C., R. G. Edwards, J. M. Pardy (1971). Fertilization and Cleavage in vitro of Preovulation Human Oocytes, *Nature, 229*, 132.

Sumner, A. T., J. A. Robinson, and H. J. Evans (1971). Distinguishing Between X, Y, and YY-bearing Human Spermatozoa by Fluorescence and DNA Content, *Nature, 229*, 231.

SOCIAL AND SCIENTIFIC PRIORITIES IN
THE USE OF GENETIC KNOWLEDGE

James V. Neel

The title assigned this presentation, "Social and Scientific Priorities in the Use of Genetic Knowledge," at first glance reads innocuously enough. How do we proceed to set up priorities in the applications of genetic knowledge. In fact, of course, what we are really discussing is the new eugenics, where I define eugenics simply as a collection of policies designed to improve the genetic well-being of our species. And I am sure the new eugenics will prove no less controversial than the old eugenics of the 1920's and 1930's. All of the value judgments and ethical issues that previously made eugenics so thorny an issue are still there, albeit with some added precision, while such recent developments as our ability to detect a variety of genetic carrier states and to engage in prenatal diagnosis have raised a number of important new social questions. In the following presentation, I shall for the most part skirt the ethical issues involved, and confine myself insofar as possible to the genetic problems.

CAN AND SHOULD WE ATTEMPT TO ESTABLISH PRIORITIES IN THIS FIELD?

Before we begin to consider how we might attempt to develop a rational system of priorities, we might do well to consider two antecedent questions. The first is: Should society at this time try to develop priorities in this area? The second, assuming an affirmative answer to the first, is: Can society develop priorities? With respect to the first, I note only that many of the developments are so new that it is not clear that we are yet ready to set priorities. To some, this will sound like the standard caveat of the paralyzed intellectual. The fact remains that we are discussing very recent developments, whose implications have yet to sink in on most of us.

With respect to the second, at this very moment the willingness of our society to assign priorities is being severely tested. While I take it that the priorities to which we are asked to direct our attention are primarily within the field of genetics, we cannot escape some concern with priorities between fields. I am sure we would agree that for the next ten to twenty years, the impact of failure to apply the new genetic knowledge to human problems is far less than failure to solve such major issues as control of pollution, decay of the cities, or a sane energy policy. On the other hand, as I believe has been apparent from previous presentations, the potential of genetic knowledge for the good (or bad) of man is really very great. Furthermore, there is a symbolism about the use of genetic knowledge to influence the genetic composition of the next generation, which readily captures the public imagination. Herein lies one of our problems in setting priorities. Right now we are something of a glamour field, as witness the pages of Life, Time, and Newsweek. We do have important contributions to make to human well-being. However, we have caught the public imagination, and it's going to take a great deal of intellectual honesty and sobriety not to take advantage of this fact.

So--let the record show that before we began our discussion of the difficult issue of setting priorities in this field, we recognized that this discussion might be considered premature, presumptuous, and naive by some. Our discussion should deserve none of these adjectives as long as we recognize this as an exercise in social and scientific judgment, approached with the necessary humility and objectivity. We will return to the "should" and the "can" of priorities after we have considered the issues involved.

WHAT ARE THE ACTIVITIES TO BE ASSIGNED PRIORITIES?

It might be well at this juncture to enumerate the sometimes interrelated developments in genetics to whose implementation we are attempting to assign priorities. We have in this conference devoted almost all our attention to just three, namely:

1. Genetic Counseling and Its Now Logical
   Extension, Prenatal Diagnosis

To what has already been said, I would add only that our experience with counseling--which goes back to the establishment of an Heredity Clinic by the University of Michigan in 1941--is not quite so dramatic as the experiences presented here. For instance, among the last 100 cases to pass through the Heredity Clinic of the University of Michigan Hospital, 32 consulted us with the question of the likelihood of recurrence of a congenital malformation which had occurred in the kindred. This would include such entities as mental retardation, Down's syndrome, severe central nervous system malformation, and other entities not regularly fitting into a simple genetic pattern. The average risk of recurrence is around five percent, and these people will for the most part proceed to parent-hood after hearing the fact. Another 43 cases involved familial occurrence of known genetic disease, both dominant and recessive. The questions raised cover a wide variety of risk situations--I imagine the mean risk of occurrence of disease in the individual of concern was 10 to 20 percent. For only two of the 43 situations which happen to be included in this particular sample (I-cell disease, galactosemia) can genetics now offer intrauterine diag-nosis in case of a pregnancy. There were 9 patients for simple karyotyping, largely either possible translocation-Down's syndromes or questionable cases of Turner's syndrome, referred because of Dr. Bloom's special interest in this field (we do not routinely advise obtaining a karyotype on all patients with Down's syndrome). There were six cases involving hereditary anemia, which I put in a special category because Dr. Rucknagel's longstanding interest in this problem undoubtedly brings us a disproportionate number of referrals of this type. We had one problem of advisability of consanguineous marriage, one of racial ancestry, and seven rather miscellaneous problems. We had one patient for amniocentesis, but this is not representative of the Hospitals' involvement in this area. The most common genetic indications for amniocentesis, sus-pected Rh disease and pregnancy in women over 40, are not regularly referred to the Heredity Clinic; the patient contacts are handled by the Department of Obstetrics and Gynecology. However, our Department cultures the amniotic fluid obtained at amniocentesis from pregnant women over 40 and has done so ten times in the past six months.

Much of our counseling, then, while certainly contributing to the understanding, acceptance, and control of genetic disease, will not produce spectacular results. You may argue that we are not putting our effort where it counts. However, in the practice of medicine one responds to the patients' perceived needs, and doctors and patients are requesting assistance with the kinds of problems just enumerated. Furthermore, it appears to me that even under the relatively favorable circumstances of highly accurate prenatal diagnosis, the impact of counseling on disease may also be modest. Consider a very simple hypothetical situation of a replacement-type population in which everyone born survives, and marries, and each couple has two children. Consider a recessive trait which lends itself to prenatal diagnosis. In the absence of the systematic and reliable detection of carriers, a "high-risk" sibship will be iden-tified by the birth of an affected child. In our hypothetical population, half of all the affected children to be born will be first-born. If we monitor second pregnancies to mothers of first-born abnormal children, one-quarter will be affected, but for every one we might detect, there will be three born to mothers whose first-born child was normal. Thus, we could expect to detect pre-natally (and possibly abort) one in eight of such children (Neel and Schull, 1972). More realistic schemes do not alter the propor-

356

James V. Neel

tions greatly (Motulsky, Fraser, and Felsenstein, 1971). For
prenatal diagnosis to be truly effective, we must be able to
identify carriers and/or high risk marriages prior to reproduction.
I believe it to be important that we ourselves make careful calculations of what prenatal diagnosis can accomplish before it is made
for us by some pragmatic public health economist. On the other
hand, I am sure that economist would be well aware that the cost of
maintaining an institutionalized child is approximately $5,000 per
annum, so that, were our hypothetical condition one requiring
institutionalization, then quite aside from humanitarian considerations, amniocentesis for the pregnancy leading to that hypothetical second sibling of an affected child would even now be a sound
procedure economically.

2. Genetic Screening

Insufficient attention has been directed to distinction
between "genetic screening" for the detection of treatable hereditary disease, which is simply an exercise in responsible public
health measures, and "genetic screening" to detect the carriers of
deleterious genes presumably for counseling purposes. With respect
to the former, on the basis of experience with such diseases as
phenylketonuria and, more recently, galactosemia (Shih et al.,
1971; Switkes, 1971; Gordon, 1971), there is already brisk debate
concerning "false positives," problems in initiating treatment,
cost, etc., and it is clear we are at the beginning of an involved
subject. With respect to the latter, in assigning priorities to
genetic programs, we must keep in mind that a screening program for
carriers that does not alter the reproductive pattern of the population concerned has failed its ostensible purpose, no matter how
interesting the data collected. And at this point it is not at all
clear just how anxious the people, screened and found to be genetic
carriers, will be to alter their reproductive behavior on the basis
of a finding which they presumably did not request. We badly need
research on how the results of genetic screening programs can be
used, but perhaps even before that, we need a good airing of the
question of what constitutes an effective program whose benefits
outweigh the costs. Furthermore, I continue to be concerned about
the wisdom of programs that locate and possibly stigmatize the
carriers of a few special genes, when in fact each of us is a
carrier for several genes which undoubtedly do us no good and were
best not transmitted to our children.

3. Genetic Repair, Either Somatic or Germinal

The repair of genetic damage is distinguished from simple
substitution or replacement therapy by the concept of altering the
genetic material of the individual concerned--in somatic or germi-

nal cells. Of all the potential developments in human genetics, this is of course the one that is most provocative. Experiments on the transfer of genetic information between somatic cells are underway in a dozen cell culture laboratories. To my knowledge, no one has yet attempted to effect a genetic change in explanted somatic tissue, followed by reintroduction of that tissue to the original donor, but this is surely to be expected within the next several decades. Conceptually, this is not too different from a renal transplant from a closely related donor to an individual with hereditary nephritis, or a marrow transplant from a sibling to a patient with lymphopenic hypogammaglobulinemia (Gatti et al., 1968). Purposive changes in human germinal tissue present very different issues, which fortunately are much less immediate than the other issues we are discussing. So also are the issues presented by cloning, or the creation of chimeras composed of a carefully selected blend of genetically superior tissues. While if the recent scientific past is any guide, these issues will be on us sooner than we anticipate, there are in my opinion more pressing matters. I should like, in the present context, to point out that whatever the ethical implications, from the standpoint of setting priorities, we should recognize that genetic manipulation of germinal tissue, if handled legitimately, will probably have substantially less impact on the human gene pool than the other developments we have just mentioned and those to which we now turn.

There are, however, four other "uses of genetic knowledge" which must be considered in any attempt to assign priorities. They have been only very briefly touched upon in our discussions thus far, so briefly I should devote a little time to each. They are--continuing our numerical sequence--4) prevention of mutation, 5) amelioration of genotype expression (euphenics), 6) "germinal choice," and 7) stabilization of the growth of the world's population, to each of which we now turn.

4. Prevention of Mutation

With respect to the prevention of mutation, we have only the roughest of estimates of the contribution of the mutational process in each generation to human disease and disability. There is a cluster of dominantly inherited abnormalities commonly used in estimates of human mutation rates (e.g., epiloia, achondroplasia, aniridia, retinoblastoma, multiple neurofibromatosis, Waardenburg's syndrome, multiple polyposis of the colon, Marfan's syndrome); their combined appearance each generation in consequence of muta-tion is in the neighborhood of 50 cases in each 100,000 births. These constitute the clearest case for the impact of mutation on human morbidity. In its 1956 Report, the Subcommittee on Genetics of the National Academy of Sciences' Committee on the Biological Effects of Atomic Radiation estimated that approximately two percent of all children born in the U. S. would, prior to sexual maturity, exhibit serious disease ultimately as the result of mutation pressure. This estimate includes a number of diseases not so well understood as the above mentioned. In its 1962 Report, the United Nations Scientific Committee on the Effects of Atomic Radiation used a figure of one percent for the same phenomenon. The various entities comprising this one to two percent will not all increase in frequency, following an increase in mutation rate, as rapidly as will the subset of dominantly inherited diseases just enumerated against which there is high negative selection pressure, but they will respond in time.

The 1966 Report of the same U.N. Committee estimated that one child out of every 200 liveborn had a chromosomal abnormality responsible for gross physical or mental defect. For the most part, these abnormalities arise anew each generation, in consequence of "chromosomal mutation," in contrast to the "point mutation" thought to give rise to the types of conditions mentioned earlier.

There has been a great deal of discussion as to whether man-made sources of radiation have increased these mutation rates; more recently, attention has shifted to chemical mutagenesis. Without attempting to delve deeply at this time into what has become a very complicated problem in evaluation, let me say that in the context of priority-setting, it would be passing strange if, while our left hand is working furiously to detect and abort genetically defective children, our right hand is condoning exposures resulting in an increase in the numbers of such children. The only excuse for such exposures is on the basis of the benefits gained; should there in fact be an increased mutation rate, very careful balancing of the over-all benefits to society from these exposures against the cost in human morbidity is called for. The monitoring of human populations for increase in mutation rates has in the past been quite unsatisfactory, but now large-scale screening for mutants at the biochemical level is possible (cf. Neel, 1971). While the mutants detected by these procedures would not be those responsible for human disease, it would appear reasonable to assume a correlation between these mutation rates and those responsible for human disease. However, again, as in previous presentations, I feel compelled to emphasize how difficult it will be to determine what particular agent in our environment might be responsible for an increase in mutation rates.

If society embarks upon a course which will result in an increase in the mutation rate, is there a coupled responsibility to the species to decrease the transmission and manifestations of known inherited diseases by whatever means we find ethically acceptable? This question raises the intriguing issue of the extent to which our collective gene pool is public property, which we hold in trust for the future, and the extent to which the very personalized packages into which it is subdivided precludes treating it as a public resource.

5. Amelioration of Genotype Expression

I have previously referred to this as "cultural engineering," as opposed to "genetic engineering" (Neel, 1961). Lederberg (1963; see esp. 1970) has referred to it as "euphenics." This involves far more than the treatment of individuals with obvious hereditary disease. Very simply, we must recognize that we are blessed with a gene pool that evolved under very different circumstances than the present, and begin to devote much more thought than heretofore to the question of the circumstances facilitating the best expression of that gene pool. We already do this on a small scale in the therapy of genetic disease, but the challenge is much greater. Individuals with α anti-trypsin deficiency, determined by homozygosity for a "recessive" gene, appear to be unusually prone to death from chronic obstructive lung disease, an entity increasing at a striking rate. There is some evidence that the predisposition is potentiated by air pollution and/or smoking. A very simple example of tailoring the environment to the person would be a survey which identified the susceptibles and, assuming the association is incontrovertible, made clear to these persons the consequences of smoking. Or, consider diabetes mellitus and hypertension. Familial and probably genetic factors are well implicated in the etiology of both. In some individuals predisposed to diabetes, obesity and lack of exercise undoubtedly contribute to realization of the genotype, while in persons predisposed to hypertension, the "trigger" may be excessive salt intake (Dahl and Love, 1954, 1957; Knudsen and Dahl, 1966). Ideally, the therapy of these individuals starts shortly after birth, with a program of physical activity or dietary restriction. And, since we cannot identify all the predisposed with accuracy, perhaps we should encourage the total population to embark upon a regime which can only result in better health for the average person.

This is a kind of genetic counseling for populations rather than individuals. And the role of the geneticist in this area is as a member of an epidemiological team, trying to understand complex genotype-environment interactions. The examples I have cited apply only to physical disease. The opportunities with respect to the functioning of the mind are even more provocative. Galton (1892) in Hereditary Genius was one of the many who have drawn attention to the population base underlying the flowering of Greece. Between 530 and 430 B.C. the district of Attica produced 14 persons whom he would classify as illustrious, namely:

Statesmen and Commanders--Themistocles (mother an alien), Miltiades, Aristeides, Cimon (son of Miltiades), Pericles (son of Xanthippus, the victor at Mycale).

Literary and Scientific Men--Thucydides, Socrates, Xenophon, Plato.

Poets--Aeschylus, Sophocles, Euripides, Aristophanes.

Sculptor--Phidias.

During that period Attica's population amounted to about 90,000 native free-born persons, 40,000 resident aliens, and a laboring and artisan population of 40,000 slaves. The above mentioned 14 persons were all drawn from the native free-born, who over a period of a century should amount to about 270,000 persons, or about 135,000 males, of whom only one-half would survive to the age of 26, and one-third to the age of 50. No matter how we criticize the sampling or the scoring process involved, or whether the estimate of population base is too low by a factor of two, clearly here was an extraordinary flowering of genius. To Galton this was a genetic phenomenon, which somehow quickly ran its course. Aware as we now are of gene frequencies and slow rates of genetic change, surely we must see this extraordinary manifestation of human capabilities as in whole or part the result of the creation of an unusual intellectual environment for unusually fine minds. It is sobering how little we really know about the heredity-environment interaction in the realm of the mind. Surely as knowledge becomes available in this field, its application will have high priority.

Incidentally, I take it to be self-evident that the principal beneficiaries of a program in euphenics would be certain minority groups; at the limit, a program in culture engineering is a program in social justice.

6. "Germinal Choice"

This development was extensively discussed by the late H. J. Muller (1967). In its simplest form, it involves nothing more than an effort, for women for whom artificial insemination constitutes the necessary and desired avenue to parenthood, to ensure that the sperm employed be from genetically superior individuals. In its logical extension, it involves a much larger fraction of the reproducing females. There would be considerable debate on the selection of genetically superior donors but otherwise, unlike some of the other developments we have been discussing, the technology is at hand. As Muller recognized, this would involve a major change in societal attitudes towards parenthood but, given the wide range of human behavior recorded by the anthropologist, such a major change is probably not impossible. Ramsey (1970) has presented cogent arguments to the effect that this development, as well as cloning, would place its practitioners outside the boundaries of the Judeo-Christian ethic, a viewpoint which a non-theologian like myself finds well buttressed. However, as a non-theologian I find I prefer the somewhat broader statement of Lord Kilbrandon (this volume) about the issues involved in cloning, genetic surgery, etc.: "It is possible that the right of free men to acquire and transmit knowledge must at some stage give place to the concept of the dignity and integrity of the human being, looked at as a fundamental requirement taking precedence of all law, learning, and ethical analyses." With the proper selection of donors, the result of artificial insemination will be better than the population average on whatever scale will be the basis for selection. However, because of genetic segregation, and because of difficulties in reproducing the environment which led to the earlier favorable expression of the parental genotype, there will be many disappointments for parents who go this route. Here, as with other possible genetic developments, it will be important not to raise false expectations.

7. Stabilization of the Gene Pool

The last development to be discussed is more commonly known in other circles as population control. I take it we are in agreement that it is unwise to assume that the world's population can continue to increase at the rate prevailing during the past century, without a wide variety of problems. I take it that the geneticists here also agree that, great though our concern for the individual unfortunate child tossed up by the vagaries of genetic segregation, we have an even greater concern for the corporate gene pool of our species. We simply cannot ignore the fact that any population policy--or for that matter, no population policy--may have implications more far-reaching for the gene pool than all the genetic counseling of the next 100 years. Graham (1971) has recently been an especially persuasive spokesman for that viewpoint.

With no population policy, large-scale famine in certain especially susceptible areas could lead to quite specific die-offs, especially if the areas which normally respond to famine relief, struggling to feed their own swollen populations, find their corn attacked by blight and their wheat attacked by rust. Some, of course, feel that with the present age structure of the world's population, even with rather optimistic predictions about population control, it is already too late to avert localized famine. This might be, but surely we must make every effort to avoid or reduce such tragedy.

And if there is a population policy, what should it be? Elsewhere I have argued that anything other than a simple quantitative policy, of the same number of children for every couple, is unworkable (Neel, 1969, 1970). Broad-scale qualitative judgments are emotionally unacceptable to society; even if acceptable, we do not possess the wisdom or knowledge to make them. This argues for a policy that will have minimal qualitative or quantitative impact on the present gene pool--without arguing against some of the possible developments discussed earlier. However, this does not mean that every couple will in fact have the same number of children. Elsewhere we have pointed out that even if society set an upper limit of three children per couple, so many couples would probably have none, one, or two children that the realized mean would be close to two (Neel and Schull, 1972).

Even such an apparently even-handed policy as this will not go unchallenged. Representatives of some of our ethnic minorities often refer to population restriction of this or any other type as "genocide." What I take to be the historical basis for this concern is shown in Table I, taken from a United Nations publication of 1953. It is an effort to reconstruct the growth of the world's population since 1650. In 300 years the total population has increased by a factor of five. However, let us consider the contributions of the major ethnic groups. To do so, I will commit some oversimplifications. I hope those who attack them will suggest improvements. We will equate Northern and Latin America and Oceania in 1650 with American Indians, Polynesians, and Australian aborigines. Even with a generous allowance for hybridization, this sub-gene pool by 1950 had increased by a factor of perhaps two. We will equate Africa with Negro; if one-sixth of the gene pool of the Americas were Negro in origin—a generous estimate—then the Negro gene pool has increased by the factor of two and one-half. Equating Asia with Mongoloids and East Indians, this gene pool has increased by about a factor of five. Finally, by this same reckoning, the Caucasoid pool has increased (last column) from an estimated 113 million persons to an estimated 935 million persons, a factor of eight. The role of us Caucasoids in the slow rate of increase of the American Indian, Polynesian, and Australian aborigine is a sordid and sickening record most of us prefer to forget. With respect to the historical role of Caucasoids in inhibiting the rate of growth of the Negro gene pool, there is no scarcity today of eloquent spokesmen, to whom I will leave the question.

Representatives of minority groups the world over will also point out that, to the extent they suffer higher infant and childhood mortality rates, this uniform policy would be to their disadvantage. Clearly this legitimate objection must be met before we can expect to move towards any general population policy. Unfortunately, in some parts of the world the situation has already deteriorated to the extent that it will be very difficult to meet this demand while populations continue to grow at the present rate.

It is clear that the percentage composition in terms of ethnic groups of the world's gene pool today is very different from that of 300 years ago, and any stabilization of population numbers will tend to perpetuate that shift. However, with all due respect for the history involved, I see no way to turn the clock back. Moreover, simply because of the distribution of resources, any failure to limit population growth now is apt to have the most dire consequences for those whose numbers have increased most slowly. I can see no alternative but to live with history and attempt to forestall the even greater inequities which might result from failing resources unable to meet the needs of the people dependent on them.

Table I. Estimates of World Population by Regions, 1650-1950 (United Nations, 1953)

Estimated Population in Millions

Series of Estimates and Date	World Total	Africa	Northern America(4)	Latin America(5)	Asia (exc. U.S.S.R.)(6)	Europe and Asiatic U.S.S.R.(6)	Oceania	Area of European settlement(7)
Willcox's estimates(1):								
1650	470	100	1	7	257	103	2	113
1750	694	100	1	10	437	144	2	157
1800	919	100	6	23	595	193	2	224
1850	1,091	100	26	33	656	274	2	335
1900	1,571	141	81	63	857	423	6	573
Carr-Saunders' estimates(2):								
1650	545	100	1	12	327	103	2	118
1750	728	95	1	11	475	144	2	158
1800	906	90	6	19	597	192	2	219
1850	1,171	95	26	33	741	274	2	335
1900	1,608	120	81	63	915	423	6	573
United Nations estimates(3):								
1920	1,834	136	115	92	997	485	9	701
1930	2,008	155	134	110	1,069	530	10	784
1940	2,216	177	144	132	1,173	579	11	866
1950	2,406	199	166	162	1,272	594	13	935

(1) Willcox, Studies in...(1940), p. 45. Estimates for America have been divided between northern America and Latin America by means of detailed figures presented ibid., pp. 37-44.

(2) Carr-Saunders, World Population (1936), p. 42.

(3) United Nations, Demographic Yearbook 1949-50 (1950), p.10; and United Nations, "The past and future growth of world population..." (1951), Table II; the 1940 figures are unpublished estimates of the United Nations.

(4) United Sates, Canada, Alaska, St. Pierre and Miquelon.

(5) Central and South America and Caribbean Islands.

(6) Estimates for Asia and Europe in Willcox's and Carr-Saunders' series have been adjusted so as to include the population of the Asiatic U.S.S.R. with that of Europe, rather than Asia. For this purpose, the following approximate estimates of the population of the Asiatic U.S.S.R. were used: 1650, 3 million; 1750, 4 million; 1800, 5 million; 1850, 8 million; 1900, 22 million.

(7) Includes northern America, Latin America, Europe and the Asiatic U.S.S.R., and Oceania.

WHAT ARE THE CRITERIA FOR PRIORITIES

These, then, are the seven principal present and potential genetic developments to which we might attempt to assign social and scientific priorities. What are the criteria by which we proceed? Where do we put the emphasis? Four kinds of scientific criteria present themselves, all of which of course have to be fitted into some kind of ethical framework, a framework whose definition--after the past several days--appears to be more difficult than the establishing of scientific criteria. We could judge the value of a development by the extent to which it accomplishes one or more of the following objectives:

1. The reduction of the proportion of persons with genetic disease, an objective with which we most readily associate genetic counseling, prenatal diagnosis and, perhaps, genetic surgery.

2. The improvement of the expression of existing genotypes, by wide-ranging medical, social and nutritional measures.

3. The creation of genetically superior individuals by artificial insemination (the germinal choice of Muller) or eventually, perhaps, cloning.

4. The protection of the present gene pool by a world population policy which will at least ensure that as little as possible of what now exists is lost and damage through exposure to mutagens is minimized.

These are all positive criteria. There is a fifth. It is becoming very clear that the human gene pool is much more complex and organized than seemed to be the case 20 years ago. Man has by now adequately demonstrated his capacity to mess up complex biological systems. Our fifth criteria, then, is a negative one: a minimum of incalculable genetic and somatic risks. On this basis, for instance, I would rule out for the foreseeable future attempts at virus transduction in man--not because they are likely to have much effect on the gene pool but simply on the philosophical grounds of so many unknown possible concomitants.

HOW WILL WE MAKE OUR PRIORITIES?

Thus far we have considered the real or pending developments in genetic knowledge which have practical implications for our species, and listed the kinds of criteria by which we might attempt to assign priorities to their implementation. Applying the criteria to the developments, what priorities emerge? There would undoubtedly be a very healthy diversity of opinion among us. In theory, we can consider each of the seven developments enumerated in the light of the four criteria for the evaluation of a development which I have suggested, and arrive at a judgment concerning the impact of that development on the quality of life. In fact, I doubt if we are ready for such an exercise. At the risk of sounding like a politician, I find all seven of the areas of possible applications of genetic knowledge that we have enumerated to be high priority areas for investigation and (excluding only genetic engineering) application, but immediately I feel obliged to enter certain caveats. Genetic screening and genetic counseling combined with prenatal diagnosis should be available in every major medical center. The increasing interest in this area by individuals with good biochemical as well as genetic training ensures a healthy growth of the field--given reasonable financial encouragement. However, we must not oversell its actual impact on disease. First, as I pointed out earlier, much of the activity of a Counseling Service, even when it has a tangible impact on reproduction, is not directed towards high risk situations. Second, even when the situation permits of decisive intervention, the numerical impact on disease will be rather modest, short of large-scale detection of carriers and programs of moral suasion of carriers more extreme than the world seems ready for. Not only are there relatively few diseases with good biochemical or chromosomal handles, but even these present problems in ascertainment.

However, while genetic counseling, with all its ramifications, has made tremendous progress in this country and is now attracting an adequate number of properly trained persons, I do not feel that some of the other areas which I enumerated are so well cared for. Let me be more specific. First, the developments concerning the mutagenic effects of radiation and chemicals of the past 40 years make it clear there may have been an increase in human mutation rates. While I personally doubt that mutation rates have greatly increased, the subject has attracted widespread comment. Some type of monitoring is indicated. Utilization of the knowledge gained from an appropriate monitoring program will be admittedly difficult --given an increase, how do we identify and remove the offending agent--but this seems no reason to shrink from the necessary studies.

Second, population control represents an important area of application of genetic knowledge. Matsunaga's (1966) systematic enumeration of the probable genetic consequences of population control include a lower frequency of Down's syndrome; a lower frequency of those congenital defects (exclusive of those due to chromosomal abnormalities) which contribute to the J-shaped curve relating maternal age to congenital defect; less disease due to maternal-fetal incompatibility, such as erythroblastosis fetalis; and a relative decline in consanguineous marriage. Beyond this, it appears that some kinds of dominant, presumably point mutations (achondroplasia, Marfan's syndrome) may be more common in the children of older parents (refs. in Neel, 1969; Murdoch, Walker and McKusick, 1972). However, if with population control the average

age at reproduction decreases, so will the interval between generations, and some of the potential impact of population control will be lost. There must be some age at reproduction which is optimal both in terms of normality of child and low rate of population growth--say 25 to 30--and if society is ready to accept some of the developments we have been considering, it should be ready to plan not only the number of children but parental age at time of childbirth. This problem needs more attention.

Finally, I return to a favorite theme of mine. Although with the diversity of human genotypes it is unlikely that any one environment could be best for the expression of all, there must be some environment which represents the best compromise for the most people, and in which the average person would do stunningly better than he does now. I use the term environment very broadly to include diet, place of living, circumstances of school, conditions of working, and absence of minority groups because of full citizenship for all. The geneticist, above all others, is trained to analyze the heredity-environment interaction. Our new knowledge is sufficient to reveal the potentiality for reducing the unfavorable expression of genetic predispositions by this approach, but only a start has been made on accumulating the necessary detailed data. I would urge that one application of our new genetic knowledge, with high priority, should be in this area. And at this point, I take a stand in strong opposition to that developed by Robert Sinsheimer (this volume), concerning the imminence and inevitability of attempts at genetic engineering. I find it incredibly presumptuous to talk of improving genetic man when our knowledge of the potentialities of our present genotype is so limited. We do not begin to know what we are now capable of. Any program of genetic engineering will be carried on in a constantly changing environment which makes evaluation of the results of any genetic manipulation, other than the creation of monsters, impossible. If there is any absolute morality in science, it is that you do not undertake an important experiment whose results you cannot evaluate. In this case, the object of the experiment is the single most precious possession man has--the double-stranded helix which, against all odds, makes us human. Paul Ramsey (1970) has coined a most appropriate sentence in this context: "Men ought not to play God before they have learned to be men, and after they have learned to be men, they will not play God." We're not losing our nerve, we're just realizing how complex the situation really is.

CONCLUDING REMARKS

These remarks have undoubtedly ranged further than the planners of this symposium anticipated. In my opinion, a narrower treatment (which followed the obvious course of urging, for example, that high priority be given to establishing a counseling center for each 200,000 persons, with provision for prenatal diagnosis) would have been a mistake. This is a worthy and defensible objective, and it would provide a clean and simple goal on which a campaign or plea for funds could be based, but as I see it--given not only the avalanche of new genetic knowledge but the critical times in which our species finds itself--we geneticists have broader responsibilities to society. Before we can assign priorities, we must have a clear view of where our special brand of knowledge can be effective. This brings us back to a thought raised at the opening of this presentation: Are we ready to make priorities? I doubt that we are. What we have been considering is all so new and of such potential significance that we should proceed on all those fronts where compelling scientific and humanitarian arguments can be brought to bear. The actual costs involved, compared with expenditures in other areas, are a pittance in relation to the ultimate possibilities.

REFERENCES

Committee on Genetic Effects of Atomic Radiation (1956). Report in *The Biological Effects of Atomic Radiation*, pp. 3-30. Washington, National Academy of Sciences, National Research Council.
Dahl, L. K., and R. A. Love (1957). Evidence for relationship between sodium (chloride) intake and human essential hypertension. *Arch. Int. Med.*, *94*, 525-531.
Dahl, L. K. and R. A. Love (1957). Etiological role of sodium chloride intake in essential hypertension in humans. *J. Am. Med. Assoc.*, *164*, 396-400.
Galton, F. (1962). *Hereditary Genius* (2nd ed.). Cleveland, World Publishing Co. Republication of 1892 edition.
Gatti, R. A., H. J. Meuwissen, H. D. Allen, R. Hong, and R. A. Good (1968). Immunological reconstitution of sex-linked lymphopenic immunological deficiency. *Lancet*, *2*, 1366-1369.
Gordon, J. B. (1971). Cost benefits of neonatal screening. *New England J. Med.*, *285*, 240.
Graham, J. (1971). The relation of genetics to control of human fertility. *Pers. Biol. Med.*, *14*, 615.
Knudsen, D. K., and L. K. Dahl (1966). Essential hypertension: Inborn error of sodium metabolism. *Postgrad. Med. J.*, *42*, 148-152.
Lederberg, J. (1963). Molecular biology, eugenics and euphenics. *Nature*, *198*, 428-429.
Lederberg, J. (1970). Orthobiosis: The perfection of man. Nobel Symposium 14: *The Place of Value in a World of Facts*, A. Tiselius and S. Nilsson, eds., pp.29-58. New York, John Wiley and Sons.
Matsunaga, E. (1966). Possible genetic consequences of family planning. *J. Am. Med. Assoc.*, *198*, 533-540.
Motulsky, A. G., G. R. Fraser, and J. Felsenstein (1971). Public health and long-term genetic implications of intrauterine diagnosis and selective abortion. In Symposium on Intrauterine Diagnosis, D. Bergsma, ed. *National Foundation Birth Defects Original Article Series*, *7*, 23-32.

Muller, H. J. (1967). What genetic course will man steer? In
    Proceedings, Third International Congress of Human Genetics, J. F.
    Crow and J. V. Neel, eds., pp. 521-543. Baltimore, Johns Hopkins
    Press.

Murdoch, J. L., B. A. Walker, and V. A. McKusick (1972). Parental age
    effects on the occurrence of new mutations for the Marfan syndrome.
    Ann. Hum. Genet. Lond., 35, 331.

Neel, J. V. (1961). A geneticist looks at modern medicine. In Harvey
    Lectures Series, 56 (1960-1961), pp. 127-150. New York, Academic
    Press.

Neel, J. V. (1969). Thoughts on the future of human genetics. Med. Clin.
    N.A., 53, 1001-1011.

Neel, J. V. (1969). Some changing constraints on the human evolutionary
    process. In Proceedings, XII International Congress of Genetics,
    Vol. 3, pp. 389-403. Tokyo, Science Council of Japan.

Neel, J. V. (1970). Lessons from a "primitive" people. Science, 170,
    815-822.

Neel, J. V. (1971). The detection of increased mutation rates in human
    populations. Perspectives Biol. Med., 14, 522-537.

Neel, J. V. (1972). Ethical issues resulting from prenatal diagnosis. In
    Early Diagnosis of Human Genetic Defects, Maureen Harris, ed.
    Washington, U. S. Government Printing Office.

Neel, J. V., and W. J. Schull (1972). Differential fertility and human
    evolution. In Evolutionary Biology 6, W. C. Steere, Th. Dobzhansky,
    and M. K. Hecht, eds. New York, Appleton-Century-Crofts (in press).

Ramsey, P. (1970). Fabricated Man: The Ethics of Genetic Control. New
    Haven, Yale University Press.

Shih, V. E., H. L. Levy, V. Karolkewicz, et al. (1971) Galactosemia
    screening of newborns in Massachusetts. New England J. Med., 284,
    753-757.

Switkes, D. A. (1971). Cost benefits of neonatal screening. New England
    J. Med., 285, 239-240.

United Nations (1962). Scientific Committee on the Effects of Atomic
    Radiation Report. New York: United Nations, General Assembly
    Official Records: Twentieth Session, Suppl. 16 (A/5216), p. iv &
    441.

United Nations (1953). The Determinants and Consequences of Population
    Trends. New York, United Nations ST/SOA/Series A. Population
    Studies, 17, p. xii & 404.

SOCIAL AND SCIENTIFIC PRIORITIES:
PROCESS AND CONTENT

David A. Kindig and Victor W. Sidel

We have been asked in this paper to address ourselves to the broad social and scientific priorities into which public policy decisions concerning genetic counseling and genetic knowledge must fit. In doing this we must disclaim any special expertise in the area of genetics. Our backgrounds lie in laboratory medicine, clinical medicine, and in the organization of medical care delivery, but neither of us has worked directly in the areas of specific concern to this conference.

On the other hand, it is perhaps fitting that two medical "generalists" address themselves to these issues on this last day of the conference. In the context of the specific genetic issues raised to this point, it is now our job to attempt to weave these issues into a broader tapestry of priorities for public policy. Since in our view all discussions of this type are based on the preconceptions of their authors, we must first state some of our biases about the social priorities of our time from which we feel the scientific priorities must flow.

In general terms, we see surprisingly little overt disagreement in the United States, at least insofar as lip-service is concerned, about certain fundamental social priorities. Stated succinctly, these priorities lie in the improvement of life for all people and the creation of the opportunity for each human being to reach the fullest achievement and happiness that his biological potential permits; a paraphrasing, if you will, of the even more succinct and much more elegant statement of human rights: "life, liberty, and the pursuit of happiness."

Some of the barriers to man's reaching this goal have also been succinctly and elegantly stated in the past: for example, as the Four Horsemen of the Apocalypse--war, famine, pestilence and death. Restated in current terms, the obstacles we must overcome include war, starvation, disease and disability, overpopulation, and the fear and hatred which divide the members of the human species. Control, if not elimination, of these threats to our well-being must be among the highest social priorities of our time.

Addressing ourselves specifically to the need to control disease and disability, there is likewise surprisingly widespread agreement in public on general principles in the provision of health care. To help meet this goal, emphasis should be placed on prevention rather than on amelioration; and medical care should be freely available, easily accessible, appropriately comprehensive, provided with full regard for human dignity, and of uniformly high quality without regard to social status or ability to pay. Many have indeed broadened the concept of health much further, as in the World Health Organization definition: "Health is a state of complete physical, mental and social well-being and not merely the absence of disease or infirmity." Thus we are forced to return, even if we had wished to limit ourselves in this conference to "medical" or "scientific" priorities, to the fundamental social priorities of the improvement of the quality of life and human self-actualization.

In our view, and we are aware that from this point on in our analysis there will be many who disagree, the setting of scientific priorities must have its foundation in social priorities. We acknowledge, of course, that research not consciously or explicitly related to any immediate practical application has on many occasions led to the acquisition of knowledge which has subsequently proved to be of great importance in the solution of social problems. In addition, it would be inconsistent with our goal of individual self-fulfillment for us to suggest that society should deny to any individual the right to seek basic knowledge in any area which turns him on--from studying the moon through an eyepiece to geological exploration of its surface--whether it has any "social usefulness" or not.

Such individual choices of scientific priorities were, however, easier to achieve and to defend when the direct cost of scientific research to the society was small. Now that society has begun to devote huge amounts of its limited resources and men and their productivity to scientific research, it is our opinion that society must make its decisions with regard to commitment of its limited resources consciously and explicitly on the basis of social priorities. The difficulty in predicting the outcome of competing investments cannot hinder our attempts, for priorities--either by difficult rational choice or as the result of not choosing--are being set every day.

As society acts to develop public policy in scientific and medical areas with priorities which best match social priorities, two distinct elements must be considered: the actual content of the policy and the process by which the content is arrived at. Both of these elements are, in our view, equally important in relating policy back to the social priorities. While the importance of the content of the policy is clear, in general less attention has been paid to the issues of process. Yet, in terms of the priorities of the importance of the quality of life and human self-actualization, the process itself may lead, on the one hand, toward alienation, disaffection, feelings of impotence, and decisions based on poor data; or on the other hand, toward integration, socialization, feelings of being in control of one's own destiny, and decisions based on the input of good data from those who will be affected. Even if soundly-conceived decision-making processes lead to poor decisions (in the sense that the priorities established do not in the short run lead toward the society's goals), the process will itself have been worthwhile in furthering these goals. However, it is our strong belief that good process is more likely to lead to public policy decisions whose content is indeed based on appropriate data and which are relevant to the lives of the people affected.

THE PROCESS OF DECISION-MAKING

If we start with the basic premise that public policy will best achieve societal goals if the decisions are made by a large number of the people in the society rather than by an oligarchy, a series of questions arises as to how a large and complex society may rationally participate in that decision-making. We know that Professor Green will be addressing himself to this issue, but if we are to fulfill our charge, we must also discuss it.

The first question which arises is how people are to be informed about the issues involved. How are they to gain the technical knowledge and the knowledge of the potential consequences of specific actions required? Given informed opinion on the part of each individual, how are the differing opinions of these individuals to be brought into public view so that the individual differences can be resolved and consensus reached or, when that is impossible, a majority point of view predominates? These questions raise others: Is it necessary for the preservation of a democratic society that when conflicts arise the majority always rules, or are there technical issues to be resolved by technicians? Beyond that, are there certain issues in which the decision ought to be made on grounds other than which side has the greatest number of votes? If one feels that there are certain issues of this type, how does society decide which ones they are and who is to make the decisions?

Another level of question arises: On which issues is policy to be made on a society-wide basis and on which should decisions be made locally? This issue has arisen repeatedly with regard to "community control" of such resources as the public schools or health institutions. To what extent is it better, because of the needs of the society as a whole and because of the greater technical resources which can be brought to bear on the decision, to make decisions on public policy with regard to education or health on a society-wide basis; and to what extent is it better, because of special local conditions and the greater extent of individual participation, to make such decisions on the basis of local community needs and demands?

The words "community control" have been regarded by some as a panacea for the cure of unresponsive social institutions. While we fully agree that most of our social institutions are indeed unresponsive and must be made responsive and accountable to the people whom they serve, this must in our view occur in a context of society-wide policy. In other words, while the people served must be full participants in, and in many cases have major control over, their own local social institutions, the policies of these institutions must be consistent with national, and eventually international, goals and priorities. To cite an example from the public school system, if a local governing board decides to segregate the schools on the basis of the race of the children, this may not be permitted in a society whose public policy has been clearly set to avoid the educational and social consequences of segregation. However, within this national policy, those served by local institutions should have the power to implement the national policy in accordance with local needs and desires.

More specifically in the area of genetics, policy-setting issues such as the rate of population growth which will be permitted, the nature of attempts to wipe out certain types of genetic defects from the population, and the nature of attempts to develop improved genetic potentialities are currently under discussion. There are some who argue that because of their consequences to civilization as a whole, those decisions clearly cannot be left to any small sub-community. To the contrary, we feel that such decisions must be brought as close as possible to the individuals affected by them. This requires, of course, that every attempt must be made to educate each citizen of the community about the technical issues and about the national and international consequences of different decisions. The sub-community and individuals must also participate in and have control over the cultural context in which education and enforcement in these areas are to be performed and the methods for enforcement of societal decisions in this area, including whether the major methods to be used are to be methods of positive reinforcement or negative reinforcement.

It must be stated that at this point the relation of genetic policies to basic social priorities, such as the fullest development of one's biological potential, is muddy. Who is to say that the prevention of the birth of a genetically-damaged individual is or is not consistent with the above goals? On the one hand, such individuals will use a disproportionate amount of society's resources and are likely to decrease the amount of resources for others. On the other hand, are they and their families not capable of fulfillment and growth to their inherent capabilities? There are few absolutes governing such decisions, but at the least we should ensure that such discussions take place in the context of the best possible information and knowledge to both individuals and policy-making bodies.

Another issue in the process of public policy-making is whether policy in largely technical fields, such as genetics, is best made by elite groups with special technical knowledge or by those with less technical training who are closer to the people and situations that the policies affect on a day-by-day basis. In this country today, major policy decisions are largely made by professionals in the field, by legislators and executives influenced by elite political pressure groups, and by institutions seeking their self-perpetuation.

Professionals make policy both by being the final pathway for its implementation as well as having technical knowledge that gives them high visibility and power. Such professional power is usually assured on the basis of degrees gained and years spent in training; often these are not especially relevant to the public issue at hand. Professionals may seek certain policies not because they are best for the population they serve, but because they consciously or unconsciously seek to perpetuate and strengthen their own power base and their own satisfaction.

Other non-professional elite groups also exist which, either by wealth or political influence, exert power out of proportion to their number in the population. Such a group, if it becomes interested in specific institutions or disease entities, can cause a disproportionate shift of resources to their area of interest. While there is no fundamental objection to groups in society organizing to fight for specific issues, we are concerned about their isolation from the people affected and their power over them.

There are similar inequities in the governmental process today. Unlike the New England town meeting, in which each individual had an individual voice in the decision-making (and which was imperfect even in small communities), in present day "representative government" those who actually make the legislation and produce the policy are far removed in many cases from the individuals whom they represent. There is thus a whole layer of not only pressure groups but of "technical experts" interposed between the people represented and their representatives. This argument obviously gets at the heart of the democratic political process of this country--and the issue of the factors that influence local legislators when in the national arena to make certain decisions. What are the factors or compromises that result in the political process when a legislator might vote against what he knows to be local wishes for a "greater good"?

Institutions created by society also become self-sustaining. Very often they continue to exist not because of any continuing need, but because an institution, when once started, is extremely hard to stop. How does the society introduce accountability within the institutions that it creates so that when the need for them either changes or ceases to exist, the institution can change or cease to exist?

The rational methods which decision-making groups can use in policy formulation in controversial areas are few and complex. Largely because it is difficult to quantify social goals, precise rational statement of attitudes is difficult at best. One method which is being explored for making such decisions is "cost-benefit analysis." In this technique, the benefits of a given course of action are converted into the same kinds of units as are the costs --usually, therefore, dollar values. This means that such things as human life and happiness must be given dollar terms. It is possible, through a modification of this technique known as cost-effectiveness analysis, to attempt to measure the outcome not in dollar terms but in terms of specific outcome. Such techniques are helpful for making policy judgments within a given area, such as which of several techniques will save more lives, but it becomes ineffective in making policy judgments between, for example, a technique which will save more life but increase morbidity vs. one which will decrease morbidity but save less life. At best, cost-benefit analysis can begin to put some of our problems into comparable terms, but its widespread applicability is yet to be demonstrated.

Finally, one of the important issues for social policy determination in this area is how the policies are to be implemented once decided upon in a goal-oriented framework. Methods of implementation range all the way from the most permissive and enlightened, such as health education which emphasizes transmission of knowledge to the public with decentralized decision-making, all the way to,at the other end of the scale, forcible, involuntary requirement of adherence to the policy. In the specific case of genetics, this would, therefore, cover the range from the education of parents to an understanding of what their risks are so that they can make informed choices, on the one hand, to that of the society forcing either abortion or infanticide, on the other. In between these two rest a whole range of mechanisms which have been developed by society for enforcing its decisions. These include positive sanctions such as subsidies, income tax credits, or the like for adherence to the policy and negative sanctions such as increased taxes and various sorts of punishments for failure to adhere.

One problem with these different means of implementation is that they often apply differently to different groups in the society. For example, if one increased the taxes for those who bore, against advice, a malformed child, this would almost always strike much more heavily on those who are poor than those who are wealthy. Even now, there are financial barriers to family planning advice and to abortion which makes it harder for the poor person than for the middle-class or affluent person to avoid a large family.

Implementation can, of course, be helped by technological improvement. For example, since it is now possible through amniocentesis to make prenatal diagnosis, one can give much more specific advice to the prospective parent. This makes it much more likely that the parent will behave in a "rational" way with regard to decision-making based on genetic knowledge. It also makes it much more rational to apply either positive or negative sanctions since the information to be given to the parent in advance is that much more specific.

THE CONTENT OF DECISIONS TO BE MADE

All of the preceding should have made it abundantly clear that we consider health professionals like ourselves to be poorly qualified to recommend the content of public policy except as consultants to, or in collaboration with, the people to be served by the policy. At most, what we should be doing is suggesting the issues which must be addressed and the mechanisms whereby they might be discussed and resolved. However, such suggestions are themselves a recommendation of public policy; the argument becomes circular. To break out of this circularity, it is necessary for someone to urge something, if only as a point of departure, and we will therefore make some specific recommendations about the content of public policy in this area as a starting point for discussion.

1. Scientific Research

If there are to be any action options for an enlightened public, medical technology must advance and continue to provide practitioners with new methods. Balanced support is needed both for basic genetic research and for applied technology such as diagnostic improvements and methods for terminating pregnancy. We reject the view that the expansion of scientific knowledge should be retarded because of uncertainty in its potential use.

2. Medical Care

Scientific knowledge is of no practical use, however, unless the information and techniques which flow from it are available to patients. A high priority policy for immediate implementation should be widespread genetic services, including those for contraception, prenatal diagnosis, and abortion. These services must be carefully integrated into a national health care system which will provide easily accessible, comprehensive, dignified care to everyone.*

---

*There is evidence that if this is not done, the more well-off in society will benefit at the expense of the poor. For example, when poliomylitis immunization was introduced, middle-class and rich people, largely white received protection earlier than the poor and black; as a result, for several transitional years polio epidemics concentrated on the poor and the black. A similar phenomenon is now being seen as a result of socioeconomic imbalance in measles immunization. For a more detailed discussion see Sidel, V. W., New technologies and the practice of medicine, in Human Aspects of Biomedical Innovation, E. Mendelsohn, J. Swazey and S. Reiser, editors (1971), Cambridge, Harvard University Press, 1971.

In addition, clinical research into the treatment of genetically-damaged individudals should also be supported. This will enable the most humane approach to the afflicted individual and his family, and allow for his comfort and development of his highest potentialities.

3. Education of Health Professionals

There must be recruited into the health field professionals who have as their attitudes and goals not their dominance over patients and community but rather attitudes and goals which permit working collegially with patients and community toward the solution of health problems. We do not allege that selection of such people is easy; we do suggest, however, that the current process of selection of students into medical schools and, to a lesser extent, into other health professional schools, often appears to recruit those who wish to foster dependence and hierarchical decision-making, and this must be reversed. After admission to school, health professionals must be taught techniques for working successfully with individual patients, with small groups, and with larger communities in mutual search for solutions to health problems. Currently the student-physician is taught, either implicitly or explicity, that he makes decisions for his patients and for the institution in which he works. He must, instead, be taught the more difficult skill of sharing decision-making with other health workers and with his patients. It is not sufficient to have the genetic knowledge; we must teach health professionals how to use the knowledge preventively and appropriately.

4. Development of New Professionals

The expansion of genetic counseling and new methods for management of hereditary disease provide the opportunity for the introduction of new types of health professionals. (See Clow et al., Management of hereditary metabolic disease: role of allied health personnel, New England Journal of Medicine 284: 1291-1298, June 10, 1971). Such professionals may be closer to their patients' cultures and problems than are physicians, and may be better able to understand and to communicate with those whom they are counseling.

5. Public Education

We urge that a widespread national campaign be undertaken to bring to the public--through elementary schools, high schools, colleges, public education and the media--the current state of genetic knowledge and its potential for good or harm. The goal of this education would be to bring to every individual in society sufficient understanding of the nature of the problems and the policy options available so that all can enter into public discussion and debate on these issues.

At the same time, there must be sufficient education so that each individual in the society can understand the implications of current genetic knowledge for his own life and the lives of any children he may have. The emphasis in this latter part of the recommendation is not on decision-making for the community but on decision-making for the individual. Individuals must be taught what the nature of their choices are, the consequences of some of them, and how to consider them. Thus, they will be better prepared, when decisions about their own procreation must be made, to make them in such a way as to maximize the quality of their individual lives.

6. Research into Public Policy Formulation

Research is urgently needed into methods for effective community involvement in the public decision-making process. Such research is exceedingly difficult, and has not been notably productive in the past. However, the need for greater knowledge in this field is immediate, and in our view much more of society's resources should be put into such research. Even when the rhetoric of "power to the people" ceases to be fashionable, we must continue to seek methods for lowering the barriers towards the acquisition of such power.

Priority setting among the six areas will largely be reflected in the amount of economic and human resources allocated to each. We do not here propose a specific formula for achieving a balanced program. However, we are strongly convinced that much more emphasis must in the future be placed on the availability and accessibility of already developed techniques and in patient and professional health education.

CONCLUSION

Finally, we wish to end where we began, with the observation that difficult scientific public policy decisions such as these must be made in full realization of the social priorities of the public that is served by them. In such a context, the people themselves must be involved and informed as early and in as much depth as possible for the effort to succeed.

We are aware that there are those who differ with us and argue that the time has come for involuntary controls on the quantity and quality of individual reproduction. While we are able to foresee crisis situations in which such measures might be required, we feel that we have far from exhausted the potential for solving such problems based on education and understanding.

The following excerpt from a letter by Thomas Jefferson to William Jarvis, in 1820, puts it more succinctly than we could write:

"I know no safe depository of the ultimate powers of the society but the people themselves; and if we think them not enlightened enough to exercise this control with a wholesome discretion, the remedy is not to take it from them, but to inform their discretion."

DISCUSSION

MURRAY: Dr. Neel, first let me comment about population control. I am sure you realize that the application at this time of the kind of quantitative restriction that you propose in child number would automatically result in the diminution of the numbers of certain groups in this country who have high birth rates, but who only maintain their proportion of the population by virtue of high birth rates. They also have higher infant mortality rates and higher death rates at all ages.

To apply the type of restriction you suggest to such a group automatically predestines that group to diminishing numbers, the degree of which we are not sure at this time. We cannot be sure because many of the figures such as infant mortality rates are only estimates.

Secondly, Dr. Jurgen Randers at MIT, a computer specialist, set up some mathematical models, in which he has attempted to correlate the factors involved with environmental deterioration. His complex model suggests that population control will not avert the crisis that is to come upon us because if our business community wants to increase the gross national product every year, pollution will continue to increase irrespective of the size of the population. So population control must be coupled with other kinds of social restrictions, particularly economic.

This suggests that the kind of man we have today, whose intellect, or whose desires, lean toward the acquisition of greater and greater material comforts, is not the kind of man to spread around the world. We might prefer to have someone whose goals are more modest, who prefers to live in harmony with his environment, as a part of it, as opposed to dominating his environment.

NEEL: Let's start with something we can agree on.

I think we will agree that the exponential character of the world's population growth cannot go on indefinitely. It has to be somehow checked.

Now, with respect to your statement that any effort to check it as I suggested would, in fact, discriminate against minority groups, I hope I made it clear what a ball of wax this whole thing is. And I can only assume that while we are working in that direction, we are also taking care of the differential mortality to which you referred.

If my memory is correct, the difference in infant mortality between the Black and the white is something like one or two percent. This is a gap that can and should be bridged in this generation.

I don't think, given reasonable improvement in the level of medical practice, which of course we are all for, population stabilization would actually result in a decrease of the minority groups. On the other hand, of course, this will not undo the historical injustice to which I directed attention.

Now finally, with respect to the type of man that we want, the whole thrust of my presentation is that so far as I am concerned, we have that potentiality within ourselves right now. We don't have to start diddling with our genes. We have got the makings of the kind of man you and I want to see.

CROW: I agree fully about the uncertainties of manipulating the genotype, but I think we also have to point out the uncertainties about manipulating the environment. Very few people foresaw the consequences of leaded gasoline, or DDT, or of a television policy that increased lung cancer and emphysema.

I want to argue that there are a number of areas in which genetic prediction is more solid than environmental prediction, and I don't want a decision to be made between them without taking their relative accuracy into account.

KABACK: I would like to address several comments to Doctor Kindig and to Reverend Eaton. Perhaps there is a myth to which we have fallen prey regarding some of the issues we are considering. I would like to take issue with the idea that there is such a thing as "the Black community" or such a thing as "the Jewish community." Recent political endeavors, at least in many urban areas of this country, would indicate that there is certainly no single voice in any of these communities. Moreover, communities may differ significantly from one geographic location to another. We must be careful when decision-making policies involving community people are developed that we do, in fact, have the community representation that we think we have. Certainly, in terms of genetics and genetic medicine, I strongly support the position that the involvement of the "community" must be included in the planning and delivery of such programs. My point is, however, that this is not a simple matter and may be quite complicated. Having a few religious leaders and a doctor whose skin is black or who is of the Jewish faith participating in such a program is by no means a clear statement of "community involvement." It may be necessary that any program at the planning and delivery stages will have to be sufficiently pliable to adapt to multiple facets of each community involved.

With the Tay-Sachs Program in Baltimore and Washington, it was my opinion that the expertise regarding the community lies in the community itself. It has become clear that there is a fragmentation into many subunits within the community and that the methods for education and delivery of this genetic service require considerable pliability and plasticity to allow for this variability.

The concept of the multifaceted community is most critical when planning evolves to policy-making levels. We must be careful not to be misled in thinking that there is such a thing as unanimity of opinion in any given community.

KINDIG: I think the word "community" ought to be dropped. My experience has been with community control of a health institution in the South Bronx; our experience there was that the representative, elective community board structure we imposed on that community to somehow transmit community information to us has not been the best way to determine what the people really want.

In my position there, I found there were two ways that we began to know what the people really wanted as far as making our health institution responsive. We got a valid source of input from the community residents we had trained to be family health workers and who were working in our institution. Such health workers knew the community but also had a commitment to the organization.

In team conference, when we heard a family health worker discuss what she thought the family health center should be all about, partly she was talking as a mother living in the community who had kids and knew what her neighbors would want, and partly she was talking as a person who had a stake in the institution. Management policies based on this kind of community participation were usually fairly responsive to patients' needs.

The other thing we found very helpful was some participant observation studies that were done in our area by a sociologist who trained community workers to go out and find out some things about what the community really thinks. This is almost a paternal way of getting some data, but we found it objective and reliable.

LILEY: I would like to develop a little further Dr. Kaback's point because I think it is a very important one, that this notion of community is a myth, that in fact we are dealing with individuals. And I am sure that I would carry Reverend Eaton with me, if I said the real problem is not how one treats black people. Rather if we treat the individual Black man, woman, and child properly, the Black minority as a concept will take care of itself.

I think there should be this attitude towards the handicapped also. The most reassuring thing about this conference as we have heard from Dr. MacIntyre, Dr. Kaback, and others, is their concern; how personal and individual their concern has been for the family and the individual child. I think in this regard, to a certain extent, public policy can take care of itself.

We have heard repeatedly expressed, of course, the question of squandering precious community resources and how much we expend in the care of the handicapped. This is a lamentation and Jeremiad that we are familiar with from our own politicians in New Zealand--just what limit, they ask, is there to the amount you can spend on education and on health services, using it in the widest sense, not just on doctoring, but all the needs of the ill or ailing or frail.

I think the reassuring answer is that there is "no limit". And I think the reason that this is reassuring is that it is related simply to a matter of how people are employed and used. There are many countries in the world today where 75 to 85 percent of the population are engaged in peasant agriculture. It takes that many people to produce enough food just to support a little group at the top in administration, in services, and in professions.

Now, in agriculturally-advanced countries--and I think I can say with some confidence in this context that the United States and New Zealand are the most advanced countries--the United States has five percent of its population engaged on primary production and New Zealand has six percent. We have one-sixteenth engaged in food production, and we produce enough to feed sixteen times the population.

As happens in many places of the world, if you do anything to increase the productivity of agriculture, if you get down to as low as not necessarily 5 or 6 percent, but even 25 or 30 percent--what happens to the remainder? Vast slums in many cities are where they go. They all flock into the big smoke, and the answer is, of course, you need to develop industry to occupy them.

But I also understand that in a country as industrially advanced as the United States, something like 47 percent of the labor force can produce all the manufactured goods that a community can conceivably need and this includes changing your refrigerators when the door handle is out of style. In this situation you have something like half your labor force engaged in actually making or producing something and the big question arises simply, from the point of view of the economist, of what do you do with the other half of the population or labor force.

Now, this other half includes your liberal professions, it includes your artists and administrators and commerce. Regrettably, also it includes armed forces--although this is perhaps not the way we would like to think of using the labor surplus of a country.

The question is: What do you find for people to do, short of paying them to do nothing? And the answer is that there is no limit to the amount that can be plowed into medical and educational service. I think the biggest advance, for instance, in geriatric medicine in my city, at least in the last 15 years, has not been in neurosurgery of Parkinson's disease, but the "Meals on Wheels" service by which volunteers deliver food to frail, elderly people who otherwise would have to be kept in the hospital at high cost. They don't need to be in hospitals, but if somebody calls every day, they have at least one decent meal. They are seen. Their simple needs can be attended to and anticipated. And this principle, I think, can be extended very widely.

When we talk about precious resources, we are not talking about the Ph.D. in biochemistry who might carry out some prodigious feat of genetic engineering, but delivery of health care at a very much simpler level, and I think I would carry Dr. Murray with me when I point out that here, in fact, is the most reassuring thing, that there is no limit to the manpower--and it doesn't even carry pollution with it--that can be put into this endeavor. And this is the goal we should have our eye on.

EATON: First, I must say I couldn't agree more. In fact, I would like to go a little farther and say there is not only the myth of the mainstream, there is the myth of individualism that is prevalent in this country that has been one of the causal factors for a breakdown in communication, if anything. The myth of individualism is a manipulative myth that goes something like this: Given the motivations, given the vast set of conditions, any man can go from janitor in a company all the way up, and all he has to do is pull himself up by his own bootstraps. Even people who don't have boots feel that way because they have been fed this individualism myth very early in school.

BLACK SCHOLAR magazine is probably the intellectual organization for the "Black community." It lists as its contributors over 80 of the top Black intellectuals in the country.

What is happening is that the many minority groups are understanding the collectivism that is patterned after the principles of Dr. Nyerere in Tanzania, which is a nationalism moving toward internationalism--a nationalism that has internationalism as its goal, and nationalism as its process. This is catching hold in the intellectual areas of the black communities, so much so that before I went to the White House Conference on Youth I met with representatives at all levels of the "Black community" to determine whether it was worth my time to pool that knowledge to carry to the conference.

I did the same thing before I came to this conference. It was many days before I could reply to your invitation. This was because I checked again with a group of people--with a peer relationship but with a cross-sectional relationship of the community. Oddly enough the consensus was--I guess because it is beautiful down here--that I should come to this conference but not go to the one at the Kennedy Center on Friday, because to do so would be too much. So the decision was made not by me independently. That decision for me to come here--and for someone else to go somewhere else, and for someone else not to go somewhere else, in terms of how many people do we have to send where--was not reached by me individually.

So in a country that is constantly talking about individuality, there are great numbers of people in minority groups who have understood the myth and the mechanisms by which the concept of individuality has been abused. So many of us are talking about this precarious balance between collectivism and individualism that one has to negotiate, so that we no longer fall dupe to the myth of individuality any more than any other societies have fallen dupe to the myth of collectivism. This is an attempt to negotiate the precarious balance between the two.

Let me show you how this reflects in some of our language and subconscious thinking. The gentleman gave a good example when he was defining "right," and I appreciate his definition. He made the statement that when you go to a store and purchase something, it is your right to possess it.

Now, in the Indian community, when it comes to land and lakes and mountains, that is not true. I may go to a real estate agent and purchase the land and say that means I have the right to that land. An American Indian would say no, I do not have the right to possess that land but I must share it.

In many of the treaties in this country, when the Indian was paid for land through his chiefs, the chiefs thought that the white man was giving him a present for the use of his land, that he would share also. It was not until the Indian found a fence around it, and not until he was chased away from the lakes for fishing, that he realized that the white man thought that he had given the land to the white man; because the Indian's mind knew that Mother Earth could not be sold or given away.

So even though in our value systems we have this thing called a "right" in our society, there are cultures within that society which interpret the word "right" differently.

CONDLIFFE: Reverend Eaton, I can only say that what you describe about the Indians is not unknown elsewhere. The same concept of land usage exists among Polynesian peoples like the Maori in New Zealand. It is the prevalent concept in many parts of the world that Western culture has come into contact with during the last 400 years.

HOTCHKISS: Reverend Eaton has in his own way covered the point I intended to make. It is perhaps not inconsistent to feel that on the one hand there is validity--and I think there is--in the concept of communities or groups, and on the other hand, in the idea that we are one great community. For me the resolution of the apparent inconsistency is in mobility and multiple choices. Looking upon my own privileges, I can, for example, think of myself as some kind of geneticist, also a sometime educator, or if I choose, as a conservationist, and a swimmer. I could be a member of this group or that. In fact, I belong to many communities and draw some of my allegiances from these, from family, and so on, partaking of many partly overlapping groups.

I enjoy, I suppose, relatively great social mobility to move among these overlapping groups and share in them. Other less fortunate individuals feel more constrained and limited by walls around them. Social mobility and freedom of choice seem to me essential factors in a sense of community. To the extent that people feel constrained, I believe they have a right to consider themselves as parts of a mosaic, as Reverend Eaton said--a subgroup rather than part of a melted, integrated community. Therefore, I think we have to recognize both views as valid and try to deal with the possibilities they raise.

If I could add one more thing; our mobility in the end may also be limited by the very intensity of working toward different worldly or altruistic goals. We may feel we would like to be a part of the establishment so that we can guide and govern or help, or on the other hand, be drawn to work more intensively within one of the struggling communites. The more of these aspirations and outward-directed impulses we have, the more we may feel frustrated and therefore, just because we grow, feel more constraint.

Young people, for example, commonly feel some lack of mobility into, and lack of contact with, what is called the establishment, and to the extent that they feel separated from the way things are caused to happen, I think they have the right to speak of an establishment.

MECHANISMS FOR PUBLIC POLICY
DECISION-MAKING

Harold P. Green

We have been discussing the processes of individual private decision-making with respect to the use of genetic knowledge and technology. Now I want to discuss the processes through which our society makes policy decisions as to the manner in which this knowledge and technology will affect the individual.

To begin with, let me make it clear that I do not regard the genetic area as in any sense unique. The issues involved in the genetic area may be different, but the mechanisms for public policy decision-making are, or at least should be, exactly the same as they are with respect to any other kind of public policy issue. The fact that science or medicine happens to be the subject, rather than economic policy or social policy, does not alter the basic mechanisms through which public policy decisions are made.

Private or professional groups, acting without some form of authority delegated by government, are not within the scope of my comments. Thus, for example, decisions made by medical societies or committees of hospitals and universities would not, even though they obviously have important public policy implications, be public policy decision-making in the sense that I use the term. On the other hand, in those areas with respect to which the government has not acted, the silence or inaction of government may be regarded as constituting a de facto delegation of authority to relevant private persons or groups to make decisions in such areas. Nevertheless, this paper is limited to the mechanisms for conscious and deliberate decision-making by government. When such decisions are made, they are embodied in what I shall term "laws." The laws may be in the form of a principle enunciated by a court or in the form of a rule promulgated by a legislative or an administrative official or agency.

In speaking of government--and I am talking about the American government--it should be understood that both the federal and state governments are involved. In the American federal scheme of government, it is only the state governments which traditionally have exercised decision-making authority over the private practice of medicine and the counseling professions. Indeed, there may be some question whether the federal government has the constitutional authority to establish universal, enforceable policies in these areas. The federal government does, however, have the authority to establish policies applicable within federal hospitals and research centers and the conditions of federal grants or contracts whereby such other activities are funded. Although not specifically enforceable, these would of course have considerable influence and exert moral force on state policy decisions.

In our democratic society, public policy decisions are made by our legislative bodies, that is, state legislatures and the Congress. This is not to say that policy decisions are not made by administrative officials as well. We all know that they are, either because the legislature delegated the policy-making function to them or because administrative officials find it necessary to act in areas in which the legislature has not acted. When administrative officials make policy decisions, however, they are always accountable to the legislature and the legislature at all times has the right to establish a corrective or superseding policy. Similarly, it should be noted that the state and federal courts, in deciding individual cases, establish a precedent which in effect constitutes a public policy determination as to how that case and similar future cases should be decided. But judge-made law is always, unless it is based on constitutional considerations, also subject to correction and supersession by legislative action.

Finally, it is necessary to distinguish between two broad categories of government policy which require decision-making. These categories are based upon two quite different roles and functions of government in the United States. The first category involves the government as umpire for resolution of clashes of interest between private persons or groups, and as the regulator of private conduct. Our socio-political system is based on the premise that individuals have the maximum latitude for doing as they please, subject to government intervention only when their actions affect the rights of others or when some regulation is deemed necessary in the public interest. In this role, government is a neutral observer and becomes involved only when necessary. Within this first category, I include governmental response to problems which may be raised by genetic counseling and privately-sponsored genetic screening programs.

The second category relates to what I shall call the parental role of government. This role goes beyond the regulation of conduct and involves positive action to improve the conditions of society. This parental role is manifest in such varied government policies as compulsory education, fluoridation of water, unemployment insurance, and vaccination requirements, to mention only a few. In more recent years, the parental function of the federal government has been manifest in massive support of scientific research and development designed to bring to the public the benefits of new scientific and technological capabilities. I consider within this category government policies relating to support of genetic research and policies which may evolve for the mandatory use of genetic knowledge in order to improve social conditions.

These two categories are not completely distinct; they overlap at various points. Nevertheless, it is useful to discuss them separately since they involve quite different kinds of policy decisions and decision-making mechanisms.

I discuss first the role of government as umpire and regulator of private conduct.

Legal responsibilities and restrictions applicable to genetic counseling reflect public policy decisions as to the manner in which counseling should be conducted. My purpose is not to answer or attempt to answer the substantive questions presented, but rather to discuss the processes through which these public policy decisions are made. Laws reflecting public policy in this area may arise in one of two ways: through regulation or standards imposed by our legislatures or through the development of judge-made law in the context of our common-law system. An example of the kind of standard which may evolve is the standard of care required of a physician, as discussed by Lord Kilbrandon (this volume). An example of regulation is our present laws which restrict abortion.

At the present time genetic counseling is, like the practice of medicine, singularly free of government regulation. This is, first of all, because of the intensely private relationship between doctor and patient, and secondly because of the sophisticated mechanisms for self-regulation adopted by the medical profession and its institutions. Our organs for public policy decision-making seem at the moment to be well satisfied with this self-regulation and it is likely that the legislature will impose standards or controls only if it perceives the existence of abuse requiring such action. Most of the legal questions which have been raised in this conference will, therefore, in all probability be raised and resolved in the first instance in the course of litigation arising in genetic counseling. Such litigation will probably take the form of a lawsuit against a genetic counselor or a medical institution by an individual who believes he has been wronged by, for example, a disclosure or a non-disclosure, an invasion of his privacy, or by erroneous diagnosis and treatment.

As such cases come before the courts, the judges will search the precedents of the past in an effort to find a rule applicable to the new issues presented in this case. Analogies to and distinctions from these precedents will be found and discussed. In effect, the court will decide the case before it on the basis of the wisdom of the past which it finds in precedents, applied in the light of contemporary standards. In formulating the rule of law applicable to this case, which in turn will become precedent for future cases, courts will sometimes look also to the future to consider the implications in future cases of the rule of law applied in the case immediately before the court. As Dr. Shaw (this volume) pointed out, we certainly can find many precedents to eliminate some of the present legal impediments to efficient and effective genetic counseling and treatment. The fact that such precedents exist, however, does not mean that a court will in fact apply them in a genetic counseling case. A court may well be troubled about the long-term implications of extending precedents so as to overcome the problem of, for example, privacy in the genetic counseling area, because such an extension may have a substantial potential impact as new precedent in other areas of privacy, including perhaps areas of privacy totally unrelated to medical care.

Formulation of public policy within the common law system takes place on a case-by-case, trial-and-error basis in the context of particular disputes in which the issues are presented to the courts by adversary parties. The outcome of any single case is difficult to predict with reliability, but the decision in that case, once made, in a very real sense becomes law. And if a decision is accepted as valid precedent by courts in future cases, the effect is that a public policy will emerge as a result of judicial decision. It is likely that most of the public policy questions discussed in this volume will, as I mentioned, be resolved through this process, and that legislative action will be taken only in the event of significant abuse which is not brought under timely control by judicial action.

Legislatures typically refrain from enacting regulatory laws until there is an obvious need for legislation. This is in part due to the implied recognition that government regulation is inherently freedom-limiting. Premature legislation regulating technology deprives society of the wisdom acquired in the course of trial and error experience and tends to cast the development of the technology in a mold which may be less than optimum. Moreover, legislatures are usually busy enough with urgent problems and are not likely to turn their attention to problems which, if real at all, lie well in the future. And even if the need for legislation is indeed compelling, the legislative process involves considerable inertia. All too often, as we all know, remedial legislation is enacted only long after the need for it has become urgent.

We are, however, living in an era in which there is considerable public apprehension concerning the adverse social consequences of technology, and this concern has already been manifest at the Congressional level with respect to biomedical technology. There seems to be a recognition by at least some members of Congress that legislation may be required to deal with genetic technology at some future date. I would expect, therefore, that Congress will from time to time hold hearings on this problem and perhaps create a commission, such as proposed by Senator Mondale, to look into these problems. Such efforts would, however, serve primarily an educational purpose and there is little reason to believe that legislation will in fact result in the near future. I would anticipate, in addition, that self-regulation will be reinforced and guided by pronouncements of public or quasi-public officials. Certainly a pronouncement of guidelines by the National Academy of Sciences, the Surgeon General of the United States, or the National Institutes of Health, although not having the force of law, would have a significant effect on genetic counseling and treatment and on the conduct of screening programs.

Self-regulation, supplemented by the development of judge-made law, hopefully will make legislative action unnecessary. It is impossible now to predict whether this will in fact be the case. In the last analysis, the need for public policy decision-making will depend on whether or not the practitioners of genetic technology will have the wisdom to conduct themselves so as to avoid a public perception of abuse.

One of the major pitfalls is the possibility that the public may come to perceive genetic technology as an occult art practiced by narrow specialists who are taking us down the road to the "brave new world." It is important, therefore, that the practitioners involve in their work and their speculations the input of those from other disciplines who can provide a form of objective auditing and advice. It is equally important that discussion of the public policy issues not be confined to elite groups. Every effort should be made to inform the public fully and candidly as to where we now are and where we may be going in the future.

I discuss now the paternal role of government which raises much more difficult and important questions.

It is possible, of course, that government may seek affirmatively to bestow the blessings derived from genetic knowledge upon the public. There has already been some discussion of the possibility of a legal requirement that every pregnant woman, or at least every pregnant woman in certain categories, be subjected to amniocentesis. It is not difficult to visualize enactment of laws requiring genetic screening of every newborn infant, or screening of adults as a condition of obtaining a marriage license. Nor is it difficult to visualize, although there may be constitutional impediments, laws making abortion mandatory when genetic examination indicates the probability that a child will be born with specified defects.

In the more distant future lurks the possibility that government may seek to use genetic knowledge on a mandatory basis for positive eugenic purposes. Such a program might be justified on public health grounds. Alternatively, it is not too difficult to visualize the possibility that genetic manipulation may be practiced to serve more narrow national interests. If it were possible, for example, through genetic manipulation, to breed supermen, the interests of the national defense or even national prestige might be regarded as justifying such a program. Or if it were possible through genetic manipulation to upgrade certain species of animals to an almost, but not quite, human level, government might conclude that such a program is warranted in terms of some national interest.

These are troubling possibilities because they relate to the very identity and dignity of man and his relationship to his society and his government. Government has, of course, a legitimate interest in improvement of its people. To this point in the history of man, however, governmental efforts to improve man have taken man as he exists and sought to enable him to cope with his environment. We stand now on the threshhold of an era in which it becomes possible to alter the intrinsic characteristics of man himself. Although this possibility, together with other biomedical possibilities, raises staggering implications, the answer to these questions is by no means clear. A free, dynamic society such as ours eagerly accepts the fruits of expanding knowledge and seeks to use these fruits constructively for its improvement. We must assume, moreover, unless we are prepared to abandon our faith in the democratic process, that in a democratic society our government will be responsive to public sentiment and the public will. We must accept the principle that the public may, if it chooses, permit its government to open this Pandora's box and let its people eat the fruit of this tree of knowledge.

In considering these issues, it should be observed that they arise only, or at least primarily, as a consequence of public policy decisions. The central problem, therefore, relates squarely to how such public policy decisions should and will be made with respect to the use of genetic knowledge. In a democracy it is not as important that correct decisions be made as it is that decisions be made in a manner that will be responsive to the informed sentiments of the public. In saying this, I recognize that few people can feel comfortable about the possibility that wrong decisions will be made, but in our form of society the making of decisions of this kind, right or wrong, based on public sentiment, seems to me to be the least worst alternative.

As we all recognize, scientific knowledge and the capacity to translate this knowledge into technological accomplishments have been expanding at an exponential rate. Similarly, potential social consequences have been expanding exponentially in the sense that technological advance affects more people more substantially and much more rapidly than in earlier times. In earlier times, as recently as only 30 or 40 years ago, the rate of scientific and technological advance was considerably slower. It was stated authoritatively in 1937 that there usually was a 30-year time lag between the early origins of invention and the time that social consequences began to be felt. We know that that is no longer true.

In these earlier days, there was more time to ponder the significance of scientific and technological advances before the next stage of advance was upon us, and more time to learn, absorb, and apply the lessons of experience. As Oliver Wendell Holmes wrote in his great work The Common Law: "The life of the law has been experience." The fact is that our present democratic form of society and our legal system are geared to the making of law on the basis of experience. The current scientific and technological revolution is bringing us technological advance which leap-frogs experience, thereby imposing immense strains on the capacity of our law-making institutions to deal appropriately and in a timely manner with the problems which technology brings us.

In a very real sense our society has become hypnotized with the notion of scientific and technological advance. We have eagerly sought the benefits of new technologies with scant regard for their potential adverse consequences. Increasingly, as the accumulation of scientific knowledge and technological advance has out-stripped the capacity of the public to comprehend and to respond, our public policy decision-makers have looked to the judgment of scientific and technological experts to resolve the public policy questions. With respect to some technologies, there has been a calculated policy of not fully informing the public as to potential adverse consequences for fear that the public would become "unduly alarmed." Indeed, I suspect that there are some scientists who would discourage public discussion and debate about potentially frightening aspects of the possible use of genetic knowledge because of their concern that such debate might lead to curtailment of their obviously beneficial research.

The basic question is how we can ensure that genetic knowledge will be developed and used by our democratic government in a manner which appropriately reflects the values, desires, concerns, and fears of our democratic society. The problem of ensuring effective public participation in the decision-making process is a difficult one. The extremely rapid rate of scientific advance, coupled with the technical complexity of the issues and the esoteric jargon of the scientists, in effect preclude informed and effective public involvement. Increasingly in recent years, our legislatures have come to rely upon and make legislative judgments based upon conclusions served to them by elite groups consisting essentially of experts in the field, supplemented by a few specialists conscripted from other disciplines, and perhaps, for window dressing, one or two generalists. Public policy decisions are therefore based on what these elite groups believe the public wants, or what they think the public should have, and what they think the public will be willing to sacrifice or pay for these benefits.

The extrememly rapid rate of advance in genetic science is due in large part to the massive commitment of federal funds in support of this advance. One way to slow the rate of advance would be to curtail or withdraw this public financial support, thereby providing more time and opportunity for public comprehension and for learning from the teachings of experience. Let me make it clear that I am not suggesting suppression of scientific research. I simply point out that scientists have no fundamental right to government support, even for obviously beneficial purposes. Although I recognize fully the value and importance of biomedical research for the betterment of our society, I do not think there is any imperative, even for finding a cure or preventative for cancer, that such research be accelerated through government funding. Imperatives for forcing scientific research may exist in certain cases, as where vital defense interests are involved or to solve problems such as contagious disease which have a devastating effect on the total community. But there is no urgency in research aimed at merely improving human conditions as opposed to protecting the public against potential catastrophe.

Of course, there is a fundamental distinction between basic research to increase the fund of scientific knowledge and technological applications. Basic research in itself is obviously beneficial and desirable and does not produce social problems. These problems arise only when the knowledge derived from basic research is translated into technology. Surely no one would deny, however, that a rapid rate of scientific advance at least tends to produce a correspondingly rapid rate of technological advance. Moreover, experience demonstrates that government agencies which obtain and dispense funds for scientific research eagerly press to have the knowledge derived from such research translated into beneficial technological applications. Not the least of the bases for their eagerness is the political necessity they perceive to justify their programs and thereby obtain a continuing flow of appropriated funds.

Experience also demonstrates a propensity to overstate anticipated benefits and to apply scientific knowledge in a manner which will make obvious benefits available, and conversely to understate potential risks and social problems which usually are more remote and speculative. All too often the prevailing attitude is that there is time enough to cope with undesirable consequences when they have become actual instead of speculative; and that if the undesirable consequences cannot be adequately limited, it is time enough to restrict the technology when this becomes apparent. This is, however, a naive attitude. Benefits are usually obvious and immediate, while the existence of adverse consequences is almost always fuzzy and a matter of dispute. Even after the existence of adverse consequences is clearly recognized, there is no button anyone can push to procure an adequate measure of social control. The legislative process is slow and uncertain and there are always powerful vested interests arguing in favor of the technology. Experience demonstrates that it is an extremely difficult exercise as a matter of political reality to turn off or restrict a technology once it has been turned on.

A government decision to support scientific research is often a decision that the knowledge derived, if beneficial, will be used. In the world in which we live, few persons would seriously argue that the government should, in fact, arbitrarily curtail or withdraw financial support for genetic research even in the area of positive eugenics. Such a policy would make no sense if, for example, the Soviet or Chinese governments are supporting such research. On the other hand, it is clear that a government decision to support genetic research is a public policy decision with profound implications. It is clear, also, that government support of genetic research in this country has already taken us a long way down the road to the "brave new world" with very little public comprehension of the issues and virtually no public debate. It is important, therefore, that the potential consequences of a future technology be considered at the time a public policy decision is made to provide government funds for research which will predictably create the capability for the technology to come into existence.

There are some who believe it is too early to debate the social implications of cloning, for example, because premature public apprehension might lead to curtailment of funds for basic research related to cloning. Unfortunately, if we wait until the basic research has progressed to the point at which there is a capability of cloning human beings for beneficial purposes, we shall have lost valuable time for public discussion and debate. Cloning of humans, at least on an experimental basis, may well have become a _fait accompli_, and in any event the problem of formulating a public policy to deal with cloning will have become, by that time, much more difficult because of the existence of vested interests.

Some new public policy decision-making mechanism must be found to involve the public in the making of decisions in this area in order to ensure that decisions will not be made by elite groups playing the role of "big brother," even a genial or benevolent one. No matter how broadly constituted such elite groups may be, they can never adequately reflect the full range of public interests which are involved. It is necessary to stimulate effective public debate on the potential implications of the use of genetic knowledge long before the knowledge actually exists in usable form and the actual problems are upon us. This is particularly true when public funding is involved because the public is entitled to and should participate in decisions as to the relative priorities for allocating public funds among competing research programs. Obviously, intelligent public participation in this process requires consideration of the long-range implications of these programs, and these implications necessarily include not only the prospective benefits but also the prospective social costs and risks.

The objective is easy enough to state but difficult to implement. The very rate of advance in the genetic area, and the fact that the potential social problems involve a highly esoteric body of scientific knowledge, make it difficult to expect that there will be adequate public comprehension and debate. Some means must be found to force the issues upon the public. These means regrettably do not lie in simple education. It is unlikely that the public will respond to a unilateral presentation of the bare facts. The public responds best to active controversy, and it is controversy and debate which should be stimulated.

There is no problem in this debate with respect to the articulation of prospective benefits since those who are actively working in the area can be relied upon to argue eagerly and fully about
the benefits their work will bring. The principal difficulties lie
in bringing about a forceful and authoritative exposition of the
social costs and risks. It is through the clash of contentions,
framed in an adversary context, that the public will be educated
and stimulated to participate in the decision-making process.

It is important in this debate that the articulation of benefits, costs, and risks not be sugar-coated; nor should the debate
be confined only to applications which are now feasible. It is
important also that the debate take place in forums readily accessible to the public and that they be conducted in language the
public can readily understand rather than in the rarefied
vocabulary of science. And finally, it is important that the
debate be focused on issues rather than on ad hominem
considerations as to the knowledge or expertise of the debaters.

Some scientists will say that it is not possible, without
introducing error, half-truth, and misunderstanding, to reduce
complex scientific knowledge to a form comprehensible to the ordinary informed member of the public. If this is true, which I
doubt, their concern is really not relevant. We have here a
problem of two cultures. In the world of science, truth and logic
prevail, and error and erroneous conclusions are intolerable. In
the world of politics, however, the object is not to make public
policy decisions that can stand the test of objective truth and
accuracy. The object of the political process in a democratic
society is to give the public what the public wants, whether this
is good or bad, right or wrong. As the Supreme Court stated in
1964, "Erroneous statement is inevitable in free debate," and the
right to make erroneous statements must be protected. As Oliver
Wendell Holmes said many years ago, "The best test of truth is the
power of the thought to get itself accepted in the competition of
the market."

These fundamental principles are no less true when the subject
of the public policy debate is science than when the subject is
foreign affairs, the busing of school children, economic policy, or
consideration of a Clement Haynesworth for a seat on the Supreme
Court. When science emerges from the laboratory and the ivory
tower and impacts on public policy, it may become the subject of
bruising political debate in which public policy decisions may be
made on the basis of spurious contentions and untrue factual allegations. Some will say that such debate would unduly or
prematurely alarm the public and result in constraints curtailing
genetic research or the ability of geneticists and practitioners to
perform "good works." But in a democratic society the public must
have the right to decide for itself, rationally or irrationally,
what benefits it wants and what price it is willing to pay for
these benefits. Errors are inevitable, but it is the faith of a
democratic people that in the long run truth will prevail.

DISCUSSION

Principal Discussant: Clark C. Havighurst

I will not directly challenge Professor Green's ringing endorsement of the democratic political process. Perhaps I am not as enthusiastic as he seems to be about the fact that that is the way things are. But I think that the system as he outlines it serves the useful and indeed essential function of requiring the people that are making portentous decisions to justify them to an aware audience and to re-examine at periodic intervals the policies that they are, in fact, furthering. Seen in that context, it would seem to be, even though perhaps unpleasant and difficult to live with, a necessary evil, and indeed in many ways a benefit.

How Critical is the Need for Policy Decisions Now?

Because of the fearsome prospect of brave new worlds to come, it is customary to think of progress in genetics as among the most threatening of technological advances. Professor Green notes the parallel to other areas in which technological progress or change is so rapid that the decision-making mechanisms of society may not be able to keep up, with the result that a large-scale disaster or calamity may occur.

The arguments for technology assessment, for institutionalized foresight embodied in such things as environmental impact statements and planning, and for wide margins of error in public health questions involving such things as suspected carcinogens in food additives, all flow from the same concerns: in each case the fear is that serious harm will occur before the society can see it coming.

The question may be asked, however, whether genetics should rank as far up our priority list--that is, our list of critical issues--as it often seems to in calls for action by concerned individuals. Even though the problem clearly has important long-run implications, it may be, as Professor Green seems to believe, that it does not now require the prompt attention of our legislatures.

There are several reasons why the problem may be less pressing than some others. The first is that genetics is so far, and for some time to come will continue to be, largely confined as a practical matter to specific diseases and their cure, treatment, or prevention. The more exotic things going on in occasional laboratories portend only that important decisions will have one day to be made, not necessarily that they must be made now. Activity focused on specific diseases and applicable to only a relatively small number of individuals may lack the potential to cause harm of a permanent and irreversible character any time soon. If the threat is not in fact immediate, and is highly speculative to boot, then probably it should not be ranked on a par as a problem with, say, heavy metals or other persistent substances released in the environment, or the possible impairment of the earth's ozone shield by supersonic transports.

Surprisingly to me, the conference has not dwelt on the worst possibilities that might flow from genetic screening and counseling. The only substantial reference to major long-term effects has been in Dr. Crow's demonstration that even the maximum efforts to reduce genetic disease, say by sterilization, would not have substantially adverse effects on the gene pool even in a generation. Presumably, Dr. Crow's talk was not to be regarded as a conclusive demonstration, but its thrust--which was, incidentally, concurred in by Dr. Kaback--was that there is ample time remaining so that we can now proceed to treat genetic disease without at the same time trying to protect the gene pool from deterioration.

Perhaps, then, any far-reaching effects to be feared from genetic screening and counseling can be depended upon to be gradual and moreover to be reversible if subsequent developments should establish the need. Of course, we must recognize that reversing any adverse effect on the gene pool involves positive eugenics, in the sense at least of restoring the human race to a condition that it once enjoyed but consciously or unconsciously allowed to deteriorate. And perhaps we should be particularly careful about doing anything now that might create pressures for adopting such measures even in the far distant future.

Another reason why it may not be necessary to move quickly to frame policy in this field is that, although careers and prestige are being committed to the field of genetics, no large capital investments and few other major commitments are being made in reliance on continuation of the present laissez-faire policies. Therefore such "vested interests," to use Professor Green's phrase, as are being created should be no more than moderate impediments to change when and if change becomes desirable.

There may also be a basis for reasonable assurance that research will continue to focus on the short- and long-run risks that may be present, and it would appear that public attention is already acutely attuned to the existence of issues and dangers in this field of research and development. I would also suppose that any dissenters who may appear will have the means available of making their case in public forums, with a high probability of being heard and heeded.

Whether we are reasonably safe in pursuing our present policies or non-policies, I cannot finally say. But I can suggest several specific criteria in the form of danger signals that should help to tell us whether the problem we have is of dire and critical, or merely of very great, importance. Moreover, the appropriateness of particular decision-making mechanisms to be adopted at this or some future point in time may be judged with reference to the presence or absence of these same factors. The list, which incorporates some of the things I have already canvassed, is as follows:

(1) substantiality of the possible harms, including those harms that are only remotely possible;

(2) immediacy of the risks in time;

(3) irreversibility of any possible harms that might occur;

(4) present foreclosure of future options (one can speculate on how sometimes what we do today prevents our doing things in a certain way in the future, and one would have to make sure that we are not foreclosing ourselves as to the future ways of handling the problem);

(5) potential creation of interests or added costs that would bar or bias future choices;

(6) the propensity for short-sightedness or tunnel vision of the primary public or private decision-makers who now influence the directions being taken;

(7) public inattention to the issue that might allow a problem to sneak up; and, finally,

(8) lack of at least an opportunity for any opponents of developments to speak for those interests that might be adversely affected.

While I am not in a position to make a final judgment, it does not seem to me that, evaluated against these criteria, genetics poses as serious a current threat as some other technologies that society is now pursuing without due regard to future risks.

Protection of Societal Values as a Predicate for Action

I have been speaking, of course, primarily about the need for immediate legislation to avert possible health hazards of a long-range character that might flow from genetic research and counseling. I would not want to be understood, however, as minimizing hazards or implications of another kind--namely, any possible adverse effects on human values that might flow from a failure to establish a policy here and now. Whether new laws are presently needed to maintain any threatened values is not clear to me. However, I must say I do not regard one of law's primary virtues to be its effectiveness is assisting a rear guard in fighting a holding action against new values that may be emerging in the society, and I would object to trying to legislate values for individuals unless third-party effects provided an independent justification. (It is interesting to note parenthetically that our ethical discussions at this conference have focused, ultimately, on whether the fetus is in fact a third party whose interests might warrant legal or other intervention in private medical decisions.)

A firm commitment to certain democratic values and correlative individual rights is, of course, embodied in the Constitution, and many specific rights and duties are established in received legal doctrine. These legal principles will allow the courts to modulate

violent swings in public policies and private or professional
behavior and to protect minorities. I hope, however, that the last
30-plus years have not led us to rely exclusively on the courts to
vindicate ultimate societal values, for judicial bulwarks can be
weakened--as the news reports this week are reminding us--and can
serve different purposes in different periods of our nation's
history. We may be on the brink of a new era in that regard.

For these reasons, it is perhaps particularly important that
the legislative mechanisms of government be called upon to defend
values and rights if they appear to be jeopardized by either public
or private conduct. Indeed, the perceived possibility of legislative intervention can provide an important and beneficial constraint on private conduct which, even though unregulated, tends to
conform to norms known to be espoused by articulate portions of the
body politic. Geneticists must surely reckon with society's
values in introducing their innovations, and it is appropriate for
them to live, if not with fear, at least with a healthy respect for
the public's right to legislate its preferences if they are not
being honored.

Professor Green treats legislative inaction as a de facto
delegation to private decision-makers, a characterization that
seems to view private conduct as occurring at the state's suffer-
ance or by its default, whereas I am suggesting that it is default
by or the failure of private institutions that invites government
to act. In any event, but particularly under his own characterization, Professor Green probably should not have excluded self-
regulatory decision-making from his scope. Indeed, although he
indicated he was not dealing with self-regulation, he in fact made
several references to the self-regulatory institutions of our
society, particularly those of the medical profession. Certainly,
genetic counselors can be expected to evolve a kind of self-
regulation by specialty certification or otherwise as a means of
responding to the public's ethical and other expectations. And
this is entirely appropriate, though as an antitrust lawyer I would
caution counselors against collective practices designed primarily
to enhance their market position.

Speculations on Potential Legislative Changes

Now I want to turn to some speculation about possible future
changes in the law as it affects genetics and particularly genetic
counseling and screening.

The case for special regulation of the provision of genetic
services may turn out to be fairly strong. The justification for
regulatory legislation would rest on the possibilities for abuse,
which may be quite considerable and of an order somewhat different
from the possibilities in medical practice of other kinds.

For a debatable but apparently immediate example, consider the
M.D. who, using presently available prenatal diagnostic techniques,

does a land-office business specializing in advising prospective parents of the sex of their unborn child and aborting those of the unwanted sex. If we as a society are not prepared for this on a large scale, then laws will have to be passed to stop it. Some legislative balancing of the population-control benefits against serious ethical and demographic consequences would seem to be called for fairly soon.

For a perhaps more troublesome example, reassurance against genetic defects could be sold to parents who had no identifiable problems but excessive fears. And, further ahead, genetic engineering services of perhaps dubious value might be sold to parents who were particularly anxious about the intelligence, height, or other qualities of their offspring.

Thus, special opportunities for abuse may reside in the fears and anxieties of expectant parents, which an unethical physician or counselor might exploit to his own advantage. Self-regulation by the profession itself might serve to minimize problems of this kind but, if such regulation is not successful, public control will be likely.

Whether we like it or not, there is a certain logic supporting FDA-type regulation of genetic engineering techniques, although it is extremely difficult to foresee how this explosive issue will ultimately be dealt with. My guess would be that an agency with scientific capability only would not be enough and that involvement of persons representative of, or "representing," a broad spectrum of society's values and interests would also be necessary. Perhaps this model of a decision-maker in fields of this kind has wider applicability, and I shall mention another use of it in a minute.

The arguments favoring voluntary screening of parents for abnormal traits seem easily extended to support making it mandatory by legislation. The arguments against mandatory screening are, first, that the counseling which follows will clearly convey the state's preferences and coerce parents into abortions, thus interfering with their freedom to bear children and, second, that compulsory abortion or sterilization will inevitably follow, if not immediately then later, as those who continue to reject the ever more popular solution of abortion appear more and more to be recalcitrants. Constitutional arguments against such extension of state power may ultimately prevail, but they are not strong on their face where the public interest in health and the gene pool and in the cost of caring for defective offspring is strong. Courts as a rule do not second-guess legislatures where a legitimate state interest appears and the legislature's chosen means do not infringe on individual rights any more than is necessary to bring about the end desired. As Lord Kilbrandon has shown us, previous eugenics legislation, dealing with incest and with compulsory sterilization of epileptics and others, has not been too skeptically received by the courts.

I would guess that genetic screening programs are likely to be sponsored by the state in the fairly near future, perhaps as soon

as a particularly good screening opportunity is presented wherein
it will not be necessary to single out a particular minority racial
group as the target. But I am not sure that the predicted infringe-
ments on parents' freedoms would necessarily follow, for I think
that the public, through its legislative representatives, will balk
at compulsory abortions or sterilizations for normal persons who
happen to be carriers of a genetic disease. The courts should be
of some help in preventing the singling out of welfare clients and
other vulnerable classes for special pressures.

Other Possible Sources of Decisions on Genetic Screening

Public policy decisions on mass screening, it should be noted,
can come from many different directions. State public health
authorities are the most logical place to find proposals origina-
ting. Federal research grants may also be used to implement
screening without state approval. Health maintenance organizations
(prepaid providers) may find that it pays to screen their enrolled
patient populations, at least by detailed family histories, and to
use the findings in an affirmative effort to reduce genetically
affected births that would be a liability to the organization,
which is of course obligated to provide the needed care. And indeed
this is simply the practice of preventive medicine, which health
maintenance organizations are expected to engage in.

Further, decisions by government and private health insurers
as to whether screening costs are reimbursable in insurance programs will also exert an influence on the extent to which screening
occurs.

Finally, courts may soon find an obstetrician negligent, and
therefore liable to the parents of a genetically defective child,
if he failed to take a detailed family history of the prospective
mother and perhaps to give other tests that would have identified a
high-risk situation. And I doubt that the Gleitman case (Gleitman
v. Cosgrove, 49 N.J. 22, 227A.2d 689, 1967) will very long be read
to prevent such a recovery, at least in a state where abortion
would have been legal. The result of any such judicial holding
would be a new malpractice hazard for doctors, which could be
expected to produce the equivalent of mass screening followed by
counseling and an offer of amniocentesis wherever indicated.

Federal Versus State Decision-making

The foregoing examples of how decisions on screening may occur
at various levels or in various branches of government call attention also to the emerging federal role in the health care system.
While it has been traditional to regard health as primarily a subject of the state police power, the federal government's involvement
in the financing of health care is quite likely to lead to a major

shift in the locus of power. Health maintenance organizations, for
example, are very likely to be exempted from state law insofar as
federal law desires to cover them.

To the extent that the states retain their authority, it may
be helpful for you to know about the National Conference of Commis-
sioners on Uniform State Laws, which promulgates uniform acts for
enactment by individual state legislatures. The drafting of such a
law is done in a careful and relatively nonpolitical manner, and
often the law on a subject of public interest will be promptly and
widely adopted, as was the Uniform Anatomical Gift Act. It is
highly likely that the National Conference, which has lately shown
an increased willingness to enter areas of controversy, will some-
day take up genetic counseling as an area for possible legislation.

Decisions on Research Directions

Perhaps the most fundamental decisions on public policy
towards genetics that are now being made, the ones which have the
most explosive potential consequences, are in the area of research
and its funding. Does or should the federal government support
research in cloning? Are ethical factors being properly incorpor-
ated? Are peer review and review by hospital experimentation
committees a sufficient check?

I would suggest that the implications of genetic research may
be enough greater than the implications of most other medical
research that it should be dealt with as a special problem.

Although I have not looked into the nature or functioning of
NIH's genetic research advisory committee, I would suggest that
consideration should be given to broadening its membership to
include not just one or two theologians or ethicists but a true
cross-section of informed opinion on the subject. The representation of minority groups would also seem highly desirable. Such a
broadened committee would have more than a scientific mission, and
it should be given more than the usual staff support, authority,
and autonomy to enable it to take some responsibility for the level
of value consciousness in genetics research.

Some of the questions for the attention of such an advisory
group seem self-evident, and Dr. Neel has admirably laid out many
less obvious issues in discussing the subject of priorities this
morning. I would suggest, as just one further example of the problems that should be confronted by a value-conscious advisory group,
the question of whether research should not be encouraged on a cure
for Tay-Sachs disease. Whatever one may conclude about Dr. Kaback's
screening program, should it and the prospect of widespread adoption of his techniques be allowed to preempt or reduce the glamor
of research in the field and the possibility that a better solution
--namely, a cure--might be found? The answer to that question and,
indeed, the matter of whether a cure would in fact be preferable,
would be something that a committee of this kind might consider.

My final point--and the one that is perhaps the most sobering of all--is simply to underline Dr. Sinsheimer's point about the international implications of genetic research. The costs of the arms and space races have so far been largely economic, though perhaps the social and human costs of the Vietnam War can be laid at the door of militaristic competition. Nevertheless, the consequences for the quality of life of an international race in genetic engineering could be even more serious than anything we have yet seen. One can only hope that our present adversaries in world politics will come to see their interests in this matter as coinciding with our own. Whether something analogous to the nuclear test ban treaty can be accomplished remains to be seen.

DISCUSSION

Principal Discussant: Kenneth M. Ludmerer

Not only today but throughout its history, genetics has been a science with numerous and varied political entanglements. This is not a surprising fact, for the intellectual content of genetics bears directly upon political matters in a way unlike that of any other science. The "nature-nurture" issue is fundamentally a biological problem, but its social and political significance is immense. A theory of the origin of the universe simply does not carry the same type of social import--for 20th century civilization, at least--as a theory of man's nature. By its very character, genetic science is intimately related to society.

Two of the topics Dr. Green so ably discussed I now wish to pursue further: the issue of genetic engineering and the question of the scientist's social responsibility. I have chosen the example of genetic engineering rather than that of genetic counseling because it better illustrates Professor Green's important observation that many of the questions surrounding genetic and biomedical research are, in fact, general problems applicable to many other perplexing general situations facing contemporary America. Afterwards, I shall conclude my remarks and the symposium by offering some general reflections on the relations of science and society.

Today, remarkable advances in molecular biology have created a dramatic new vision of man's future. With the structure and principal mechanisms of the gene having been elucidated, bold visionaries predict, and in some cases anticipate, a day when physicians will dispense test-tube babies and even prevent hereditary conditions by genetic surgery! The idea of genetic engineering has arisen from unquestionably brilliant scientific work--indeed, from Nobel Prize-winning discoveries. It seems to me that this is its weakness as well as its strength. The hazard is that enthusiasts of genetic engineering may be approaching the subject too objectively, too scientifically. Many are convinced that man's understanding of genetics far exceeds his wisdom to apply that knowledge ethically and beneficially. Some fear that proponents of genetic engineering regard it so much an intellectual problem that they neglect to consider its effects on the individual and society. One well-known investigator has urged, "If this investigation (work in genetic engineering) is done with man, the study should be made with collaborators who can protect genetics from public scorn by having scientists working with articulate sociologists and psychologists who plan for a long time before doing the engineering." Eugenically-minded individuals have performed an about-face from an earlier era in which their predecessors were reproached for not being objective enough in approaching the genetics of man.

It is not surprising that some enthusiasts have been accused of approaching genetic engineering too objectively. Genetic engineering is in fact a genetic technology, and as a form of technology it suffers from the same problem of "technology without a 'logos'" that Herbert Marcuse has described for other forms of technology. Marcuse has discussed the tendency for science and technology to become the instrumentalities of "experts" who are so interested in "making it work" that they neglect to ask the value questions--"for what?" and "for whom?" Engineers might come to consider "building the perfect bridge" an end in itself, not caring whether a bridge in a certain site is needed; surgeons might become obsessed with the idea of "the perfect operation" or "the perfect transplant," forgetting that medicine's task is to save lives. With this perspective it thus becomes understandable why the tendency to some is so great to treat genetic engineering wholly as a scientific matter--this is the manifestation of a general dilemma affecting much of the rest of technology as well.

Another dilemma surrounds genetic engineering, a general one facing all of American society: the problem of differentiating problems of "technique" from problems of "value." Since World War II, science and technology have played such important roles in American affairs that for a while many regarded them (and some still do) as "cure-alls" for any problem. Recently it has been increasingly recognized that not all problems can be solved by technique and expertise--that underneath certain apparent questions of methodology and technology lie questions of value. It has been suggested, for example, that the solution to the ecological crisis does not depend solely upon the development of better laws and more sophisticated equipment to clean pollution, but also upon making a fundamental ethical and moral conversion to the view that saving the environment is an imperative--a switch analogous to the moral conversion abolitionists made in relinquishing slave ownership as a "natural property right" of man. Laws and equipment are necessary to resolve the ecological crisis, but so also is the re-examination of underlying political and philosophical beliefs, such as whether air and water are free commodities and whether land and its resources may be used in accordance with the unrestricted desires

of their private owners. In discussing the use of any science,
including genetics, to solve social problems, it therefore becomes
important to demarcate clearly the limit that scientific technique
may be expected to contribute to the final solution. Small wonder,
then, that the debate over genetic engineering has been so muddled
and confused.

Many current workers in genetics and human genetics have
attempted to guide the public discussion of genetic engineering.
They believe, as L. C. Dunn remarked in 1962, that "the social and
political misuse to which genetics applied to man is peculiarly
subject is influenced not only by those who support such misuse,
but also by those who fail to point out, as teachers, the distinctions between true and false science." Accordingly, in recent
years there has been an outburst of symposia and publications,
intended for the public as well as the scientific community,
discussing the genetic future of man. Such efforts have been
beneficial, but unresolved problems still remain. Despite
geneticists' attempts to evoke widespread discussion of genetic
engineering, the public often seems more inclined to accede to the
views of the authorities than to debate the issue. The tendency is
very great indeed to assume that a man with the technical knowledge
of a field is somehow more qualified to pass judgment on its
applications, even if he claims he is offering only his personal
opinions. Today, when mass media enables the views of the famous
to be heard everywhere, this tendency may even be accentuated. A
famous biologist might describe his "view of the future" on one of
the network television "talk shows" before millions of home
listeners; even if he disapproves of that view, he runs the danger
of being thought to condone it and thereby unintentionally helping
to bring it about. Statements on genetic engineering carry the
risk of becoming self-fulfilling prophesies.

As Professor Green has suggested, in cases of genetic applications it is imperative that workers in the field fulfill their
social responsibility. By a scientist's social responsibility, I
mean his duty to inform the public of the scientific facts of a
public question concerning the application of science or technology
to social problems so that an enlightened citizenry may more
knowledgeably make important political, ethical, or social
decisions. The term implies something other than the mere
participation of a scientist in politics. From this perspective, a
scientist lobbying in Congress for partisan purposes, such as
increased federal support of scientific research, would not
necessarily be exercising social responsibility. Neither would a
scientist expressing his views on general political issues, such as
the Vietnamese War. The term also suggests a necessary distinction
between an investigator's role as scientist and as citizen. A
scientist has human limitations; in exercising social
responsibility properly he must make no pretense of possessing
greater moral insight into the beneficial use of science than the

non-scientist. Many investigators have personal views as to how science should be used, but these are their views as "citizens," not as "scientists." Social responsibility demands the analysis and elucidation of scientific knowledge, not the prescription of social policy.

Though some might disagree, I believe that scientists are capable of manifesting social responsibility as here defined--that they can reasonably separate their scientific and social views. I am not suggesting that an investigator's social presuppositions will not influence his interpretation of scientific evidence, or his scientific views will not influence his position on social issues. On the contrary various studies have shown social and scientific attitudes often to be significantly interrelated. I am suggesting, however, that frequently the distinction between political and scientific problems may be made with reasonable ease. Consider the views of physicists toward nuclear energy at the end of World War II. In 1945 almost all physicists agreed on the scientific question of what atomic energy is and what it can do, but their ranks were markedly divided over the political question of whether to use the bomb. A poll of 150 physicists at the Chicago Metallurgical Laboratory showed one faction demanding that the bomb not be used at all, another that the bomb be exploded on an unpopulated location as a warning to the Japanese, still another that the bomb be dropped on Japan in order to end the war promptly. In this instance there was no confusing the scientific and the political issue.

In discussing social responsibility, complex ethical and moral questions arise, particularly if an investigator's views on the social applications of scientific discovery do not coincide with public opinion. Are there areas of knowledge which, because of their disquieting social implications, should not be investigated? To what extent is an individual scientist entitled reasonably to withhold his knowledge from society on the grounds of moral or value judgment? Does the scientist possess some absolute right to interpose his value system between the fruit of his work and the undesirable application of his discoveries to offensive social objectives? Has he the right of veto or the right to act as a concurrent majority in the John C. Calhounian tradition, negating the will of the social majority? To what extent may society compel a scientist to cooperate against his will in the application of his skills to social goals he finds revolting, or at least morally objectionable? Who possesses the obligation to bring a professionally-trained person to task whenever he brings discredit upon the scientific community--even in the furtherance of a socially popular cause? With whom is to reside the ultimate authority and responsibility for the social applications of science, and what shall be their criteria? The crux of these questions seems to be the difficulty of defining a universal code of scientific conduct acceptable even to members of the scientific community, not to mention politicians who may seek to control them.

What will be the future of eugenic applications in the United States? A survey of contemporary American society offers no certain answer, only ambiguous and contradictory signs. Contemporary medical research is concentrating more and more earnestly on controlling hereditary conditions, having developed techniques and procedures which make possible the in utero detection of fetuses afflicted with certain "inborn errors." At the same time, however, medical interest has not diminished in the conquest of disease by conventional environmental methods of surgery, diet, and medication--an approach which if completely successful theoretically would eliminate the need for any type of eugenic elimination of the particular deleterious genes. As mentioned in reference to genetic engineering, some current problems of human genetics are possibly in danger of being approached too objectively; yet the furor now raging over the suggestions of Stanford physicist William Shockley and Berkeley psychologist Arthur Jensen that blacks are intellectually inferior to whites indicates that other problems of human genetics are still laden with emotion. Of course, there is no reason why eugenic and environmental approaches cannot be pursued simultaneously, but so far there is no concurrence regarding their relative desirability or potential effectiveness. Moreover, at a time when American society must determine how to permit individual expression without inviting lawlessness or civil disobedience and how to control crime and violence without instigating repression, the ancient problem of defining the responsibility of the individual to the group and of the present generation to posterity is as unresolved as ever; on no other issue is agreement so fundamental a prerequisite to the enactment of wide-scale eugenic measures.

Today the eugenics question is but one of many biological matters which are political problems as well. The 1970's opened with marijuana, narcotics, the pill, the psychological effects of pornography, and ecology among the major political issues of the day. In discussion of these issues it is apparent that there exists a very pronounced tendency to fit facts to policy rather than to build policy upon facts. The recent testimony of a host of scientific and medical experts that the harmful effects of marijuana have been greatly exaggerated made little noticeable impact upon Congressmen. Conviction remains a felony, and legal technicalities have made research into the drug's properties exceedingly difficult to carry out. The conclusions of President Nixon's Commissions on Pornography (and on Campus Violence) were denounced by many, including the President himself, before the studies were officially released. Without having read the reports, numerous citizens and politicians, emotionally committed to conflicting views, challenged the commissions' "competence" and "authority." Scientific argument cannot overcome irrational sentiment against a position, though it can be used effectively when scientific fact and sentiment happen to coincide. Perhaps it is not surprising that this is so, for the tendency to fit facts to policy is undoubtedly traceable to human nature--which, it would appear from the record afforded by history, has not changed in substance and which rises to throw askew the best-laid plans of politicians, generals, yes, and scientists too!

During the present controversy over applications of genetics, many geneticists are meeting their social responsibility by helping to guide public discussion of the issues. Though such efforts are needed, it must be realized that the exercise of social responsibility also involves certain dangers. Scientists may not always be able to safeguard themselves by distinguishing between their roles as scientists and citizens. A public accustomed to respect the authority of scientists may find it difficult to realize that some of their occasional remarks are imprecise and non-scientific. In important, emotionally-laden issues a bewildered and anxious citizenry, noting that scientists in possession of the same facts hold contradictory opinions, may feel that science has somehow failed. In addition, some scientists may capitalize on the public's regard for them as experts to speak on issues outside their areas of authority, or they might inadvertently pass off speculation as fact. Though social responsibility is generally considered desirable, it would seem that it also carries the danger of being abused, and if this happens science may thereby incur some of the mistrust that traditionally belongs to politics.

Some feel that this is already happening today. There is a growing disillusionment with science among the young--a decreased enrollment in university science courses, renewed interest among youth in astrology, mysticism, and the occult. Such a revolt against science does not necessarily have to occur. At the heart of the problem lies not the failure of science but this century's unrealistic faith that science is without limitations. With such high expectations the disillusionment with science is correspondingly greater when it does not perform as anticipated. The solution, I think, lies in a more thorough education of the public on the true nature of science--on its limitations as well as its capabilities, on the degree to which it may reasonably be expected to contribute to the solution of social problems, on the important distinction between fact and interpretation or speculation. The public must be taught to respect the scientific method and scientific fact without being duped into believing that they are omnipotent. With such an approach, it may be expected that science in America will continue to occupy a position of esteem.

General Discussion

HIMSWORTH: It seems to me that there is one factor which keeps coming up repeatedly, and that is the problem of the integration of expert knowledge into public policy and the role of the expert in this.

If the public is to make wise decisions on matters that are scientifically based, it must have access to the most accurate and the best information possible. That, I think, is self-evident.

But I was very taken with Dr. Kindig's quotation from Thomas Jefferson about the position of the public in these matters. As you know, Thomas Jefferson never wrote a sentence without weighing every word. You will notice that he said the safeguard was that the public should have the ultimate responsibility--and I suggest that in this connection, 'ultimate' is the operative word.

This is the point. To produce reliable and expert assessments on which these ultimate decisions can be made and to integrate these into the machinery of public policy is the great question facing human societies since science became effective and not just a scholastic exercise.

Dr. Green referred to the opinions of scientists, the experts. He drew some rather severe strictures upon them, saying how the man who is enthusiastic in a particular field is apt to exaggerate its beneficial potential. That, I think, is very understandable, and it is a corollary of the specialization forced upon scientists as a result of the great increase of knowledge. But it does mean that an individual expert may present a biased or incomplete picture.

Now, there is a danger in this situation with which Dr. Green may not agree, but I know it exists. It is the danger of what is called the predictable expert--that is, the expert who is selected by the administrator or the politician because he knows what advice he is going to give.

The point I wish to make with respect to science and public policy is this: Scientifically based matters that are politically important are never concerned with established knowledge. They are always concerned with fields where possibilities and opportunities have been opened but certainly have not yet been established. And the assessment of those fields is a highly expert job. That is why the predictable experts and the enthusiasts selling themselves are really potential social dangers. I am not suggesting muzzles. I am suggesting they need to be assessed expertly and that it is an expert job in itself to do this.

When you have a field where there is not the established, mission-oriented knowledge to lock into the practical problem to give the answer, you will find scientists saying, "Oh, you can't answer that question." That is often not true.

Dr. Neel remembers the days when we worked together, doing something that had never been done before. We were answering the question, "What are the effects on man of test explosions?" I chaired the UK committee and Dr. Detlev Bronk chaired the one on this side. But putting together the whole range of knowledge from radiotherapy at one extreme to DNA chemistry and the transformation of elements in it at the other, we each made an assessment which I think still stands in its broad perspectives. On both sides of the

Atlantic, we came to the same conclusions, and there was no collusion.

To produce such broad-based, expert assessments and to interpret them to government is, I think, one of the most important and expert jobs in science. And we need an instrument that we acknowledge for the purpose.

Expert knowledge was not possible until men came to live together in organized communities. When they did, they were able to specialize in their interests, and specialized occupations and professions arose in consequence. This had the social consequence that men were no longer self-sufficient; they had to rely and be dependent upon each other. So the problem of integrating expert knowledge into social policy is one inherent in the human situation.

With the evolution of expert occupations and the further growth of knowledge, there came the need for another instrument-- one to give a period of preliminary training. In our own field, the first example of a device for that purpose was the medical school at Salerno. From this coming together of such specialized schools, the universities arose. So the growth of knowledge brought into existence a further instrument, one for teaching and the further advancement of knowledge. Later, with the further expansion of knowledge, there came the need for another instrument. Various trials were made and that is how the device, the instrument of a scientific society or academy, arose in the 17th century.

I am suggesting that we are now in a new age. Scientific knowledge has become effective, and it is no longer possible to say that we can only go blindly forward in the faith that following the knowledge for its own sake will work out. Now we can do things with more purpose than before. We need an instrument to relate expert knowledge to public purpose.

I think that the first kind of instrument that emerged with this object was a purpose-directed foundation like Rockefeller. The other manifestation of it in the public field is the national research organization, like the National Institutes of Health. That is the kind of instrument for the integration of knowledge and the assessment of information which is wanted--an instrument that covers the whole range from the mission-oriented to the basic.

One of the things that I have met repeatedly over on our side of the water is that a man distinguished in science thinks ipso facto he can understand social policy and public policy; he doesn't need to learn anything; he hasn't another language to learn. That, I think, is very dangerous. I was very interested the other day to see an academician, not devoid of wit, speaking about this in relation to the Russians. He put amongst the top priorities of science--first, the acceptance by scientists that the integration of their knowledge into public policy was as much a duty as publishing their results. Second, he put the need to breed a new race of people, a new profession within science. And he took the analogy of the theatre. He said, "If you are producing a ballet, you don't send for the business manager to put on the show. You breed a race of actor-managers."

I think we have to have a new profession in science. There must be some machinery for making the most considered judgments possible, and I think we need a race of actor-managers to tie that into government. I don't hesitate to say this because I think you in this country have produced one of the greatest. His name is James Shannon.

One final point about the nature of the assessments--it is from recent experience. Two years ago there was a great deal of concern in our country because the police had used CS (a new type of irritant tear gas) on rioters in Northern Ireland. There were not lacking scientists who said it was completely harmless, others to say it would produce the most serious damage. I was impounded to head up an independent inquiry. My committee found that this was another of those cases in which one had to range from clinical medicine to recondite chemistry in order to make an assessment of the situation.

When our report appeared, it was said to be scientifically irreproachable, but we were criticized by some on one score. We had said we had conceived our task to give a professional assessment of the possibilities of this agent so that public and government might make an informed decision as to whether it should be used for controlling civil disturbances.

The criticism was that we had avoided expressing an opinion on the morality of using CS. But that is not a professional responsibility, and it is professional assessments, I think, that we have to insure the government gets.

CAPRON: I would like to pick up on a comment of Dr. Ludmerer's which has broader implications. He raised the question whether scientists have any right or ought to exercise any authority over the use of knowledge which they develop when they find the knowledge is being used in a way of which they do not approve.

As I have always understood the scientific method, it involves the publication and free dissemination of ideas. In fact, an idea hasn't in many ways been "discovered" until it is communicated to one's colleagues, both for reasons of practical priority and because if a man is looking for truth, he needs his colleagues to tell him the answer to the question: Is this an important fact which contributes to our understanding of the world? So it would certainly pose a practical difficulty for a scientist to hold onto knowledge, and once it is part of the public domain, it is obviously difficult for him to control.

I think it comes up in a different way in the question of who "owns" knowledge, as such, in even the particular counselor-patient relationship where knowledge is gained by the application of certain techniques to, say, a blood sample, a leukocyte sample, a serum sample, etc., supplied by the patient. Who, then, owns knowledge in that situation? It is knowledge about someone, and it really is inherent in them. It is truth about them, and yet it is held momentarily, at least, by the scientist involved.

LUDMERER: Of course, once the paper is published, it is public property. I had in mind two types of situations prior to publication. One is the case where a scientist might not want to pursue an area of research deemed important by society and public opinion. The other and more dramatic situation is the case where the government might try to compel a certain group of scientists to work on a project it considers important to the nation's welfare.

BERGMANN: I think Mr. Capron made a very important point. The genetic counselor takes a history and puts it in the computer bank. He also takes a blood sample and puts it in the deep freeze. And from the point of view of confidentiality, I would suggest that there is much more information in the deep freeze than in the computer bank, and I think that point should be appreciated by the lawyers and everyone else.

SINSHEIMER: I would like to take issue with a point you made, Dr. Green, about imperative claims for the support of scientific research, because that implies a judgment as to what is imperative. The examples you gave were contagious disease or defense. One might quarrel with some aspects of defense, certainly. And one might also, to make a parochial case, suggest that research on improvement of crops is an imperative matter in view of the population situation, and certainly persons who have relatives suffering from cancer might argue that research on cancer is imperative. So, I think there are subjective elements in any such determination.

HAVIGHURST: I think it would be useful to follow up Sir Harold's comments about the need for improved mechanisms for bringing scientific expertise into governmental decision-making. It is a subject of immense importance which I think neither Professor Green nor I have dealt with in the detail we might have.

We are all aware that there are frequent and increasingly more frequent examples in this country of expert committees being appointed for purposes of bringing outside specialists' attention to bear on problems of public policy. For example, we find more and more often the National Academy of Sciences being called in to appoint a committee for the purpose of studying a particular environmental hazard or public health problem that is before the public. The techniques of creating such advisory committees, the constitution of them, the delineation of their charge, and the administration of a committee's activities are all subjects that have not been studied and understood to the appropriate degree.

I think that probably we could have another conference on the subject of how scientific expertise, ethics, and other policy inputs can be blended in the decision-making process, how advisory committees can be used to advantage, and how the scientific community, and particularly the National Academy of Sciences, should view its role. There is, of course, a high probability that the government uses prestigious advisors for the purpose of adding credibility to decisions that have already been made, and it is fair to ask how far this can legitimately be carried. Also, there are questions whether the advice that is obtained is in fact disinterested, whether there may be subtle influences acting on the experts, consulted professionally for their opinions, whether they may not be so flattered by the invitation that they tend to give the statesmanlike opinion that everyone knows the decision-maker wants to have.

The other day I had occasion to ask a law school seminar whether the National Academy of Sciences should have its own legal advice in setting up its advisory committees. Even as law students, they were reluctant to say "yes," apparently perceiving no risk to the Academy in operating without legal counsel. However, the Academy's prestige and continuing credibility are very much at stake in some of these situations, and because the Academy is subject to being used by political operatives as a scapegoat or a shield behind which to hide, I would suggest that legal advice could be extremely helpful in particular cases, especially if the Academy sees itself as increasing its role in providing inputs into decision-making on hard questions of science and policy. A lawyer could apply his instincts to the political and legal context and warn the Academy to structure its role so as to maximize the benefits of its participation and to keep it out of political traps. In the past, and I have particularly in mind the Drug Efficacy Study, the Academy has accepted the policy-maker's delineation of the problem and the approach, and has failed to tailor its role to its capability and to the legal and political context. The form of the question put and of the advice given seems to me--as it does to Sir Harold--to be all-important, and I hope I will be forgiven if I suggest that scientists may plunge in a bit naively on occasion.

All of this is, of course, to agree with Sir Harold's point about the need to improve the process of accumulating and communicating scientific information to political decision-makers and the public for appropriate action.

GREEN: I think the point that Sir Harold makes runs directly counter to the main thrust of my paper. What he is suggesting is that we should find some mechanism, some kind of an agency, which is going to provide more or less definitive answers to scientific issues.

HIMSWORTH: Uncommitted.

GREEN: Uncommitted, if possible, which I doubt--and serve these answers to the government where they will then be rather uncritically accepted, and because of their authoritative nature will be largely insulated from political debate.

Now, I would suggest there are a number of factors which in my mind militate against such an arrangement. I think it is extremely difficult to get an uncommitted group of people to perform this function. The job may be easy if all you are talking about is scientific fact, but when you get into the realm where there is any uncertainty, the resolution of uncertainty involves value judgments--judgments as to what value you are going to give to certain elements of uncertainty.

I am concerned about the back-scratching phenomenon. Many segments of our society today are tainted by the expectation of receiving public funds. I think there is some tendency on the part of some people to say, "We are not going to say anything bad about Dr. X's project because we want him to say good things about our project when our project comes up for review."

So I think it is hard to get uncommitted people. I think, moreover, there is a tendency in groups of this kind to try to compromise whatever differences they have. My own experience with the reports of various kinds of scientific advisory committees is that they come out in rather sterile form, expressing only conclusions which are reached through a process of compromise, so that the real issues which have been compromised are not fully revealed.

I come back, also, to the other point I made. There is nothing unique about science. Surely every day the United States Congress enacts very important legislation which involves fundamental questions of economics. We are not concerned about whether the economics which are reflected in legislation are valid or invalid. We have little concern as to whether Congressional decisions in the economic sphere may be based on scientifically false premises. If we can tolerate this kind of inaccuracy in the sphere of economics, I cannot understand why we cannot tolerate it in the sphere of science and technology.

And in the very nature of our political processes, as I pointed out in my paper, the primary concern is giving the public what the public wants, rationally or irrationally, right or wrong, good or bad.

In my view, error and erroneous debate are not only inevitable, they are necessary. Take, for example, a simple issue, which I think is useful in this context, "Should Clement Haynesworth sit on the Supreme Court of the United States?" In that debate, as in most political debates, there were a number of statements made which, if not false, were exaggerated and were not made in any kind of an objectively valid context.

On the other hand, if one says that the exercise was really not one of considering whether this man was fit to sit on the Supreme Court, but rather the issue really was whether the public wanted someone with his political views sitting on the Supreme Court, I suppose people who hold that view ought to have every conceivable opportunity to keep him off the court, even if the process of political debate in achieving that does involve some erroneous statement or exaggeration.

This is the way our political system works. And I don't think science ought to be in any kind of a sacred preserve, insulated from this process of error and erroneous decision.

CALLAHAN: I would just like to raise one issue, Sir Harold. First, part of the success of this meeting has been that we have not adopted toward each other the position of adversaries. Certainly, I think many of us came with the conception that in certain areas we were adversaries. Part of the advantage of talking issues through is we find we are or we are not adversaries in one respect or another, and in many respects we end up changing roles. This, to my mind, raises the very large question: At what point ought the kind of issues we are concerned with here become politicized issues? My feeling on many of these problems at the moment is that it would be a terrible thing if they all got directly into the political arena. It seems to me that Dr. Green is quite right that people should be given what they want, but I think there is a need to have an opportunity to be informed about what one might and ought to want before finally deciding what one does want.

Second, it would seem to me fairly critical to make some progress in deciding just what it is that is at stake. The course of political debate is often quite precipitate about what the actual issues are. And I am not certain in this field that one should make an analogy to the Judge Haynesworth type of situation. There, somebody was being put up for a seat on the Supreme Court. A judgment had to be made instantly. I don't know that that is the case in this particular field. I don't know quite how to avoid sounding elitist here, but if the public is to make any kind of informed judgment on these issues, there has to be an awful lot of preparatory discussion in order that the issues will be sensibly presented. If polarities eventually develop, they will at least be reasonable and sensible polarities.

CONDLIFFE: In conclusion may I say that it has been very illuminating to listen to people in this field talk about these issues. Inside the NIH there is enormous debate and not a little anguish and trouble over our own role as scientific administrators in this kind of problem. I don't mean just genetics, but a whole host of problems that confront a large governmental organization which has relationships to the people who provide the money in Congress, to its political directors, and their agents.

I do believe there ought to be perhaps more public debate of this kind of issue, as Professor Havighurst said, because so often

the composition of the councils that help make decisions is almost
a hidden matter, in my belief, from the general public or even
Congress. They tend to be made inside the bureaucracy or at least
at the political summit of the particular section of the
bureaucracy, and they are not Presidential appointments which are
debated in the Senate or anything else.

I think it is an unresolved question, and I would rather leave
it as an unresolved question. I don't know that I would ever
organize a conference on such a subject.

PARTICIPANTS

CONFERENCE ON

ETHICAL ISSUES IN GENETIC COUNSELING
AND THE USE OF GENETIC KNOWLEDGE

October 10-14, 1971
Airlie House Foundation
Warrenton, Virginia

Dr. Henry D. Aiken
Department of Philosophy
Brandeis University
Waltham, Massachusetts

Dr. Duane Alexander
National Institute of Child Health
  and Human Development
National Institutes of Health
Bethesda, Maryland

Dr. Alexander G. Bearn
Department of Medicine
The New York Hospital
Cornell Medical Center
New York, New York

Dr. Fred Bergmann
National Institute of General
  Medical Science
National Institutes of Health
Bethesda, Maryland

Dr. Donald Bergsma
National Eye Institute
National Institutes of Health
Bethesda, Maryland

Mr. Burton Berkley
Office of the General Counsel
National Institutes of Health
Bethesda, Maryland

Dr. D. J. H. Brock
Department of Human Genetics
University of Edinburgh
Edinburgh, Scotland

Dr. Daniel Callahan
Institute of Society, Ethics
  and the Life Sciences
Hastings-on-Hudson, New York

Mr. Alex Capron
Yale Law School
New Haven, Connecticut

Dr. James Carmody
Health Services and Mental Health
  Administration
Rockville, Maryland

Dr. Cedric O. Carter
Institute of Child Health
Medical Research Council
London, England

Dr. Lars L. Cederqvist
Department of Medicine
The New York Hospital
Cornell Medical Center
New York, New York

Dr. Ronald Chez
National Institute of Child Health
  and Human Development
National Institutes of Health
Bethesda, Maryland

Dr. Jerry W. Combs, Jr.
National Institute of Child Health
  and Human Development
National Institutes of Health
Bethesda, Maryland

Dr. Peter G. Condliffe
Fogarty International Center
National Institutes of Health
Bethesda, Maryland

Dr. James F. Crow
Department of Medical Genetics
University of Wisconsin
    Medical School
Madison, Wisconsin

Dr. Felix de la Cruz
National Institute of Child Health
    and Human Development
National Institutes of Health
Bethesda, Maryland

Reverend David Eaton
All Soul's Unitarian Church
Washington, D.C.

Dr. John Fletcher
Interfaith Metropolitan Theological
    Education, Inc.
Washington, D.C.

Dr. Mark Frankel
Program of Policy Studies
    in Science and Technology
George Washington University
Washington, D.C.

Dr. F. Clarke Fraser
Department of Biology
McGill University
Montreal, Quebec, Canada

Dr. Ernst Freese
National Institute of Neurological
    Diseases and Stroke
National Institutes of Health
Bethesda, Maryland

Professor Charles Fried
Harvard University Law School
Cambridge, Massachusetts

Professor Harold P. Green
The National Law Center
The George Washington University
Washington, D.C.

Dr. Robert E. Greenfield
National Institute of General
    Medical Science
National Institutes of Health
Bethesda, Maryland

Dr. Zora J. Griffo
National Institute of Dental
    Research
National Institutes of Health
Bethesda, Maryland

Dr. James M. Gustafson
The Divinity School
University of Chicago
Chicago, Illinois

Dr. Judith Hall
Department of Pediatrics
Johns Hopkins Hospital
Baltimore, Maryland

Canon Michael Hamilton
Washington Cathedral
Washington, D.C.

Dr. Maureen Harris
Fogarty International Center
National Institutes of Health
Bethesda, Maryland

Professor Clark C. Havighurst
Duke University School of Law
Durham, North Carolina

Mr. Bruce Hilton
Institute of Society, Ethics
    and the Life Sciences
Hastings-on-Hudson, New York

Sir Harold Himsworth
Secretary, Medical Research Council
    (Ret.)
14 Hamilton Terrace
London, England

Dr. Magda G. Hotchkiss
Rockefeller University
New York, New York

Dr. Rollin D. Hotchkiss
Rockefeller University
New York, New York

Dr. R. Rodney Howell
Department of Pediatrics
Johns Hopkins University
School of Medicine
Baltimore, Maryland

Dr. David Yi-Yung Hsia
Loyola University
Stritch School of Medicine
Maywood, Illinois

Dr. Cecil B. Jacobson
Department of Obstetrics &
  Gynecology
The George Washington University
School of Medicine
Washington, D.C.

Dr. Michael M. Kaback
Department of Pediatrics
Johns Hopkins University
School of Medicine
Baltimore, Maryland

Dr. Leon R. Kass
Committee on The Life Sciences
  and Social Policy
National Academy of Sciences
Washington, D.C.

The Honorable Lord Kilbrandon
House of Lords
London, England

Dr. David A. Kindig
National Health Service Corps
Health Services and Mental
  Health Administration
Rockville, Maryland

Dr. Harold P. Klinger
Department of Genetics
Albert Einstein College of Medicine
Bronx, New York

Dr. Marc Lappe
Institute of Society, Ethics
  and the Life Sciences
Hastings-on-Hudson, New York

Dr. Jerome Lejeune
Chaire de Genetique Fondamentale
Institut de Progenese
Paris 6, France

Professor A. W. Liley
Postgraduate School of Obstetrics
  and Gynecology
National Women's Hospital
Auckland, New Zealand

Dr. John W. Littlefield
Genetics Unit
Massachusetts General Hospital
Boston, Massachusetts

Dr. Herbert Lubs
Department of Pediatrics
University of Colorado
Medical Center
Denver, Colorado

Mr. Kenneth Ludmerer
Institute of the History of Medicine
Johns Hopkins University
Baltimore, Maryland

Dr. M. Neil Macintyre
Department of Anatomy
Case Western Reserve University
Cleveland, Ohio

Dr. Joel M. Mangel
Office of the General Counsel
Health Services and Mental
  Health Administration
Rockville, Maryland

Dr. Anne McLaren
Department of Genetics
University of Edinburgh
Edinburgh, Scotland

Dr. William J. Mellman
Hospital of the University
  of Pennsylvania
Philadelphia, Pennsylvania

Dr. Barbara Migeon
Department of Pediatrics
Johns Hopkins Hospital
Baltimore, Maryland

Dr. James R. Missett
Health Services and Mental
  Health Administration
Rockville, Maryland

Dr. Robert S. Morison
Professor of Science and Society
Cornell University
Ithaca, New York

Dr. Samuel Moss
Division of Research Grants
National Institutes of Health
Bethesda, Maryland

Dr. Arno Motulsky
Division of Medical Genetics
University of Washington
Seattle, Washington

Dr. Robert Murray, Jr.
Howard University
College of Medicine
Washington, D.C.

Dr. James V. Neel
Department of Human Genetics
University of Michigan
Medical School
Ann Arbor, Michigan

Dr. Paul Ramsey
Department of Religion
Princeton University
Princeton, New Jersey

Dr. Richard Roblin
Infectious Disease Unit
Massachusetts General Hospital
Boston, Massachusetts

Dr. Joseph Schulman
New York Hospital
Cornell Medical Center
New York, New York

Dr. J. E. Seegmiller
Department of Medicine
University of California, San Diego
La Jolla, California

Dr. Margery W. Shaw
M.D. Anderson Hospital
  and Tumor Institute
The University of Texas
Houston, Texas

Mr. Daniel Singer
General Counsel
Federation of American Scientists
Washington, D.C.

Dr. Robert L. Sinsheimer
Division of Biology
California Institute of Technology
Pasedena, California

Dr. Tracy Sonneborn
Department of Zoology
Indiana University
Bloomington, Indiana

Dr. James R. Sorenson
Department of Sociology
Princeton University
Princeton, New Jersey

Dr. Arthur Steinberg
Department of Biology
Case Western Reserve University
Cleveland, Ohio

Dr. DeWitt Stetten
National Institute of General
  Medical Sciences
National Institutes of Health
Bethesda, Maryland

Dr. Laurence R. Tancredi
Health Services and Mental Health
  Administration
Rockville, Maryland

Dr. Carlo Valenti
Department of Obstetrics and
  Gynecology
Downstate Medical Center
Brooklyn, New York

Professor E. A. Vastyan
Department of Humanities
The Pennsylvania State University
Hershey, Pennsylvania

Dr. Robert M. Veatch
Institute of Society, Ethics
  and the Life Sciences
Hastings-on-Hudson, New York

Dr. Elliot S. Vesell
Department of Pharmacology
Pennsylvania State University
Hershey, Pennsylvania

Dr. Joseph Warkany
Children's Hospital Research
  Foundation
University of Cincinnati
Cincinnati, Ohio

Dr. Katherine S. Wilson
Division of Research Grants
National Institutes of Health
Bethesda, Maryland

Dr. Omar C. Yoder
Division of Research Grants
National Institutes of Health
Bethesda, Maryland

GLOSSARY

A Priori--Presupposed by experience; relating to or derived by reasoning from self-evident propositions.

Ablation--Removal of a part of the body, especially by cutting.

Abolitionist--An advocate of the abolition of slavery.

Aborigine--An indigenous inhabitant especially as contrasted with an invading or colonizing people.

Abortion--The expulsion of an embryo or fetus prematurely, or before it is capable of sustaining life on its own; **criminal abortion**, an illegal attempt to produce an abortion, "causing or procuring abortion" is the full name of the offense.

Abortus--A fetus weighing less than 17 oz. at the time of expulsion from the uterus, having no chance of survival.

Academician--A member of an academy for promoting science, art, or literature; a follower of an artistic or philosophical tradition or a promoter of its ideas.

Achondroplasia--A hereditary, congenital, familial disturbance causing inadequate bone formation and a peculiar type of dwarfism.

Acute--Having a sudden onset, sharp rise, and short course (as in a disease); not chronic.

Adversary--A litigant (party to a lawsuit)-opponent; the opposite party in a writ or action.

Albinism--Congenital absence of pigment in the skin, hair, and eyes.

Alkaptonuria--Excretion in the urine of alkapton bodies (substances with an affinity for alkali) which cause the urine to turn dark on standing, or on addition of alkali; sometimes associated with arthritic symptoms.

Allele--One of two or more contrasting genes which determine alternative characteristics in inheritance, such as presence or absence of pigmentation in albinism.

Amino Acid--An organic acid containing an amino group, especially any of the alpha-amino acids that are the chief components of proteins.

Amniocentesis--Perforation of the uterus to permit removal of amniotic fluid, which is produced very early in pregnancy; also called **amniotic puncture**.

421

Amnion--A thin membrane forming a closed sac (placenta) about the
embryo and containing the amniotic fluid in which the embryo is
immersed.

Amphibia--A class of vertebrated animals that are able to live both on
land and in water; it includes frogs, toads, and salamanders.

Animism--The obsolete doctrine that the soul is the source of organic
development; attribution of conscious life and purpose to all objects;
belief in the existence of spirits separable from bodies.

Aniridia--Absence of the iris (circular pigmented portion) of the eye.

Anomaly--Marked deviation from the normal standard.

Anthropology--The science of man, especially the study of man in relation
to distribution, origin, classification, and relationships of races,
physical character, environmental and social relations, and culture.

Antibiotic--A chemical substance which has the capacity to inhibit the
growth of or destroy bacteria and other microorganisms; used largely
in the treatment of infectious diseases of man, animals, and plants.

Antigen--Usually a protein complex which, when foreign to the blood-
stream of an animal, on gaining access to the tissues of such an
animal stimulates the formation of specific antibody and reacts with
its corresponding antibody.

Apert's Syndrome--A congenital malformation consisting of a pointed shape
of the top of the head and webbing of the hands and feet; also called
acrocephalosyndactylia.

Aphasia--The defect or loss of the power of expression by speech, writing,
or signs, or of comprehending spoken or written language, due to
injury or disease of the brain centers.

Apocalypse--One of the Jewish and Christian writings of 200 B.C. to A.D.
150 marked by the expectation of an imminent cataclysm in which God
destroys evil and raises the righteous to life in a messianic kingdom.

Arginine--An amino acid produced by the digestion of proteins. It is
injected intravenously in coma due to hepatic disease.

Argininosuccinic Aciduria--A condition resulting from a genetically determined defect in metabolism and accompanied by mental retardation.

Artificial Insemination--Introduction of semen into the vagina by
artificial means; donor insemination, when the semen used is that of
a man other than the woman's husband; homologous insemination, when
the husband's semen is used.

Ascetic--Practicing strict self-denial as a means of religious discipline.

Ashkenazi Jews--One of the two great divisions of Jews comprising the
    eastern European Yiddish-speaking Jews. See Sephardic Jews.

Assault--An intentional attempt, by violence, to do bodily injury to
    another.

Asthma--A disease marked by continuous or paroxysmal labored breathing,
    wheezing, a sense of constriction in the chest (due to spasmodic
    contraction of the bronchi), and attacks of coughing or gasping.

Astrology--The divination of the supposed influences of the stars upon
    human affairs and terrestrial events by their positions and aspects.

Astrophysicist--A specialist in astrophysics, the branch of astronomy
    dealing with the physical and chemical constitution of the celestial
    bodies.

Ataxia Telangiectasia--A hereditary, familial failure of motor coordination
    associated with frequent pulmonary infections and abnormal eye
    movements.

Atherosclerosis--A chronic disease characterized by abnormal thickening
    and hardening of the arterial walls due to increased deposits of
    fibrous tissues and fatty substances.

Autoimmunization--Production by an individual of antibodies against
    constituents of his own tissues; this is a possible cause of a number
    of serious and apparently incurable diseases.

Autosome--Any ordinary paired chromosome as distinguished from a sex
    chromosome.

Barbiturate--A salt of barbituric acid, whose derivatives are barbital and
    phenobarbital (used especially as sedatives or hypnotics).

Battery--The unlawful beating of another.

Biogenesis--The theory that living organisms can originate only from
    organisms already living; a supposed tendency for stages in the
    evolutionary history of a race to briefly occur during the develop-
    ment and differentiation of an individual of that race.

Biosynthesis--The production of a chemical compound by a living organism.

Blastocyst--In mammals, the modified blastula - an early stage of the
    embryo having the form of a single layer of cells surrounding a fluid-
    filled cavity.

Canon Law--The rules and regulations by which the Roman Catholic Church
    is governed. Canon law has no standing in civil or criminal courts.

Carcinogen--Any cancer-producing substance.

Carrier--In human genetics, an individual who harbors in his body one
    gene for a specific genetic trait, the manifestation of which requires
    the gene to be present on both members of a chromosome pair. The
    individual does not display the trait but does act as a carrier and
    distributor of the gene to his progeny.

Cataract--A clouding of the crystalline eye lens or of its capsule,
    obstructing the passage of light.

Causative Gene--A dominant gene which produces an effect in the organism,
    regardless of the state of the corresponding allele.

Caveat--A legal warning to a judicial officer to suspend a proceeding
    until the opposition has a hearing; a warning enjoining from certain
    acts or practices; an explanation to prevent misinterpretation.

Ceteris Paribus--Other things being equal; if all other relevant factors
    remained unaltered.

Chediak-Higashi Syndrome--A rare, fatal, inherited syndrome characterized
    by decreased pigmentation of the skin, eyes, and hair; also called
    hereditary leukomelanopathy.

Chimera--An individual, organ, or plant consisting of tissues of diverse
    genetic constitution.

Cholesterol--A fatlike, pearly substance which constitutes a large part
    of the most frequently occurring type of gallstones and occurs in
    hardening of the arteries.

Chondrodystrophia Fetalis Calcificans--A rare condition characterized by
    bone irregularities, usually present at birth. The infants frequently
    are stillborn or die of associated abnormalities in the first year.

Chromatin--The part of the cell nucleus that stains intensely with basic
    dyes. It is a nucleic acid attached to a protein structure base and
    is the carrier of the genes in inheritance.

Chromosome--A large nucleic acid which stains darkly and as a more or less
    rod-shaped body in the nucleus of a cell at the time of cell division.
    Chromosomes contain the genes, or hereditary factors, and
    are constant in number in each species. The normal number in man is
    46, with 22 pairs of autosomes and 2 sex chromosomes (XX or XY).
    Chromosomal aberrations are associated with various abnormalities.

Chronic--Persisting over a long period of time (as in disease); not acute.

Citrulline--An amino acid formed as an intermediate in the conversion
    of ornithine to arginine (also both amino acids) in a living organism.

Citrullinuria--A rare disorder involving the urea cycle in which the
    levels of citrulline (an amino acid) in the blood, cerebrospinal fluid,
    and urine are elevated. The disorder is accompanied by mental re-
    tardation.

Civil Law--The body of law relating to private rights or remedies
    sought by action or suit, as distinct from criminal law.

Cleft Lip--A longitudinal opening or fissure of the lip; also called
    harelip.

Clone--To establish or initiate a strain of cells asexually from a
single cell.

Collectivism--A political or economic theory advocating collective
control especially over production and distribution, or a system
marked by such control.

Common Law--The whole body of the law of England as distinguished
from the civil and canon laws; the common jurisprudence of the
people of the United States. It was brought by the colonists from
England and established in the United States insofar as it was
adaptable to their institutions and circumstances.

Communicable Disease--A disease that can be transmitted from one
person to another.

Comparative Jurisprudence--The study of the principles of legal science
by the comparison of various systems of law.

Compensation--Correction of an organic inferiority or loss by
increased functioning of another organ or unimpaired parts of
the same organ.

Conceptus--The whole product of conception at any stage of development,
from fertilization of the ovum to birth.

Congenital--Existing at, and usually before, birth; referring to
conditions that are present at birth, regardless of their causation.

Consanguinity--Descended from the same ancestor; related by blood.

Consensual Contract--A term derived from the civil law, denoting a
contract founded upon the mere consent of the contracting parties,
without any external formality to fix the obligation.

Contraception--The voluntary prevention of conception or impregnation.

Convulsion--An abnormal violent involuntary contraction or series of
contractions of the voluntary muscles.

Co-opt--To choose or elect as a fellow member or colleague; to appoint
or deputize.

Cord Blood--Blood contained within the umbilical cord at the time of
delivery of the fetus.

Cost Accounting--The systematic recording and analysis of the costs of
material, labor, and overhead incident to production.

Criminal Law--That branch or division of law which treats of crimes and their punishments.

Cystic Fibrosis--A hereditary disease that usually appears in early childhood and involves dysfunction of the exocrine (excreting externally) glands. It is especially marked by chronic pulmonary disease, deficiency of pancreatic enzymes, and excessive loss of salt in the sweat.

Cytology--A branch of biology dealing with the study of cells, their origin, structure, and functions.

Cytopathology--The study of cells in disease.

De Facto--Exercising power as if legally constituted, such as a functioning government, which may not be permanently established or recognized. See de jure.

De Jure--By a lawful title, distinguished from de facto.

de Lange's Syndrome--A form of congenital muscular and motor disturbance and mental deficiency. Death usually ensues early.

Defamation--The offense of injuring a person's character, fame, or reputation, either by writing or by words.

Deglutinate--To extract or remove gluten, an albuminous element found in animal tissues.

Dehydrogenase--An enzyme that accelerates the removal of hydrogen from metabolites and its transfer to other substances.

Demography--The statistical study of human populations, especially with reference to size and density, distribution, and vital statistics.

Deoxyribonucleic Acid--A nucleic acid found in all living cells and comprising the genetic materials in chromosomes; also called DNA.

Depression--A psychoneurotic or psychotic disorder marked by sadness, inactivity, and self-depreciation; a lowering or decrease of functional activity.

Diabetes--A deficiency condition marked by habitual discharge of an excessive quantity of urine.

Diabetes Mellitus--A metabolic disorder in which the ability to oxidize carbohydrates is more or less completely lost; symptoms include thirst, hunger, emaciation, weakness, and finally coma.

Disjunction--The moving apart of chromosomes during meiosis, a form of cell division occurring in maturation of egg and sperm cells.

Down's Syndrome--See Mongolism.

Duodenal Atresia--Absence or closure of the duodenum (small intestine).

Dystrophy--Any of several neuromuscular disorders arising from defective or faulty nutrition.

Ecology--The science of organisms as affected by the factors of their environments.

Egalitarianism--A belief in human equality especially with respect to social, political, and economic rights and privileges.

Ehlers-Danlos Syndrome--A condition characterized by overextensibility of joints, hyperelasticity of the skin, fragility of the skin, and pseudotumors following trauma.

Electrocardiogram--A graphic tracing of the electric current produced by the contraction of the heart muscle.

Electrophoresis--The movement of charged particles, suspended in a liquid on various media (e.g., paper or starch gel), under the action of an electromotive force applied to electrodes in contact with the suspension.

Emphysema--A condition characterized by air-filled expansions of body tissues, such as a condition of the lung marked by distention and frequently by impairment of heart action.

Encephalogram--An X-ray picture of the brain.

Ensoul--To endow or imbue with a soul.

Entropy--Diminished capacity for spontaneous change; the measure of that part of the heat or energy of a system which is not available to perform work.

Enzyme--An organic compound, primarily protein, that is produced by living cells and brings about or accelerates reactions at body temperatures without itself undergoing marked change in the process.

Epilepsy--Any of various disorders marked by disturbed electrical rhythms of the central nervous system and typically manifested by convulsive attacks usually with clouding of consciousness.

Epiloia--A familial disease characterized by brain tumors, progressive mental deterioration, and epileptic convulsions; also called tuberous sclerosis.

Epistemology--The study or a theory of the nature and grounds of knowledge with reference to its limits and validity.

Erythroblastosis Foetalis--An anemia of the fetus or newborn infant caused by the transplacental transmission of maternally formed antibody.

Ethicist--A specialist in ethics, the discipline dealing with what is
good and bad and with moral duty and obligation.

Etiology--The study or theory of the causation of any disease; the sum
of knowledge regarding causes.

Eudaemonism--A theory that defines moral obligation by references to
personal well-being (happiness) through a life governed by reason.

Eugenics--The study and control of various possible influences as a
means of improving the hereditary characteristics of a race.

Eukaryosis--Having a true nucleus.

Evolution--A process of development in which an organ or organism
becomes more and more complex by the differentiation of its parts; a
continuous and progressive change according to certain laws.

Ex Post Facto--Done after the fact; an ex post facto law makes criminal
an act that, when it was committed, was not criminal or imposes a new
punishment for an act that, when it was committed, merited a different
punishment.

Factor VIII--A coagulation factor, present in blood plasma and not in
serum. A primary deficiency of this factor causes classical, sex-
linked hemophilia.

Familial--Occurring in or affecting different members of the same
family.

Favre Disease--A virus disease characterized by an initial lesion,
usually on the genitalia; a venereal disease; also called venereal
lymphogranuloma.

Felony--An offense punishable by death or by imprisonment in a State
prison.

Feticide--The destruction of the fetus in the uterus.

Fetish--An object believed among a primitive people to have magical
power to protect or aid its owner.

Fibroblast--A connective tissue cell which forms the fibrous tissues
in the body, tendons, and supporting and binding tissues.

Flagellate--A form of microorganism observed in the blood of typhoid
patients.

Fluoridation--The addition of fluoride to the public water supply as
part of the public health program to prevent or reduce the incidence
of dental cavities.

Friedrich's Ataxia--An inherited disease, usually beginning in childhood or youth, marked by hardening of the spinal cord, irregularity of muscular action, and speech impairment.

Fucose--Found in algae (seaweed), some gums, and certain polysaccharides, bacterial as well as those of blood group-specific substances from animal and human sources.

Galactosemia--A hereditary disorder involving inability to properly metabolize galactose and characterized by vomiting, diarrhea, jaundice, poor weight gain, and malnutrition in early infancy.

Gamete--A reproductive element; one of two cells, male and female, whose union is necessary, in sexual reproduction, to initiate the development of a new individual.

Ganglion--A mass of nerve tissue containing nerve cells external to the brain or spinal cord. A small cystic tumor connected either with a joint membrane or tendon, as in the wrist.

Gene--The biologic unit of heredity, self-reproducing and located in a definite position on a particular chromosome.

Gene Pool--The gametes of all mating individuals which comprise a gene pool from which the genes of the next generation are drawn.

Genetic Counseling--Providing the most complete and recent medical knowledge in the field of genetics to the patient and his family.

Genetic Counselor--A trained professional adviser who must be well versed in the medical, legal, and psychological implications of such procedures as contraception, sterilization, abortion, artificial insemination, and adoption.

Genetic Engineering--The chemical alteration or reinforcement of defective genes by addition of new genetic material; synthetic fashioning of elementary genes.

Geneticist--A specialist in genetics, the study of heredity.

Genocide--The deliberate and systematic destruction of a racial, political, or cultural group.

Genome--The complete set of hereditary factors, as contained in the chromosomes.

Gentiles--Of or relating to the nations at large or Christians as distinguished from the Jews.

Geriatrics--That branch of medicine which treats all problems peculiar to old age and the aging, including the clinical problems of senescence and senility.

Germ Cells--The cells of an organism whose function it is to reproduce the kind.

Germ Plasm--The reproductive and hereditary substance of individuals
which is passed on from the germ cell in which an individual
originates in direct continuity to the germ cells of succeeding
generations. By it new individuals are produced and hereditary
characteristics are transmitted.

German Measles--An acute contagious virus disease milder than typical
measles but damaging to the fetus when occurring early in pregnancy;
also called rubella.

Germinal--Being in the earliest stage of development; pertaining to a
germ cell or early embryo.

Gestalt--A structure of physical, biological, or psychological
phenomena so integrated as to constitute a functional unit with
properties not derivable from its parts in summation.

Giemsa Stain--A dye used to stain, among many cellular parts, the
chromosomes during metaphase before cell division.

Glycogen--The chief carbohydrate storage material in animals. It is
largely stored in the liver and is also called animal starch.

Gynecologist--A person skilled in gynecology, the branch of medicine
which treats the diseases of the genital tract in women.

Haploid--An individual or cell having only one member of each pair of
homologous (corresponding in structure, position, and origin)
chromosomes, or having one complete set of nonhomologous chromosomes.

Helix--A coiled, spiral structure.

Hemangioma--A benign tumor made up of new-formed blood vessels.

Hemoglobin--An iron-containing protein respiratory pigment occurring in
the red blood cells of vertebrates and in some plants (yeasts).

Hemophilia--A hereditary tendency to uncontrollable bleeding.

Heterogeneity--The state or quality of being composed of dissimilar
elements or ingredients; not having a uniform quality throughout.

Heterozygote--An individual possessing differing alleles (contrasting
genes) in regard to a specific characteristic.

Heuristic--Encouraging or promoting investigation; valuable for empirical
research but unproved or incapable of proof.

Hexosamine--A nitrogenous sugar.

Hippocratic Oath--Written by Hippocrates of Cos in the late fifth
century B.C., it is an oath embodying the code of medical ethics,
usually taken by those about to begin medical practice.

Histopathology--A branch of pathology (the study of disease) concerned
with the tissue changes characteristic of disease.

Hoffman-Werdnig Syndrome--A hereditary spinal muscular atrophy.

Homologous--Corresponding in structure, position, and origin; derived
   from an animal of the same species but of not necessarily identical
   genotype.

Homozygote--An individual possessing an identical pair of alleles
   (contrasting genes) in regard to a given characteristic or characteristics.

Humanism--A doctrine, attitude, or way of life centered on human
   interests or values; a philosophy that asserts the dignity and worth
   of man and his capacity for self-realization through reason.

Huntington's Chorea--A chronic disease characterized by a wide variety of
   rapid jerky but well-coordinated movements, performed involuntarily.

Hybrid--An animal or plant produced from parents different in kind,
   such as parents belonging to two different species, breeds, or
   varieties.

Hydrocephalus--A condition marked by abnormal accumulation of fluid in
   the cranial vault, enlargement of the head, prominence of the
   forehead, atrophy of the brain, mental weakness, and convulsions.

Hyperacusis--Abnormal acuteness of the sense of hearing, or a painful
   sensitiveness to sounds.

Hypercholesterolemia--An excess of cholesterol (a fatlike substance) in
   the blood.

Hypertension--Abnormally high strain or tension; especially high blood
   pressure.

Hyperuricemia--An excess of uric acid (urine) in the blood.

Hypogammaglobulinemia--An abnormally low level of gamma globulin (blood
   plasma rich in antibodies) in the blood.

Hysterotomy--Surgical incision of the uterus, e.g., cesarean.

I Cell Disease--Characterized by a notable increase in intracellular
   lipid (fat).

Implantation--Attachment of the embryo to the lining of the uterus,
   occurring six or seven days after fertilization of the ovum; the
   insertion of a part or tissue in a new site in the body.

In Utero--Within the uterus.

Inanition--The condition which results from complete lack of food.

Inborn Error of Metabolism--Referring to any of a number of genetic
   diseases in which abnormal metabolism of chemicals in the body occurs.

Infanticide--The taking of the life of an infant.

Institutes of Justinian--One of the four component parts of the Corpus
    Juris Civilis, a treatise on the Roman law, first published November
    21, 533.

Interim Ethics--Originally, principles enunciated by Christ for
    governing the conduct of the disciples during the anticipated brief
    span of time before the coming of the second advent and the end
    of the world.

Intrauterine Device--A birth control device implanted within the uterus;
    also called a coil or IUD.

Ipso Facto--By the very nature of the case.

Karyotype--A systematized arrangement of the chromosomes of a single cell
    by number, form, and size.

Kinetics--The branch of mechanics which comprises the phenomena of
    motion as affected by force.

Klinefelter's Syndrome--A condition associated with an abnormality of
    the sex chromosomes (XXY sex chromosome constitution) and characterized
    by the presence of small testes and an increase in urinary gonadotropins
    (which stimulate the sex glands).

Laissez-Faire--A doctrine opposing governmental interference in economic
    affairs beyond the minimum necessary for the maintenance of peace and
    property rights; a philosophy characterized by abstention from
    interference with individual freedom of choice and action.

Laparoscope--An instrument for visualizing the peritoneal cavity,
    especially the liver and the peritoneum.

Larceny--The unlawful taking and carrying away of personal property with
    the intent to deprive the rightful owner of his property permanently;
    punishable by imprisonment in a state prison.

Law--A uniform or constant fact or principle; a binding custom or practice
    of a community; a rule of conduct or action prescribed or formally
    recognized as binding or enforced by a controlling authority; the
    whole body of such customs, practices, or rules.

Leber's Optic Atrophy--A hereditary form of optic or retrobulbar neuritis
    (inflammation in that portion of the optic nerve which is posterior
    to the eyeball) which is often sex-linked.

Lesch-Nyhan Syndrome--Characterized by mental retardation, weakness, and
    compulsive self-mutilation; most patients die in childhood.

Leucine--An amino acid (the chief component of protein) essential
    for optimal growth in infants and for nitrogen equilibrium in adults.

Leukemia--A fatal disease of the blood-forming organs, characterized by a marked increase in the number of white cells in the blood. The disease is attended with progressive anemia, internal hemorrhaging, and increasing exhaustion.

Leukocyte--Any of the white or colorless nucleated cells that occur in blood.

Liable--Obligated according to law or equity.

Libertarian--An advocate of the doctrine of free will; one who upholds the principles of liberty of thought and action.

Lobby--To conduct activities aimed at influencing public officials, especially members of a legislative body, on legislation and other policy decisions.

Logos--In ancient Greek philosophy, the belief that reason is the controlling principle in the universe.

Lymphopenia--Decrease in the proportion of lymphocytes (a variety of white blood corpuscle) in the blood.

Lyon Hypothesis--A theory that the two X chromosomes of a female are not both operative in any one cell; only one X functions while the other is suppressed. Therefore, if a female receives one color-blindness gene and one normal one she might have defective color vision to a greater or lesser degree.

Marfan's Syndrome--Unusually long legs and fingers, often with deformities of the chest cage and eye lenses.

Malpractice--A dereliction from professional duty or a failure of professional skill or learning that results in injury, loss, or damage.

Mandibulofacial Dysostosis--A congenital condition characterized by abnormalities of the face and jaw.

Mannose--A simple sugar similar to dextrose in general properties.

Maori--A Polynesian people native to New Zealand; the Austronesian language of the Maori.

Maple Syrup Urine Disease--An inborn error of metabolism in which there is an overflow of amino acids in the blood and urine. If untreated, most patients die during the first months of life, and the survivors are severely retarded. Treatment consists of a diet very low in the three amino acids involved; also called Menkes disease.

Marihuana--The dried leaves and flowering tops of the Cannabis sativa plant that yield cannabin and are smoked in cigarettes for their intoxicating effect.

Meiosis--A type of cell division, occurring only in the germ cells,
   in which the resultant cells contain only one member of each pair
   of chromosomes of the parent cell.

Mendel's Law--In the inheritance of certain traits the offspring are
   not intermediate between the parents in characteristics, but inherit
   from one or the other parent in varying genetic combinations.

Metabolic--Undergoing metamorphosis; of, relating to, or based on
   metabolism (the sum of all the physical and chemical processes
   by which living organized substance is produced and maintained).

Metallurgy--The science and technology of metals.

Metaphysics--A division of philosophy that includes ontology (the
   nature and relations of being) and cosmology (dealing with the
   universe as an orderly system) or ontology and epistemology
   (the nature and grounds of knowledge).

Metastasis--The transfer of disease from one organ or part of the
   body to another not directly connected with it.

Methemoglobinemic Cyanosis--A condition present at birth and occurring
   predominantly in males, characterized by a bluish discoloration of
   the skin and mucous membranes due to excessive concentration of
   reduced hemoglobin in the blood.

Microassay--Very small-scale determination of the purity of a substance
   or the amount of any particular constituent of a mixture.

Microcephaly--Abnormal smallness of the head.

Miniaturization--The act or process of designing or constructing in
   small size.

Mitosis--A type of cell division, consisting of a complex of various
   processes - prophase, metaphase, anaphase, and telophase - in which
   the chromosome set of the resultant cells is identical to that
   of the parent cell. See meiosis.

Molecular Biology--The study of biological molecules which arises out
   of developments in four fields: genetics, biochemistry, physical
   chemistry of macromolecules, and chemical physics.

Mongolism--A condition characterized by moderate to severe mental
   retardation and associated with a chromosomal abnormality. The
   child is born with slanting eyes, a broad short skull, and broad
   hands with short fingers; also called Down's syndrome.

Monism--The view that there is only one kind of ultimate substance or
   that reality is one organic whole with no independent parts.

Morality--Conformity to ideals of right human conduct; a doctrine or
   system of morals.

Morbid--Of, relating to, or characteristic of disease; affected with or induced by disease.

Morphology--The science of the forms and structure of animals and plants.

Morquio's Syndrome--A familial condition marked by peculiarities in bone formation, dwarfing, and bodily deformities; also called eccentro-osteochondrodysplasia.

Mucopolysaccharides--A group of carbohydrates which contain hexosamine (a sugar), which may or may not be combined with protein and which are components of many types of mucus.

Mutagen--A chemical or physical agent that induces genetic mutations (changes).

Mutagenesis--The induction or production of genetic change.

Mutation--A permanent transmissible change in the genetic makeup of an individual such that the characteristics of an offspring are different from those of his parents.

Myocardism--A tendency toward the development of weakness and degeneration of the muscular tissue of the heart.

Myopia--A condition in which the visual images come to a focus in front of the retina of the eye resulting in defective vision of distant objects; also called nearsightedness.

Mysticism--A theory postulating the possibility of direct and intuitive acquisition of ineffable knowledge or power; a religion based on mystical communion.

Narcotic--An agent that produces insensibility or stupor.

Natural Selection--A natural process tending to cause the survival of individuals or groups best adjusted to the conditions under which they live, and being equally important for the perpetuation of desirable genetic qualities and for the elimination of undesirable ones by recombination or mutation of genes.

Naturalism--The doctrine that scientific laws are adequate to account for all phenomena.

Neonate--A new-born infant, up to about four weeks after birth.

Neoplasm--Any new and abnormal growth, such as a tumor.

Nephritis--Inflammation of the kidney, caused by infection, degeneration, or vascular disease.

Neurofibromatosis--A familial condition affecting the nervous system, muscles, bones, and skin.

Nexus--A link between members of a series or group.

Nucleic Acids--Substances of high molecular weight which constitute the prosthetic groups of the nucleoproteins, and contain phosphoric acid, sugars, and purine and pyrimidine bases.

Nucleotide--One of the compounds of which nucleic acid is composed.

Obstetrician--One who practices obstetrics, that branch of surgery which deals with the management of pregnancy, labor, and the puerperium (the condition of a woman immediately following childbirth).

Occult--Of or relating to supernatural agencies, their effects, and knowledge of them.

Oligarchy--A government in which a small group exercises control, especially for corrupt and selfish purposes.

Omphalocoele--Protrusion at birth of part of the intestine through a large defect in the abdominal wall at the umbilicus.

Ontogeny--The complete developmental history of the individual organism. See phylogeny.

Osteogenesis Imperfecta--An inherited condition in which the bones are abnormally brittle and subject to fractures.

Ovogenesis--The origin and development of the ovum; also called oogenesis.

Ozone--An active form of oxygen used as a disinfectant and antiseptic; formed when oxygen is exposed to the silent discharge of electricity or by the energy from the sun's rays.

Pap Smear--A method of staining smears of various body secretions, particularly the genitourinary tract, to detect the presence of a malignant process; also called Papanicolaou's stain.

Parkinson's Disease--A disease of late life, progressive in character and marked by a tremor of resting muscles, a slowing of voluntary movements, and weakness of the muscles; also called paralysis agitans and shaking palsy.

Parturition--The act or process of giving birth to a child.

Paternalism--A system under which an authority treats those under his control in a fatherly way especially in regulating their conduct and supplying their needs.

Pediatrician--An expert in pediatrics, that branch of medicine which treats of children and their development and care and of the diseases of children and their treatment.

Pedigree--An account or register of a line of ancestors; lineage, descent, and succession of families.

Penetrance--The frequency with which a heritable trait is shown in individuals carrying the principal gene or genes conditioning the trait.

Peptic Ulcer--An open sore on the mucous membrane of the esophagus, stomach, or duodenum, caused by the action of the acid gastric juice.

Periodontal--Situated or occurring around a tooth.

Perjury--The making of a false oath to a material fact by a witness in a judicial proceeding as part of his evidence.

Petri Dish--A shallow glass receptacle for growing bacterial cultures.

Pharmacogenetics--The scientific study of the effect of genetic factors on the individual organism's response to drugs.

Phenocopy--An individual whose phenotype (outward, visible, hereditary constitution) mimics that of another genotype (fundamental, hereditary constitution), but whose character is determined by environment and not heredity.

Phenomenon--An object or aspect known through the senses rather than by thought or intuition; a fact or event of scientific interest susceptible to scientific description and explanation.

Phenotype--The outward visible expression of the hereditary constitution of an organism.

Phenylalanine--A naturally occurring amino acid (the chief components of protein) essential for optimal growth in infants and for nitrogen equilibrium in human adults.

Phenylketonuria--A rare genetic irregularity in man marked by inability to oxidize phenylpyruvic acid (which is found in the urine) and by severe mental deficiency; also called PKU.

Philanthropy--Goodwill to fellow men; active effort to promote human welfare.

Phylogeny--The evolution of a genetically related group of organisms as distinguished from the development of the individual organism. See ontogeny.

Placenta--The organ within the uterus which establishes communication between the mother and child by means of the umbilical cord.

Plaintiff--The complaining party in an action at law.

Platonism--The philosophy of Plato stressing that actual things are copies of transcendent ideas and that these ideas are the objects of true knowledge apprehended by reminiscence.

Pluralism--A theory that reality is composed of a plurality of entities; a state of society in which members of diverse ethnic, racial, religious, or social groups maintain an autonomous participation in and development of their traditional culture.

Polyandry--The practice of having more than one husband at one time.

Polycystic--Containing or made up of many cysts, or sacs containing liquid or semisolid material.

Polygamy--Marriage in which a spouse of either sex may possess a plurality of mates at the same time.

Polygenic--Pertaining to or influenced by several different genes.

Polymer--A compound, usually of high molecular weight, formed by the combination of simpler molecules and consisting essentially of repeating structural units.

Polynesians--Inhabitants of the islands scattered over the eastern Pacific Ocean; their language is traceable to Malay and their origins are thought to be Asian.

Polyposis--The development of multiple polyps (protruding growths) on any mucous membrane.

Pompe's Disease--A recessively inherited glycogen storage disease characterized by excessive accumulation of glycogen in the heart and skeletal muscles; usually fatal in infancy.

Populationist--An advocate of population control.

Pornography--The depiction of erotic behavior (as in pictures or writing) intended to cause sexual excitement.

Porphyria--A pathological state characterized by abnormalities of porphyrin (a metal-free substance obtained from chlorophyll or hemoglobin) metabolism by excretion of excess porphyrins in the urine, and by extreme sensitivity to light.

Positivism--A theory that theology and metaphysics are earlier imperfect modes of knowledge and that positive knowledge is based on natural phenomena and their properties and relations as verified by the empirical sciences.

Postnatal--Occurring after birth; also called postpartum.

Prenatal--Existing or occurring before birth; also called antenatal.

Prescience--Foreknowledge of events; omniscience with regard to the future.

Proband--The original person presenting with a mental or physical disorder and whose case serves as the stimulus for a hereditary or genetic study; also called propositus.

Prognostication--The forecasting of the probable outcome of an attack of disease.

Prophylactic--An agent that tends to ward off disease; a device for preventing venereal infection; a contraceptive.

Prosencephalon--The part of the brain developed from the anterior of the three primary divisions of the embryonic neural tube; also called forebrain. The most anterior of the three primary divisions of the neural axis of the embryo.

Prototype--The original type or form after which other types or forms are developed.

Pseudocholinesterase--An enzyme which catalyzes the hydrolysis (reaction with water) of acetylcholine (a base).

Psychodynamic--Of or relating to mental or emotional forces or processes developing in early childhood and their effects on behavior and mental states.

Pyloric Stenosis--A narrowing of the opening leading from the stomach into the intestine (pylorus); can be a congenital malformation.

Quadriplegia--Paralysis of the arms and legs.

Rabbinate--The office or tenure of a rabbi; a group of rabbis.

Radiotherapy--The treatment of disease by means of X-rays or radioactive substances.

Raison d'Etre--Reason or justification for existence.

Recessive Gene--A gene that will produce an effect in the organism only when it is transmitted to an offspring by both parents.

Reformation--A 16th-century religious movement marked by rejection or modification of much of Roman Catholic doctrine and practice, and establishment of the Protestant churches.

Reprobate--To condemn as unworthy or evil; to foreordain to damnation.

Retinitis Pigmentosa--A disease, frequently hereditary, attended by contraction of the field of vision and hemeralopia (defective vision in a bright light).

Retinoblastoma--A tumor of the retina arising from retinal germ cells and believed to be hereditary.

Rh Factor--A factor present in the blood; a blood type antigen (a protein complex which can stimulate the formation of specific antibodies); also called Rhesus factor.

Ribonucleic Acid--A nucleic acid found in all living cells; assumes the genetic role in the absence of deoxyribonucleic acid (DNA), another nucleic acid; also called RNA.

Riley-Day Syndrome--A familial condition characterized by defective lacrimation, skin blotching, emotional instability, motor incoordination, and weakening of the reflexes; also called dysautonomia and familial autonomic dysfunction.

Rubin's Test--A test for patency of the fallopian tubes made by transuterine insufflation with carbon dioxide; infertility test.

Schizophrenia--A psychotic disorder characterized by loss of contact with environment and by disintegration of personality.

Scienter--A degree of knowledge that makes an individual legally responsible for the consequences of his act.

Secretor--An individual possessing A or B type blood whose saliva and various other body secretions contain the particular (A or B) substance.

Senescence--The process or condition of growing old.

Sephardic Jews--The Occidental branch of European Jews originally settling in Spain and Portugal, or one of their descendants. See Ashkenazi Jews.

Serum--The watery portion of an animal fluid remaining after coagulation; immune blood serum that contains specific immune bodies (antitoxins or agglutinins).

Sickle Cell Anemia--A hereditary, genetically determined anemia, occurring mainly in Negroes, characterized by acute attacks of abdominal pain.

Somatic--Pertaining to or characteristic of the body.

Spermatogenesis--The process of male gamete formation and transformation of the four resulting spermatids into spermatozoa.

Sphingolipidosis--A general designation applied to a disease characterized by abnormal storage of sphingolipids (occurring in particularly high concentrations in brain and nerve tissue), such as Tay-Sachs disease.

Spondet Peritiam Artis--He promises the skill of his art; he engages to do the work in a skillful or workmanlike manner.

Statutory Law--A statute is a law passed by a legislative body - Congress (act), State legislature (statute), City council or municipal body (ordinance).

Sterilization--Any procedure by which an individual is made incapable of reproduction, such as castration, vasectomy, or salpingectomy.

Stigmata--Bodily marks or pains resembling the wound of the crucified Christ and sometimes accompanying religious ecstasy. Any mental or physical mark or peculiarity which aids in the identification or in the diagnosis of a condition.

Streptococcus--Any of a genus of nonmotile, chiefly parasitic, gram-positive bacteria that divide only in one plane, occur in pairs or chains, and include important pathogens of man and domestic animals.

Supernumerary--In excess of the regular or normal number; superfluous.

Supersonic--Having a frequency above the human ear's audibility limit of about 20,000 cycles per second.

Surd--A voiceless speech sound.

Synthesis--The production of a substance by the union of elements or simpler chemical compounds or by the degradation of a complex compound.

Talmud--The authoritative body of Jewish tradition comprising the Mishnah and Gemara.

Tay-Sachs Disease--A genetic disease characterized by progressive neurological degeneration due to accumulation of gangliosides in nervous tissues and leading to death by early childhood.

Technocracy--Government by technicians; management of society by technical experts.

Teratogenic--Tending to produce irregularities of formation or development in offspring.

Testicular Feminization Syndrome--A condition in which the patient has female external development, including secondary sex characteristics, but with presence of testes and absence of uterus and tubes.

Test-Tube Baby--Theoretically, a baby produced by insemination and development of an egg cell outside of the womb.

Tetraplody--The state of having four sets of chromosomes.

Thalassemia--A hereditary, genetically determined anemia with familial and racial incidence.

Thalidomide--Used commonly in Europe as a sedative and hypnotic. In
    the early 1960's it was discovered to be the cause of serious congenital
    defects in the fetus when taken by a woman during early pregnancy.

Theologian--A specialist in theology, the rational interpretation of
    religious faith, practice, and experience, dealing with God and His
    relation to the world.

Thomism--The scholastic, philosophical, and theological system of St.
    Thomas Aquinas, and the explanations and developments made by his
    followers.

Tort--A violation of a right not arising out of a contract, for which a
    civil action may be taken.

Transduction--The transfer, generally by a virus, of a genetic fragment
    from one cell to another.

Translocation--The shifting of a segment or fragment of one chromosome
    into another part of a homologous chromosome, or into a nonhomologous
    chromosome.

Treponema--A genus of microorganisms, some of them being parasitic and
    causing disease in man and other animals.

Trichloroacetic Acid--A strong pungent acid used in medicine as a
    caustic and astringent.

Trisomy--The presence of a third chromosome in a cell usually containing
    two.

Trypsin--An enzyme occurring in pancreatic juice.

Tuberous Sclerosis--A familial disease characterized by tumors on the
    brain, mental deterioration, and epileptic convulsions.

Turner's Syndrome--Retarded growth and sexual development;
    associated with an abnormality of the sex chromosomes (XO chromosome
    constitution).

Ultrasound--Vibrations of the same physical nature as sound but with
    frequencies above the range of human hearing.

Utilitarianism--A theory that the aim of action is the largest possible
    balance of pleasure over pain or the greatest happiness of the
    greatest number; a doctrine that the useful is the good.

Vaccinate--To inoculate a person with cowpox virus in order to
    produce immunity to smallpox; to administer a vaccine by injection.

Vasectomy--Surgical removal of the vas deferens (a spermatic duct) to
    induce permanent sterility.

Venipuncture--Surgical puncture of a vein for the withdrawal of blood or for intravenous medication.

Viability--Ability to live after birth.

Virology--That branch of microbiology which is concerned with viruses and virus diseases.

Wallenberg's Syndrome--Impaired sensory perception to touch, position, and vibration sense; tongue paralysis.

Wilson's Disease--Progressive degeneration of the lens of the eye.

Zero Population Growth--A social proposal that couples have no more than two children, thereby stabilizing the present population level rather than increasing it.

Zoology--A science that deals with animals and is the branch of biology concerned with the animal kingdom and its members as individuals and classes and with animal life.

INDEX

Abnormal child, the, 188-90, 216-17, 218

Abortion, 26-27, 49, 50, 52, 85, 95, 113-14, 119, 153, 186-88, 191-92, 195-97, 202-20, 251-52, 285, 289-90, 308-10, 318-19, 322-25, 339, 343, 345, 374-75
compulsory, 399
ethics of, 2, 4-5, 49, 56-57, 67, 85, 108-10, 113-15, 117, 180, 185-99, 277, 324
for heterozygotes, 207
in Down's syndrome, 85, 211
in Tay-Sachs disease, 134, 211
legal aspects, 4, 15, 21, 31, 54-55, 186, 189, 202-204, 232-37, 251, 387, 389
relation to amniocentesis, 54, 156, 157, 203, 205, 213, 289, 309-10, 339
relation to screening, 164, 165, 167
religious aspects, 178, 202, 320-21
risks, 49
spontaneous, 96
therapeutic, 123, 130, 275

Acatalasemia, 46 (Table II)

Achondroplasia, 357, 365

Alkaystonuria, 90

∝ anti-trypsin deficiency, 359

American Society of Human Genetics, 13

Amino acid disorders, 46

see also metabolic disorders

Amniocentesis, 7, 10, 17, 21, 25, 44 (Table II), 48, 50-53, 68, 73, 91, 152-58, 166, 186, 187, 190, 212, 261, 285, 289, 290-91, 301, 303, 307, 308, 317, 322, 339, 345, 374, 375
ethics of, 54, 56, 71, 108, 187, 193, 201, 202, 206, 220, 305-306 (Fig. 1)
economics of, 356
hematological disorders, 48
in chromosome disorders, 43-45
in screening programs, 148, 151-52, 154-58, 163, 271
in Tay-Sachs disease, 22, 133, 340
legal aspects, 55-56, 189, 251, 389
metabolic disorders, 45-46 (Table IV)
RH factor, 355
relation to abortion, 54, 156, 157, 203, 205, 213, 289, 309-10, 339
relation to maternal age, 40 43, 52, 355
relation to sterilization, 339
religious aspects, 320
risks, 43-44, 49, 53-54, 316-17
role of counselor, 207, 209, 314-15, 338
tetraploidy in amniotic fluid cells, 45 (Table III)
translocation, 43-45